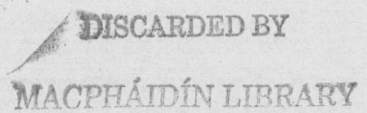

The Uncertain Course

sipri

Stockholm International Peace Research Institute

SIPRI is an independent institute for research into problems of peace and conflict, especially those of disarmament and arms regulation. It was established in 1966 to commemorate Sweden's 150 years of unbroken peace.

The Institute is financed mainly by the Swedish Parliament. The staff, the Governing Board and the Scientific Council are international.

The Board and Scientific Council are not responsible for the views expressed in the publications of the Institute.

Governing Board
Ambassador Ernst Michanek, Chairman (Sweden)
Egon Bahr (Federal Republic of Germany)
Professor Francesco Calogero (Italy)
Dr Max Jakobson (Finland)
Professor Dr Karlheinz Lohs
    (German Democratic Republic)
Professor Emma Rothschild (United Kingdom)
Sir Brian Urquhart (United Kingdom)
The Director

Director
Dr Walther Stützle (Federal Republic of Germany)

sipri

Stockholm International Peace Research Institute

Pipers Väg 28, S-171 72 Solna, Sweden
Cable: Peaceresearch, Stockholm
Telephone: 08-55 97 00

The Uncertain Course

New Weapons, Strategies and Mind-sets

Edited by
Carl G. Jacobsen

sipri

Stockholm International Peace Research Institute

OXFORD UNIVERSITY PRESS
1987

Oxford University Press, Walton Street, Oxford OX2 6DP

Oxford New York Toronto
Delhi Bombay Calcutta Madras Karachi
Petaling Jaya Singapore Hong Kong Tokyo
Nairobi Dar es Salam Cape Town
Melbourne Auckland

and associated companies in
Beirut Berlin Ibadan Nicosia

Oxford is a trade mark of Oxford University Press

Published in the United States
by Oxford University Press, New York

© SIPRI 1987

British Library Cataloguing in Publication Data

The Uncertain course: new weapons,
  strategies and mind-sets.
  1. War 2. Peace
  I. Jacobsen, Carl G. II. Stockholm
  International Peace Research Institute
  327.1 JX1952
  ISBN 0–19–829115–9

Library of Congress Cataloging in Publication Data

The Uncertain course.
  "Stockholm International Peace Research Institute."
  1. Military art and science—History—20th century.
2. Weapons systems. I. Jacobsen, C. G. (Carl G.)
II. Stockholm International Peace Research Institute.
U42.U53 1987 355'.02'0904 86–33278
ISBN 0–19–829115–9

Set by Wyvern Typesetting, Bristol
Printed and bound in
Great Britain by Biddles Ltd.,
Guildford and King's Lynn

Contents

Part 2.   New military capabilities, new doctrines

Part 3.   New complications for international security

Part 4.   Beyond the security dilemma

The uncertain course: introduction

New strategic, doctrinal and military-technological dynamics are changing the nature and likelihood of war. They promise to revolutionize military affairs as fundamentally as gunpowder and the atomic bomb once did. We are entering a new, vastly more complex nuclear and post-nuclear age. *The Uncertain Course* presents the first comprehensive analysis of the most important of these separate yet interdependent and mutually reinforcing dynamics: exotic technologies and battle management; space weapons; the cruise missile explosion; new naval reach; the US Army's forward Air/Land doctrine; Soviet 'Operational Manoeuvre Groups' and 'Theatres of Military-Strategic Operations'; and new challenges complicating international security calculations. Mind-sets are also discussed: we have twenty-first century weapons and nineteenth century mind-sets. Computers and artificial intelligence lessen our comprehension and control. The risks of inadvertent war and inadvertent cataclysm are increasing, even as the risk of deliberate war may be diminishing.

Historically, periods of very rapid technological advance combined with old concepts of strategy have always been dangerous. Technology outrunning strategy—the single most notable characteristic of today's strategic environment—has proved particularly dangerous. Uncertainty can be breeding ground for restraint, or for paranoia. Space deployments as an outgrowth of terrestrial doctrines bring to mind earlier dysfunctions, such as naval cannons using land tactics—periods of volatile change, and surprise.

'The 'risk of war' is changing. The risk of war as a political act is decreasing. The risk of war as a consequence of dysfunction between control and complexity is increasing. War by accident is a greater danger than war by design.

The Uncertain Course focuses on the interlocking dynamic of rapidly evolving technologies and strategies. Defence ministry and public debates tend to centre on single issues, or issue clusters, such as space militarization, 'counterforce' missiles and forward deployments that cut an opponent's reaction time. Yet, sometimes developments within one cluster may, in fact, impact more dramatically on the potential of another. The grandiose dreams initially associated with the Strategic Defense Initiative, for example, now appear ephemeral and unrealizable. But technological innovations fuelled by these dreams have other, realizable ramifications. They dramatically change prospects for war at sea, and blur the distinction between naval and land combat. In the crucial Barents and Okhotsk Sea regions, in particular, these developments have immediate consequences for Soviet 'Theatres of Military-Strategic Operations' (usually referred to by their Russian acronym, TVD). And these consequences, in turn, affect the confrontation between TVD postures and Western Air/Land doctrines on the central front. By concentrating on single issues and clusters, we see the trees, but not the forest. It is the interlocking totality of today's strategic-military-technological revolution that must be appreciated if we are to retain control.

Greatly improved speeds, accuracy, mobility and C³I—command, control, communication and intelligence—tempt strategic pre-emption. But they also compel the judgement that the opponent's growing and ever-more diversified retaliatory capabilities cannot be thwarted. The very dynamics that make pre-emption plausible also make it futile. Yet history cautions that crisis and desperation lead to different concepts of rationality. What is a cost-benefit calculation in peacetime becomes a damage-limitation exercise in crisis. Quick crisis redeployments to guard deterrence (and hence retaliatory potential)—a quintessential defensive action—may have high-tension implications for the opponent. Without strategic defences of substance, the increasing likelihood of more potent and multi-faceted retaliation will probably deter. With strategic defences in place, crisis decision-making may favour pre-emption.

We are used to thinking about a superpower arms race. We should instead be talking about arms rivalry or arms competition. The word 'race' is misleading. It diverts attention from other propellents, like inter-service rivalries, the lobbying power and vested interests of military-industrial combines, research laboratories and bureaucracies, and cultures that associate technological advance with progress. If the actors are racing, they are doing so on different tracks, tracks separated by a hill; or, as suggested by another scholar: one side is playing on a US football field, the other on a soccer field—if the ball from one falls on the other field, it causes consternation and confusion. A race can be regulated, or called off. Independent processes are difficult to harmonize.

Past arms control efforts have focused on the outputs from these processes. The outputs were never strictly comparable. The United States, for example, traditionally preferred fewer, but higher-technology and more costly units, while the Soviet Union—partly from choice and partly of necessity—focused on simpler, more easily replaceable and more numerous units. Nevertheless, the units, whether missiles, planes, tanks or personnel, were analogous. But lasers, particle beams and other exotic technologies, computer software and artificial intelligence (AI), cruise missiles and other weaponry designed to embody qualitatively different options—nuclear and conventional, strategic and tactical—defy easy categorization. They obfuscate both the nature and the number of units of relevance.

The coincidence of rampant technological change and adversarial doctrines poisons political relationships, increases the stakes and makes prospects for arms control more difficult. Arms control efforts during the 1960s and 1970s were essentially confidence-building measures that sought improved communication and avoidance of unnecessarily provocative and destabilizing deployment patterns. Arms control regulated the competition. It connoted control. It did not retard the pace of the competition. Instead, it suggested that an intensified pace was safe. The early and mid-1980s brought no regulatory advance. There was less real negotiation than at any time since the 1950s. Arms control meetings and protestations were spurious. Yet they retained their anodyne effect. The pace of the arms competition intensified further.

Is negotiated arms control necessary? If the propellants driving the arms competition are domestic, the main regulators may also be. The inter-service rivalries that balloon requirements at times of financial largesse, may dampen or diffuse them under the pressure of financial stringency. There can be unwitting arms control. Self-restraint and less provocative procurement strategies are not necessarily incorporated into and do not necessarily emanate from a formal negotiating process.

Yet nuclear and 'post-nuclear' arms are not self-regulating. Requirements of budget control, technological 'friction' and other factors may impose restraint. But considerations of threat control and uncertainty control demand tacit or formal agreement with the adversary. Whether informal, formal, non-negotiated or negotiated, control ultimately requires management. Control and restraint must, in the final analysis, be reciprocal in nature. It must be codified, though it may not have to be in treaty form. Serious arms control must legitimize modernization. Arms control cannot be seen as a final outcome. It is a process. It is not control. It is a vehicle for control. It is not arms reduction or disarmament. It is a step back from the dangers of unregulated competition, and paranoia, no more, no less.

Arms control of the 1960s and 1970s concentrated on quantity, on units of output, because the control of quality appeared too difficult. Today, the output is becoming so complex that qualitative arms control may prove easier and more efficacious. Qualitative arms control can never be truly comprehensive. Intrusive arms control that covers design and laboratory research is not feasible. Incremental modernization cannot be denied. But the threat of more precipitous destabilizing change can be eviscerated or diffused. Warhead designs and targeting accuracies, for example, can evolve without testing. But confident evaluation of new generation devices that promise more dramatic change demands testing.

Today's phenomenon of increased strategic mobility, security-threatening to proponents of counterforce, is security-enhancing to advocates of deterrence, and those reconciled to the reality and inevitability of mutual assured destruction (MAD). In much the same way, the uncertainties that would attend a test ban, anathema to proponents of counterforce, because it would undermine the targeting confidence that is a *sine qua non* of counterforce (and pre-emption), would, for that very same reason, be confidence-boosting and security-enhancing to those reconciled to MAD.

The choice is, in fact, becoming starker. The perhaps inexorable trend towards militarization of space and the unquestionable trend towards a proliferation of nuclear and chemical-biological capable cruise missiles on planes and aboard naval vessels and, in the Soviet case, probably civilian vessels, suggests a future in which the United States also will face the unpalatable reality of hostile 'forward-based systems' around its periphery, and less and less warning time. Without qualitative restrictions that clearly limit confident extrapolations of theoretical targeting abilities, fears of crisis pre-emption will fester and grow. Another corollary is that the United States will be forced to reject the intercontinental-range definition of strategic weaponry, and embrace that of the Soviet Union, Britain and France, which classifies all mass-destruction weaponry capable of striking home territory as strategic.

Technologies developed and pursued during the 1980s in the hope that they would circumvent the moral dilemma of MAD now promise instead to embed it, as the unavoidable reality also of the foreseeable future. MAD's apparent imperviousness to technological fix or finesse establishes the foundation for and possibility of negotiation and adjustment. Domestic restraints and unilateral measures do not suffice to ensure control. Effective control cannot be unilateral. Arms control without arms control is not possible.

The pace and character of today's developments emasculate many of the traditional spectres of doves, arms controllers and hawks—the fears of 'roll back communism' advocates, the 'action–reaction' arms race postulate and 'the Russians are coming' appear divorced from new and emerging realities. Their survival reflects the dysfunction between old mind-sets and new weapons.

We focus on counterforce, on temptation and fear arising from new targeting options against military installations and stationary and less mobile force elements. Yet, we sometimes forget that counterforce scenarios fail to negate the opponent's more important countervalue capabilities—the ability to strike population centres and economic targets. Unsatisfied with mere deterrence, for it emasculates us as effectively as it stymies them, we seek the edge that gives relative leverage. We seek 'extended deterrence' and the means with which to pursue compellent strategy. The latter, embraced by the Reagan Administration, has many antecedents, on both sides of the divide. Historically, the posture has had successes, but only against lesser opponents, and in peripheral regions. Today, the extraordinary diversity and survivability of superpower strike options relegate relative advantage in one or more areas to the realm of the superfluous; the concept of meaningful advantage has become a mirage, itself dangerous.

MAD mocks notions of decisive big-power war. And the military, as institutions, have learned that 'small' commitments tend to grow. Yet, doctrines now in place call for escalatory nuclear engagements, and the ability to go anywhere and do anything.

The complexities that ensure countervalue retaliation and mock the counterforce mirage that attends sophisticated targeting options also break the bounds of comprehension—and make advanced control illusory.

Crisis stability is a contradiction. The term fosters only the illusion of control. We must instead seek to stabilize the arms competition, an environment of neither excessive temptation nor provocation. Technology is not autonomous. It has been used to escalate the pace of competition and to increase uncertainty; it can be used to dampen that pace and to increase confidence. We need to reduce forces that suggest pre-emption. The counter-force syndrome—the temptation and fear—must be excised; current and foreseeable developments compel the conclusion that it is unrealizable. Acceptance of this conclusion would ease military planning. And, it would alleviate strategic requirements. Deterrence requires far less than compellence or counterforce.

Today's strategies and doctrines derive from pre-nuclear experience and reality. They have evolved, but their essence echoes the big-power postulates of a world safe for war. The environment has altered, qualitatively and decisively, and the clock cannot be turned back, but mind-sets and action patterns remain mired in an older era. Evolution or extinction? Mankind may face the ultimate Darwinian challenge.

The papers that follow look at the most important new trends and dynamics. The authors have been chosen for their expertise and detachment; the focus is on pragmatism, not idealism, though the former may ultimately demand a measure of the latter. The emphasis on new is deliberate, to steer away from the arguments of the past and to help orient debate towards newer realities. This emphasis is relaxed only in the papers that analyse Soviet developments, because their history is less well known and because some appreciation of their antecedents is a necessary prerequisite for evaluation and judgement.

Many new weapon systems are not discussed. No paper deals with the problems of chemical-biological warfare, nuclear proliferation (though this may be affected by technological change), regional security or terrorism. These are issues that may alter individual or regional prospects for life or death. They are less likely to alter prospects for global life or death.

The book addresses only those new strategic, doctrinal and military-techno-logical dynamics that impact most immediately on the nature and likelihood of major war. Coverage in breadth of all issues of importance has been sacrificed for coverage in depth of the crucial new dynamics that now alter the character of the risk of war—major war—in our times. The book aspires to provide an overview and to lay the foundation for detailed follow-up studies of particular weapons and doctrinal nuances.

Part 1 presents the context of superpower relations during the early and mid-1980s; an evaluation of the pioneering, but national and less than comprehensive 'Arms Control Impact Statements' mandated by the US Congress; and a historical essay on strategy and ethnocentricity—the impact on strategy of differing mind-sets and different national prisms.

Parts 2, 3 and 4—the heart of the book—discuss new weapon systems, evolving strategies and doctrines, new complications and new (all-too-often reincarnations of old) mind-sets.

Acknowledgements: To Barbara Adams for her conscientious editorial assistance; to Nenne Bodell, who hunted down and doublechecked our most obscure references; to Anna Helleday and Åsa Pihlstrand for organizing a most productive workshop; to Åsa Pihlstrand, again, for also having helped type the papers; and to families and friends, who sustained us—the authors are grateful!

Stockholm,   CARL G. JACOBSEN
November 1986

List of contributors to this book

Dr Ken Booth
Senior Lecturer
Department of International Politics
University College of Wales
Aberystwyth SY23 3DB
UK

Dr Allan M. Din
Senior Research Fellow
SIPRI
Pipers väg 28
S-171 73 Solna
Sweden

Dr Richard W. Fieldhouse
Research Fellow
SIPRI
Pipers väg 28
S-171 73 Solna
Sweden

Professor Carl G. Jacobsen
Senior Research Officer
SIPRI
Pipers väg 28
S-171 73 Solna
Sweden

Dr David R. Jones
Director, Russian Micro-project
Killam Library
Dalhousie University
Halifax, NS
Canada

Dr William H. Kincade
Adjunct Professor of National
  Security Studies
Georgetown University
National Security Studies Program
Intercultural Center
Washington, DC 20057
USA

Professor Jacob W. Kipp
Soviet Army Studies Office
US Army Combined Arms Center
Fort Leavenworth, KS 66027–5000
USA

Mr Edward A. Kolodziej
Director, Program in Arms Control,
  Disarmament, and International
  Security
University of Illinois
330 Davenport Hall
607 Mathews
Urbana, IL 61801
USA

Mr Michael Krepon
Senior Associate
Carnegie Endowment for
  International Peace
11 Dupont Circle, NW
Washington, DC 20036
USA

Ms Laurel C. Schneider
Assistant Director, Educational
  Programs
Women's Action for Nuclear
  Disarmament
691 Massachusetts Avenue
Arlington, MA 02174
USA

Dr Gerald Segal
Lecturer
Department of Politics
University of Bristol
12 Priory Road
Bristol BS8 1TU
UK

Dr Phil Williams
Lecturer
Department of Politics
University of Southampton
Highfield Southampton SO9 5NH
UK

Dr Nicholas J. Wheeler
Lecturer
International Politics
University College of Wales
Aberystwyth SY23 3DB
UK

The Uncertain Course

Edited by Carl G. Jacobsen
Oxford University Press, Oxford, 1987, 374pp.
(Stockholm International Peace Research Institute)

ISBN 0–19–829115–9

Abstracts

PAPER 1.1. International dynamics: arms
defiant

Carl G. Jacobsen

This paper, which discusses current international dynamics, provides a background for this book. It traces, from 1980, the evolution of US and Soviet military-political postures, strategies and doctrines, and it analyses their interrelationship and import. Interests that appear to compel great power accommodation are juxtaposed to other interests that continue to thwart, undermine or dilute the prospect of lasting accord.

PAPER 1.2. Arms Control Impact
Statements (ACISs): critique and
prescription

Laurel C. Schneider

In the early 1970s, the US Congress initiated the Arms Control Impact Statements (ACISs) in an attempt to analyse the implications of new weapon technologies on prospects for arms limitation. As they are now structured, the ACISs have failed in their mission because they have not adequately or effectively established the negative link between current weapon innovation and future arms control.

This analysis of the ACISs explores the concept of arms control impact and, through an examination of structural flaws in the ACIS process, identifies some basic requirements for impact assessment. The failure of the ACISs reveals underlying contradictions in US policy and the arms control process. Impact assessment requires a degree of objectivity that is not native to governmental agencies, but it is a pursuit that is essential to eventual arms limitation.

PAPER 1.3. New challenges and old mindsets: ten rules for empirical realists

Ken Booth

Although we live in a 'war system', our understanding of threats remains very limited. In addition to the inherent problems of weighing ambiguous information and future possibilities, threat perception and assessment have been confused by four powerful and regressive mindsets: ethnocentrism, the doctrine of Realism, ideological fundamentalism and strategic reductionism. In order to overcome these and replace them by 'empirical' or 'sophisticated' realism as an approach to international politics, 10 rules are suggested to stimulate thought and encourage a closer matching of our images and the world 'as it is'. In the course of discussing these rules, it is suggested that there is less to the Soviet threat than meets the eye and that we need to reconsider who are the real 'realists' confronting today's international challenges.

PAPER 2.1. The sources and implications
of new military capability

William H. Kincade

Innovation in military technology, techniques and tactics produces new military capability, which alters the security situation and creates pressure for change in institutions, attitudes and doctrines. The complex processes leading to and engendered by new military capability are little examined and less understood. In general, new military capability relaxes constraints involved in specific operational tasks. It arises from a significant advance in a basic or component technology, achievement of a synergistic effect by the interaction of either two or more basic technologies or two or more weapons, or by some combination of these developments. The impact of new military capability is highly variable and context-dependent; for example, new capability may be evolutionary in development and revolutionary in its consequences or vice versa. Two predisposing images or attitudes that influence responses to new military capability are the *command technology* model and the *autonomous technology* model.

facto recognition of the doctrine of mutual assured destruction (MAD) and, subsequently, a switch of focus from strategic nuclear systems back to the conventional battlefield. The paper concludes by considering the implications of this switch for Soviet conceptions of strategic defence, especially in space, and for their attitude to both the Strategic Defence Initiative (SDI) and the future of arms control.

PAPER 2.2.   Strategic defence and international security

Gerald Segal

The concept of strategic defence is not new in strategic studies, but the expectations for the Strategic Defense Initiative (SDI) are the most ambitious yet. This paper assesses the three main variants of strategic defence in the West, including the perfect SDI, more limited ballistic missile defence, and the European Defence Initiative (EDI). It concludes that no programme is anywhere near to fruition, and yet the very serious consideration given to the plans risks undermining international security. The impact on arms control is also a major cause for concern. The paper concludes with four scenarios for the future, suggesting that the most likely is the quiet shelving of SDI in its original population defence and its missiles (only)-protecting Ballistic Missile Defence (BMD) modes.

PAPER 2.3.   Soviet military doctrine and space in the 1980s

David R. Jones

The capabilities of the Soviet Union's existing strategic air defence (PVO) network are first examined quantitatively and qualitatively in terms of their technological levels and ability to defend the Homeland against US air-breathing weapon systems. Attention then turns to the related themes of ballistic missile defence (BMD; or, the Russian acronym, PRO) and space-war (the Russian acronym, PKO) weaponry, both of which were considered aspects of air defence until 1976. The writer then argues that the Soviet General Staff's negative assessment of these capabilities was one factor in the doctrinal revision that began around 1976 under Marshal V. I. Kulikov. Gaining momentum under Marshal N. V. Ogarkov, this review gradually brought the more or less open Soviet acceptance of the reality of nuclear parity, a *de*

PAPER 2.4.   Conventional force modernization and the asymmetries of military doctrine: historical reflections on Air/Land Battle and the Operational Manoeuvre Group

Jacob W. Kipp

Over the last decade there has been an increasing concern about the role of conventional military forces in deterrence. This essay examines the very different ideological, geostrategic, political and military context in which the Soviet military art and US military doctrine have addressed the problem of conventional force modernization in the post-war period. The current debate about Air/Land Battle, the Operational Manoeuvre Group and Follow-on Forces Attack is best understood within the historical context of the evolution of Soviet and US military art/military doctrine in the post-war period. This evolutionary process can be broken down into four periods: post-war assimilation of lessons learned during World War II and emergence of the Cold War, the nuclear-rocket revolution in military affairs and the decline in importance of conventional military power, conventional forces within the context of mutual nuclear deterrence, and the resurgence of interest in conventional force modernization as a strategic option. In each period, the different socio-political and geostrategic contexts of each power's military system led to radically different solutions to the dilemmas created by the perceived threat and the anticipated impact of new techology upon force structure, tactics and operational art.

In the West, this latest period has been dominated by concerns regarding the Soviet military's ability to engage in a blitzkrieg-line, theatre-strategic operation against the North Atlantic Treaty Organization (NATO)'s Central Front. This issue has shaped the current debate regarding the ability of NATO's defences to withstand such a threat without immediately resorting to nuclear weapons. The recent increase in conventional military capabilities, associated with precision-guided munitions, air-mobile forces, and automated command and control has complicated the problem of deterrence and left unresolved the uncertainty in the linkage between the employment of such forces against the other power and escalation to theatre nuclear and strategic levels. Such capabilities have, however, made it imperative that both sides address the problem of reducing the risks of surprise attack and doctrinal misunderstanding.

thus is an integral component of Soviet military power. Whereas the Navy's only vital force from the 1960s through the early 1980s was its submarine-launched ballistic missiles (SLBMs), today other branches of the Navy are assuming comparable importance.

PAPER 2.5.   US naval strategy and nuclear weapons

Richard W. Fieldhouse

Since the mid-1980s, the US Navy has been proposing, debating and implementing a new offensive naval strategy—one for fighting a global, protracted conventional war against the USSR. While both the US and Soviet Navies are thoroughly armed with nuclear weapons, the new strategy seems to ignore intentionally this fundamental reality; thus the danger that a superpower naval conflict could involve the use of nuclear weapons increases. Accordingly, numerous elements of the evolving strategy are controversial, including the goals of making any conflict global, sinking Soviet ballistic missile submarines, and launching strikes against Soviet territory. This chapter examines the new US naval strategy in light of these issues and suggests the need for an alternative.

PAPER 2.6.   Soviet strategy: the naval dimension

Carl G. Jacobsen

The historical evolution and ambitions of the Russian and Soviet Fleets are traced in this paper, within the larger context of historic Russian–Soviet strategy, doctrine and geopolitical realities. Historically, forward deployment is not novel for the Russian Navy; it has had several brief periods of relative flexibility. But in its quest to find a role for itself, the Soviet (and predecessor) Navy has always had its more ambitious instincts curbed by the state. The pattern of expanded naval influence threatened again in the 1970s and early 1980s, only to be tempered by the traditional land orientation of the military. Today, the Soviet Navy is being successfully integrated into the combined-arms Soviet military system, and

PAPER 2.7.   Future cruise missiles: nature and impact

William H. Kincade

Cruise missile technology dates to World War I and was employed by Germany in World War II. Yet it was only with the advent of improved guidance, propulsion and warhead technologies in the 1970s that this aerodynamic projectile amounted to a new and versatile military capability. Among many advantages is its compatibility with a variety of existing land, sea and air weapon platforms. Already proven in limited conflicts, first-generation versions of modern cruise missiles show great potential for a variety of applications—tactical, theatre and strategic—and for future development into stealth-configured, supersonic weapons. Coupled with advances in other types of air-breathing weapon, they may have the effect of changing military strategy, both conventional and nuclear. Difficult to detect with confidence, cruise missiles reflect the larger trend towards weapons that cannot be monitored by existing or foreseeable surveillance technology. Besides posing problems for military intelligence and arms control, cruise missiles increase the vulnerability of all classes of target.

PAPER 2.8.   The implications of increased mobility, force diversification and counterforce capabilities for strategic arms control

Michael Krepon

Three interconnected trends in Soviet and US nuclear forces—mobility and diversification of nuclear weapon launchers, and the continued accumulation of counterforce capabilities—have generated concerns over strategic stability and prospects for arms control. Currently mobility and diversity have outpaced counterforce growth, and retaliatory forces on both sides have grown. But strategic force requirements have also increased, driven largely by war-fighting doctrines of deterrence. An extension of these trends means accelerated nuclear arms competition, particularly with decisions to deploy space-based strategic defences. Successful arms reduction agreements will depend on relaxing counterforce requirements, and non-deployment of space-based defences. Future agreements will have to address limitations of mobile land-based missiles and sea-launched cruise missiles. Alternative approaches are discussed.

PAPER 3.1. Modernization of British and French nuclear forces: arms control and security dimensions

Edward A. Kolodziej

French and British nuclear modernization poses serious arms control and security problems for· the superpowers. Possessing essentially second-strike invulnerable forces, each appears to have the capacity to inflict intolerable damage on the Soviet Union; each also hampers superpowers in their attempt to define a stable nuclear balance.

Four conditions have been implicitly and explicitly cited by British and French officials, with varying degrees of intensity, as prerequisites for their participation in arms control talks. First, neither will enter into negotiations in the absence of significant reductions in superpower offensive nuclear capabilities. Second, both reject the incorporation of European nuclear forces into an exclusively European zone lest the superpowers agree to a sanctuarization of their homelands at the expense of Western Europe. Third, little progress (add the French) can be made on nuclear issues unless there are significant reductions of superpower conventional forces, especially those of the Soviet Union. Fourth, neither superpower can be permitted an advantage in the development of defensive systems against nuclear attack.

PAPER 3.2. Chinese nuclear forces: overview and ambitions

Richard W. Fieldhouse

China is the most recent and most obscure nuclear weapon state. It has built a nuclear arsenal of some 300–400 nuclear weapons, deployed in a 'triad', to assure a retaliatory capacity against a Soviet nuclear attack. Although China has incentives to avoid a major military competition, it appears that it will take such steps as it deems necessary to maintain some form of nuclear sufficiency. If the USA and the USSR continue their nuclear and strategic defence competition, it may compel China to embark on new nuclear weapon programmes to maintain its nuclear sufficiency. If, however, the superpowers can forgo the deployment of strategic defences and reduce the theatre nuclear forces in Asia, the way to relaxed nuclear tensions and improved relations between China and the USSR could open up. China's nuclear ambitions are thus in flux.

PAPER 3.3. Strategy, security and advanced computing

Allan M. Din

The decision-making processes that are required to implement current strategy and security concepts are becoming increasingly complex. The time-urgency of many decisions compels the large-scale use of computers and advanced computing techniques, including artificial intelligence techniques. The impact on strategy and security is analysed for some military applications where computers and automation are playing, or might come to play, an important role.

PAPER 3.4. Emerging technology, exotic technology and arms control

Phil Williams

This paper identifies several major trends in weapon technology—increasing miniaturization, improved accuracy, greater fungibility, improved surveillance capabilities and development of exotic technologies—and assesses their impact on the strategic environment of the 1990s and beyond. Although increased command, control, communications and intelligence (C^3I) capabilities could provide an illusion of controllability, the overall result will be a blurring of thresholds and an increased likelihood of escalation from conventional to nuclear hostilities. The key problem is unbridled technological enthusiasm, especially in the United States, and this will make it difficult to devise effective arms control arrangements for the 1990s and beyond.

PAPER 4.1.   Control of war, crisis and armed peace: new challenges

William H. Kincade

The increased scale, pace and potential destructiveness of modern warfare pose challenges to the political and military control of the use of force that will intensify in the future. The improved control of weaponry contrasts sharply with lags in the control of war itself. The information revolution has changed but not alleviated the problem of fog of war or battle; the new battle management systems—crucial to conflict and escalation control—are vulnerable to disruption by attack, deception or internal failure modes. Information warfare may thus be decisive in many types of future conflict. Beyond nuclear scenarios, little effort has been made to evaluate control systems, especially in human and institutional terms, and to link their effectiveness to the many demands they face. Future analysis must address a far broader array of interactions, contingencies and system elements or qualities.

PAPER 4.2.   Beyond the security dilemma: technology, strategy and international security

Nicholas J. Wheeler and Ken Booth

The international system is anarchic, but far from being exclusively characterized by Hobbesian security dilemmas. Other paradigm conditions are possible, including insecurity traps and security communities. Lasting international security requires the creation of a 'legitimate international order', one in which states behave with moderation, and recognize the rights of others without requiring changes in their domestic order. Restraint and reciprocity are necessary and possible, though the historical record of such periods has not been encouraging. The interplay of strategy and technology with international security is a complex one, and it admits few generalizations, except that there are no technological fixes to what are fundamentally political problems and that order is more likely to be achieved in periods of technological restraint rather than in those where states seek unilateral advantage through rapid innovation. In the light of this, prevailing superpower mind-sets can be seen as representing a fundamental challenge to a lasting international order in the future.

Part 1.   Old mind-sets, new weapons

Paper 1.1. International dynamics: arms defiant

CARL G. JACOBSEN

I. Introduction

Secretary of State George Shultz's January 1985 meeting with Foreign Minister Andrei Gromyko, to re-establish an arms control dialogue, drew a sigh of relief from most of the world's media. The October 1985 summit meeting between President Ronald Reagan and General Secretary Mikhail Gorbachov, in which the two leaders agreed that 'nuclear war cannot be won and must never be fought'; Gorbachov's startling arms cut proposals of early 1986; and the tantalizing, yet elusive, siren call of the Reykjavik arms reduction package heightened expectations. The early 1980s saw the doomsday clock of the *Bulletin of the Atomic Scientists* twice move closer to midnight.[1] Both powers reviled the other. Arms negotiations broke off. US arms spending rose and the USSR's did not abate, even though scientists estimated that just 2 per cent of existing arsenals would suffice to threaten nuclear winter. Now, however, pessimism is joined by hope.

A number of domestic, economic and external alliance considerations compel both sides to embrace visions of dramatic arms cuts. But, the respective visions rest on incompatible premises. And, current arms dynamics threaten to relegate apparently sweeping cut-back agreements to the realm of spurious arms control. Established weapon programmes chafe against the Strategic Arms Limitation Talks (SALT) limits. The modernization pace outstrips older system retirement possibilities; in December 1986 the USA crossed the SALT threshold for strategic delivery systems. At the same time, today's exotic weapons-driven revolution in military affairs and very different deployment options suggest that otherwise advanced components may be redundant. Hence, even sizeable cuts if agreed, might yet be spurious.

Arms stabilization and arms control prospects are hostage to obviously contradictory policy dynamics in Washington, and to less obvious but analogous dynamics in Moscow. These need to be addressed.

II. US policy dynamics

In 1981 the incoming Reagan Administration projected a deliberately exaggerated image of Soviet power. Yes, the Soviet Union had acquired a lead in certain crude quantitative categories of power, and in some cases crude units may even be more effective and reliable than over-sophisticated ones. The USSR had also acquired some distant power projection capabilities—air and sea.

But the US Office of the Under Secretary of Defense for Research and Engineering and the US Office of Technology Assessment both confirmed (and still do) significant US advantage in most areas of basic technology. And US Defense Department statistics still show a US lead in the five most important categories: total warhead numbers; overall accuracy, far more important than yield; warhead miniaturization technologies, which allow more on smaller missiles; readiness norms—the US Navy's percentage of battle-ready sub-marines is four times higher than the Soviet Navy's, and similar discrepancies affect other force elements; and vulnerability, with three-quarters of the USSR's strategic arsenals land-based, and theoretically vulnerable, compared to less than 20 per cent of the USA's.[2]

Some areas of asserted Soviet quantitative advantage were sleight-of-hand projections. The Soviet Navy had and still has more ships, but an aircraft carrier is not equivalent to a coastal patrol craft. The US Navy retains a two-to-one lead in tonnage and in the ability to sustain distant voyages. The Soviet Union does have more tanks; however, figures that include Soviet reserves and not the North Atlantic Treaty Organization (NATO)'s and that ignore quali-tative factors (e.g., NATO tanks' twice-higher average firing rate) are not helpful.[3]

Distortion and/or exaggeration of enemy strength is a universal phenomenon, especially when defence budgets are presented to legislatures. In this case, however, the effort went beyond established norms. And it apparently did so, at least in part, because the driving ambition was stronger, less restrained.

Reagan was openly disdainful of arms control when he assumed office. Two decades of arms control had not slowed growth in offensive nuclear capabili-ties. He feared that the process had lulled people into a false sense of security. He was surely partly sincere when he described the USSR as an 'evil empire'. This puritan heritage, this conceptualizing of the world as divided between GOOD and EVIL, gave arms control a sinful connotation. US–Soviet arms control is predicated on a willingness to concede bottom-line parity. The biblical vision (like that of Karl Marx) calls for unremitting struggle.

Some elements of the Reagan Administration's defence programme, such as the MX, the Trident, the B1 and Stealth bombers, and cruise missiles, all initially funded, researched and/or developed by previous administrations, could be seen as emblematic of the traditional US drive to maintain an edge. But previous administrations, both Republican and Democratic, recognized that the edge was relative. They conceded the present and likely future reality of MAD (mutual assured destruction), and hence the need for arms control.

The Reagan Administration, however, was not resigned to MAD, or to the concomitant thesis that arms control was a vehicle for systems stability. It appeared instead to set for itself the goal of re-establishing meaningful US superiority.

The administration's embrace of nuclear utilization theories (NUTS) fuelled Pentagon procurement programmes explicitly designed to render accumulated Soviet weapon stocks 'obsolete'. The thrust found political expression in the forward deployment of Pershing II ballistic missiles in Europe. The deployment defied a tacit 20-year agreement not to deploy shorter-range ballistic missiles up against the other's territory. The denial of reciprocal Soviet rights in Cuba underlined the challenge: the Soviet Union must accept disadvantage or precipitate crisis.[4]

But the more important military moves lay elsewhere. One was the adoption of new doctrines for war-fighting in Europe, for quick-response deep penetration and nuclear interdiction (Air/Land). Another, perhaps more crucial, was the procurement of new carriers and naval task forces assigned to target the established jugular of Soviet defence systems, the Barents and Okhotsk sanctuaries that harbour her submarine-launched ballistic missiles (SLBMs), her retaliatory forces, her deterrent.[5] Complementary air and other support facilities in Norway, Iceland and Japan were upgraded and modernized.

Finally, the most dramatic ambition: the USA's Strategic Defense Initiative (SDI, or Star Wars). Laser, high-energy particle beam, anti-ballistic missile and other technologies integral to (multi-layered) space defence visions received priority funding. The USA's population was to be made immune from nuclear horrors.[6]

The Pershing deployment, the Soviet Union's move of some additional missile subs closer to US shores, the dynamics of forward deployment and assertion, and the promise of space systems programmed for automatic action/ response caused widespread concern. US warning systems still spawn false alarms every month. Soviet systems may be more prone to malfunctions. The squeezing of time—time to verify and consider—is deeply perturbing.

Arms controllers nevertheless found some cause for solace. There had been fear that the USSR might feel forced to adopt a launch-on-warning strategy in response to the minimal flight time of the Pershings, or that it might prove defiant enough to move SS–20s to Cuba. But there was no evidence of the first (perhaps because the concept was utterly alien to Soviet doctrine, and tradition), and the measured choice of submarines as primary deployment response was one that made the military (if perhaps not the political) point without forcing immediate confrontation.

The appointment of Paul Nitze as Shultz's primary arms control adviser also appeared propitious. Nitze, the USA's senior conservative nuclear strategist and the Reagan Adminstration's negotiator on theatre-nuclear arms in Europe, before these talks broke off, was co-architect of the 'walk in the woods' formula. This formula, vetoed in Washington (and in Moscow, apparently in response to the US decision), called for Soviet Euro-missiles to be balanced by slower US cruise missiles, not ballistic Pershings. Nitze's reemergence suggested support for the thesis that Moscow's Pershing phobia must be accommodated if agreement is to be reached.

There was complementary caution on the ground. Reload missiles for the 108 Pershing II launchers were not deployed, in deference to German opposition. Furthermore, most warheads are stored off at observable distance from the missiles; only about 25 per cent are armed and on alert. This reflects non-strategic practice and is far below the readiness norms of US intercontinental ballistic missiles (ICBMs) and other strategic forces targeted on the Soviet Union.

Arms controllers also found grounds for optimism in the fact that internal US Navy documents evinced extreme scepticism concerning the Barents/Okhotsk mission.[7] Navy Secretary Lehman appeared undeterred, as did his Naval commander-in-chief.[8] But if in-house US Navy professionals found the task of all-out challenge to be overly daunting, then the Soviet Union might be presumed to feel some confidence—and therefore be less jittery. Some US attack submarines did penetrate into the Barents, near Soviet base complexes, and did threaten fleet components. Without supporting surface and air elements, however, they did not suffice to jeopardize the overall viability of the SLBM fleet. The limited attrition threat against single SLBM units furthermore came at a time of increasing Soviet confidence concerning ICBM survival trends; with more secure land-based second-strike potentials, SLBMs are no longer sole guarantors of retaliatory might. Underwater US prowling in the Barents may help Soviet Naval funding more than it undermines Soviet survival prospects.

Finally, a veritable who's who of the USA's most prominent scientific luminaries expressed doubts about the feasibility of a truly comprehensive 'Star Wars' defence system. To get there from here made the route from the Wright brothers' first plane to the 747 appear both short and easy. Remaining technological problems and plausible cost estimates (of up to a trillion dollars and more) appear equally prohibitive. Countermeasures are likely to prove cheaper, whether they take the form of laser-reflecting materials, nuclear mines 'parked' near space defence installations, increases in warhead numbers to offset the degradation potential of the defence system, and/or a mushrooming of supersonic, ground-hugging cruise missiles darting under the supposed defence shield. More importantly, however, it appears inconceivable that either side would tolerate completion of such a system by the other. No US President would acquiesce in a Soviet space defence system that would grant Soviet immunity and assign the USA to the ranks of lesser powers. No Soviet leader can accept the reverse.[9]

By 1985 the more grandiose vision/threat had receded. The ultimate ambition was constantly reaffirmed, and the plethora of technologies funded, propelled by its promise and fear, promise dynamic consequences across the whole gamut of military systems and services, not least the navy. But administration spokesmen confirm that the shorter- and medium-term focus has narrowed; practical efforts concentrate on 'point defence' of missile silos and command posts, and on interception during the terminal phase of strategic and perhaps tactical ballistic missiles.[10] These ambitions appear more feasible. They also concede MAD; population defence remains unattainable.

There thus opened a 'window of opportunity'. Pentagon officials conceded that the dream of absolute superiority and release from nuclear horrors appeared illusory. Arms controllers called for renewed efforts to regulate the arms competition.[11] Yet the goal of compellent advantage, though now again relative, a matter for subjective interpretation rather than objective necessity, continues to thwart acknowledgement of parity.

Two other motivational and explanatory approaches must be probed, one essentially psychological, the other part ideological, part economic. The psychological interpretation of White House motives suggests that the goal was not the ephemeral one of absolute military security, but, rather, psychological security.[12]

One might infer support for this view from the nature of the administration's unprecedented increases in defence spending. Congressional passage was secured through references to the 'Soviet threat'. But defence programmes were not focused on areas of real or perceived imbalance, real or perceived threat; nor were they focused on programmes that might lead to superiority, such as SDI, or the naval ambition to strike the Barents and the Okhotsk. The defence largesse was initially spread across the board, from military bands to fighting units.

1981's 'window of vulnerability' may have been a myth. But the USA's armed forces did suffer problems. Viet Nam's legacy, drugs and sometimes poor morale remained. The Rapid Deployment Force was being built up, but the army did not have general-issue canteens large enough to hold the daily water rations required for desert regions. The navy wanted more ships, but existing ships could not sail because of a shortage of technicians and specialists. The Reagan Administration's first-term efforts did improve morale, and drug addiction apparently did decrease. But the canteen problem remains. And improved specialist retention rates may owe more to economic uncertainties than to government policy. Ironically, one can argue that many of the real problems of 1981 have not been addressed; the financial windfall has passed them by.

This may have been due to Presidential disinterest. In his third year of stewardship, as President and Commander-in-chief, Reagan acknowledged that he was unaware of some of the central underpinnings of strategic reality: that the Soviet Union is disproportionally dependent on land-based missiles; that bombers and cruise missiles carry nuclear warheads; that submarine-launched missiles cannot be recalled.[13] He also appeared unconcerned.

The psychological explanation accounts for such anomalies. According to it, Reagan's primary concern is not the reality of Soviet power, but its image, and specifically the image it derived as a consequence of prevailing perceptions of US power. Reality matters less than perception. The perception of the USA's lack of resolve had to be addressed. What President Carter called the 'American malaise' had to be exorcized.

If this was the true goal of the defence effort, then it was achieved. This interpretation also augurs well for arms control. The perception of strength might be as illusory as the unnecessarily self-deprecating doubts of old. But if the administration should wish to pursue arms control, it is clearly now much freer to do so, with confidence.

The 'ideological/economic' approach, however, continues to thwart arms control aspirations (in concert with compellent strivings). It combines a view of inevitable, unremitting struggle with the conviction that the Soviet economic system will fail if forced into an all-out arms competition; arms agreements that temper the pace of the competition serve only to alleviate the Soviet burden and extend the menace to the United States. Richard Pipes, a nineteenth century historian who served as the National Security Council's Director for East European and Soviet Affairs during 1981–82, and Richard Perle, the Assistant Secretary of Defense, whose visceral opposition to military, economic and other accords with the USSR never wavered, are the main apostles of this thesis.[14] The professional Soviet Studies community is deeply sceptical on both counts. And there is the historical fact that wars are more often initiated by nations under pressure, in decline, or fearing decline or the passing nature of advantage than by nations confident of status and security. The premises underlying the ideological/economic thesis may prove a more dangerous lodestar if true, than if false.

III.   Soviet policy dynamics

The US Central Intelligence Agency (CIA)'s 1983 re-evaluation of Soviet defence spending trends, a re-evaluation confirmed and reiterated in 1986, confirmed dramatically lower estimates than previously accepted.[15] Soviet military spending growth was limited to 2 to 3 per cent annually, from 1970 to 1985. 1985 saw a near 12 per cent increase in the official budget (operational expenses), purportedly in response to SDI. Yet there was no increase in budget accounts thought to cover other categories of military spending, and there was no further increase in 1986. The 1985 figure suggested alternative options; the 1986 figure reflected continued restraint.

The restraint pre-dated and can therefore not be ascribed to poor growth in the general economy (though possibly contrary ambitions during the first half of the 1980s may have been impeded by the leadership's increased emphasis on economic and social reform). The CIA confirms that Soviet military procurement rates show no growth since the mid-1970s. Total outlays for the Strategic Rocket Troops and Air Defence actually 'declined in absolute terms after 1977'. The estimated growth in Soviet defence expenditures reflects high research, development, testing and evaluation (RDT&E) assumptions (described as 'least reliable').

Considering so-called lead time, the time needed to research, develop and test new weapons, it is evident that the decision to decelerate strategic investments dates back to the late 1960s or early 1970s—that is, the time leading up to the signing of SALT I. This suggests basic Soviet satisfaction with the balance struck by SALT, and Soviet acceptance of the thesis that Mutual Assured Destruction—its central tenet—was likely to endure.

In terms of military doctrine, the early and mid-1960's Soviet stress on the suicide implications of nuclear war initiation had been followed by a contrary stress on war-fighting and war-winning.[16] General Secretary Brezhnev's Tula speech and Marshal Ogarkov's appointment as Chief of the General Staff, in 1977, signalled emphatic return to the earlier posture.[17]

Ogarkov's tenure saw ever-increased emphasis on the mutuality of the cataclysm that would necessarily and inevitably attend the unleashing of strategic nuclear war. He heaped scorn on the illusions of those who thought such wars could be either contained or controlled. Strategic nuclear weapons could have no other purpose than to deter their use by others. They promised doomsday and had no military utility. If the dynamics of local land or sea conflict did bring nuclear weapons into play, then there was only one possible escalatory fire-break: the inviolability of superpower homelands.[18]

Ogarkov stressed new, 'smart' and exotic technologies which, with novel operational concepts, might circumvent the nuclear impasse. He emphasized that new non-nuclear technologies promised to achieve the military tasks once assigned to nuclear weapons, without the latter's attendant threat of collateral self-destruct.

The priority assigned to technological innovation spanned offensive and defensive realms (though re-invigorated pursuit of orthodox and unorthodox ballistic missile defence potentials continued to focus on ground basing). It also gave credence to high RDT&E estimates.

The late 1970s and early 1980s saw extensive organizational changes affecting Soviet force structures, changes designed to increase conventional flexibility and options and to allow at least for the possibility of large-scale conventional war. Soviet forces were made more mobile and more aeromobile across the board. Combined arms 'theatre' groupings incorporating armies, fronts and, where appropriate, fleets were established in 1978. Subsequent years saw extensive development of rapid-deployment Advanced Guard (or 'Operational Manoeuvre Group') composites, designed to penetrate and rove deep behind enemy lines.[19]

The launching of SDI in 1983 brought Soviet warnings that it might spark 'an uncontrollable race in strategic offensive weapons', and compel 'retaliatory measures in both offensive and defensive weapons'. And the 1985 defence budget increase may have covered stepped-up research efforts. But it caused no change in the fundamental tenets of the Soviet Union's post-1977 posture. The 'Ogarkov themes' were reiterated by the Marshal himself—in articles and in a noteworthy 1985 book—and by other Soviet authorities.[20] The considered military view appeared to be that SDI would not negate MAD; it could be countered. On the other hand, the research profligacy that it unleashed would spawn dynamic and potentially destabilizing technological innovation across the board, impart greater urgency to developmental programmes, and increase the pace and momentum of technological change and organizational adjustment.

The US challenge may have precipitated one rather startling development. In late 1984 Marshal Ogarkov left his post as Chief of the General Staff (he was succeeded by his deputy, Marshal Akhromeyev), to take command of the Western combined-arms *Teatr Voyennykh Deystviy* (TVD), or Wartime Theatre of Strategic Military Operations.[21] This is the most crucial TVD, responsible for the central front in Europe; central and northern tier Warsaw Pact forces are subordinate to it. The southwestern, southern and eastern TVDs were also assigned commanders. The quintessential wartime TVD designs, with supreme high command representatives taking direct charge of the most vital sector(s), have never before been fleshed out in peacetime. The decision surely reflected appreciation of the time-urgent corollaries of emergent datalinks, arms and strategies.

In the political realm, the Soviet Union welcomed Reagan's November 1980 election victory. President James Carter's initial human rights crusade, his late born-again bellicosity, and his inability to control Congress exasperated the USSR. It preferred consistent conservatism. It was able to deal constructively with Presidents Richard Nixon and Gerald Ford. Reagan's ideological pronouncements were dismissed as electioneering fodder. Once in office, he was expected to revert to traditional republicanism.

During Reagan's first years, the USSR took care to appear accommodating. The Pentagon justified its pursuit of strategies and weapon systems designed to 'prevail' in a nuclear war in part through assertions that this merely answered the Soviet Union's challenge—the USSR's emphasis on the destructiveness of nuclear war was termed a smoke-screen, designed to obscure continued adherence to the dictum that war is a rational continuation of politics. Soviet leaders protested vigorously. Nuclear war was branded 'a threat to the whole of civilization . . . to life in our world'; nuclear war, once unleashed, would inevitably escalate; attempts to present such a war as rational were 'criminal'.[22]

Established Soviet nuclear programmes did proceed. But the Soviet Union downplayed their importance. It insisted that its SS–20 deployments in Europe constituted normal modernization; newer, accurate, small warhead missiles replacing older, less accurate, and higher-yield SS–4s and SS–5s. The SS–20s' mobility was seen as security-enhancing. The immobility of the SS–4s and SS–5s translated into vulnerability, which ordained early use.

By 1982, however, NATO, which initially accepted the modernization thesis, appeared determined to press ahead with counter-deployments.[23] The USSR was deeply perturbed at the prospect of Pershing IIs. But the growing West European opposition to US missile deployments, an opposition that swept churches, trade unions and town halls, and reached into the inner sanctums of parties and governments, appeared to afford the Soviet Union an opportunity to split the NATO alliance. Against Reagan's gunslinger image, the USSR juxtaposed one of apparent Soviet moderation. General Secretary Brezhnev announced a moratorium on new SS–20 base construction.

But the Reagan defence buildup, and Pershing deployment preparations, continued unabated. NATO solidarity held, in spite of the fact that majority opinion throughout NATO Europe remained opposed. West European alienation proved largely impervious to Soviet blandishment. Moscow's support for peace campaigns did more to spur independent (though far smaller) peace movements in the East than it did to increase Soviet influence over those in the West. The Kremlin was to become as leery of 'peace' as the White House.[24]

The last months of the Brezhnev regime saw pressures for increased Soviet defence spending. They were deflected. The consensus that coalesced behind Yuri Andropov focused on domestic socio-economic problems. The priority was buttressed by scepticism about the security impact of a new arms race. Moscow's détente posture survived.

Andropov's USSR appeared to recognize that the chances of an end-run through influence manipulation was slight. This, and deep concern about the Pershings, was evident in the concessions that Moscow offered during the winter/spring/summer of 1982–83.[25] Andropov offered to slash Soviet Euro-missiles, and warheads, to British and French levels, with no allowance for the USA's 'Forward Based Systems'; Soviet nuclear forces targeted on Western Europe would be cut to the level of the late 1950s. He affirmed Soviet willingness to accept some on-site inspection. NATO's 'dual-track' decision had succeeded.

Summer 1983 offered an indisputable 'window of opportunity'. The Reagan Administration, however, was not ready to reciprocate. Rising pressure to do so, from Allies and Congress, became the most important casualty of the downing of Korean Airlines flight 007.

The vitriol that flowed from that (still not fully explained) tragedy slammed the window shut. Pershing deployment proceeded. Moscow withdrew from negotiations, as expected. The confrontation sharpened, symbolized on the one side by the unbridled pursuit of SDI and forward deployment, and on the other by the ominous preparation of full-fledged TVDs.

Both powers increased pressure on allies to conform (though allied reluctance was manifest).[26] Both became more assertive within their own 'spheres', the USSR in Afghanistan and the Warsaw Pact; the USA in Grenada, Central America and Western Europe. Yet, there was a sharp difference. The Soviet Union protected its existing positions; the United States pursued outward assertiveness. The USSR gave aid, but refused commitment to Managua; the USA demanded that the Sandinistas 'cry uncle', and extended the list of Sandinista actions that would be deemed to constitute *casus belli*, and hence justify intervention.[27]

The positions of the two superpowers have in a sense reversed. US strategy evolved from Eisenhower's doctrine of massive retaliation, to war-fighting, and finally to war-prevailing and war-winning. Soviet strategy evolved from assertions, however questionable, of inevitable victory, through ambiguity and the tentative embrace of war-fighting, to something akin to massive retaliation. The reversal is not total. The Soviet Union deploys new tactical nuclear missiles in Europe. The nuclear option remains. But the contrary predilection, indeed imperative, of current Soviet strategic doctrine is emphatic.

IV.   Renewal of talks

President Reagan's accommodating November 1984 campaign rhetoric, perhaps a response to public concern (the lingering legacy of 'peace' and 'freeze' movements), brought the Soviet Union to the bargaining table. The USSR's disenchantment with peace movements, and recoil from the prospect of a stepped-up arms race in space, surely influenced the decision. But it was the change in atmospherics that tipped the scales. The Soviet Union had adopted the mantle of reason. It might have doubts about US motives. But it could not dismiss the USA's professed willingness to address ALL outstanding issues without impugning her own. The Soviet Union dropped its demand for prior dismantling of Pershings; the United States agreed that SDI was a subject for discussion.

Yet suspicion and distrust ran deep on both sides. There was little progress. The most important initiatives of the early 1980s, from forward naval designs to Pershings and Star Wars, came from the United States, and to this extent the ball is in the USA's court. The United States showed no inclination to compromise. The Geneva summit statement that nuclear war cannot be won and must not be fought eased public fears, but there was no progress towards arms control.

General Secretary Gorbachov orchestrated a new Soviet arms control offensive.[28] He announced a moratorium on Soviet nuclear testing before the Geneva summit. In January 1986 and through the spring and summer, he presented a series of proposals. The centrepiece 15-year plan to eliminate nuclear weapons countered SDI's justificatory vision: instead of a scientifically dubious and draining quest likely to propel an escalating arms race, why not instead seek security through negotiations and mutual cuts?

Other elements appeared constructive. The strategic first step—halving US and Soviet strategic arsenals—was tied to US willingness to shelve space defence deployments (hostile defences inevitably spur offsetting offensive increases). The United States had embraced deep cuts as its primary strategic objective. The Soviet Union accepted continued research into new defence technologies. And it accepted the Western definition of strategic: weapons with a range of 5500 kilometres or more. This excludes US medium-range missiles in Europe.

The old demand for simultaneous cuts in the arsenals of Britain, France and China was dropped. They must refrain from increases, but nuclear tests and some modernization (British Tridents and French multiple independently targetable re-entry vehicles [MIRVs] could proceed. They need not join the reduction process until superpower arsenals have been halved. This accommodates British, French and Chinese positions that their forces are minimal, that proportional cuts would therefore be inequitable, and that the superpowers must initiate the process. France and China previously declared that US–Soviet cuts of 50 per cent would trigger their participation.

Gorbachov extended the unilateral Soviet testing moratorium, and called again for a comprehensive test ban treaty with international monitoring, seismic verification stations and on-site inspection. The Reagan Administration insisted that national security considerations necessitated continued testing.

Trident, MX, Pershing II and cruise warhead designs had already been fully tested. Advanced diagnostic testing methods mean that even new warheads often require no testing. Only more radical concepts must be tested. The US Department of Energy funds five such weapon programmes: X-ray lasers, optical lasers, particle beams, hypervelocity pellets and microwaves, all nuclear-driven.[29] The first, Excalibur, starred in space defence visions. Early tests were not as promising as reported. And administration spokemen concede that 200 or more tests might be needed to develop it. In fact, the development stage alone of each one of these five programmes is likely to require 200 or more tests. The uncertainty of radical designs, both in terms of feasibility and in terms of strategic impact, encouraged those who wished to accept and codify the Soviet offer. But Excalibur and its brethren, though elusive, remained sacrosanct to those opposed to codifying parity.

Gorbachov also called for the total elimination of so-called theatre-range missiles in Europe, the Soviet SS–20s and the USA's answering Pershing II and cruise missiles. After two years of unremitting opposition to President Reagan's 'zero option', Moscow accepted its central argument. The zero option called for a global ban on theatre nuclear forces (TNF), but it was aimed at Europe.

The Soviet Union emphasized that the elimination of theatre-range superpower missiles in Europe could be negotiated separately from a US–Soviet test ban. They are not linked either to each other, to strategic arms reductions or to the space defence abstinence or restraint (the Reykjavik caveat that final ratification must await resolution of the SDI issue was subsequently rescinded). The only negotiating condition is that British and French missiles are not increased and that Pershings and cruise missiles are not transferred to their control.

SS–20 missiles in Europe, and their infrastructures, would be destroyed. Fear of redeployment from Asia appears disingenuous. SS–20 mobility is limited; it needs prepared facilities.

The United States vacillated in the face of the North Atlantic Treaty Organization (NATO) allied and Far Eastern concerns; European allies had only recently forced through unpopular deployment decisions and feared the political fall-out from a change of heart; and China and Japan expressed concern that a European arrangement would leave them exposed. The Soviet Union was unwilling to dismantle Asian SS–20s targeted on China and on US bases in Japan, Korea and Taiwan, but redundancies and the fact that some Asian deployments had been designated part of Moscow's package response to Pershing and cruise missile threats left room for compromise. At Reykjavik, President Reagan and General Secretary Gorbachov agreed that each of their countries would retain 100 theatre-range missiles on home soil, outside Europe.

The Soviet Union agreed to forgo explicit British and French commitments. Soviet–US agreement will inevitably focus attention on Britain and France, and undermine the rationale for their expansion plans. The Soviet Union will presumably stipulate that unbridled British and French expansion will alter the agreement's premise and compel countermeasures.

The Soviet Union added another inducement: shorter-range tactical missiles in East Germany might also be withdrawn, if agreement is reached. This, however, is clearly contingent on British and French reciprocity.

France was the most reluctant, though force-expansion plans could be deferred. The argument that Pershing presence equates with US commitment to Europe is scarcely credible. The real French fear is that removal of Pershings may encourage German neutrality and lead, ultimately, to the reunification of Germany. But this spectre is neither inevitable nor likely.

V. Prospects

Prospects for arms control negotiations of substance remain highly uncertain. Both sides made concessions—to reopen formal talks, to convene the Geneva Summit and to chart strategic cut-backs in Reykjavik—but the concessions were cosmetic and/or conditional. Further-reaching, more startling proposals held aloft the beacon of possible breakthrough(s), but negotiators were loath to follow up.

Continuing allegations of cheating, on both sides, keep alive the possibility of failure.[30] General Secretary Gorbachov charged that US refusal to engage in real negotiations on Star Wars violated the January 1985 formula for combined offensive/defensive talks. The USA side-stepped the charge in favour of accusations that the USSR was violating past accords. The USSR's MX-equivalent SS–X–24 was joined by another, smaller, mobile, single-warhead missile, the SS–X–25, akin to the USA's projected Midgetman. The SS–X–25 was said to be a second new missile (as the Midgetman would also be), contravening SALT's limit of only one new design. The Soviet Union described the SS–X–25 as the sanctioned successor to the older SS–13s. The United States insisted that it exceeded agreed size-increase formulas, though admitting uncertainty concerning exact SS–13 specifications.

The Soviet Union described Pershing deployment as a gross circumvention of SALT limits. SDI research was said to violate the spirit of the Anti-Ballistic Missile (ABM) Treaty; SDI tests would constitute blatant violations of its word. The United States dismissed the former, but allowed that the ABM accord might have to be revised.

The Soviet phased-array radar near Krasnoyarsk was said to be a 'battle-management' facility, defying the ABM Treaty provision that such radars must be located on a country's periphery, facing outward. The USSR denied the purpose and offered to allow US inspection upon completion. The offer was ignored. The Soviet Union then suggested the facility might be traded for US missile-tracking radars, thus acknowledging analogous capability, if not intent. The USA insisted that the former was illegal, the latter legal—yet Thule and Fallingdale radars defied stipulations mandating location on a member state's periphery, while others, on the periphery, were designed to provide some inland coverage as well.

The Soviet Union was accused of encrypting missile test transmissions, violating SALT verification strictures. The Soviet Union asserted that its telemetry encryption extended only to data not covered by SALT—although the USA's refusal to ratify deprived the provisions of legal force. The USSR did flaunt missile 'pop-up' techniques, suggesting reload intent; on the other hand, US intelligence officials acknowledged that Egyptian surface-to-air missile (SAM) fields, inspected after the Soviets' ouster, contained 50 per cent dummies. Soviet 'maskirovka' obscures both strength and weakness.[31] But satellites and other national means of verification leave little scope for deceit. Ratification and activation of already-agreed-to verification and on-site inspection formulas would close most loopholes. And Gorbachov's avowed readiness to go further suggests that de facto transparency can be ensured.

The two sides also focused on apparently different strategic perceptions, especially as concerns stability. The United States professed fear that the USSR's disproportionate number of large land missiles might tempt a first strike against US land forces: large ICBMs were destabilizing. The Soviet Union professed fear that new accurate Trident II submarine-launched ballistic missiles (SLBMs) might launch a first strike, from closer range, and thus with less warning: SLBMs were more destabilizing. But the accuracies and co-ordination prowess necessary for a first strike belonged to the realm of theory and staged tests. They were not likely to be replicated in a real-life environment. The SLBM threat also is potential and theoretical, and not easy to realize. Both spectres can be countered, through mobility, super-hardening of silos and/or other measures. They did serve a purpose, in highlighting the instability that inevitably attends arms competition momentum. Yet the ethnocentric choice of focus, only on the other side's advantage, undermined protestations of sincerity.

Arms control breakthroughs are clearly conceivable. But the crucial question of will is not synchronized. The lack of will in the Reagan Administration may not influence a successor. But Soviet will may also prove ephemeral, dissipated by contrary dynamics.

VI.   Conclusion

Research programmes and weapon systems acquire lives of their own, quite apart from strategic rationale. They acquire bureaucratic constituencies. The arms literature is replete with examples of weaponry, on both sides, that once passed a certain stage of development received continuous funding regardless of performance.

Determined strategic intent is needed to deflect the momentum. Yet key Washington policy-makers continue to embrace a contrary strategic intent.[32] The USSR's public posture, however, asserts emphatic willingness to change course. Yet decreased fear of SDI's ultimate vision may ironically make the Soviet Union more ready to embrace its pursuit tacitly. The Soviet Union has conceded US penetration (and can tolerate no jeopardy to its own), but it has never accepted that the same penetration certainty must be conceded to France or China. Soviet ballistic missile defence research concentrates on the goal of ensuring a measure of immunity *vis-à-vis* third powers; her established programmes, in fact, constitute a limited-ambition SDI.

If left unfettered, the momentum may open a veritable Pandoras's box of new weaponry, new systems and new mind-sets, spur an immensely draining arms race, and compel even more determined and perhaps crippling efforts on the part of lesser nuclear powers. But there are those who believe that destabilizing dynamics can be managed and that arms control is constricting. The choice may be made consciously, or not.

Notes and references

* Earlier versions of this study appeared in Jacobsen, C. G., 'Arms control; last chance, or lost chance?', ed. J. O'Manique, *A Proxy For Trust: Views on the Verification Issue in Arms Control and Disarmament Negotiations* (The Norman Patersen School of International Affairs, Carleton University: Ottawa, 1985); and in Jacobsen, C. G., 'Soviet-American arms control: hope or hoax?', *Current History*, vol. 84, no. 504, 1985, pp. 317–20.

[1] See e.g. 'Editorial', *Bulletin of the Atomic Scientists*, vol. 40, no. 1, 1984.

[2] For US Government documents and/or references, see Jacobsen, C. G., *The Nuclear Era* (Oelgeschlager, Gunn & Hain: Cambridge, MA, 1982 and The Bertrand Russell Foundation: Nottingham, 1982), chapter 3.

[3] Jacobsen (note 2).

[4] Invocation of NATO's 1979 dual-track decision was misleading. International Institute of Strategic Studies (IISS)'s *Military Balance 1979–80* estimated that 270 SS–20s, if accompanied by phase-out of older missiles, would in fact not upset the European nuclear balance; new NATO systems would be required only if the tally went above 270. By late 1983 European SS–20s remained below that figure. The USSR's offer to cut missile and warhead numbers further, to the 1950s levels (see note 25), in effect meant that NATO's 1979 decision had succeeded; a US Administration committed to MAD would have changed course accordingly.

[5] See *US Department of Defense Authorization Act, 1983*, Committee on Armed Services, House of Representatives (US Government Printing Office: Washington,

DC, 1982); and the Congressional Budget Office (CBO) (US Government Printing Office: Washington, DC, 2 Apr. 1982).

6 Garwin, R. L., Pike, J. and Velikhov, Y. P., 'Space weapons', *Bulletin of the Atomic Scientists*, vol. 40, no. 5, May 1984, Special Supplement inserted in journal.

7 See e.g., *The Washington Post*, 2 May 1982, and *Newsweek*, 17 May 1982.

8 Watkins, Admiral J. D., 'The maritime strategy', *The Maritime Strategy*, US Naval Institute Proceedings, Supplement, Jan. 1986, pp. 3–17: see also pp. 41–7 (Swartz, P. M., 'Contemporary U.S. naval strategy: a bibliography?').

9 Garwin, Pike and Velikhov (note 6); and Bethe, H. A., Garwin, R. L., Gottfried, K. and Kendall, H. W., 'Space-based Ballistic-Missile Defense', *Scientific American*, vol. 251, no. 4, 1984, pp. 37–47. See also 'Soviet scientific paper calls space defenses vulnerable, *New York Times*, 8 Jan. 1985.

10 Brzezinski, Z., Jastrow, R. and Kampelman, M., 'Defense in space is not Star Wars', *New York Times Magazine*, 27 June 1985; note also Lord Zuckerman's exquisite review, 'The wonders of Star Wars', in *The New York Review*, 30 Jan. 1986.

11 See, e.g., Axelrod, R., *The Evolution of Cooperation*, reviewed in the *New York Times Review of Books*, 28 June 1984, and Thomas, L., 'Scientific frontiers and national frontiers: a look ahead', *Foreign Affairs*, vol., 62, no. 4 (1984), pp. 966–94.

12 Lemann, N., 'The peacetime war', *The Atlantic Monthly*, vol. 254 (Oct. 1984).

13 Talbot, S., *Deadly Gambits* (Knopf: New York, 1984).

14 The thesis is prominently displayed in *Soviet Military Power,* US Defense Department, 1981–86 editions, and in 'Threats, Military Balances and Net Assessments', *Report of the Secretary of Defense Caspar W. Weinberger to the Congress*, 5 Feb. 1986, pp. 55–71.

15 Jacobsen, C. G., 'Soviet military expenditures and the Soviet defence burden', *World Armaments and Disarmament, SIPRI Yearbook 1986* (Oxford University Press: Oxford, 1986), pp. 263–74; Kaufman, R. F., 'Causes of the slowdown in Soviet defense', *Survival*, vol. 27 (1985), pp. 179–92.

16 McConnell, J., 'Shifts in Soviet views on the proper focus of military development', *World Politics*, vol. 38 (1985), especially pp. 320–4; K. Bochkarev's article in *Voennaya Mysl'*, no. 9 (1968), exemplifies the nuclear warfighting school. Note: The author of this book is indebted to Mary C. Fitzgerald, also of the US Center for Naval Analysis, for her pioneering work on Ogarkov. Some will appear in a forthcoming issue of *International Security*. See also Fitzgerald, M. C., *The Soviet Union and Nuclear War* (Academic International Press: Gulf Breeze, FL, forthcoming).

17 'Comrade L. I. Brezhnev's Speech', *Pravda*, 19 Jan. 1977, p. 2; Ogarkov, N. V., in *Sovetskaya Rossiya*, 23 Feb. 1977, p. 2; Ogarkov, N. V., 'Military Strategy', *Sovetskaya Voennaya Entsiklopedia* (Soviet Military Encyclopaedia) (*Voenizdat*: Moscow, 1979), Vol. 7, p. 564; and Ogarkov, N. V., 'Military science and the defence of the socialist fatherland', *Kommunist*, no. 7 (1978), p. 117.

18 MccGwire, M., *Soviet Military Objectives* (The Brookings Institution: Washington, DC, 1987, chapters 1, 5 and 7.

19 Ogarkov, N. V., *Vsegda v Gotovsnosti k Zashchita Otechestva* (Always in Readiness to Defend the Homeland) (*Voenizdat*: Moscow, 1982); and Jones, D. R. (ed.) *Soviet Armed Forces Review Annual* (SAFRA), Vols. 6 and 7 (Academic International Press: Gulf Breeze, FL, 1982 and 1983).

20 Ogarkov, N. V., 'The defence of socialism: the experience of history and the present day', *Krasnaya Zvezda*, 9 May 1984, p. 3; Ogarkov, N. V., *Istoria Uchit Bditelnost* (History Teaches Vigilance) (*Voenizdat*: Moscow, 1985), pp. 24, 47 and 88; Ogarkov,

N. V., 'The unfading glory of Soviet weapons', *Kommunist Vooruzhiennikh Sil* (Communist of the Armed Forces), no. 21 (1984), p. 25; Gareyev, Colonel General M. A., *M. V. Frunze—Voyennyy Teoretik* (*Voenizdat*: Moscow, 1985), pp. 239–41 and 380–1.

[21] Hines, J. G. and Petersen, P. A., 'Changing the Soviet system of control', *International Defense Review*, vol. 19, no. 3 (1986), pp. 281–9; see also Ogarkov, 1984 and Gareyev, 1985 (note 20).

[22] For Chernenko, Ogarkov and other quotes, see Jones, D. R., 'Nuclear war and Soviet policy', *International Perspectives* (Nov./Dec. 1982), pp. 17–20.

[23] See note 4.

[24] The continuing strength of the 'Peace' movement, alluded to in the second paragraph of this text, was indicated by Fine, M. and Steven, P. M. (eds.), *The American Peace Directory 1984* (Institute for Defence and Disarmament Studies: Brookline, MA, 1984), which listed 922 organizations; it is also evident, e.g., in the various issues of the *END Bulletin*, London, and the *Nuclear Times*, New York. The degree of public pressure brought to mind Eisenhower's parting prophesy; see 'Dwight D. Eisenhower, 1960', *Public Papers of the Presidents*, p. 1038 (National Archives and Records Service, US Government Printing Office: Washington, DC, 1961).

[25] See e.g., *New York Times*, 22 Dec. 1982

[26] den Oudsten, E., 'Public opinion on peace and war', *World Armaments and Disarmament, SIPRI Yearbook 1986* (Oxford University Press: Oxford, 1986), pp. 17–35.

[27] *Hearings* before the Western Hemisphere Sub-Committee of the House of Representatives Foreign Affairs Committee, 28 Feb. 1985; see also the *New York Times*, 4 and 5 May 1985.

[28] *Tass*, 15 Jan. 1986; and Jacobsen, C. G., 'Superpowers' arms control reaches a crossroad', *The Miami Herald* (*& Knight Ridder*), 20 Apr. 1986, Op-ed page.

[29] *Energy and Water Development Appropriations for 1986*, House of Representatives Committee on Appropriations, Subcommittee on Energy and Water Development (US Government Printing Office: Washington, DC, Feb. 1985), p. 138; see also *Christian Science Monitor*, 25 Apr. 1986, p. 1.

[30] 'Arms control and the Russians: battle of compliance heats up', *New York Times*, 7 June 1985, provides a good summary; see also *New York Times*, 11 and 12 June 1985, and *Pravda*, 24 Apr. and 12 May 1985, and 5 June 1986.

[31] Jacobsen (note 15).

[32] Jacobsen (notes 2 and 15).

Paper 1.2. Arms Control Impact Statements (ACISs): critique and prescription

LAUREL C. SCHNEIDER

I. Introduction

An elusive relationship exists between new weapon technologies and future arms control. This relationship can be defined as the impact of technological advancement on arms control and the arms race. The link between production and prospects for limitation establishes the basis upon which arms development and acquisition can be controlled. But to the detriment of actual arms reductions, this connection is seldom made in the politically static environment of arms negotiations. Impact assessment implies a reasoned estimate of future events and future political attitudes towards restraint. The United States has made an attempt to both recognize this relationship and institutionalize its analysis in the form of Arms Control Impact Statements (ACISs). However, the original vision of impact analysis that was to be embodied in those statements is more fully represented in the following chapters of this book than in the actual ACISs themselves. As they are now structured, the ACISs have failed in their mission because they require a degree of self-examination and criticism to which no government will voluntarily submit itself.

It is useful to examine the US impact statements for the purpose of understanding both the relevance of impact analysis and the problems associated with its implementation. New weapon technologies beget new political pressures and attitudes which in turn influence the very concepts of strategy and security that form the underpinnings of international rivalries. Impact and implication are fundamental words that transcend structural questions of how to cope with them. The impact of new weapon technologies on prospects for limiting or eliminating those technologies remains the same whether arms control is codified into a chronic legal proceeding, or whether it follows the political whim and panic of nuclear competitors. Like arms control, impact analysis does not have to imply a specific structure for the achievement of its end, but arms reductions will occur only when the arms producers are able to perceive the negative implications of their weapons—and of the political mind-sets which generate them—for security and international stability.

Impact analysis has an important role to play in any form of arms control. The following discussion examines the US impact statement process and its usefulness in the weapon acquisition cycle. In addition, in light of the real relevance of impact assessment in arms control, this paper goes on to identify some of the minimal requirements for impact statements that are valid regardless of the limitations imposed by the US Government on its own ACIS process. The failure of the US arms control impact statements gives us some valuable clues to the problem of forging the link between new weapons, new mind-sets and arms control in a manner that will indeed reverse the current trend of robust production and faltering limitation. Regardless of whether impact analysis can take place effectively within a governmental setting or whether it can take place effectively in a non-governmental setting, it is essential that it take place.

II.   US arms control impact statements: critique

Arms Control Impact Statements (ACISs) are congressional documents intended to inform national decision-making processes concerning arms development and acquisition. ACISs are produced in the United States for the US Congress by the Arms Control and Disarmament Agency (ACDA), and they have at various times been proposed in the Federal Republic of Germany, the United Kingdom and in Norway.[1] The US statements, in accordance with section 36 of the Arms Control and Disarmament Act, are submitted annually for the purpose of enhancing 'both executive branch and congressional decisionmaking regarding the potential impact of defense and nuclear programs on arms control policy and negotiations'.[2] Controversy concerning the effectiveness and quality of the impact assessments has simmered both within and outside of the US Government and since the first statements were submitted in 1976. The statements have never fully realized the non-partisan, analytical role originally envisioned for them, and particularly in recent years, the ACISs appear to be a means of securing support for administration defence goals.

Completed US Fiscal Year Arms Control Impact Statements consist of a compiled series of documents, each analysing a nuclear weapon programme included in the budget submitted to the US Congress by the President. The Fiscal Year 1986 ACIS contains, for example, impact statements for the following seven military developments: Strategic Defense Initiative (SDI); sea-launched cruise missiles (SLCMs); airborne strategic offensive systems; intercontinental ballistic missile (ICBM) programmes; ballistic missile-equipped nuclear-powered submarine (SSBN)/submarine-launched ballistic missile (SLBM) programmes; and space defence and chemical warfare. The structure of analysis within each document involves a breakdown into six sections: (a) introduction; (b) programme description; (c) stated military requirements; (d) funding; (e) analysis; and (f) summary and overall arms control assessment. Together, these programme components are intended to provide a comprehensive outline of the proposed weapon programme and an analysis of its various consequences for arms control. The 1987 format is somewhat revised, with fewer technical and budgetary details, but it does not alter the findings of three early reviews of the impact statements, sponsored by Congress after each of the first three annual submissions, which revealed serious flaws both in the preparation process and in the ability of the responsible executive organs to serve as impartial critics of administration policy.

The first series of ACISs were submitted by the Department of Defense and the Energy Research and Development Agency (ERDA) in late 1976. After analysis by the Congressional Research Service, they were not accepted by the Senate Foreign Relations Committee and the House Committee on International Relations. The committees returned the statements, stating that they 'do not comply with the law and are unacceptable'.[3] The impact statements were resubmitted by the executive branch in 1978 and were again reviewed by the Congressional Research Service (CRS). This time, Charles R. Gellner, the senior CRS analyst, described what he felt Congress was looking for in an impact statement:

Analysis implies an examination of such matters as causes, effects, purposes, accompanying circumstances, alternatives, reasons in favor or against, costs vs. benefits, and historical evolution. To put it another way, an analysis of impact might explore historical, political, economic and military factors, or it could be concerned with long-range, or medium- and short-term elements. These are some of the categories of information, among others, that are necessary for Congress to make its own appraisals and to participate meaningfully in the formulation of arms control policy.[4]

Gellner reported that the 1978 impact statements fell far short of these criteria. In his review of the second series of statements, he questioned 'how Congress could rely upon them exclusively or even largely to make its own independent appraisal or for assistance in making a Constitutional input to foreign policy relating to arms control'.[5] Following in-depth analysis by the CRS, the Foreign Relations and International Relations Committee rejected the second set of statements as they had the first, stating that the documents still did not comply with the law and were 'neither complete nor adequately analytical'.[6]

ACISs have failed from the very beginning to meet the minimal criteria set out for them by Congress. As Gellner's comments indicate, the problems with the documents run much deeper than poor editing or inadequate preparation. The failure of the first two series of statements revealed structural flaws in the impact assessment process itself. Representative Clement Zablocki, Chairman of the House Committee on International Relations, noted in correspondence addressed to the President's Assistant for National Security, Lt General Brent Scowcroft, that '[we] were frankly appalled at the statements . . . They dealt only at the shallowest level with impact on arms control and disarmament negotiations and they do not deal at all with impact on policy.'[7]

The third set of US ACISs finally gave complete descriptions of proposed weapon systems and passed inspection in 1979. However, the statements still fell short of arms control impact assessment, and it appears clear that the Committees on Foreign Affairs and International Relations gave up or were unable to pursue further their efforts to produce in them a valuable analytical tool. Subsequent ACISs, although improved to the level of minimal compliance with the law, still deal at only the shallowest level with impact on arms control, and do not deal at all with impact on policy. The structural flaws inherent in the impact statement process remain in place, indicating that early observations by the CRS and congressional committees were not heeded.

ACISs embody an opportunity for law-makers to evaluate far more than the specific military and economic consequences of a given weapon system. The statements were originally intended to assess a broad range of consequences, encompassing the international and intranational links between military, political, technological, economic and social realities and relationships. According to Michael Krepon, former CRS researcher assigned to the impact statement studies and author of paper 2.8 in this book, another important rationale for ACISs was 'to provide the Arms Control and Disarmament Agency with a "need to know" about defense programs'. This means that ACISs can be the vehicle by which ACDA personnel establish crucial links to the Pentagon and thus review defence programme material not otherwise sent to ACDA offices.[8]

Under the Carter Administration, ACISs fulfilled this 'need to know' function. According to an independent report commissioned in 1979 under the auspices of the President's Reorganization Project, Carter sought to improve the role of ACDA in national security planning by eliminating ACISs and replacing them with an institutionalized role for ACDA and the State Department in the existing Department of Defense (DOD) acquisition process, the Defense Systems Acquisition Review Council (DSARC).[9] Carter was not re-elected, and the reorganization project came to naught. The Reagan Administration had no interest in expanding ACDA's role in defence-acquisition planning and the ACIS posed no threat to the President's planned buildup because the administration possessed editorial control over ACIS preparation. It is, in fact, possible that during the first years of the Reagan Administration, the cumbersome ACIS requirement provided a good distraction for the small agency.

III.   The problem of definition

It is clear that whatever role the arms control impact statements are meant to fulfil is thwarted by the serious procedural and structural flaws inherent in the assessment process. The first of these flaws is definitional. The ACISs employ some important concepts, all of which remain ill-defined or entirely ignored in the final documents. Three of these concepts—arms control, impact and purpose—will be discussed here because of their particular centrality to the purposes, procedures and effects of arms control impact statements.

Arms control

The first of these concepts—arms control—establishes the mission and scope of the entire impact analysis. Congress intended that the statements assess and report the consequences of a given military innovation on arms control. A major impediment to the accomplishment of this task has been the lack of any single, coherent definition of arms control. Particularly in recent years, there has been little consistency in the uses and understanding of the term. For many representing the US Department of Defense, arms control constitutes an active verb, meaning the restraint of ongoing arsenal growth to the minimum required to maintain, for example, strategic advantage (or at least a conclusive level of parity) *vis-à-vis* the Soviet Union. Many members of Congress, however, believe that arms control refers only to the current set of actual, ongoing negotiations in Geneva or elsewhere. Still others set arms control up as the catchword for all governmental activities relating to the monitoring, restraint and removal of weapons, particularly nuclear weapons. But arms control encompasses a broader range of international political, military and strategic variables than the preceding three definitions allow: it is a co-ordinating, stabilizing activity, a means of initiating and sustaining mutual security and international stability. The evidence of this activity is found in the military sphere, which is the source of the greatest threat to mutual security and general stability, but the motivation and sustaining energy of arms control are political, rooted in the mutuality of competition and co-operation.

The authors of the US Arms Control Impact Statements do not specify their definition of arms control. The 1977 Congressional Research Service review of the second ACIS took the position that the DoD and ERDA, then the principal authors of the statements, had chosen so narrowly defined concepts of arms control that the scope and usefulness of the statements were severely limited. CRS cited 'reducing the destructiveness of war if it should occur, lessening the economic burden of armaments, and inhibiting arms races' as aspects of arms control not covered by the ACIS.[10]

In addition, the CRS reviewers made an important note of the role that national image and perceptions of security play in arms control. They referred to 'the political effects of impact of . . . the international image projected by the correlated defense and arms control policies by the United States'.[11] The place of the public image of nations in the success or failure of limiting arms development and deployment is very little understood. Because the maintenance of deterrence relies so heavily upon projected images of strength, an analysis of the effects of military innovations on international public perceptions is integral to the concept of arms control.

In the context of ACISs, the most useful concept of arms control is one that takes an inclusive look at governmental activities relating to general military procedures and developments in the arms race, with an emphasis on the international environment and current progress towards limiting arms. This perceptive draws most heavily on the perception of arms control as a co-ordinating activity. Arms control was originally introduced to provide some ballast in superpower competition and the global political system. Arms control therefore encompasses not one prescribed set of actions, but a range of actions guided by a constant search for dynamic stability in the relationships between competitive nations. A stable equilibrium in these relationships provides the structure within which communication, trade and other interactions essential for peace can operate.

For the purposes of an ACIS, the consequences of a weapon system for arms control are as broad as those forces contributing to stability in the international political system. A comprehensive analysis requires that all of the elements of the arms control environment be considered. The political, social, strategic, diplomatic, technological and economic components of arms control are most fruitfully viewed from the perspective of international security. Attention and corrective measures can be given to those aspects of the international system most vulnerable to erosion or collapse. ACISs therefore serve the goal of security best when they are most critical of possible consequences to stable relations—and general lines of communication—between superpowers. Only by exposing every relevant cost to stability can a clear range of priorities, and informed decisions concerning arms control, emerge.

Impact

The second concept that needs clarification in the impact statements is impact itself. As the preceding discussion of arms control has indicated, the environment studied by ACISs is broad and fluctuating. An impact to this environment is the set of specific phenomena that alter the particular constellation of variables comprising the arms control environment. It is significant that the US impact statements make no systematic definition of the term and this may explain the failure of each ACIS to identify and assess arms control impacts.

In his letter of submittal of the Fiscal Year 1986 ACIS, Kenneth Adelman, Director of ACDA, claims that 'the administration has concluded that while many of these programs will require continuing review, all of the programs analyzed in the fiscal year 1986 budget are consistent with current US security and arms control policy'.[12] Consistency constitutes the nearest reference to impact in the ACIS. While consistency with official policies can be viewed as one aspect of impact on arms control, it is vastly incomplete as a guiding definition. Indeed, Adelman's words are potentially misleading, for if consistency with current administration policies is synonymous with arms control impact, then the resulting impact analysis will illuminate only a small portion of the arms control picture.

The yardstick of consistency can measure only internal effects—the extent to which a proposed programme will contradict or enhance official government policies. Consistency is unable to measure the potential responses of other governments or the potential disruptions of US goals in the numerous external arenas which will feel the effects of a new programme. In other words, consistency is unable to determine the 'impact' of any new policy in so far as that policy relates to international affairs. As the single criterion of impact, consistency short-circuits the value of the statement as a reasoned assessment of the international system in which governments must act and defend themselves, transforming the document into a policy platform for the President.

A somewhat more useful definition of impact has been provided by the members of the Congressional Research Service. They argue that to 'have an impact, a weapons system or defense program must cause some change in policy, negotiations or an existing or potential agreement'.[13] The correct emphasis here is on change rather than consistency. An impact is a change, and it is changes in arms control prospects to which Congress and the President must respond in their efforts to make progress in arms control.

The impact statement is an early warning system for any substantial alterations in the arms control environment. An impact can be defined as the substance of any change in the system, extrapolated out to all relevant effects. Arms control, as defined earlier, is the maintenance of system stability between hostile nations and among allies. The forces which make up this stability are dynamic, produced by the myriad of governmental and non-governmental interactions which span the distances between nations and anchor them in steady relationship. Unequal displays of force can weaken the links and aggressive displays dissolve them. An impact is a significant change in the system of interaction, either positive or negative, which has implications for overall stability.

The quest of the United States and the Soviet Union for security through deterrence has complicated the arms control environment. Since 1945, they have succeeded in keeping nuclear weapons out of warfare, and they have succeeded in avoiding attacking each other directly. The question remains unanswered, however, whether they have succeeded in providing any real basis for peaceful relations in the presence of nuclear weapons. Johan Holst has pointed out that in 'a world of sovereign nations and no accepted authority with the means to police the conduct of those nations, security is unattainable in any absolute sense. *Bezopasnost*, the absence of danger, remains a dream. Any nation which strives for absolute security inevitably creates dangers for other nations.'[14] Striving for absolute security is the instinctive activity of national leaders, but the maintenance of international stability is a necessary one. Weapon innovations are a product of the former, arms control a product of the latter. Impact assessment reflects the attempt to strike a balance between the two.

Purpose

The third important concept which has not been adequately defined in the US impact statements is purpose. It does not figure quite so centrally as the concepts of arms control or impact, but its importance in the impact assessment process requires some discussion. In each of the fiscal US impact statements, the purpose of a weapon system is described in vague terms as the military capability of the technology involved. In the context of an impact assessment, this is too limited a concept of purpose. The specific design intentions of a technological innovation are important for programme description, but they provide no explicit information pertaining to the particular role of the programme in securing overall security and stability, nor in achieving the ultimate purpose of arms control.

Presumably, the striving of US leaders for national security would ensure that all new weapon programmes are evaluated in terms of their ability to provide security in its broadest sense. Regrettably, this does not often happen. Weapon innovations and programmes acquire a life and momentum of their own which admit few questions of purpose. A new weapon system can, for example, easily serve the required military purposes of increased accuracy or greater invulnerability, yet undermine the broader, more compelling purposes of national security and international stability.

IV.   The problem of perspective

The second structural flaw in the ACIS process is the subjection of the statements to executive control. The value of an impact statement rests in its capacity to report all potential consequences of a proposed weapon system, negative as well as positive. Even if the authors of the statements were to put to use substantive and accurate definitions of arms control and impact, compelling them to examine the underpinning network of political, military and social forces governing the arms race, the results could still be warped by their lack of incentive to weigh and accurately document the various probable impacts.

This problem has already been identified by several observers and participants in the process, including ACDA itself. The 1978 CRS review stated quite clearly that the conditions imposed on the statements by the partiality of the DoD and ERDA reduced their viability as a comprehensive analysis. 'CRS has noted in previous memoranda the dilemma faced by such agencies as DoD and ERDA (now DoE) in making a recommendation for a weapons or defense program, while at the same time being under a technical obligation of impartiality weighing the arms control advantages or deficiencies of such a program. It seems unlikely that any agency would normally concede that a recommended defense program had serious arms control disadvantages.'[15]

An additional disincentive to impartiality in the ACIS is the fear that criticisms may come back to haunt the President. When in 1985 the Reagan Administration hotly defended its 'official' interpretation of the 1972 Anti-Ballistic Missile (ABM) Treaty as permissive of SDI programmes, previous ACIS passages were produced contradicting the reinterpretation. This is an embarrassment no President suffers a second time if it can be helped.

Mindful of the limitations imposed by executive self-interest, the CRS reviewers advocated the inclusion of a more objective perspective in the ACIS process. They claimed that 'unless a dominant voice in the preparation of the arms control impact statements as an impartial "third" party which does not have a vested interest in the defense programs recommended to Congress, it would not appear that the Executive impact statements could be fully depended upon to be untendentious'.[16] The CRS arguments strike at the centre of the ACIS dilemma. At the time of the review, the statements were virtually useless to Congress as impact assessments, although they contained, and have continued to contain, detailed information on the bevy of new weapon systems in the legislative pipeline. Unfortunately, the implementation of the practical suggestion put forward by CRS, namely that ACDA become the recommended third party, has had disappointing results. As an executive agency, ACDA has been subject to many of the same pressures and limitations of all other executive agencies and departments, and thus has not succeeded in imparting an unbiased and critical voice to the statements. It is curious that CRS would make note of the fact that 'it seems unlikely that any [official] agency would normally concede that a recommended defense program had serious arms control disadvantages' and then predict that an executive branch agency (ACDA) might constitute the recommended impartial perspective.[17]

The lack of impartiality on the part of ACDA may not, however, be the fault of ACDA itself. Before submission to Congress, each ACIS is reviewed, edited and then approved by the combined forces of the Department of Defense, the Department of Energy, the Central Intelligence Agency, the Joint Chiefs of Staff, the State Department, the Office of Management and Budget, and the National Security Council. What may easily begin as an acceptably impartial and comprehensive statement could well erode beyond recognition in circulation through these various executive departments.

In 1979, testifying before the Subcommittee on Arms Control, Oceans, International Operations and Environment of the Senate Committee on Foreign Relations, Barry M. Blechman, then Assistant Director of the Weapons Evaluation and Control Bureau of ACDA, referred to ACISs as 'agreed administration documents'. He noted that 'moreover, to some extent, the purpose of this process has become to prepare an acceptable document, rather than to prepare an independent, comprehensive and objective analysis'.[18] The impartiality of ACISs therefore reflect, to some extent, the tolerance of criticism by the executive office. The statements are subject, through the review process, to every disincentive on the part of the executive branch and its military planners to issue doubts regarding programmes that they are promoting. Blechman raised some of these issues in his congressional testimony:

After all, what the Congress is asking of the administration, is that it provide arguments against the very programs the administration has already decided to pursue, after evaluating the relative weight of military and political needs versus pertinent arms control considerations to its own satisfaction. Realistically, such statements always will be phrased quite gingerly and require excessive staff work before the document can be agreed to.[19]

Blechman makes reference not only to the impossibility of producing an incisive analysis under the constraints of the present inter-agency edit and review process, but he underscored the clear limitations involved in a self-critical discipline imposed on a governmental institution. In his book *Politics of Arms Control*, Duncan L. Clarke notes that 'any administration will generally put a high premium on presenting a united front to Congress. No President will be entirely content to have his Secretary of Energy seeking funds for a neutron warhead while his ACDA Director castigates the program.'[20] Although in-house reviews and impact analyses ensure the minimal participation of Congress in decision-making on arms control and military development, the quality and value of these analyses are crippled by the bonds of executive control.

V.   The problem of timing

The third flaw in the ACIS preparation involves poor timing. From his statements before the Congressional Subcommittee, it is clear that Blechman was wishing to bring attention to the problem of timing in the ACIS and arms production cycles. His agency was asked to produce impact statements after the essential executive decisions had been made, which often meant after the technology was approved by the President for research and supplied with some initial funding.

The executive is instructed to submit the ACIS along with major requests for funding in order to provide Congress with maximum information prior to making allocation commitments. For strictly legislative purposes, the timing of the impact statement production is basically adequate. Congress has the statements in hand at the point that budgetary questions are taken up and at the point that serious commitments to new weapon systems are made. The problem lies in the fact that the President and executive branch will have already adopted the new programme and its own momentum will have accelerated, independent of congressional approval.

The poor timing of the impact statements contributes to the problem of bias and thus affects the actual content of the documents. Because the impact statements correspond to the President's budget requests, ACDA prepares them after the President has made prior commitments to the technologies. The production of the impact statements by executive agencies comes on the heels of executive adoption of the programme, dissolving the value of the statement to the executive decision-making process and, as explained by Blechman in his testimony, curbing the liberty and incentive of the administration to provide complete information.

Given the current structure of the ACIS process, there is little that can be done to alleviate this problem, unless the administration was willing to take the potentially risky step of ordering impact statements prior to the conclusion of its own decision-making process. The benefit of this alternative to the executive is that the administration could be informed by the statements in formulating arms policies. It should not be assumed, however, that the lack of complete information and analysis in the impact statements means that the President does not have access to it elsewhere, and it is possible that the political costs of producing an earlier impact statement could be high. An ACIS prepared prior to executive commitments and submitted to Congress could well provide compelling arguments against the President's eventual budget proposals for weapon developments.

Except for the executive branch's own need for adequate information on arms control impacts (to which it presumably has access, regardless), there is little incentive for the President to send to Congress an ACIS that damages the budget request that it accompanies. The most effective hedge against allowing the ACIS to impede budget goals is to time its preparation in such a way that executive interests and budget proposals are most fully protected.

Even if the timing problem were to be eliminated and the President ordered by Congress to prepare impact statements much earlier, it is hardly likely that the volumes which emerge from the current executive and military approval mill would be phrased any less gingerly than they are now. Timing is important in assuring complete information at the critical points in the arms production and approval cycle, particularly since the vast machinery of the arms race picks up momentum all too quickly, assuring the production and deployment of even the most destabilizing innovations.[21] Timely impact statements can better equip Congress to make deliberate, well-reasoned decisions about arms development, but timing can do little to enhance the quality of content in the statements.

VI.   The problem of scope

The last major flaw in the arms control impact statements that will be discussed in this paper can be referred to as the problem of scope. An arms race, by definition, involves more than one producer of weapons. A nation by itself needs neither arms to protect itself from other nations nor a policy of arms control whereby arms development and procurement are measured and controlled.

It stands to reason therefore that the arms control environment is necessarily multipolar. With five acknowledged nuclear powers and several other suspected powers, the arms control environment of the 1980s is decidedly international. The explicit nuclear arms race is mirrored in the race of numerous small powers, most notably in the Third World, to acquire nuclear weapons and achieve the status—or just capability—of a nuclear weapon power.

The complete lack of an international perspective is a severe limitation in the arms control impact statements. Not only do they fail consistently to address links between nuclear developments in the United States and the Soviet Union, but they fail to investigate deeper links between the superpower arms race and the conventional arms race gripping the rest of the world. Global arms transfers have multiplied in recent years and the militarization of the developing nations has accelerated at a similar pace. The implications of both of these trends, linked through various routes to the nuclear arms race, are important to those countries preparing arms control impact statements. The stability and livelihood of the European nations are directly at stake in the buildup of nuclear weapons, and the European 'theatre' is a chip often cashed in for arguments in favour of new weapon technologies. The US ACISs fail to look beyond the usual claims of a Soviet threat in Europe to impacts of renewed rounds of the arms race on European security and stability.

The problem of bias in the impact statements is multiplied in the context of the international arms control environment as a whole. It is possible that the failure of the current US ACIS process to produce results of any policy value for Congress in terms of US options in arms control implies that it may be impossible for one country to produce within its administration an ACIS which is both adequately objective in perspective and international in scope.

Every impact statement represents an agreed administration document. Agreement is not the objective laid out by the US Congress in section 36 of the Arms Control and Disarmament Act. The Chairman of the Senate Foreign Relations Committee claimed that Congress had 'envisioned that the statements would be of considerable value in executive branch and congressional decisionmaking and would promote a more informed public discussion . . .'.[22] Informed discussion and decision-making in the mutable world of arms control depends not upon agreed representations of reality, but upon adequately comprehensive debate concerning the nature of that reality. The widest range of relevant possibilities—what may occur as a result of a new weapon technology—must be made available for scrutiny. It is useless to establish what should occur strategically or politically as the result of a new weapon programme. Actual impacts do not respond to normative conditions.

The 1977 study by the Congressional Research Service took note of the importance of an international perspective in establishing the proper scope for the impact statement. '[A] relevant part of an appraisal of arms control aspects of a U.S. weapons system is to assess what the response of other countries, including adversaries, might be to U.S. decisions regarding that weapon system.'[23] Subsequent ACISs, with varying degrees of success, did attempt to include some mention of likely Soviet escalatory responses to the proposed technology, but they failed to provide any analysis of this crucial impact. The 1983 ACIS, for example, supplied the following overall arms control assessment for intermediate-range nuclear missile systems and the sea-launched cruise missile (SLCM):

The Pershing II, GLCM (ground-launched cruise missile) and SLCM programs are consistent with U.S. arms control policy and related presidential decisions and are not constrained by existing arms control agreements. The effect of U.S. modernization programs on current and prospective arms control negotiations has already been demonstrated in the INF talks. In the face of Allied resolve to go forward with INF deployments, the Soviets dropped their preconditions for entering into negotiations with the U.S. U.S. modernization programs could engender further modernization of Soviet TNF. On balance, however, there would be little prospect for concrete arms control results involving INF in the absence of NATO's decision to modernize these forces.[24]

As usual, consistency with US policy is the first matter of concern and only passing reference is made to possible escalatory action on the part of the Soviets in response to the proposed action. The 'agreed administration document' approach states that impacts are equated only in terms of US force capability. To say, therefore, as each ACIS assessment for each weapon programme has said, that the programme is consistent with US policies and will enhance US capability means that this assessment is the sum total of the impact of the programme on arms control prospects and, according to the administration, constitutes a sufficient fulfilment of its legal requirements concerning the ACIS.

The arms control assessments of the 1986 ACIS contain no references to arms control impacts other than US force capability and additional leverage hoped for by the administration in future negotiations. The conclusion of the arms control assessment for SSBN/SLBM programmes in 1986 states that 'modernization of the U.S. sea-based strategic forces is consistent with the U.S. policy of restoring the strategic balance, enhancing stability through survivability, and creating incentives for the Soviets to enter into meaningful negotiations for arms reduction treaties'.[25]

So-called incentives, hinting at a closer approximation to actual arms control impact, are neither explained nor analysed for the purpose of illuminating US strategic implications, real or perceived threat experienced by other nations, or additional implications for arms control in the case of possible adversary responses. All of these factors are essential to the scope of the impact statement.

The 1983 cruise missile arms control assessment represents the most comprehensive analysis that the US ACISs have to offer. The brief five-paragraph assessment concludes with the acknowledgement that 'like any nuclear modernization program, however, [the US Pershing II, GLCM and SLCM programmes] entail political costs and carry with them important arms control implications'.[26] This is the nearest approximation to a declaration of impact available in the seven existing US statements. It is not enough, however, for an impact statement to indicate that costs or important arms control implications are involved. It is the central task of the impact statement to enunciate clearly what those costs and implications are. If an impact statement has not done this, taking into account the entire international arms control environment, it has failed to state arms control impacts in any meaningful form.

VII.   Minimal requirements

In establishing the ACISs, the hope of the US Congress was not to hinder arms acquisition, but to ensure that arms acquisition did not hinder arms control. There may also have been a hope to prod the President into giving the tiny Arms Control and Disarmament Agency a larger role in defence planning. The ACIS process has succeeded in giving permission to ACDA to take something of a role (if only as an informed observer) in US arms acquisition. It is fairly clear, however, that the impact statements have not ensured the advancement of arms control. The absence of explicit concepts of arms control and impact, the over-abundance of executive control and the limitations imposed both by poor timing and by a parochial scope indicate that some minimal requirements must be met before a comprehensive ACIS can be prepared. The Congressional Research Service began to establish some of these requirements in 1978 and 1979, but the majority of the CRS recommendations were not implemented. Carter left office before he could take advantage of any of the Odeen recommendations and Reagan found no use for a system of checks and balances in the weapon acquisition process.

If the ACIS process is to be effective under any condition, there are seven requirements for analysis which can be distilled from the failures of the current evaluation process: (1) preparation and authorship by an independent, non-governmental agency; (2) identification and analysis of the impact environment; (3) programme purpose statement; (4) programme description and funding; (5) impact analysis; (6) review of alternative actions; and (7) inclusion of outside, expert opinion. Taken together, these requirements may sound the death knell for intragovernmental, executive impact assessment. They need not do so, but under current circumstances they must be presented as the ideal, as well as minimal, basis for arms control impact analysis.

1.   The first requirement, preparation and authorship by an independent, non-governmental agency, recommends a severing of executive control over the impact assessment process. ACDA, as an executive branch agency, is not fully capable of providing independent analysis, particularly when such analysis involves criticism of executive policies. Although ACDA has access to details which are otherwise classified, the qualitative nature of the information that is publicly available is sufficient for the kind of assessment needed for arms control decision-making and policy formulation. A non-governmental, international agency, freed from the political constraints of an official mandate, can better provide a balanced, incisive analysis of the range of possible consequences that the international arms control environment is liable to suffer.

One of the problems associated with independent authorship is that the results rarely enter the legislative process directly. However, a study conducted extra-governmentally can still inform the public and give indirect guidance to legislative or parliamentary bodies. Although the proposed requirements discussed here are best put to use by independent scholars, they are applicable to the ACDA process and to the potential impact statement procedures established by other governments, in so far as those governments seek to develop objective, comprehensive impact assessment tools. Legislators are much more in need of objective, expert analysis concerning future developments than they are of executive promotional platforms.

2.   The second requirement calls for the identification and thorough examination of the impact environment. In the case of arms control, this environment is primarily political, and attitudes, strategies, perceptions, cultural filters, military ambitions and technological incentives are all present.

As defined in the beginning of this paper, the term impact implies the existence of a particular environment which is capable of change upon introduction of a new component or variable. This means that the specific impacts in question— those which will define arms control prospects—are dependent upon the particular, case-specific constellations of political, social and technological variables in the international arms control environment.

The ACISs were first conceived in the United States by legislators who had had experience with environmental impact statements.[27] The National Environmental Policy Act (NEPA) is legislation which requires impact state- ments to be prepared prior to approval of a 'major federal action' affecting the natural environment, such as hydroelectric dams or hazardous waste facili- ties.[28] Since the passage of NEPA into law, these impact statements have provided a means by which a growing environmental concern in the United States can legitimately express itself, and the statements have supplied Con- gress with a compilation of expert opinion on the effects of the proposed projects on constituents, the ecosystem, wildlife and, by extrapolation, on the local economy, tourism and other factors dependent to some degree upon environmental welfare. The idea for ACISs emerged from this experience, and those who supported the concept sought to achieve the same kind of forecast- ing analysis in the politically charged atmosphere of national security and military procurement.

An evaluation of impacts upon the natural environment, however, is a far more straightforward process than an evaluation of impacts upon the temperamental conditions governing arms control. The biosphere consists of a primarily tangible set of variables, but the variables which comprise the arms control environment are difficult to pin down. What exactly is the arms control environment? This question is central to the impact assessment process. An environmental impact statement for a hydroelectrical facility must identify valleys and habitations that exist in a proposed site before it can determine what will be covered with water, and an arms control impact statement for a new weapon system must describe the international political, military and technological landscape before it can evaluate any potential impacts upon arms control.

For the purposes of an ACIS, the arms control environment can be broken down into general technological, diplomatic and political categories. The technological category encompasses the current state of scientific advance- ment, the rate of change in that advancement and the current allocation of economic, military and intellectual resources to military research. A basic understanding of these factors makes it possible for Congress to answer the important question of what will happen to military technology after significant resources have been committed to a particular new programme.

President Reagan's Strategic Defense Initiative provides a good illustration. Prior to SDI, the development of military technology absorbed a certain amount of economic and intellectual resources, and proceeded along paths determined to a large extent by earlier developments in nuclear bomb physics and weapon design. The introduction of SDI will alter this technological landscape in three potentially significant ways. SDI will draw upon a far greater number and variety of scientific minds than former military endeavours, with lasting implications for universities and for civilian industries. SDI will cost a prohibitive amount of money, even in military terms, with obvious implications for other defence and general budgetary needs. Finally, SDI will have an effect, as do all major conceptual departures in science, on the future of weapon conception and design.

Moreover, the arms control environment consists of the range of diplomatic activities related to arms control. The state of existing international arms agreements and of current, ongoing arms control negotiations are of critical relevance. General diplomatic relations are also important however, not only between the superpowers themselves, but between all other nations. These relations are a part of the arms control environment in so far as they are susceptible to change upon the introduction of new technologies and strategies.

Each military innovation of the superpowers causes ripples within the military alliances of the North Atlantic Treaty Organization (NATO) and the Warsaw Pact, but in recent years non-aligned nations have felt the impact of advancing weapon technology and have begun to exercise influence in response to superpower military activities and the arms race. The far-reaching impacts of nuclear explosions of any kind have made the weapons a concern of each nation, and to the extent that these nations exercise any influence in the international system, the development of new military technology has given them a place in the arms control environment.

The final major category of the arms control impact environment—and perhaps the most important—encompasses the fluid forces of social behaviour, political strategy and threat perception. Arms control is the offspring of political necessity, and the success or failure of arms control efforts is dependent more upon the political environment than upon the skills of diplomats sent to the bargaining table. The arms control environment is governed in part by the symbolic commitment of political leaders to arms control (commonly referred to as political will),[29] which is born out of social pressure. It is also governed by the strategic mind-sets of military personnel, the political lenses of governmental institutions, and the overall perception of threat, goodwill, motives and reliability on the part of all parties to the arms control process.

The non-static nature of strategic doctrine means that perceptions of the arms race change, carrying with them the whole of the arms control environment. A minor shift in the threat perceived by one superpower, or even by a third country, can radically alter the climate in which arms control must function. The political and perceptual forces governing the arms race are the most compelling set of factors making up the arms control environment. They determine the will and ability of the superpowers to make progress at the bargaining table, to respect existing agreements and to pursue confidence-building measures. A technological innovation which will alter these forces alters the arms control environment and therefore possesses serious ramifications for the prospects of arms control.

3.   The third minimal requirement for comprehensive ACISs is the inclusion of a general security-oriented statement of purpose. As already mentioned, the statement of purpose serves as the guiding principle of the assessment. The value of stating a purpose in terms of national or international security lies in the important distinction which it causes to arise between the particular programme under consideration and overall national strategic and security needs.

The statement of purpose as a vital component of the impact process has not been incorporated in any consistent fashion in the US statements. An explicit statement of purpose provides a clear understanding of the objective of the proposed programme. More importantly, it identifies a specific military or strategic need which must be filled. Too often, weapon systems are developed and deployed with little informed discussion about whether the adopted systems appropriately address the security needs of the government. An impact statement which starts from a general security purpose statement rather than from a specific technological purpose statement is better able to address the question of whether the specific technology is the best out of a range of reasonable options for addressing the overall security needs of the government. An effective, comprehensive impact statement cannot assume that the proposed programme is the best one.

Again, the SDI impact statement in the 1986 ACIS offers a useful example. Although there is no explicit statement of purpose in the document, one can extract an approximate purpose statement from the presidential speech quoted in the introduction: 'On March 23, 1983, the President called for the exploration of new technologies with the aim of substantially reducing U.S. dependence on the threat of nuclear retaliation.'[30] The stated purpose, therefore, is to reduce substantially US dependence on the threat of nuclear retaliation. Presented clearly in this manner, the logical question that must follow such a statement is 'what is the best means by which to achieve this purpose'. Using our example, SDI is then available as an optional rather than a mandatory solution. Its impact can be assessed in terms of its ability to reduce US dependence on nuclear retaliation, rather than in terms of its ability to perform specific military functions. In this light, the impact statement takes on an important new function. It identifies a purpose first (to reduce US dependence on the threat of nuclear retaliation as a strategic policy) and a technical solution (SDI) second. This approach makes room for the essential process of weighing and measuring national and international security needs. It also acknowledges that the achievement of security and international stability should take precedence over the adoption of a particular technology.

In fact, the introductory purpose statement issued by President Reagan in the 1986 SDI ACIS is submerged under the immediate promotion of the SDI programme itself. The sentence following his quote indicates the direction that the rest of the document takes: 'Defense technologies have the potential for enhancing both deterrence and strategic stability by reducing significantly and eventually even eliminating the military utility of ballistic missiles . . . the U.S. has developed a technological research plan to support this effort termed the Strategic Defense Initiative Program'.[31] In this case, even if the programme's statement of purpose was to eliminate the military utility of ballistic missiles (perhaps more manageable than reducing the threat of nuclear retaliation), a pre-emptive promotion of a solution bypasses both the enormity of the original challenge stated in the purpose and potentially endangers the security of the international arms control community by cauterizing the debate at the very point that it should flourish. A statement of purpose such as the one proposed by the President, taken as a starting point for enquiry rather than as a justification, provides the forum out of which the most effective solutions can emerge.

4.   The fourth minimal requirement for the ACISs is that they outline the specific programmatic attributes and structures of each proposed innovation, including costs and funding. This is what currently comprises the bulk of the US ACISs and is a fairly straightforward exercise. The most important aspects of a new weapon for impact analysis are accuracy levels, payloads and general delivery capabilities.

5.   The fifth requirement, analysis of impact, is far more complicated. This section of the impact statement provides an opportunity to observe, hypothetically, the new programme in action, bringing together the known properties of the innovation and the many variables of the arms control environment for the purpose of revealing important alterations to that environment. Each dimension of the arms control environment—the technological, diplomatic and political—must be discussed and analysed in the presence of the new programme. Desired modifications (for example, how the Soviet Union should respond, what the innovation ought to do for security, and so on) are irrelevant and potentially distracting to this analysis. Instead, potential changes to the social and political forces governing arms control and possible reactions of other governments should be noted and examined in the light of current arms control prospects.

In the technological environment, possible new avenues for the arms race should be identified. In the diplomatic area, possible reactions of, for example, the Soviet Union or Warsaw Pact—particularly in terms of further arms developments—should be offered, as well as potential changes to their perceptions of threat, strategies, doctrines or levels of communication with the West. In addition, the consequences of third-party reactions to US strategy and doctrine are an important element of the political assessment.

6.   The sixth minimal requirement for the impact statements is that they include available alternatives to the proposed programme. In environmental impact statements, this requirement takes the form of three basic options: (a) implementation of the proposed programme; (b) implementation of a modified or alternative programme; or (c) no action. In the environmental statements, reasons for or against all three of these options must be provided. This requirement has not made its way into the ACISs in any form. It is possible that

a different configuration of alternatives than that employed by the environmental statements would be better suited to the arms control setting, but a review of alternative actions is certainly appropriate to the ACIS.

The inclusion of a discussion of alternatives expands the parameters of choice for legislative bodies, for the public and indeed for the military. The necessity of justifying an action in the presence of alternative actions forces the argument to be of higher quality than if no alternatives are considered. In addition, it is the alienation of arms control considerations and deliberation of alternative actions from the military procurement process which serves to fuel the arms race.

7.   The last requirement makes the claim that an ACIS produced either by an independent, international organization or by governmental mandate, benefits from the presence of expert, outside opinion regarding the viability of new weapon programmes and the impact they will have on arms control. A presentation of opposing views could take the form of an appendix to the statement: a forum where various arguments can illuminate the arms control environment and broaden the base of the debate. In official settings, outside opinion could well be gathered through congressional or parliamentary hearings, the transcripts of which are published officially and are available to the public.

In either case, a balancing of views adds a valuable aspect of perspective to the volatile material presented in the ACISs. Arms control impact statements can only exist as a tool for decision-making. They can be tools of value for decision-makers, planners and the general public, but the worth of the statements is dependent entirely upon the depth and integrity of their contents. In the case of arms control, the contents are varied and complicated, but a reasoned, objective approach to the analysis of impact can better ensure the establishment of conditions essential for the achievement of stability in the international system and for progress towards genuine arms control.

Notes and references

[1] Clarke, D. L. and Brauch, H. G., *Decisionmaking for Arms Limitation: Assessments and Prospects* (Ballinger: Cambridge, MA, 1983). See chapters 5, 6 and 7 regarding arms control decision-making in the United Kingdom, the Federal Republic of Germany and Norway.

[2] The President of the United States and the Arms Control and Disarmament Agency, *Fiscal Year 1983 Arms Control Impact Statements* (US Government Printing Office: Washington, DC, 1983), Forward, p. 3.

[3] Congressional Research Service (CRS), 'Letter from Sparkman to Warnke', *Analysis of Arms Control Impact Statements Submitted in Connection with the Fiscal Year 1978 Budget Request* (US Government Printing Office: Washington, DC, 1977), p. IV. The 1987 ACIS has implemented a new, briefer format, eliminating most of the budgetary data and statistics which gave some substance to the former documents. According to the Arms Control and Disarmament Agency, these changes are designed to make the document more 'readable' for Congress, focusing more on policy than on budgetary and technical detail.

4 CRS (note 3).

5 CRS (note 3).

6 CRS (note 5).

7 CRS (note 3).

8 Personal correspondence, Michael Krepon to Carl Jacobsen (for affiliations, see list of contributors to this book, pages xvii–xviii), 3 Mar. 1986.

9 Odeen, P., *National Security Policy Integration: Report of a Study Requested by the President Under the Auspices of the President's Reorganization Project* (Coopers and Lybrand: Washington, DC, Sep. 1979).

10 Odeen (note 9).

11 Odeen (note 10).

12 The President of the United States and the Arms Control and Disarmament Agency, *Fiscal Year 1986 Arms Control Impact Statements* (US Government Printing Office: Washington, DC, 1986), Letter of Submittal, p. V.

13 CRS (note 3), p. 6.

14 Holst, J. J., 'On how to achieve progress in nuclear arms negotiations', *Bulletin of Peace Proposals*, vol. 16, no. 2 (1985).

15 CRS (note 3), p. 7.

16 CRS (note 3).

17 CRS (note 3).

18 Committee on Foreign Relations. *Arms Control Implications of Current National Defense Programs*. Hearing before the Subcommittee on Arms Control, Oceans, International Operations and Environment (US Government Printing Office: Washington, DC, 1980), pp. 3–4.

19 Committee on Foreign Relations (note 18), p. 4.

20 Clarke, D. L., *Politics of Arms Control: The Role and Effectiveness of the U.S. Arms Control and Disarmament Agency* (The Free Press: New York, 1979), p. 202.

21 Christoph Bertram refers to the problem of momentum in technological change in the arms race in terms of arms control negotiations. '. . . given both the inherent speed of technological innovation and the wide-spread tendency of politicians, analysts and the media to speed it up further in their minds by assuming that a known technology is a deployed one, the intervals between agreements would have to become very brief indeed'. *Arms Control and Technological Change: Elements of a New Approach*, Adelphi Paper No. 146 (The Intenational Institute for Strategic Studies: London, 1978).

22 CRS (note 3), Forward, p. 111.

23 CRS (note 3), p. 10.

24 ACIS (note 2), pp. 183–4.

25 ACIS (note 12), p. 200.

26 ACIS (note 2), p. 184.

27 Clarke (note 20), p. 190.

28 See Patten, II, B. M., *Environmental Review of Nuclear Weapons Systems: Current Policies and Opportunities for Change* (Resource Policy Center: Hanover, NH, 1985). See also National Environmental Policy Act (US Government Printing Office: Washington, DC, 1969).

29 Myrdal, A., *The Game of Disarmament: How the United States and Russia Run the Arms Race* (Pantheon Books: New York, 1976), p. 25.

30 ACIS (note 12), p. 4.

31 ACIS (note 12), p. 34.

Paper 1.3. New challenges and old mind-sets: ten rules for empirical realists

KEN BOOTH

Let me repeat the analogy . . . about the drunk who lost his watch in a dark alley but was found looking for it under a lamp post because there was more light there. The light provided by our knowledge of technological capabilities and our capacity for sophisticated strategic analysis is so dazzling as to be almost hypnotic; but it is in those shadowy regions of human understanding based on our knowledge of social development, cultural diversity and patterns of behaviour that we have to look for the answers.

(Michael Howard)[1]

I.   Introduction

We live in what is variously called a 'threat system' or a 'war system'; yet our understanding of threats remains painfully limited. The interrelated processes of threat perception (the cognitions which make us aware, rightly or wrongly, of challenges to our interests) and threat assessment (how we evaluate those challenges) are both complex and prone to mistake and misperception. Several years ago one expert in the business rightly described thinking about threats as 'one of the most primitive areas of statecraft'.[2]

II.   Old Mind-sets

The analysis of threats, in most situations, is notoriously difficult. It is one of those not unfamiliar problems in international politics which seem relatively simple until they are prodded beneath the surface. But even then there is no escaping the difficulty of the business, for when we think about threats we have to handle what is usually ambiguous information and what is always an unknowable future. Even those who may be challenging us do not know what they will be doing (though they will undoubtedly have hopes) in five months or five years. When thinking about the present and future, about which we know so little, it is sometimes comforting to remember the extent to which historians disagree about the past, about which we know so much.

The importance of accurate threat perception and assessment should be as obvious as the difficulties involved. The direct and opportunity costs of errors can be enormous. They can affect the fate of nations. That being so, it is surprising that the problem has been given such limited theoretical attention by policy-makers and academics whose professional lives involve the vicissitudes of thinking about and trying to survive passably well in a threat system. Well-established approaches leave much to be desired. There is a preference for crude formulae (a 'threat' equals 'intentions' multiplied by 'capabilities'), for simple rules-of-thumb ('since intentions can change overnight it is safer to concentrate on capabilities') and for the concrete rather than the intangible (such as the preference for computing the quantifiable rather than speculating about the unquantifiable, and for thinking about technology rather than perceptions). Security, both national and international, requires that we look beyond these traditional approaches, and that we concentrate on investigating the 'shadowy regions' of the subject.

When individuals or groups think about threats, it is striking that the criterion of validity for so many people is other than empirical. The mixture of empiricism and preconception will vary between individuals and groups, but there can be no doubting that threat perception and assessment is heavily determined by a range of ideological, psychological and theoretical considerations. These provide the framework for whatever knowledge is acquired; and they are often left to explain and fill in whatever gaps exist in our knowledge. Information is sought and used selectively to confirm old mind-sets. With most people when it comes to threats, it is not a case of seeing is believing; it is a case of believing is seeing.

Threats in international politics constitute a relationship between two or more nations. As such, they are susceptible to all the factual and analytical problems that attend the assessment of inter-group relationships. In international relations, as in interpersonal relations, it is essential to try to understand the psychological realities of those with whom we deal. Human relations at all levels are full of people who are unable or unwilling to understand and act upon the different needs, fears, hopes and ambitions of others. In international politics this problem largely manifests itself in the inability or unwillingness of individuals and groups to follow through the implications of the fact that we live in a multi-cultural world.

Perceptual mechanisms which distort our understanding of the facts are important because there is no clear dividing line in social life between image and reality. The reality of our strategic world is inextricably linked with our manner of conceiving it—with our image of it. The perceiver brings something to the facts of strategy, just as the perceiver brings something to a work of art. Strategic reality, like beauty, is in the eye of the beholder. And our behaviour in strategy, as in other parts of our life, is based upon what we believe to be true, not what is actually true. The ease with which we cope with our problems will not be unrelated to the extent to which our psychological realities match objective reality.

Our images of threats are shaped by many considerations, but there are four old mind-sets in particular that hold sway. These are ethnocentrism, Realism, ideological fundamentalism and strategic reductionism. These mind-sets are not mutually exclusive. But either singly or together they have significantly affected threat perception and threat assessment, and they have generally had a deleterious effect on the game of nations.

Ethnocentrism

Ethnocentrism is a basic problem in the theory and practice of strategy.[3] In its broadest sense, it is a synonym for being 'culture-bound'; this refers to the inability of one individual or group to see the world through the eyes of others. The consequence is an inability to emphathize or to recreate another's psychological realities. There are two other rather more particular aspects of ethnocentrism. First, in its original meaning, it describes attitudes of national superiority and importance; one's own group is seen as the centre of everything. And second, it involves the habit of interpreting the thoughts and behaviour of those from other cultures in terms of one's own. Ethnocentrism is a universal phenomenon, but its grip on thinking varies considerably between individuals.

Awareness of the significance of ethnocentrism for the theory and practice of strategy has risen since the 1970s. There is still considerable room for improvement however. Some strategists accept intellectually that the world is multicultural, but they write and behave as if it were not. Nearly two centuries ago, Clausewitz did not have to apologize for elaborating at great length and with metaphysical complexity the hardly novel point that war is a continuation of politics; equally today, nobody need apologize for stressing the need to reduce the problems which result from culture-bound thinking. Once Clausewitz's central thesis about the unity of war and politics is internalized, then one never looks at war in quite the same way again. Similarly, once one has understood the nature and implications of ethnocentrism in strategy, then the game of nations is henceforth interpreted through new eyes. For one thing, it appears increasingly like a 'tragedy' and decreasingly like a struggle between 'right' and 'wrong'.

Realism

The second mind-set that pervades the theory and practice of international relations, and greatly affects the way we have come to think about threats, is the doctrine of political Realism. This mode of thinking purports to see world affairs 'as they are' as opposed to 'as they ought to be'. The latter is said to be the failing of liberals and idealists, who are criticized for placing excessive faith in the role of reason, law and morality in human relations. Realists play down or ignore these dimensions and stress that politics is about preserving or increasing power in the pursuit of group interests. In international politics this outlook is accompanied by a conservative view of the state system and its processes; Realists therefore stress the primacy of states as actors in the system, the importance of sovereignty, the inevitability of war, the prevalence of expediency rather than principle and the absence of 'happy endings'. International life is 'nasty, brutish and short'. Realists are neo-Hobbesians.

Realists captured the debating high ground when they tied to their philosophical flag-staff a designation ('Realism') which connotes common sense, concreteness and objectivity. However, the Realist flag should not distract us from the fact that Realism is not necessarily realistic, objectively speaking. Realism is ideology. And like other ideologies, it seeks to legitimize and naturalize the status quo; it portrays as natural and immutable what are described as the prevailing conditions in the system. Thus Realists tell us that this is the best of all possible worlds. It is therefore 'natural', and their views are therefore 'realistic'. But this is simply doctrine. So, when somebody describes himself or herself as a 'Realist', it often tells one more about the beliefs of the individual than it does about the 'actual' nature of the world he or she may be describing. Like the idealists they scorn, Realists are also prisoners of their preconceptions.

There are too many Realists in contemporary strategy, but there is not enough actual realism. As both Hans J. Morgenthau and Edward H. Carr, the masters of realism in international politics knew, the ideology of Realism is not enough. And this is never likely to be more so than in the next few difficult decades. As we contemplate the new challenges ahead, the question we have to ask ourselves is: who are the 'real' realists and who are the real 'non-realists'.[4] Realism has always been a regressive doctrine, in the sense that it has always stressed what was not possible and has pointed to futures which are out of reach. But as William T. R. Fox has argued, the future is 'semi- but only semi-determined', and in the 1980s, we need to devote as much effort to 'determining what can be done as what cannot'. He then made an important distinction, between what he called 'empirical realists' and 'doctrinal realists', and he suggested that it is the empirical realist rather than the doctrinal kind (the Realists described above) which is best equipped to meet the new challenges.

The distinction between the two kinds of realist is fundamental to understanding how changeable is future change. The doctrinal realist asserts the basically Hobbesian world. Eternal conflict, he says, is structurally determined; there is, he maintains, no escape from the security dilemma; and the quest for national security foments all round insecurity in a gigantic and unending negative-sum game. The doctrinal realist does not need to examine how nation-state actors really behave by virtue of their nation-stateness in a multi-state world system. The empirical realist by contrast looks to see how they actually behave and perhaps beyond that to examining the possibilities for tolerable coexistence.[5]

Doctrinal realism is regressive; empirical realism is an imperative.

Ideological fundamentalism

Ideologies are theories or belief systems about man and society, and they consist of analytical and operational aspects. Some ideologies are flexible in their nature; others are far less so. In relation to the present discussion—the attribution of enemy status—we are particularly concerned with fundamentalist tendencies in ideologies; these are tendencies of individuals or groups to be drawn towards the most basic beliefs, doctrines, analyses and programmes upon which their particular ideology rests. In short, we are concerned with the extremists and radicals, be they on the political right or political left. Fundamentalists are conservatives who refuse to change their outlooks just because the world changes; they find it difficult to accommodate new information, or adjust to changing ways of thinking. New information is ignored or it is used selectively to confirm existing beliefs and justify existing prescriptions.

It is one thing to talk ideologically but act pragmatically, but it is another matter entirely to believe and act in a fundamentalist fashion when actual realities have changed. All ideologies provide a more-or-less coherent, more-or-less robust analytical framework which shapes the ideologue's thinking about the essential forces in world affairs, and which offers guidelines for analysis and prediction. Fundamentalism is irrational because it limits thought about change and about how to deal with the inevitable problems which politics throw up. Ideologies therefore not only shape interpretations but also establish boundaries on thought and action.

Ideologies have other implications which are relevant to threat perception. One important function they perform is to bind groups together by their words, beliefs and symbols. And for fundamentalist believers this objective may well be more important in any particular instance than the inherent truth, realism or reasonableness of what is being discussed. Thus, fundamentalists insist that people stand either with them or with the enemy on an issue. Democracy and rational debate are lower values than loyalty. Naturally, ideologues exhibit a strong 'us and them' mentality, which has a powerful effect on threat perceptions; with fundamentalists 'devil images' of the enemy are projected. Ideological fundamentalists know who they are, who the enemy is, and they are sure that things have to be that way, as part of man's natural lot, as part of the historical process. Being sure of all this is a consolation. They also know where their duty lies in response to the challenge.

Strategic reductionists

Ideologues may or may not be strategic reductionists, the last of the mind-sets under discussion. This term has been coined to describe those who look at strategy in a technical and mechanistic way, based on a simple conception of what politics among nations is all about. These strategic reductionists are obsessed by the military balance, state-of-the-art technology, windows of vulnerability, orders-of-battle, and questions of inferiority and superiority. Strategy is reduced to a numbers game. The concomitant political obsessions are with opportunism, temptation, power politics and the belief that marginal differences in overkill can have enormous politico-strategic effects.

International politics is seen by strategic reductionists as a rather crude and mechanistic process of power politics. 'How many divisions has the Pope?' asked Stalin. The calculation based on Soviet doctrine of the correlation of forces as the basis for action is merely the 'scientific' variant of Stalin's cruder approach. The North American equivalent of such an approach can be seen in the technical strategists who discard values, law, morality and cultural diversity in their outlook and concentrate instead on the abacus of warfare. Thus, for example, these technical strategists see nuclear parity as fundamentally unacceptable to the United States. It is a cause of anxiety which can be overcome only by the achievement of US superiority. Safety comes through strength, not politics.

Strategic reductionists take the politics out of strategy and reduce it to technology. They are not 'neo-Clausewitzians'; they are anti-Clausewitzians. In thinking about the Soviet threat, for example, there is no attempt to comprehend the complexity of the adversary; the problem is reduced to assessing relative military strengths. So, rather than ask people to try to cope with the nuances, ambiguities and uncertainties of political affairs, understanding is promised, clarity is imposed and common sense is invoked by the reductionist argument that a threat is essentially a surplus of capabilities and a hostile intent. The more distant one is from the history and culture of the country concerned, the easier it is to be taken in by such views.

Taken together, these old mind-sets act as cultural, philosophical, political, and strategic blinkers on the way individuals and groups think about international politics in general and the problem of threats in particular. These mind-sets freeze international relations into crude images, portray its processes as mechanistic responses to power, and characterize other nations as stereotypes. The four mind-sets described are not mutually exclusive. Indeed they are often mutually reinforcing. This can be seen in the outlook of that group of influential opinion-formers and policy-makers who have so dominated the US defence debate since the late 1970s: they are 'strategic fundamentalists'.[6] Their organizational embryo was the Committee on the Present Danger, and today they are in key positions throughout the political establishment. Their counterparts are less easy to distinguish in the Soviet Union because they more thoroughly pervade the political system.

III. Empirical realism

If the mind-sets just discussed act as blinkers on threat perception and assessment, what is the sensible alternative? There is one, and there have been signs during the more intense defence debating in the West since the late 1970s that growing numbers of people are moving towards it. Some are former policy-making insiders who have changed their minds; some are in the peace movement; some belong to the armed forces or government; some are in universities and research institutions; and others are concerned citizens who have discovered that the old mind-sets are part of our problem, not the solution. The best term to describe this alternative approach is that of William

Fox's used above, namely 'empirical realism'. Charles Manning, somewhat earlier and in a different context, called for 'sophisticated realism' when approaching international politics.[7] Such an approach, according to Manning, is grounded in the study of mankind as a whole from a global perspective and is sensitive to cultural relativism. This approach understands the significance of the human factor in its numerous manifestations and also the implications of the fact that states operate in an anarchic but not chaotic international system. A strategist with such an intellectual background should be able to avoid, in Mannings's words, 'the stultifications of fanaticism on the one hand and of pale non-alignment on the other'. Thus an empirical or sophisticated realist will base his or her thinking on evidence rather than on the preconceptions of old mind-sets; will be clear about the interests of his or her own state, but will be sensitive to those of others; will be aware of the sources of misperceptions between governments and nations; will have a sense of what is achievable; and will exhibit an ability and willingness to look at issues through the eyes of other nations. An empirical realist sees things as they are and tries to push matters in a benevolent direction, that is, towards coexistence and away from using force as a means of settling conflicts between states (though for the foreseeable future this will remain an option which cannot always be eschewed). Strategists who attempt to become empirical realists cannot guarantee success, but, to paraphrase Andrew Jackson on generals, they will conduct themselves so as to deserve it.

Reducing the grip of regressive mind-sets will not quickly produce a world of philosopher-kings and peace on earth. As in other areas of human behaviour, the game of nations is too complex to admit panaceas. But reducing the impact of these mind-sets should minimize the conflicts exacerbated by misperception, while at the same time producing policies based on educated guesses rather than incuriosity and ideology. Despite years of mass education, there is still a marked lack of knowledge in most countries about the outside world; and this in turn encourages insensitivity to the values and thoughtways of other nations. If minimizing the impact of old mind-sets does not guarantee peace, neither will it produce 'warm thoughts' about the world. Stands must still be taken; there are some ethnocentric values about which we need not apologize; we should avoid what Adam Ulam has called 'the immorality of unrealism';[8] there is no immediate or even foreseeable escape from the insecurity trap of the international system; and as long as armed forces exist, strategic thinking (including that of a technical kind) cannot be avoided.

Those who want to make life more secure have to begin from where we are. There is no better starting point for this than eschewing old mind-sets and adopting empirical or sophisticated realism as one's approach to international politics, that is, looking at the world as it is based on empiricism, cultural relativism and open-mindedness, rather than interpreting it through the distorting lenses of ethnocentrism, Realism, ideological fundamentalism and strategic reductionism.

IV.   Ten rules for empirical realists

Strategy is ultimately a practical business, and trying to liberate one's self from regressive mind-sets is the basis for rational practical activity in the changing and multi-cultural world we inhabit. At its most basic, what is being proposed in this essay is simply an elaboration of one of the oldest maxims in the whole of strategy, namely 'know thine enemy'. The importance of the maxim is obvious, but the history of war has shown with tragic regularity that it has not always been put effectively into practice.

The 10 rules discussed below are meant for mental stimulation rather than learning by rote. In strategy, as in other areas of political life, the art of judgement is more important than the slavish adherence to rules. The rules proposed may sound over-simple, have an aphoristic quality, be open to the discovery of exceptions and possibly encourage the bringing forward of counter-aphorisms. None of this matters, as long as the end product is deeper thinking about the perception and assessment of threats.

The 10 rules are applicable to any potentially adversarial relationship between states. However, the illustrations used have all been taken from recent Soviet–US relations, and, within that, overwhelmingly from the US side. This apparently lopsided presentation is not meant to imply that US policy-makers are more prone to regressive mind-sets than others. They are not. But US policy-making is visible and accessible. It is also crucially important, since US power, and hence responsibility, means that it is the single country with the most ability to nudge strategic history in a favourable direction—or the opposite.

1.   Threat assessment is a level-of-analysis problem

A 'threat' is an intention, perceived or otherwise, on the part of one state to inflict injury, in some circumstances, on the interests and values of another. 'Enemies' are those who manifest, or who are thought to manifest, such intentions.

If we conceive threats as a level-of-analysis problem, then several confusions will be minimized.[9] At the outset, we should always make a distinction between the foreign policy level of threat and the military contingency level. The former is concerned with *probabilities*: that is, what action might the other country perceive as being in its interests in a particular situation? The latter is concerned with *possibilities*: that is, what could the other country do in a military sense? What is seen as a 'threat' at a lower level might not be significant at the upper level. What a contingency planner might define as a possible threat in the event of conflict might have little or no significance from the perspective of the foreign policy analyst. To believe that it has is to demonstrate what Michael MccGwire has dubbed the 'colonel's fallacy'.

The simple distinction between levels of threat should help us think about some aspects of the military confrontation in Europe. The size and offensive orientation of Soviet forces is a North Atlantic Treaty Organization (NATO) contingency planner's nightmare; but this Soviet military posture is not incompatible with an overall Soviet strategy based on deterrence and a desire to avoid war. An offensive strategic doctrine can operate alongside a status quo foreign policy (though naturally this will always be more provocative to neighbouring countries than a more obviously 'defensive' posture). The fact that the Soviet Union has always made extensive and serious preparations for war does not mean that it 'wants' war. Rather, this fact signifies that it regards the threat of war as finite, that it is serious about what it does, that it intends to talk from a position of strength in international affairs, and that it is determined to do its best to prevail (whatever that means in modern conditions) if war comes about. The evidence does not suggest that the Soviet Union wants war in Europe, that it believes that such a war would be politically winnable, or that it thinks that the risk is presently 'high' (though it has thought the risks to be greater in the 1980s than they were in the 1970s). Foreign policy analysts must give due weight in their forecasts to Soviet aims and interests, and not simply to what Soviet forces can do in certain circumstances. In this regard it must be recognized that the threat of nuclear war-fighting (even war-winning) is simply the Soviet theory of 'deterrence'. Through the 1970s it became much more explicitly the doctrine of the United States as well. This represents the traditional military approach to deterrence: deterring the opponent into inaction by the threat of a successful attack.

The level-of-analysis idea is also helpful when contemplating force modernization. Confusion about how to think about threats caused unnecessary uncertainty in the West when it was faced by the need to react appropriately to the arrival and growth of Soviet SS–20s in the late 1970s. In what sense, if at all, did the SS–20 change the nature of the threat to the West?

At the outset, everyone can agree that the buildup of SS–20s has greatly complicated the calculations of NATO contingency planners. For them, the Soviet 'threat' has obviously increased. However, this has not led to an increase in the Soviet 'threat' at the higher foreign policy level. There is no reason to suppose that the introduction of the SS–20 signified a change in Soviet political intentions, and hence the character of the 'threat' at the foreign policy level. Indeed, the evidence suggests great continuity on the part of the Soviet Union in its attitude to theatre nuclear systems. It is therefore probable that the SS–20 was introduced simply as a modernization of the ageing SS–4s and SS–5s. Of course, modernizations involve improved specifications. Thus, the SS–20 was a more accurate and less vulnerable system than those it was replacing and could better threaten a range of adversary targets. This, British readers will recognize, is exactly the same rationale that the Thatcher Government has used on behalf of buying the Trident system as a replacement for Polaris; it is a modernization, not an escalation. There was another reason for not being alarmed. Since the SS–20 is mobile, it is not immediately vulnerable to attack, and so its operators need not have itchy trigger fingers in a crisis or at the outset of war. This represents an improvement in stability over the vulnerable SS–4s and SS–5s, where the pressure in a crisis would be to use them before they were destroyed. Again, readers in the West should appreciate this rationale, for it was one of the justifications for NATO's deployment of cruise missiles.

Without doubt, modernizations complicate the life of an adversary's contingency planners, but threat analysts at the higher level should hestitate before screaming 'escalation!'. Modernizations have to take place periodically, but they do not necessarily indicate a change in adversary intentions. The threat of mutual assured destruction (MAD) will remain the basis of the superpower relationship for the foreseeable future. The cautioning effect which this produces means that it is necessary neither to defer to unfavourable nuclear disparities nor demand immediate matching responses to every modernization.

2. Listen to area specialists

One way to improve one's understanding of the relationship between the various levels of analysis ('Will improved theatre capabilities lead to changed policy aims?') is to listen to area specialists. This might seem an obvious point, but the essence of good advice has always been that it is never heeded.

Many politicians and strategists are incurious and ignorant of the outside world. They are not notably improving with the passage of time. Whatever their other skills, for example, some of the leading members of the Reagan Administration will not go down in history because of their extensive knowledge and understanding of other countries. But they are by no means unique. Among academic strategists, few mainstream nuclear theorists have devoted much of their great energy to the systematic study of Soviet affairs, though the 'Soviet threat' is the framework for their thinking and prescriptions. Doctrinaire realists are content to massage their predispositions about the Soviet Union by scanning newspaper headlines.

Area specialists are precious, yet in recent years a crisis has been allowed to develop in the United States (and Britain) in the provision of Sovietologists. This is hardly the outcome one would expect from rational societies which expend significant portions of their scarce public money on 'defence' against the Soviet 'threat'. A cynic might suggest that this is a case of governments not wanting to have their beliefs clouded by facts. The widespread lack of sophisticated knowledge about the Soviet Union in the early 1980s did enable the White House and Downing Street to escape too easily with their outdated Cold War Sovietology.

Area specialists must not only be acquired, they must also be used. Here again, there is much room for improvement. Recent history furnishes plenty of examples of area specialists whose skills were wasted. The way George Kennan, the dean of US Sovietologists, was ignored after his period of service in Moscow is one example.[10] Another is the way the US Central Intelligence Agency (CIA) south-east Asian specialists were ignored in the 1960s'.[11] In both these instances, knowledge and advice could have been offered which might have saved the United States from errors, both great and small. And how would Western deterrence theory have developed had Soviet specialists been present at its creation?

Area specialists add knowledge and nuance. They will differ in interpretations among themselves, and theirs need not be the final word, for wider considerations may have to be taken into account. But there can be no doubt that they should have a word. Serious consultation with relevant area specialists is an essential foundation of rational policy-making. (Having said that, area specialists should not be listened to uncritically. This is especially the case when an area falls into the hands of a particular group with deep emotional commitments, such as the way US Sovietology fell into the hands of Eastern European *émigrés* after World War II.)

Area specialists (other than *émigrés*) usually have the reputation of being smitten by the country or region which they study. This is a justifiable warning in some cases, but even where it is there is much to be said for having one's own nationals explaining with conviction the outlook of those foreigners with whom one has to deal. But overcoming ethnocentrism does not necessarily lead to defending the other's cause, or to taking a more relaxed view of affairs. Middle Eastern specialists in recent years, for example, have been more nervous about the long-term instability of that region than have Western policy-makers.

The opposite has been the case in Soviet affairs. Here, with one or two prominent exceptions, the Soviet Studies community in the West has been much more relaxed about the Soviet 'threat' than those in policy-making circles. Few in the Soviet Studies community have endorsed official claims about the degree of Soviet military 'superiority' which is alleged to exist; have been willing to underwrite assertions about Soviet confidence regarding the fighting and winning of nuclear wars; or have supported arguments about Soviet 'adventurism', 'expansionism' and 'strategic momentum' in the Third World. On this last issue, for example, the picture painted by most Soviet area specialists has differed greatly from that of the White House. They show that despite persistent Soviet efforts in the Third World over 30 years, there is no gathering strategic momentum. Viewed in perspective, the Soviet Union has missed the bus in the Third World, and there is no evidence that widespread opportunities will open up in future.

3. Numbers do not necessarily add up

If area specialists should be given more attention in threat assessment, technical strategists ('bean counters') should be given less. When it comes to human behaviour, numbers do not necessarily add up. An individual who puts his head in the icebox and his feet in the oven is not, on average, likely to be comfortable.

We cannot think about particular strategic relationships without thinking about numbers, but we must recognize that there is at least as much politics as mathematics in the arithmetic of the military 'balance'. All states play the numbers game in their presentations of their case, for budgetary and propaganda reasons. And even with the best will in the world, computing relative orders-of-battle is not easily done. Whose numbers can one trust? Which systems should be compared with which? What is the qualitative balance? What is the significance of the electronic black boxes which are so crucial in determining the performance of weapon systems these days? We ask these questions, but for the most part are left to accept on faith the conclusions of the standard sources.[12] And then we must get on with the business of thinking as best we can. 'What is truth?', said the jesting strategist, and would not stay for an answer.

Given the uncertainty of the business, there has been a preference in threat assessment for giving undue weight to what on the face of it appears to be 'hard' numerical indicators. But numbers are an uncertain foundation on which to construct expectations about behaviour.

Intentions cannot be directly deduced from capabilities. The explanation for a particular order-of-battle is likely to be multi-causal, the result of a combination of service traditions, economic constraints, technological possibilities, inter-service rivalry, and so on, as well as rational intentions in the face of a perceived adversary. Furthermore, relative military strength does not necessarily translate into military aggressiveness. Aggressors have rarely been fully ready for war, in terms of both weapons and ambitions. As a result, if one waits until an aggressor has achieved an optimum level of preponderance, the chances are that one will be taken by surprise, earlier than expected. Equally, relative weakness cannot be taken to signify peaceful relations; the relatively weak in all societies can be the most aggressive. And neither is the bean counter's favourite rule-of-thumb ('intentions can change overnight, therefore it is safer to rely on enemy capabilities') based on the record of the past. Capabilities can change at least as quickly, and sometimes more quickly, than intentions. This is not to say, of course, that the actual number of vehicles in a nation's tank parks or of its missiles in their silos can suddenly increase or decrease overnight. But what can and does change overnight are the estimates of them made by other nations, and it is these estimates that determine the other nations' expectations and hence behaviour. Capabilities changing overnight, in this fashion, have occurred on a number of occasions in the past 25 years.[13] Meanwhile, the intentions of great powers on the great issues of peace and war have shown considerable continuity. There have been some 'technical' (tactical) surprises, but there have been few, if any, of a 'behavioural' or radical kind.[14]

In the East–West confrontation it is important that the NATO allies guard against believing their own propaganda about Soviet strengths and 'superiority'. The inflation of adversary strengths (which serve a variety of budgetary, bureaucratic and propaganda purposes) can encourage wasteful arms races or defeatism. Threat inflation can also encourage a fatalistic belief that there is nothing to be done except rely on the threat of piling up ever-greater amounts of nuclear overkill. If one ignores some official threat inflation regarding the strategic 'balance', one can clearly see that there exists what Zbigniew Brzezinski some years ago called an 'ambiguous equivalence' about the inventories of the superpowers. This means that in some categories of weapon the Soviet Union is ahead, but in others the West is; as a consequence, neither side has the capability, or foreseeably can acquire the capability, of being able to succeed in a military strike against its adversary without suffering overwhelming destruction in retaliation.

Nuclear weapons, by their nature, wipe out the military significance of even larger disparities in orders-of-battle. This could be used to encourage more-relaxed attitudes about the superpower relationship, and the exploration of ways of accommodation. But for some groups in both countries, these attitudes have not proved appealing. Instead, these strategic reductionists advertise scares about 'gaps' of one sort or another; or spread excitement about 'windows of vulnerability'. Such was the behaviour of the influential Committee on the Present Danger. So far, however, the only people who have jumped through 'windows of opportunity' to dominate the American people have been aspiring presidential candidates. No doubt it will happen again.

4. Never discount intentions

Because counting capabilities is an imprecise science, and assessing their significance is a difficult art, it is important to think much more systematically about adversary intentions. A sophicated realist will integrate both intentions and capabilities in the assessment of a threat, and will give more weight to intentions (based on a study of words and deeds through history) than realists or reductionists would contemplate, while, for different reasons, ethnocentrics and ideologues would be incapable of doing the task well. That others cannot do it perfectly does not invalidate the effort of trying.

An attempt to understand intentions is necessary because the hopes and fears of other nations are every bit as real in politics among nations as their tanks and ships. Too much emphasis was given to capabilities rather than intentions when their potential targets thought about Hitler in the mid-1930s, about Egypt in the early 1970s, and about Argentina in the early 1980s. It does not mean, just because something is 'in the mind', that it is not real.

It would be foolish to claim that one can fully understand the intentions of foreign governments. How many of us can be confident that we understand our own leaders? A start can be made, however, by trying to identify the negative interests of an adversary; if dreams and ambitions might be unclear, it is usually not difficult to list the developments an adversary hopes to avoid. Thus the Soviet leadership clearly wants to avoid general nuclear war; it does not want dangerous confrontations with the United States; and it does not want to lose orthodox party control in the USSR or in Eastern Europe (or the loss of Soviet control there). If the Soviet leadership believes that the country is about to be attacked or if they are about to lose a vital position (and see no alternative to military force), then there is little doubt that they will act violently. But they will normally try and avoid actions which will put their interests at risk. They might miscalculate, but that is a different matter. When we are thinking about threats, we must normally assume rationality on the part of the adversary, while not ruling out the possibility of the opposite.

Soviet leaders have miscalculated Western positions on several occasions in the post-war period. We do not face an infallible chess player. Generally, however, when they have contemplated or used the military instrument, their behaviour has been cautious and has avoided risks. To the extent the Soviet Union has a reputation for being adventurous, it is largely confined to Nikita Khrushchev's behaviour between 1958 and 1962. Khrushchev, significantly, was more conscious of his weaknesses than of his strengths during these years. He believed that time was running out over Berlin, in his relations with China, and in the strategic balance. Pushed into a corner, Khrushchev was willing to take great risks in order to escape. His insecurity was the fundamental threat to the West, not his rockets.

5. Analogies are not proof

One much-favoured way of thinking about intentions is by drawing upon analogies. It is a habit of practitioners as well as armchair strategists. Everybody is familiar with the way Anthony Eden, the British Prime Minister of the day, identified Nasser in the mid-1950s with Hitler 20 years earlier, and so brought about Britain's worst foreign policy disaster since 1945. Even more disastrously, we saw in the 1950s and 1960s the obsession in some American minds with the 'Munich syndrome'. This led to the idea of defending San Francisco on the Mekong, and of trying to preserve US democracy by protecting dictatorships in far-away countries about which Americans knew little. The result was the war in Indo–China—the one great tragedy in two centuries of US foreign policy.

Analogies do not prove anything. At best they only illustrate. And, even when illustrating, one must be aware of the differences between situations and not be tempted by superficial similarities. They are a poor guide for policy-making.

Of all the analogies which have been politically significant in the past 10 years, none have been more important than the attempt to liken the Soviet threat with that of Nazi Germany. Both regimes have been described as warlike; both are said to share a commitment to territorial acquisition by means of military expansion; and both are totalitarian dictatorships. This analogy has been propounded by important members of the Reagan Administration,[15] and therefore presumably plays some part in how they think of dealing with the Soviet Union. Like so much of the thinking behind the Reagan Administration's foreign policy, this analogy is flawed.[16] The nature of the Soviet threat and the character of Soviet expansionism is too large a topic to be dealt with in a few words, but for present purposes it is sufficient to draw attention to Michael Howard's distinction between 'militarist' and 'bellicist' states, the Soviet

Union belonging to the former category, Nazi Germany to the latter. According to Howard's distinction, a 'militarist' state such as the Soviet Union invests in huge military efforts, but does so in order to avoid war, not because it is planning to bring one about. There is no 'cultural disposition' to go to war in the Soviet Union—to use Howard's phrase—as there clearly was in the hyper-violent culture of Nazi Germany.[17]

The preceding paragraph does not mean that the Soviet Union is not a military problem or even 'threat' to its neighbours. It does, for it is a great power, and like all great powers it tends to want to dominate its neighbours, possess preponderant military power, acquire the best weapons, define its 'vital interests' expansively and demand more extensive rights than others. And, like all great powers, it will go to war if its government thinks it must. But the record does not suggest that the Soviet Union will go looking for war, as did Nazi Germany. So far at least—and it remains to be seen whether matters might change if its relative power increases—the Soviet Union has been rather cautious when asserting its military weight beyond its borderlands.

The analogy between Soviet Russia and Nazi Germany is fed by the idea that the Soviet military buildup through the 1960s and 1970s represents the working out of a blueprint,[18] and that what has been acquired represents more than the Soviet Union 'needs' for its legitimate self-defence. The obvious implication we are supposed to draw from such arguments is that Soviet military power has been acquired for offensive purposes. The actual explanation for the situation is much more complex.

The Soviet military buildup since the 1960s was not the product of a single decision. It was rather the result of a variety of interacting considerations: the various branches of the Soviet forces responded to different external challenges at different times; inter-service, economic and bureaucratic factors had an impact; tradition played a role; and the processes of technological obsolescence had their effect. The different lead-times involved in the innovation cycles of weapons happened to work together to produce a step-up in Soviet military power in the second half of the 1960s, but this was coincidence rather than a master plan. Furthermore, the buildup was not self-generated; it was instead largely a response to a variety of military challenges thrown down by the West and the United States in particular. These included the increased nuclear potential of the US Navy represented by the deployment on carriers of aircraft with greater strike ranges, the deployment of Polaris, the accelerated strategic buildup during the Kennedy Administration and NATO's shift to flexible response. Once underway, the Soviet military response, in typical fashion, just kept rolling along. As a result, the Soviet leaders by the late 1960s had acquired military options which they had not previously possessed. Today their military power is even more varied. This is a problem for Western contingency planners, but devising the best response will not be assisted by imputing false motives to the Soviet buildup. Bad history makes bad strategy.

The Soviet Union is a handful enough for the West without professional threat inflaters frightening everybody with sloppy history and ethnocentric biases. But the situation is not helped by the fact that the Russians themselves can be their own worst enemies, for they periodically feed the appetites of those in the West who are prone to frightening analogies by their obsessive toughness and secrecy. The Soviet political élite, for example, probably has no conception of the extent to which its own behaviour in the 1970s—its military buildup and opportunistic tactics in the Third world—helped legitimize the Reagan phenomenon in the United States. This problem was again illustrated by the Korean airliner incident in 1983. Anti-Soviet appetites had already been whetted by such 'normal' and understandable Soviet actions as their interven-tion in Afghanistan in 1979. This action, a move largely to try to protect a friendly regime on its southern border, was simply the stuff of great power behaviour. The Soviet Union was being as true to great power type as it had been in its decision to attack Finland in 1939. Such actions were comparable to the tough US behaviour—of which there has been much over the years—in Central America. However, to those who have what Kissinger calls an 'inherent bad faith'[19] model of the Soviet Union, there is no attempt to understand such actions from the Soviet point of view (or even in terms of great power norms); instead such behaviour is simply categorized according to favoured demonic analogies.

The problem of analogies in East–West relations is compounded by the fact that Soviet thinking is probably even more oppressed by them. Western behaviour towards the Soviet Union today is still likened by Soviet commen-tators with that of the imperialist predators who, in Soviet legend, tried to strangle Bolshevism at birth. Soviet thinking along these lines is not entirely fanciful, however, just as some Western analogies contain some plausible comparisons. Soviet observers have had every reason for not feeling relaxed when they have listened to the hectoring of the Reagan Administration to the effect that the Soviet Union is an 'evil empire', that its position in Eastern Europe is not legitimate, that it is a nation of cheats and liars and that it is based on a bizarre doctrine which is doomed to fail. When leading members of the most powerful nation on earth carry on such verbal hostility, and in the background instigate an enormous military buildup, it is not likely to encour-age Soviet leaders, and the people of a proud nation, to feel relaxed or to forget old analogies. It is only likely to rekindle historic fears, make them feel edgier, and build up a determination to fight back.

6.   Think before (and after) worst-case forecasting

Analogies are one way by which people try to comprehend complex affairs. Worst-case forecasting is another method and is used by strategic planners. Robert McNamara, when US Secretary of State for Defense, advised that a strategic planner must always be conservative; he must always prepare for the worst plausible case.[20] This means thinking about what the enemy *can* do, not what he might do. If you assume the worst, you do not risk mistaking an enemy for a friend. This was the trap into which Little Red Riding Hood fell. Her lack of sense of danger led her to see benevolence in threatening signals.

But adopting the opposite posture is not without problems, especially if other states act on the same worst-case assumptions. If this occurs, the outcome is what McNamara called an 'action–reaction process'; this lead to arms-racing and less security for all at higher levels of cost and destructive power. Worst-case forecasting has a propensity for being self-fulfilling. As George Kennan noted, those one treats as enemies tend to behave like enemies.[21] The counter-moral to the story of Little Red Riding Hood can be drawn from the tale of King Arthur's last battle. At a peace conference one of the knights drew his sword. He intended to kill a snake, but his action was misinterpreted. Others sprung to their own defence, and in a contagion of fear the knights fell upon each other, causing virtual annihilation.[22] Those who live by the worst-case forecast may die by the worse-case forecast.

In the US–Soviet confrontation, worst-case forecasting on the US side has had deleterious effects. Some influential people have come to regard the technique of worst-case forecasting as synonymous with the truth. The result is that 'implicit enemy images' are compounded and opportunities are missed to nudge the relationship in a safer direction. Negative points about the Soviet Union get repeated, as if in a catechism. Typical of this is the misconceived assertion—by spokesman after spokesman—that the Soviet Union has more military power than it needs for its own legitimate self-defence. This is ethnocentrism at its insidious worst. How can we tell whether the Russians have too much? What are the standards of comparisons? If one genuinely attempts to step inside the boots of a Soviet defence planner, one is unlikely to come up with any conclusion other than that the Soviet Union does not have enough military power to deter its multiple enemies, compete with technologically and economically more advanced states, dominate Eastern Europe and support foreign policy concerns elsewhere. From the Soviet point of view, the United States has more military power than it needs for its legitimate self-defence needs.

It is the tendency to be over-impressed by worst-case forecasts that leads some people to become over-excited about small gaps in capability; this has been seen in the alarms about windows of vulnerability turning into windows of opportunity, through which the Russians will jump. These ideas are also fed by the tendency to see international relations as simply a strategic game, where the significance of marginal vulnerabilities become inflated beyond reason. Such faulty reasoning was evident in the thinking of the Committee for the Present Danger, and is evident in the arguments of those who interpret and predict Soviet behaviour in terms of the state of the military balance.[23] When politics between nations are seen as narrowly as a strategic game, common-sense questions are ignored: What interests can be served by military action? What are the risks? What are the costs? What is it all about?[24] In trying to cope with the blizzard of information, contemporary strategists can easily be blinded, and so fail to consider the first-order questions in their business. In this respect, the revived peace movement in the West since the late 1970s has performed a most valuable democratic function. It has forced those on the inside of the policy process, academic strategists and others to ask more fundamental questions about our predicament. It has raised the level of the defence debate.

7.   Fear the man who fears you

A healthy corrective to worst-case forecasting, which concentrates on one's own fears, is to try to recreate the fears which one's adversaries may have; that is, think worst-case for others. In this context the old Jewish saying 'Fear the man who fears you' is of special relevance. Among other things, it reverses the idea of the 'security dilemma'.[25] Rather than an increase in one state's security provoking insecurity on the part of others, here we see that an increase in one state's insecurity can promote insecurity elsewhere.

In order to try to understand the fear felt by others, it is necessary to undertake the always difficult task of trying to see ourselves as others see us. In the strategic context this means trying to see ourselves as a threat. Since all nations believe themselves to be the most peaceful, and know that they are the good guys, this is clearly a difficult task. But those who do not attempt this, or who do it badly, miss a crucial dimension of international reality. Edmund Burke said that 'nothing is so fatal to a nation as an extreme of self-partiality and the total want of consideration of what others will naturally hope or fear'. To know what others naturally hope or fear, it is necessary to understand their psychological realities. This cannot be done by those with an 'extreme of self-partiality'; the latter, unfortunately, is the natural condition, perhaps the privilege, of superpowers. In recent years the leaderships of neither superpower have shown a flair in seeing themselves through the eyes of others. Their own self-image, and that of foreigners, would not recognize each other if they collided on the street.

We are familiar with Western fears about the Soviet Union, but not with Soviet fears about the West. This is a crucial weakness from an analytical and policy-making point of view, for there are strong grounds for arguing that the starting point for any examination of Soviet thinking about defence should be the deeply ingrained sense of insecurity which arises from Russia's turbulent past. Insecurity, it must be stressed, can lead to threatening behaviour and expansionism, as well as hedgehog passivity.[26]

There are historical, geographical, psychological and ideological dimensions to the Soviet Russian sense of insecurity, though without doubt the Soviet Union today is stronger than in the past and has much less reason to fear old-style invasion. While accepting the latter, we must understand that as Mikhail Gorbachev looks out from the Kremlin, he has plenty of reason for anxiety, even without indulging in worst-case scenarios. The Soviet Union over the past 40 years has done an impressive job in catching up with the United States (in a military sense at least), but it still sees itself confronted by a technologically superior adversary which rejects its right to exist; it sees itself opposed by a relatively united and relatively prosperous Western world (including Japan, an economic superpower in the East); there is chronic instability in bordering areas of the Middle East; there are worrying problems in the socialist world with the Eastern European bloc running out of steam on the one side and China modernizing with the help of the West on the other; and at home there is the chronic problem of trying to prod an unwieldy country and a rusting socialist system to work more effectively. The West thinks of Soviet foreign policy as something calculated to produce headaches for us; from the viewpoint of a foreign policy planner in Moscow, the Soviet Union is a rather harassed socialist superpower whose external relations leave much to be desired.

Soviet defence planners also face a difficult job. Over the years, the Soviet Union has made heroic strides in overcoming challenges and in catching up with opponents. Despite all the sacrifice and exertions, however, Soviet planners are still confronted by numerous problems and have good reason for feeling more insecure than their Western counterparts. Consequently, one does not have to spend much time trying to see the world through Soviet eyes in order to understand why they try to over-insure in a military sense. Of course, Soviet spokesmen exaggerate external 'threats' for propaganda reasons; and for the same reasons they play the military 'numbers game' when they can. Such behaviour is simply the gamesmanship of the international system. But there is often more than a kernel of truth in the Soviet position. It is not all 'disinformation'. If we do not attempt to understand the element of 'truth' that exists in Soviet statements, then we will be dealing with a Soviet Union of our prejudices rather than the real world, one which has a complex of fears as well as ambitions.

Take the intermediate nuclear force (INF) issue, for example. Accepting the Soviet view that their SS–20 deployment was a modernization of obsolete systems (which up to that point NATO had not thought it necessary to 'balance' by the deployment of US land-based missiles in Western Europe), we should be able to appreciate that the NATO deployment of cruise and especially Pershing II represented in Soviet eyes a dangerous 'escalation' which cut down their warning time to a minimum. The Soviet position on INF in the late 1970s and early 1980s was not something dreamed up for the arms control negotiations, but was the outgrowth of a policy pursued for 20 years.[27] They believe, with justification, that the INF crisis was created by the West. But then they are also unable to see themselves as others see them. Like us, they find it difficult to imagine how their own actions, such as periodic weapon modernizations, can excite such fear in others.

An excellent illustration of the West's inability to see itself through Soviet eyes is evident in the differing interpretations of the decline of détente.[28] The standard Western interpretation of superpower relations in the 1970s stresses that this was a period of relentless Soviet arms-building, of growing Soviet assertiveness and intervention in the Third World, of Soviet hypocrisy about matters such as human rights and arms control, and of an attempt by the Soviet

Union to use détente as a smoke-screen behind which it could successfully pursue its cold war designs. Thus the Soviet Union did not live up to either the spirit or the letter of détente; this was confirmed by its aggressive invasion of Afghanistan in 1979.

The Soviet interpretation of this period is an almost exact mirror image. It sees the 1970s as a period of US arms-building, of a US lack of seriousness about arms control, of US hypocrisy about agreements and a period characterized by US assertiveness in the Third World. From the Soviet point of view even the ragged détente of the late 1970s was worth hanging on to. It was the United States that ditched it: it never really accepted the idea of superpower equality; it failed to ratify SALT II; it engaged in unprecedented arms-racing; and it conducted the superpower relationship through what a former US Ambassador in Moscow called 'gutter language'. It was US behaviour that heralded the period of 'new cold war'.

Future historians will undoubtedly include elements of both interpretations in their explanation of the decline of détente in the 1970s. Like the onset of the cold war before it, this episode was less a case of absolute good versus absolute evil, and more a case of two suspicious powers, each seeing itself as being in the right, and each unable to believe that the other's increasingly hostile behaviour was largely a response to its own actions, rather than a manifestation of its basic hostile intentions. At the start of the 1970s, both superpowers had attempted to loosen the insecurity trap they were in, but by the end of the decade, the interplay of circumstances and suspicions had led to its tightening. Had the West had a better understanding of the world through Soviet eyes, their expectations about détente would not have been as high originally, while later on the deterioration in relations could probably have been handled with more skill. Had the Soviet leaders better comprehended how their behaviour appeared to the West, they would more clearly have understood why the United States elected Ronald Reagan.

The West has to fear the Soviet Union because that traditionally insecure state fears it. And Soviet fear is not only in the military-strategic arena. It is also political. The very existence of liberal democracies represents a standing political challenge to an authoritarian leadership of a socialist superpower whose industrial and agricultural production leaves plenty to be desired; whose ability to satisfy domestic consumer wants falls well short of desirable; and whose arrival at the gates of communism is constantly postponed. What John F. Kennedy called 'the disease of liberty' represents a persistent fear for Soviet leaderships; they are particularly worried about the contagion spreading within the socialist commonwealth. This morbid political insecurity means that a state in Eastern Europe does not have to present a direct military threat to the Soviet Union to have Soviet tanks rolling over it. Czechoslovakia discovered this, at great cost, in 1968. The 'Prague Spring', with its 'socialism with a human face', was a severe political challenge to the whole Moscow-dominated edifice. If it was not stamped out there, where would it end? Like the White House with respect to Central America in the early 1980s, Soviet leaders in the late 1960s feared falling political dominoes in their own backyard. Recognition of this Soviet fear is important when Western countries compose their policies on Eastern Europe or on the human rights issue.

The West has therefore to fear the Soviet Union because the Soviet Union fears the West both in a military and political sense. The historical record clearly suggests that Western security is not obviously improved by our stoking the fears of a deeply suspicious, ethnocentric and chronically insecure nation. Stimulating insecurity will be particularly dangerous if ever a Soviet leadership comes to feel strongly that time is running out. And Western observers must not merely recognize Russia's historical insecurity at an intellectual level; they must also act on that cognition. If this is done, one will eschew the words of those who say, in effect: 'Yes, I accept that Soviet Russia has had a terrible history, but they still have more military power than they need'. In practice Western policy should give more attention in its strategic posture to reassurance and less to intimidation; and a more sympathetic ear should be given to Soviet fears and rights. This is not a call for appeasement; it is the basis for a final normalization of the relationship.

8.   Guard against wishful thinking

Whatever one's interpretation of the present state of East–West relations—and the argument so far has pointed to a more relaxed view of the Soviet threat—it is always important for analysts to ask themselves whether the psychologically comfortable evidence is being chosen about the adversary. That is, is 'best-case forecasting' being undertaken? Are one's arguments being affected by wishful thinking? Are one's verdicts about the trends and prospects being based upon what one wants the future to be, so that one's policy prescriptions will appear rational and logical? Typically, for example, nuclear deterrers reduce the risk of general nuclear war virtually to zero, in order that they might sleep soundly in their beds, confident in the rationality of their commitment to nuclear overkill. Unilateral nuclear disarmers in Britain, on the other hand, usually dismiss the likelihood of military Soviet behaviour, so that they too can sleep content that their recommendations will not lead to the collapse of that security which their recommendations were supposed to uphold. Both groups have been reluctant to have their thinking disturbed by the contemplation of uncomfortable possibilities.

Since everybody searches for cognitive consistency, the tendency just described is one we all share, to a greater or lesser extent. In order to minimize the problem, we must act as our own devil's advocates. This means that those of us who take a relatively relaxed view of the Soviet threat must remind ourselves about Soviet ideology, the suppression of human rights, the Gulag, the episodes of adventurous Soviet behaviour in the past, the steady commitment to military research and development, the fact of enormous Soviet military strength, and all those negative aspects of Soviet behaviour which make the prospect of living together a bumpy prospect (chronic Russian mistrust of outsiders, secrecy and so on). And neither must one forget the very size of the Soviet Union; this came about not as the result of a geographical accident, but through the expansionist use of military force. The Soviet Union is a superpower and, when appropriate, will behave like one. Equally, those who are more relaxed about the risks and consequences of nuclear war than about the Soviet threat should ask themselves appropriate questions about their ideas, and ask whether and where wishful thinking might be operating.

In trying to guard against wishful thinking, we must be ready to reassess our assumptions periodically. The challenges thrown up by international affairs are complex and changeable, and we must not be afraid to change our minds as appropriate. Not to do so is tantamount to claiming that all the ideas one had in one's student days were correct, and that nothing one has learned since has had any effect, save that of consolidating one's beliefs.

9. Expect surprises

The easy thing in strategic affairs is to predict today what was predicted yesterday.[29] Assuming 'the threat' can be dangerous, without periodic reassessment, for it can lead to unwarranted assumptions about the character of the adversary's behaviour, and the faulty categorization of individual elements of it. When one's own preconceptions become more powerful than new knowledge, a state can be in trouble, as Israel discovered in 1973. Thus, while it might seem a contradiction to advise 'expect surprises', it should be taken as a warning against possibly fatal complacency.

The practice of international politics is humbling in part because it is so unpredictable. Strategic history is full of people being caught out. The final piece of advice given by Philip Crowl to those on the threshold of careers as strategic planners was along these lines:

After all your plans have been perfected, all avenues explored, all contingencies thought through, then ask yourself one final question: 'What have I overlooked? Then say your prayers and go to sleep—with the certain knowledge that tomorrow too will bring its share of nasty surprises.[30]

These surprises may be 'technical' or 'behavioural', to use Knorr's earlier distinction, but there should be few of the latter for strategic planners who have done their work thoroughly.

Strategy is not generally an area of human relations that permits confident and detailed predictions. It is an art, and one wherein even the skilled get it wrong for some of the time. Most Soviet specialists over the past 30 years were taken by surprise by such major developments in Soviet strategy as the speed of their technological innovation in nuclear weapons and missiles, their naval buildup, the extent of their support for national liberation movements in the 1970s, or their intervention in Afghanistan in 1979. Having noted that, it should also be said that some observers of the Soviet scene have been periodically surprised by how cautious, reasonable and rational the Soviet leadership can be. The inherent bad faith model, allied with the image of the Kremlin as a rational unitary actor, also leads some to be surprised that, like their Western counterparts, Soviet policy-makers can also be incompetent. Because of the widely held inherent bad faith model of the Soviet Union, the negative surprises about the Soviet Union only confirm existing negative beliefs, while positive signals are usually dismissed as merely tactics to further ambitious intentions. As a result, positive surprises are rarely seized upon in order to try to nudge East–West relations in a favourable direction.

10.   Remember the system

Lest it be thought that the previous nine rules exaggerate the importance of misunderstandings and misperceptions—what Kenneth Boulding called the 'illusory' incompatibility between nations[31]—it is important to conclude with a reminder that the 'anarchic society' in which states exist is in part a 'threat system'. So, even if there were to be in the second half of the 1980s an outbreak of 'understanding' between the superpowers—a sunny mirror image of that stormy outbreak of mistrust between them, which has characterized their relationship since the late 1970s—the result would not be 'positive peace'. The next few decades do not promise the prospect of massive disarmament or an end to reciprocal nuclear targeting.

Something can and should be done to minimize the problems caused by and exacerbated by misperceptions, but we must also avoid the largely liberal fallacy that all conflicts are basically the result of 'misunderstandings' between nations. Competition over resources and security is rooted in the very dynamics of an international system where national interest is king and where each state is the arbiter of its own case.

Clashes of national interest sometimes cannot be resolved by any means other than fighting. And war occurs because international society, unlike its domestic counterpart, does not have powerful law enforcers. Fighting is bound to occur over issues that are regarded as 'vital', unless one state is willing to surrender. But states are rarely willing to do that. Surrender produces a kind of peace, but nations rarely place the highest value on peace at any price. They do not want 'peace' alone: they want peace with security, peace with justice or peace with rights. And for security, justice and rights, they are willing to forgo peace and go for war.

The international system has been called a 'war system' or a 'threat system' not because of the propensity of nations to misunderstand each other, but because of the very structure and processes of the international system. This clash of interest rather than of understanding was illustrated with both wit and simplicity by Francis I. When asked what differences accounted for the constant wars between himself and Charles V, he replied: 'None whatever. We agree perfectly. We both want control of Italy'.[32] The same sentiment would be completely understood today by a Prime Minister of Israel or a leader of the Palestine Liberation Organization (PLO). There are no significant misunderstandings between these two nations. They understand each other perfectly. They both want control of the same thing.

As between the United States and the Soviet Union, there have obviously been misunderstandings over the years, but that is only part of the conflict. Since the outbreak of the cold war, they have also been replaying the traditional competition between the most powerful states in the system. There would still be some sort of East–West conflict, even if 'misunderstandings' disappeared. In any case, it is a mistake to think that misunderstandings always lead to conflict. The reverse can be true. In the first half of the 1970s, Soviet–US relations flourished as a result of the dose of misunderstanding which Americans had swallowed regarding détente. Many misunderstood the Soviet conception of détente; instead they saw it in terms of 'live and let live' rather than in the narrower Soviet philosophy of 'peaceful coexistence'. As a result, it was easier for most Americans to feel friendlier towards Soviet Russia during this period of misunderstanding than it proved to be later in the 1970s when they had come to grasp that détente in the Soviet conception did not mean 'peace and goodwill', but 'peace and ill will'.[33] Suddenly misunderstanding disappeared: but so did the friendly relationship. This was an exact parallel with the relationship which had developed between the Western democracies and Nazi Germany. In the early 1930s, their relationship was amicable. It remained so as long as Hitler was misunderstood. When his ambitions and power became understood, war quickly followed.

The illustrations above show that reducing the incuriosity, the culture-boundness and the false expectations that come from trying to overcome the problems of misperception between nations will not inevitably lead to peace and harmony. The case for attempting to reduce misperception does not rest on any belief that it is a panacea for the problems of peace and war. It only promises to lead to a better understanding of 'reality'; that is, it will produce a closer fit between the images in our heads and what is happening out in the world of affairs. One of the effects of this should be the pursuing of more consistent policies. As a result, there should be no repeat of the excessive swing that were evident in US attitudes towards the Soviet Union between 1972 and 1982; that is, the swing between the excessive optimism of the early détente period and the excessive hostility of the Reagan period. More consistency should help to improve everybody's security.

V.   Conclusion: old mind-sets versus the future

Nobody imagines that the decades ahead will be easy ones in international politics. The interaction of political, economic, social and strategic trends—some of which are examined in this book—threaten a future with an overkill of new challenges. They need not be rehearsed here. Suffice it to say that security issues will remain at the top of national agendas, and the world's, since civilized life can no longer survive another of those general breakdowns of the international system which have characterized the past. A general war would be catastrophe beyond imagination, but even 'conventional' wars are now devastating for the lands being fought over. In these circumstances we need to counter every tightening of the insecurity trap that may bring such possibilities closer, and we should not forget the daily drain of scarce human and material resources away from our ability to meet a world full of human miseries. The importance of perceiving and assessing threats accurately should therefore be self-evident; we have problems enough without compounding them by sometimes avoidable errors and misperceptions.

The accurate perception and assessment of threats, like so much in international politics, scoffs at rigid 'rules' and 'principles'. The theory and practice of human relations at all levels is an art, not a science. But that is not to say that we cannot be helped by sensible advice, and if the rules discussed above are used with discretion and judgement, they might help us avoid some of the mistakes and much of the waste of the past. The empirical or sophisticated realism towards which we should reach is neutral. Sometimes it will help nations to adopt a more relaxed attitude towards their international problems. On other occasions it will put them on guard. Empirical realism improves a nation's options: to live together with others if it can, or to fight them if it must. What is on offer, therefore, is not a guarantee of peace; it only guarantees the basis for more rational policy-making. Having said that, peace is the only rational course for East–West relations, and in order to achieve that over a prolonged period, the replacement of old mind-sets by empirical realism is a necessary but not sufficient condition. Other conditions, such as less provocative defence policies, are also necessary, but they lie outside the scope of this essay. Replacing one set of beliefs with another will not be easy: ethnocentrism, Realism, ideological fundamentalism and strategic reductionism have all exercised a deadly grip on human affairs.

Turning to the substantive aspects of East–West relations discussed in this paper, the main conclusion that should be drawn is that the Western powers have cause to adopt a more relaxed attitude than has generally been the case in the past. This essay has argued that the Soviet Union is a threat in some senses, and at some levels but not at others. There are aspects of Soviet society which are not liked in the West; there are clashes of interest between Western states; the Soviet military system has targeted the West; the USSR has sometimes behaved in a dangerous manner; and Soviet leaders consistently fail to recognize the extent to which their own behaviour stimulates Western fears and thus its rushing to the military, diplomatic and propaganda barricades. Part of the continuing East–West conflict is historical and political; part of it is system-induced; but part of it is the result of exaggerated fears—on both sides. The mutual suspicion that exists between both societies probably cannot be completely eradicated in any time-scale worth thinking about, and indeed each side has good reasons for not eradicating its suspicions. Genuine conflicts of interest do exist and the legacy of historical antagonisms, not to mention recent hostility, is powerful. Even so, the conflicts of interest and other problems just mentioned need not rule out the possibility of both societies being able to live together without war. Soviet policy-makers are not lacking in rationality; the operational aspects of their ideology have been de-radicalized; and the nation knows full well the dangers of war and the need for coexistence. Warfare between the greatest powers of the day can no longer be regarded as a solution: it is functionally obsolete, though some people talk and act as if it were not so. The Soviet Union is a threat in some ways and at some levels, but so are our own mind-sets and well-established ways of behaving.

Ill will will remain between the East and the West for years to come, but living together is an imperative. In these circumstances, crisis prevention is a priority of the highest importance. This involves, among other things, working through diplomacy and strategy to minimize the occurrence of dangerous situations and to reduce the likelihood of misperception. At present the primary responsibility for acting along these lines lies with the West. There is now a more sophisticated and possibly more flexible—in sum a more empirically realist—leadership in Moscow than we have seen for years, but the constraints on the Kremlin are enormous. The security of the West cannot wait for the Soviet Union to change its domestic politics in ways we find desirable. At this stage, therefore, initiative and reciprocation between East and West must be asymmetrical. In this regard, the major conceptual change necessary on the part of the leaders of the West is a replacement of the confrontational posturing, which doctrinaire realists find so comfortable, by a full recognition that Western security is and will remain intimately and indefinitely tied up with the security of the Soviet Union; this means, above all, endorsing the idea that increases in Soviet insecurity will not necessarily improve Western security. Being solicitous about Soviet security is in the Western interest. As a result, those who frame Western policy must attempt to appreciate how and to what extent they themselves are a threat, attempt to comprehend the psychological realities of Soviet policy-makers, and attempt to deal without prejudice with Soviet words and actions. If we do not understand the Soviet side of the matter, we cannot claim to understand contemporary strategic reality. If that is the case, can we claim to be 'realists', or think of our policy-making as 'rational'?

Many of the points elaborated in this essay are heretical to the strategic fundamentalists who have been in the driving seat in Washington since the second half of the 1970s. Their criticisms of this approach are likely to result in simple labels being attached to it, just as they caricature the Soviet Union. Those who read this essay carefully, however, will not have seen anything in it which suggests that: to attempt to 'understand' the Soviet Union equates with 'excusing' all Soviet behaviour; to argue that the Soviet Union has legitimate interests is the same as arguing that the Soviet Union is always benevolent; to suggest that the Soviet Union has a case is the same as advising appeasement; or to believe that a particular Soviet position is honest is equivalent to proposing that there is no political or moral difference between the Soviet and US positions. Such extrapolations are mistaken and illogical, but they are ones that ethnocentrics, Realists, ideologues and reductionists not infrequently make. Furthermore, the rules discussed are neither wishy-washy nor naïve.

They can be used as the basis of a set of quite specific proposals for dealing with—*living with*—the Soviet Union. The themes and conclusions of this essay are not neutralist, anti-American, appeasing or pacifist. They are quite simply the basis for empirical realism in a dangerous, independent and multi-cultural world.

Notes and references

1 Howard, M., 'The future of deterrence', *RUSI Journal*, vol. 131, no. 2 (June 1986), p. 10.
2 Knorr, K., 'Threat perception', *Historical Dimensions of National Security Problems*, ed. K. Knorr (Allen Press: Lawrence, KS, 1976), p. 97.
3 This is the theme of Booth, K., *Strategy and Ethnocentrism* (Croom Helm: London, 1979).
4 Fox, W. T. R., 'E. H. Carr and political realism: vision and revision', *Review of International Studies*, vol. 11, no. 1 (1985), p. 12.
5 Fox (note 4).
6 For a critique of strategic fundamentalists, see Booth, K., 'Nuclear deterrence and World War III: how will history judge?', *Journal of Strategic Studies* (special issue in honour of Bernard Brodie; forthcoming).
7 Manning, C. A. W., *The Nature of International Society* (Macmillan: London, 1975), p. 216.
8 Ulam, A. B., *The Rivals: America and Russia since World War II* (Viking Press: New York, 1971), pp. 383–95.
9 This idea was first made clear to me by Michael MccGwire. See 'Prologue: the level of analysis and its effect on assessment', *Soviet Naval Developments: Capability and Contest*, ed. M. MccGwire (Praeger Publishers: New York, 1973), pp. 1–5.
10 Kennan, G. F., *Memoirs 1925–1950* (Little, Brown and Co.: Boston, MA, 1968), pp. 310–11, 395, 403 and 497–8.
11 May, E. R., *'Lessons' of the Past: The Use and Misuse of History in American Foreign Policy* (Oxford University Press: New York, 1973), p. 174.
12 An imaginative and original initiative in this regard is the World Weapon Database, which will fill a dozen volumes and cover all major weapons produced world-wide since 1945. See *World Weapon Database*, series ed. R. Forsberg, Institute for Defense and Disarmament Studies (Lexington Books: Lexington, MA, forthcoming).
13 The best known examples were the changing estimates that turned the dangerous bomber and missile 'gaps' into US leads. Kissinger has written about the drastic and confusing alterations in (US estimates of) Soviet capabilities in the mid-1950s, and Hoffman has explained a similar pattern in US–Chinese relations. See Kissinger, H. A., *The Troubled Partnership* (McGraw-Hill: New York, 1965), and Hoffmann, S., *Gulliver's Troubles: Or, The Setting of American Foreign Policy* (McGraw-Hill: New York, 1968), p. 160.
14 The distinction is Klaus Knorr's. See his 'Failures in national intelligence estimates: the case of the Cuban missiles', *World Politics*, vol. 16, no. 3 (Apr. 1974), pp. 455–67.
15 See Scheer, R., *With Enough Shovels: Reagan, Bush &-Nuclear War* (Secker & Warberg: London, 1983), pp. 14 and 37–8.
16 See Booth, K. and Williams, P., 'Fact and fiction in U.S. foreign policy: Reagan's myths about detente' *World Policy Journal*, vol. 2, no. 3 (Summer 1985), pp. 501–32.

17 Howard, M., *The Causes of War* (Unwin Paperbacks: London, 1983), pp. 157–9.

18 For example, Haselkorn, A., *The Evolution of Soviet Security Strategy, 1965–1975* (Crane, Russak & Co.: New York, 1978).

19 Kissinger, H. A., *Necessity for Choice* (Chatto and Windus: London, 1960), p. 194.

20 See Freedman, L., *US Intelligence and the Soviet Strategic Threat* (Macmillan: London, 1977), p. 85.

21 Kennan, G. F. ('X'), 'The sources of Soviet conduct', *Foreign Affairs 1947*, reprinted in Kennan, G. F., *American Diplomacy 1900–1950* (Secker and Warburg: London, 1953), p. 111.

22 The illustration is suggested by Garnett, J. C., 'Disarmament and arms control', *Strategic Thought in the Nuclear Age*, ed. L. Martin (The Johns Hopkins University Press: Baltimore, MD, 1979), p. 204.

23 See, e.g., Luttwak, E. N., *The Grand Strategy of The Soviet Union* (Weidenfeld and Nicolson: London, 1983).

24 Brodie, B., *War & Politics* (Cassell: London, 1973), chapter 1.

25 Jervis, R., 'Cooperation under the security dilemma', *World Politics*, vol. 30, no. 2 (Jan. 1978), pp. 167–214. See also Butterfield, Sir Herbert, 'The tragic element in modern international conflict', in Butterfield, Sir Herbert, *History and Human Relations* (Macmillan: New York, 1952).

26 See Booth, K., 'Soviet defence policy', *Contemporary Strategy, Vol. II*, eds J. Baylis *et al.* (Holmes and Meier: New York, forthcoming).

27 See Holloway, D., 'Theatre nuclear weapons: the Soviet doctrine', *Disarming Europe*, eds. M. Kaldor and D. Smith (The Merlin Press: London, 1982), pp. 89–104.

28 Shulman, M. D., 'U.S.–Soviet relations and the control of nuclear weapons', *Rethinking the U.S. Strategic Posture*, ed. B. M. Blechman (Ballinger Publishing Co.: Cambridge, MA, 1982), pp. 77–100.

29 Knorr (note 2), p. 113.

30 Crowl, P. A., 'The strategist's short catechism: six questions without answers', The Harmon Memorial Lectures in Military History, Number Twenty (US Air Force Academy: Colorado Springs, CO, 1978), p. 11.

31 Boulding, K., 'National images and international systems', *Journal of Conflict Resolution*, vol. 3 (June 1959), p. 130.

32 Quoted by Garnett (note 22).

33 The phrase is Peter Vigor's, see 'The Soviet concept of peace', *The Soviet View of War, Peace, Neutrality* (Routledge and Kegan Paul: London, 1975), chapter 3.

Part 2.   New military capabilities, new doctrines

Paper 2.1.   New military capabilities: propellants and implications

WILLIAM H. KINCADE

I.   Introduction

Military-technological innovation—in combination with new techniques and tactics for utilizing armed forces—gives rise to new military capability. Along with political and psychological factors, it also contributes importantly to the dynamics of that symbolic conflict known as arms competition. As pervasive as technical change has been during the past century and as central as it has been in all aspects of military affairs, the literature on the process of innovation, as it applies to the distinctive military realm in general, is remarkably sparse. Most analyses address trees rather than the forest.

A full treatment of this diverse and complex process in its military dimension alone would require a separate volume, at least. Nevertheless, a few broad observations on the subject are both possible and useful as a backdrop to analysing the weapons and other factors that will dominate future security concerns and policy. The following pages set forth a simple paradigm for dissecting the process and impact of military innovation. Included is a brief discussion of the attitudinal component of innovation, for it must not be forgotten that technical change is a deeply human phenomenon, much like artistic creation, and it is therefore heavily influenced by the various preconceptions we bring to it.

II.   The elements of technological change

Technology can be subdivided into its constituent elements and processes almost endlessly and under any number of classification schemes. The crystal in an old radio set or the silicon chips in a modern video-cassette recorder are technologies in themselves, and their production and use imply a host of other technologies as well. In this analysis, however, the focus is on technologies more broadly construed.

Four major categories of military technology are employed, as follows:

1. *Basic technologies* (or *basic technological families*). These are the building blocks from which components of systems (weapons or associated military equipment) are created. Examples are: electronics, turbines, rocket engines, explosives, and so on. These basic building blocks, of course, are in

turn based on even more fundamental technological fields such as ceramics, metallurgy, and so on.

2. *Component technologies*. These are made up of one or more basic technologies. They are elementary systems in the sense that they do not usually constitute a weapon or piece of other usable military equipment alone, although they may be quite complex in themselves. Examples are: propulsion systems, guidance, destructive devices, aerodynamic surfaces, and so on.

3. *Generic technologies*. This term refers to complete systems of component technologies classified by *general* military functions; that is, platforms, projectiles, delivery vehicles, communications systems, and so on.

4. *Functional technologies*. These, too, are complete systems of technologies classified by specific military purpose or mission, such as armoured systems, anti-tank weapons, surface vessels, anti-submarine weapons, and so on.

There is, of course, some overlapping in this approach to the classification of military technology, but it provides a useful means of discussing trends and consequences of innovation without becoming bogged down in the taxonomy (or the metaphysics) of technology.

New military-technological capability, to state the obvious, is normally achieved by: (*a*) a significant advance in a basic or component technology; (*b*) a synergistic effect arising from the particular interaction of two or more basic technologies, wherein the resulting whole is greater than the sum of the parts; (*c*) the similar synergistic or interactive effect of combining two weapons (or a weapon and a piece of associated equipment) in a highly complementary way; or (*d*) a combination of all of the foregoing. However, changes in tactics and techniques are also often required to exploit the potential of new technological capability. A few examples will help to illustrate these principles.

Advances in electronics are probably among the most notable contributions to improved weaponry; among other things, gains in this basic technology have improved the component technology of guidance systems across the range of modern weaponry. More specifically, improvements in electronics have led to their miniaturization, allowing more of the payload of projectile weapons to be devoted to other uses.

Improvements in the yield-to-weight ratios of nuclear explosive devices have likewise led to shrinkage in their size, so that a ballistic missile warhead can carry more of them or carry other useful devices, such as decoys or other penetration aids, and even more elaborate guidance systems. The result, to simplify, has been the development of multiple, independently targetable re-entry vehicles (MIRVs) and manoeuvrable re-entry vehicles (MARVs), a significant net gain in military-technological capability.

Exemplifying the synergistic effect of combinations of weapon systems are the deadly fires which resulted in World War I from the complementarity of improved artillery and machine guns and from the interaction in World War II of advanced dive bombers and tanks. The first combination ground up, not only a great many lives, but also the pre-war notions of offence-dominated tactics and strategy. The idea of the decisiveness of '*élan vital*' and the 'attack to the utmost' were among the first victims of this combination. The failure of a generation of senior officers to realize this early in the conflict was the proximate cause of the subsequent carnage.

Only towards the end of World War I was the tank developed, first by the British, as a means of returning mobility to the battlefield and breaking up the defensive impasse caused by the combination of artillery and machine-gun fire. But its immediate impact was constrained, not only by the limitations of the first-generation armoured technology, but by the very rudimentary state of tank tactics, to which the Royal Navy (initially involved in tank development owing to its experience with armour) could contribute little.

These deficiencies were partially remedied in the inter-war period. But only a few military men saw the potential of armour as an offensive weapon and even fewer saw its synergistic possibilities in conjunction with the improved dive bomber. This combination permitted blitzkrieg (or 'lightning war') and changed the shape of combat once again in World War II. Part of the reason for this oversight was the general fascination with heavy bombers and 'airpower doctrine'. In the event, however, these failed to live up to the inter-war expectation that they would make future wars short, if highly damaging.

The failure of strategic bombing, compared to the success of blitzkrieg, is not attributable alone to the fact that governments and peoples proved much more resistant to industrial and terror bombing than airpower doctrine anticipated. It arises also from the fact that, while the technologies of bombs and bombers had advanced between the wars, important ancillary technologies—such as bomb-sighting, navigational equipment, and target acquisition and discrimination capability—had not advanced or had not improved at the same pace. Basically, strategic bombing suffered from an inability to know with precision what the targets were, where they were, and how to get to them, a problem that was not truly corrected until after the advent of satellites in the late 1950s.

This conceptual and historical background proves instructive in examining the contemporary cruise missile case, for it shows both how the uneven rate of change across different technologies or different categories of technology affects actual military capability and how prevailing strategic or tactical doctrine influences, and often obscures, the import of technical developments. As a result, the interactive implications of technologies may be largely missed, ignored or partially understood.

To summarize, there was little appreciation for the relationships among embryonic, emerging, evolving, or evolved (mature) technologies.[1] Thus, attention focused on the strategic bomber, which combined evolving platform and projectile technologies with embryonic targeting technologies. Yet the synergism of armour and tactical air, both of which represented more mature functional technologies, was generally underrated. Moreover, tactical and strategic uses of armour and tactical air were fairly well developed by the eve of World War II, in Germany at least, whereas the concept of strategic bombing remained just that—an untried concept.[2] Both the constraints imposed on strategic bombing by the relative immaturity of the associated targeting technologies and the complementarity of the more mature tank and dive bomber were largely overlooked owing to: (a) doctrinal fashion; and (b) simplistic understandings of military-technological innovation.

III. Impact of new military capability

A new military capability may be defined as a development that relaxes existing constraints or limitations in carrying out specific operations or tasks (although it may also create additional problems or aggravate old ones). Such developments may favour the offence or the defence and involve advances at the level of basic, component, generic or functional technologies, or all of them at once. The internal combustion engine, nuclear fission, and large-scale rocket engines all provided new military capabilities. Yet a new military capability may also stem from the synergistic use of two or more technologies, as in the case of the tank and tactical aircraft.

In general, the impact that a new military capability has on operations, institutions, strategy and tactics, force planning and composition, and other aspects of war preparation and on war itself (including the outcome) is a complex product of how that capability arises and the environment in which it reaches maturity. The Dreadnought-Class superbattleships represented the consolidation of a variety of mature technologies in a new platform with the advantageous addition of newly developed gunfire control systems. Its impact on force planning and composition was revolutionary, in the context of the Anglo-German naval competition, although its influence on naval warfare turned out to be less than expected.

The intercontinental ballistic missile (ICBM) likewise had a revolutionary impact on force planning and composition, following steady but hard-won gains in rocket propulsion. The evolving long-range attack submarine, on the other hand, tended to represent a neglected albeit new military capability, even in the countries most advanced in and potentially benefitted by this technology.

Atomic weapons, while a revolutionary development, did not change military strategy or force composition overnight, however. They were assimilated in airpower doctrine; indeed, they validated it. Even political strategy did not immediately change to accommodate this new capability. In an earlier case, that of the heavy bomber, strategic thinking outpaced the actual evolution of the requisite technologies.

The new military capability represented by improvements in machine guns and artillery was persistently ignored in terms of strategy and tactics, even after it became evident on the battlefield. The implications of the similarly new capability represented by the use of tanks and armoured vehicles in conjunction with tactical air (both arising from the mechanization of warfare owing to the internal combustion engine) were recognized by the Germans and Russians in the inter-war period, partly because of limitations on their military capability generally. But they were neglected by the British, French and US military institutions for a variety of reasons.[3]

These examples, however drastically abbreviated here, nevertheless illustrate several general responses to new military capability:

1.   Evolutionary technological developments may have revolutionary consequences in some dimensions of military endeavour but not in others (e.g., altering force composition but not doctrine or institutions).

2.   Revolutionary advances may not cause equally dramatic or sudden changes in military thinking, forces, operations, and so on.

3.   New military capability arising from evolutionary, revolutionary or synergistic progressions may not be *visible* short of combat and may not be readily *seen* even in combat.

4.   Technological innovation may suggest possibilities beyond what the available technology can actually deliver (i.e., the new military capability is overanticipated, usually owing to a failure to assess supporting technologies).

5.   Recognition of new military capability may be retarded by past experience and assumptions (e.g., the World War I fixation on frontal assault) or by premature future projections (e.g., the inter-war fixation on airpower doctrine) which divert attention and resources.

6.   New military capability may be more readily recognized and exploited in some nations and military institutions than in others owing to various factors of experience, resources, and so on.

The different requirements of armed peace and actual conflict also affect the development and integration of new military capability. In peacetime, the potential of advances in unglamorous weapons without service or national constituencies, such as naval mines, may go unexploited. Attention, perhaps too much attention, on the other hand, may be paid to refining and improving at the margins weapon systems which are preferred by the armed services or specific branches of them and which command political support because they are deemed to symbolize the apex of military power. Dreadnoughts and ICBMs appear to reflect this phenomenon. Furthermore, it is possible that the doctrinal and other dimensions of nuclear weapons would have developed more rapidly had they been introduced at the beginning of World War II instead of at the end (assuming, probably unrealistically, that such early introduction did not result in a quick cessation of hostilities).

Of course, some of the variation seen in the historical cases is less likely to be so great in the contemporary period. The need to rely on standing forces rather than on mobilization capability—arising both from the advent of nuclear weapons and the doctrinal imperatives of deterrence and compellence—means that military institutions are at greater pains to exploit new potential and to match or overmatch any increase in adversary potential.[4] This 'demonstration effect' creates a general kind of convergence in force composition, if not specific force-matching in every respect or identical doctrines and weapons.

Additionally, the capacity to manufacture complex weapons, formerly reserved to a few advanced countries, is spreading to a larger number of nations. Thus, there is a rudimentary global weapon culture which tends to facilitate the rapid spread of the 'homogeneous level of technique' that has always been a feature of military-technological progression, but, in the past, proceeded unevenly and with significant time-lags.[5] Technology transfer, intended or unwanted, is nevertheless inescapable and reinforces the convergence effect mentioned earlier.

Despite these new factors creating a more evenly distributed integration of new military capability, responses to technological opportunities and limitations or to a potential gain in military capability remain varied and difficult to predict. This is particularly so in peacetime and in the near- to middle-term, before the demonstration effect and the new global capacity for technology exchange have their full impact. Projecting future weapon developments and the particular manner in which technical potential will be exploited simply on the basis of linear trends or the availability of technological opportunities—as is often done—thus stands a good chance of producing erroneous forecasts.

IV.   Models of technological innovation

Also influencing technical hopes, fears and forecasts is our basic conception of the relationship between humans and the technology they create to carry out tasks more efficiently. How we regard the man-machine interaction helps to define our objectives or expectations and the way in which we evaluate results. At a very general level of analysis, there are contrasting, and usually implicit, models of this interaction. Such abbreviated portrayals, however, cannot do full justice to the complexity of the several perspectives one finds in analysing technological paradigms.

One conceptual model can be described as the *command technology* paradigm, in which it is assumed that technological innovation is largely under human control and obedient to its needs and wishes.[6] This view emphasizes the determinative role of intentions in technological evolution, and, while it does not exclude the impact of unforeseen developments and occurrences, it does tend to view innovation as an instrumental value, that is, technological innovation largely is directive and conforms well to human management.

This approach is well illustrated in the US view of technology generally. Indeed, it is not only reflected in, but reinforced by, the unfolding of the Manhattan Project to develop atomic weapons and the original space programme objective of placing a man on the moon inside a decade. Characteristic of the command technology model is a tendency to reason from successes in past programmes and projections and to neglect failures, the reasons for past changes in goals, and for delays in achieving desired results.

Also associated with this approach is a propensity to generalize from experience in the area of civilian technology. Civil technological progress is perhaps not greatly different from military-technological innovation. Indeed, in some ways the distinction is arbitrary. What makes it worth observing is that civil technology does not involve the offence–defence interaction, so that a civilian technical problem, once solved, is solved for all similar cases, whereas a military-technical solution may only beget countermeasures that create new problems.

The command technology model is particularly well illumined in the assumption that the Soviet Union also constructs its technology development programmes with a highly instrumental sense of the opportunities of innovation. Those holding this view, for example, tend to consider that Soviet technological outcomes are foreseen and pre-planned; that is, nothing happens that is not anticipated. Hence, Soviet 'heavy missiles', to take one prominent example, are seen as intentional outcomes rather than the product of technical circumstances and exigencies. The tendency of this model, then, is to overrate the ability of humans to direct the technological future.

The other major model or paradigm of technological innovation and its effects tends to stress the autonomy of technology, that is, its ability to stimulate consequences unwanted, unintended or unforeseen by those who presume to direct it. This school of thought, of course, is often concerned with imposing political controls on the artifacts and effects of military-technological innovation. It tends to see the unintended consequences of technological change as more determinative than the intended goals and as comprising an autonomous variable in international relations.[7]

Although usually more sensitive to the impact of the offence–defence interaction on the course of innovation, those who view technology in this light are often, although not uniformly, inclined to magnify the meaning of early failures and set-backs in technology development programmes. In other words, if the command technology paradigm too often depreciates the impact of engineering problems and delays, the *autonomous technology* model treats them as validation of the uncontrollability of technology and overlooks the fact that, over the longer term, such obstacles are often resolved.

According to this approach, Soviet 'heavy missiles' are not the predictable consequence of Soviet technological planning but an outcome of largely uncontrollable factors—the particular state of Soviet technology at the time it entered into the nuclear arms competition imposed by the necessity of responding to US technological and numerical leads.

The purpose here is not to formulate a synthesis of these models but simply to observe that, while both have a certain validity, each misses some important factors in military-technological innovation. The command technology model overrates the ability of individuals or institutions (including governments) to control technology and its consequences, while the autonomous technology paradigm overestimates the unintended effects of technical evolution and the impact of normal developmental problems on ultimate capability.

The different expectations of these two models of the nature of technological innovation are well reflected in one of the most celebrated cases of centrally directed and self-conscious technological innovation in the twentieth century: the development of the Dreadnought-Class superbattleship in 1906. On the one hand, it was considered that the many innovators involved in this development, especially Admiral Sir John Fisher, knew precisely what they were doing and largely accomplished their objectives. On the other hand, there is considerable evidence to support the view that this innovation created a ripple effect that influenced naval warfare technology—the premier strategic technology of its time—and naval tactics and strategy in a manner largely unforeseen by Admiral Fisher and other innovators.[8]

Which approach creates greater errors in technological forecasting can only be evaluated in terms of specific technical developments, owing to the fact that other military and political factors enter into the technology assessment process. Neither model, therefore, can be understood in its technological terms alone. Each will stress the controllability or uncontrollability of technology *per se* according to the political and military objectives it cherishes most.

V.   Conclusion

Thus, finally, the models or preconceptions that we bring to technological innovation are subservient to, but also influence, larger policy interests and postures. They are a central part of the perceptual milieu that is addressed by Ken Booth in paper 1.3 of this volume and that plays such an important if unspoken and often unrecognized role in the determination of and reaction to security policy initiatives. Yet only by trying to discern the latent models of innovation that underlie decisions and responses (as well as the various technical styles encountered in different institutions, nations and administrations) can we begin to form a complete picture of the sources and implications of new military capability.

Notes and references

[1] This conceptualization of stages of technological maturity is explained in an appendix to the author's 'The future of Star Wars and arms control', paper prepared for the Conference on Strategic Defense and Soviet–American Relations, The Woodrow Wilson International Center for Scholars, Washington, DC, 10–11 March 1986; it will be published in the conference proceedings (Ballinger Publishing Company: forthcoming in 1987).

[2] For the development of thinking about armour, see Simpkin, R., *Race to the Swift: Thoughts on Twenty-First Century Warfare* (Brassey's Defense Publishers: London, 1985), pp. 15–17 and chapter 2.

[3] Simpkin (note 2).

[4] For the distinctions between deterrent and compellent threats and the use of the latter in superpower policy, see Kincade, W. H., 'Arms control or arms coercion?' *Foreign Policy*, no. 62 (Spring 1986).

[5] The concept of the 'homogeneous level of technique', and an admirable demonstration of its operation, is to be found in McNeill, W. H., *The Pursuit of Power: Technology, Armed Force, and Society since A.D. 1000* (University of Chicago Press: Chicago, IL, 1982).

[6] The concept of 'command technology' is also developed extensively in McNeill (note 5), *passim*.

[7] The idea of technology and technique as autonomous factors is treated in Winner, L., *Autonomous Technology: Technics-out-of-Control as a Theme in Political Thought* (MIT Press: Cambridge, MA, 1977) and in Ellul, J., *The Technological Society*, translated from the French, Wilkinson, J., *La Technique* (Alfred A. Knopf: New York, 1964).

[8] This sceptical view of the conventional wisdom regarding the foresightedness of the developers of the Dreadnought may be found in Barnett, C., *The Swordbearers* (Indiana University Press: Bloomington, IN, 1973). The more standard appreciation of the development of the Dreadnought Class of battleships is conveyed in Lautenschlager, K., 'Technology and the evolution of naval warfare', *International Security*, vol. 8, no. 2 (Fall 1983).

Paper 2.2.   Strategic defence and international security

GERALD SEGAL

I.   Introduction

A great illusion of modern strategic studies is that new technology necessarily revolutionizes military and political strategy. The recent debate about strategic defence reminds us that even illusions can be damaging to international security.

To be sure, the invention of nuclear weapons and the means for their swift delivery did revolutionize strategy. A new strategic orthodoxy developed that stressed a few basic facts of nuclear life:

1.   The only protection against a nuclear threat is a nuclear counter-threat. This process is called deterrence.

2.   Deterrence functions when the counter-threat is credible and is communicated clearly.

3.   Nuclear deterrence is so clearly credible because the devastation that can be wrought by even the smallest portion of the superpowers' arsenal is so awesome, that anything beyond the use of these first few weapons would be utterly redundant.

Nuclear weapons are therefore not useful instruments of policy except for deterrence. One might have thought this was all terribly obvious, even after 40 years of life with nuclear deterrence. Not so it seems.

A minority voice persisted in the belief that the nuclear revolution was not so revolutionary. They saw nuclear weapons as useful instruments of compellence, not deterrence, if only sufficient defence could be provided to minimize the impact of a nuclear strike. Although defence in the nuclear age has been persistently proven to be unobtainable, the supporters of war-fighting strategies in both Moscow and Washington have not given up hope. The latest and most ambitious demonstration of that hope, the Strategic Defense Initiative (SDI), is the result of a mixture of motives, combining believers in compellence with those who believe deterrence is failing and needs fixing.

Of course, officially, no superpower subscribes to a strategy of compellence. Thus the two superpowers, and most recently and vociferously the Reagan Administration, want us to believe that deterrence is not robust and that the basic rules of the nuclear age can and should be rewritten. For a hefty price in political and economic terms, we are offered a childlike cartoon of a 'peace-shield' that will protect us from the nuclear threat. It is the contention of the following analysis that the so-called Strategic Defence Initiative is both overpriced and oversold.

But as much as one might be inclined to dismiss the entire project as infantile, the political and military consequences of SDI could be considerable. SDI, and indeed a similar Soviet programme, if it should ever make significant progress, can cause havoc on: (*a*) arms control; (*b*) superpower stability; (*c*) defence spending; (*d*) budget deficits; and (*e*) relations with allies. The argument that follows will eschew detailed discussions of technical issues, largely because few people, if any, are qualified to judge what is undeniably a highly speculative SDI research programme. If, at some near future date, SDI can be proven to have imminent prospects of success, then the debate can become more practical and detailed. For the time being, it is misleading to suggest certainty by arguing in purely scientific terms. What is essential, is the potential impact of SDI, whether or not it proves technologically feasible, on the politics of international security.

Before turning to the impact of SDI, with special emphasis on arms control, a number of major complications need to be pointed out. First, not only is there both a US and a Soviet SDI programme, but the United States seems to have several different types of SDI plan, and there are even signs that the Europeans are talking about their own version. The analysis that follows will concentrate on: (*a*) the perfect SDI; (*b*) SDI as ballistic missile defence (BMD) of land-based missiles; and (*c*) a European Defence Initiative (EDI). What is more, it is impossible to be comprehensive about the impact of such developments on arms control across the board because there is such a range of arms control agreements and negotiations to be considered.[1] The intricacies of each agreement will not be discussed in great detail here, but rather this paper will stay focused on the larger, and far more important political arguments.

II.   The utopian dream

It is hard to feel entirely secure and comfortable with a world where stability is supposed to be guaranteed by Mutual Assured Destruction (MAD). The dangers of deterrence have already been well catalogued, and even most believers in MAD shift uncomfortably in their seats when asked to justify why the world should be expected to continue living rationally. But, they argue: what choice do we have?[2] Simply giving up nuclear weapons, whether unilaterally or by agreement, is foolish because the technology to build them is widely known and the weapons cannot be uninvented.

The proponents of SDI reply that there is another option. Instead of MAD we can have a Mutual Utopian Dream (work out the acronym yourself) of an effective defence in the nuclear age. Nuclear weapons will no longer be useful because, for the first time since 1945, we will have given the defence the advantage over the offence.

One can doubt whether this utopian dream was ever seriously believed. Of course, there have always been supporters of such a perfect defence, if only as a way to regain US superiority and allow it to dominate the Soviet Union 'like in the good old days' before détente. Utopia certainly figured prominently in President Reagan's inaugural SDI speech (23 March 1983), but then that was a year when anti-nuclear protests were taking to the streets in Europe in large numbers and even US politicians were taken by the 'freeze' campaign. The best way to fight utopia was with utopia, and some cynics felt the idea would be shelved after the 1984 Presidential election. Far from it. Instead, billions of dollars are being thrown on it, even while other sectors of the US defence budget are being cut to cope with the broader budget deficit crisis.

The utopian version of SDI remains very much alive. In its final form, it is supposed to protect the United States and its allies (including in Europe, Asia and presumably anywhere else in the Third World) from nuclear attack. The technology would then be sold to the Soviet Union (according to President Reagan) if Moscow had not already developed its own SDI. The entire territory of SDI-protected states would be safeguarded, unlike earlier anti-ballistic missile (ABM) schemes which were mainly only designed to protect missiles. If successful, such a 'peace-shield' would make nuclear weapons obsolete.[3]

But the problems in getting from here to utopia are daunting. The technical and financial issues are being debated by 'experts', but even the proponents of SDI accept that the hundreds of billions of dollars ('only' $26-billion of seed money in the first five years) that will eventually be spent will have to overcome daunting engineering and computer-software challenges. The fate of the nation will be largely taken out of the hands of politicians and handed to a gargantuan computer (or computer network) that would have to react accurately in minutes, if not in seconds. Even if the gadgetry could cope, would we want it to take such momentous decisions about our fate without human involvement?[4] As Lord Carrington reminds us, this is the mind-set of 'nuclear accountancy'. What is worse, the enemy is unlikely to stand still and will try to underfly, overwhelm and outfox the system.[5] No one suggests that an effective, perfect SDI is anywhere but in its very early research stage. The system is not going to be developed suddenly and deployed overnight. Therefore, most discussion of SDI has shifted to interim systems (to be discussed below). But before moving on, it is useful to reflect on the strategic impact of such a utopian dream, if it should ever become reality.

If such a system were ever deployed successfully, strategic weapons arms control would be properly obsolete. Who needs a Strategic Crossbow Arms Limitation Agreement in the age of the musket? However, there would be an even greater need for conventional arms control agreements because with the nuclear deterrent made obsolete the world would be made 'safer' for conventional war. The pre-Hiroshima world was hardly a happy place, and it is a matter of opinion whether Europeans, on whose territory the last world wars were fought, would prefer to return to the dangers of the 1930s rather than the early 1980s.

Arms controllers might also have to focus on Strategic Suitcase Arms Limitation Talks because with nuclear technology already well tested and understood, what would stop the enemy from planting a nuclear device in a suitcase in New York's Grand Central Station. If the United States could hide the Manhattan Project in the 1940s, the Soviet Union or Libya could hide the strategic suitcase arms-manufacturing process. How many suitcases would constitute assured destruction?

III.   Ballistic missile defence (BMD) of land missiles

Since SDI is obviously not deployable in anything like the near future, its adherents argue the need for its future development in stages. The immediate likely response by an enemy would then certainly be to add incrementally to its own offence. But SDI proponents argue that the defence will be incrementally cheaper than the offence. If so, the obvious solution would be to have a joint US–Soviet SDI programme. According to some members of the Reagan Administration, the Soviets are supposed to be far advanced in their own SDI research, and thus it would make sense for both superpowers to spend their money on defence instead of offence. Of course, it is hard to believe that the United States would offer the Soviet Union billion-dollar contracts for SDI research, or the USA's most advanced military technology.

The idea is preposterous, in part because neither side is seriously moving towards the utopian version of SDI. What the research on both sides is aiming at is ballistic missile defence (BMD) of stationary offensive missile emplacements. Unlike the utopian dream of replacing MAD, this BMD is intended to enhance the assured destructive capability of silo-based intercontinental ballistic missiles (ICBMs), thereby reinforcing MAD. The origins of this plan lay in the by-now discredited assertion that the Soviet Union had a 'window of opportunity' in military terms that made the United States vulnerable to a pre-emptive Soviet first strike. Back in the late 1970s, it was thought that the mid-1980s would find the United States at its weakest strategically because the Soviet Union would be able to eliminate the USA's entire ICBM force in a first strike. The concern was that the United States would then have no sufficiently accurate weapons of its own to respond with a counterforce strike against the Soviet Union. The Soviet Union would have 'escalation dominance'. All Moscow had to do in a moment of political crisis was to threaten to 'send its missiles through the window' and the United States would back down.

Of course that is the kind of exaggerated nightmare that defies logic and gives strategic studies a bad name. Why the Soviet Union should ever imagine that the United States would not respond if, say, 90-million Americans died in the collateral damage of a Soviet 'counterforce' strike, or that the United States would not use its marginally less-accurate submarine-launched ballistic missile (SLBM) fleet and its Strategic Air Command (SAC) to retaliate, certainly defies all common sense, if not also strategic logic. Of course, the most rational approach was simply to scrap the US ICBMs and put more of its punch, in the form of new Trident submarines with highly accurate warheads, out to sea where it would be less vulnerable to pre-emptive attack. But the triad of strategic forces has always been central to US posture and radical reorganization of the strategic arsenal was never contemplated. What remained was the firm US belief that ICBMs have to be protected. Hence (limited) BMD.

So for the sake of closing an imaginary window, and one that certainly no longer exists with the deployment of more accurate US Trident SLBMs, the United States is developing a 'point-defence' BMD as a first-stage SDI. According to the Reagan Administration, such a BMD could enhance strategic stability if deployment takes place in conjunction with massive cuts in superpower arsenals negotiated at the strategic arms reduction talks (START). Without such cuts in the weapons it must cope with, the BMD's task may well be too great, and certainly very expensive. Yet it is difficult, given current Soviet hostility to the USA's SDI programme, to see how one can simultaneously get both cuts and the deployment of a BMD. Until the Soviet Union has its own 'point-defence' BMD, it has no incentive to agree to limit its offensive forces.

In fact, the problem of unreal expectations is one that dogs the BMD plan in three fundamental ways:

1.   It is unreal to expect the Soviet Union to play by the old arms control rules. It takes no subtle strategist to imagine the Kremlin's response to SDI and therefore the likely fate of arms control. To begin with, the 1972 ABM accord would be killed outright.[6] For the time being, what goes on in scientists' minds and experimentally behind closed laboratory doors is not a violation of the ABM agreement. But testing of nearly all but 'exotic' technologies would be a violation of the ABM Treaty, and there can be no BMD without testing. If the strict interpretation of the ABM agreement is accepted (and for the time being the United States has agreed to see it that way),[7] then the ABM agreement would have to be renegotiated, or abandoned by the United States. What many people have seen as the jewel in the arms control crown would certainly be destroyed if even limited BMD deployment were to take place.

Next, a unilateral US pursuit of SDI would mean the Strategic Arms Limitation Talks (SALT) accords would be violated and the START process would STOP. Moscow would have every reason to add new weapons to its arsenal and try to overwhelm the US defence with added offence. Moscow would also have every reason not to negotiate an anti-satellite (ASAT) agreement, preferring to keep its options open in the expectation that some part of the US programme will be space-based, and therefore able to be countered by a Soviet ASAT system.[8] Unless the defence was indeed cheaper than the offence, BMD would die. The paradox is by now obvious: BMD needs arms control to survive, but unilateral BMD would kill arms control.

Even if (limited) BMD turned out to be cheaper than the offence, the Soviet Union would only be encouraged to move to greater countervalue targeting. And, even if the Nuclear Winter stories are vastly exaggerated, very little countervalue strikes are needed to destroy civilization as we know it. The 'safe' ICBMs would be left standing, but without admirers.

2.   The second unreal expectation is that the United States can afford a BMD, let alone a full-scale SDI. Some proponents of SDI no doubt do believe that the United States can spend the Soviet Union into the stone age by a BMD race. But could the US economy stand the strain either? Of course the US economy is doing well, outgrowing most of its allies and the Soviet bloc in recent years. But the cost of a higher defence budget is either a huge budget deficit, or vastly increased taxes and an end to growth. The impact of the budget deficit so far has been devastating both in the United States and abroad. The Gramm-Rudman-Hollings budget-cutting bill of 1985 is a sign of just how anxious Americans have become. Defence spending in 1986, apart from on SDI, was held constant in real terms; unrestrained growth was over. Conventional weapons will not be procured as fast as the North Atlantic Treaty Organization (NATO) needs them. The opportunity costs are a law of economics that US generals appreciate. If forced to choose, they would probably prefer more bullets to a partial BMD.

But beyond reduced 'normal' defence spending, the most damaging impact of the budget deficit is higher interest rates. In the end, the higher rates stifle domestic growth and threaten to bring down the international banking system. The debt problem in the developing world, and in Latin America in particular, could all too suddenly destroy the USA and the international banking system. The recent fall in oil prices has given many non-oil debtor nations breathing space, but for some (such as Mexico which depends on oil revenues to pay debts), it brings the crunch closer. Further cutting of US interest rates is a matter of urgency, or else the debt bomb will explode. The depression of the 1930s would look mild, and all for the sake of a (limited) BMD designed to close an imaginary strategic window of vulnerability. Politics is supposed to be about sensible priorities.

3.   Finally, it may be an illusion to believe that the United States can carry its allies (in Europe, Asia and the scattered ones in between) with them on the BMD issue. NATO has only just begun to recover from the intermediate nuclear force (INF) squabble, when the question was whether the United States would defend its allies in time of nuclear threat. It is true that a complete SDI defence would make the United States more likely to come to the defence of Europe. There would be no risk to Boston if Bonn were under threat. But if the United States only had a (limited) BMD system, Boston would be at even greater risk because the Soviet Union would have fewer counterforce targets to hit. Thus a partial SDI, such as the envisaged BMD, would only reinforce European fears about a fortress United States and again raise the issue that motivated the INF deployment decision—decoupling of the United States from Europe.[9]

But even if Moscow faced US 'escalation dominance' and was therefore unable to strike at the United States (a non-credible supposition), it would only take us back to where we were in the 1950s before ICBMs. In the pre-ICBM age, the Soviet Union held Western Europe hostage for the USA's good behaviour. Europe was a more dangerous place than in the decades following the ICBM. Remember those nasty surprises in Berlin. The NATO allies know only too well that a US (limited) BMD could bring more political or indeed military crises in Europe.

What is worse, if both superpowers have some form of strategic defence, then central Europe becomes 'safe' for conventional and nuclear war. SDI may eventually be able to cope with ballistic missiles, but it is an even longer way from being able to knock out cruise or Pershing-II missiles, let alone the supersonic bomber. As the quip goes: 'we fought World War I in Europe, we fought World War II in Europe, and if you dummies in Europe let us, we will fight World War III in Europe.' As worried as the NATO allies were with the INF issue, with SDI they would undoubtedly be more anxious about the risks of war in Europe.

Worst of all from the NATO perspective is the effect that spending on BMD will have on spending on conventional weapons. The most pressing priority for the alliance is to move away from a strategy that relies for its deterrent on the first-use of nuclear weapons in the case of a Soviet conventional breakthrough in Europe. NATO has recognized for decades that only by matching Warsaw Pact conventional strength can Western Europe be defended conventionally, and the nuclear threshold raised. Some progress has recently been made in moving from first-use to no-early-use, but the cuts in US conventional defence spending from 1986 will abort that process. BMD will make Europe 'safer' for conventional war just when NATO spends less on conventional weapons.

Not surprisingly, therefore, even the USA's staunchest allies in Europe have balked at loyally supporting SDI. Even Prime Minister Margaret Thatcher made it clear that while research was possible, testing and deployment were not because they would risk ruining the structure of arms control.[10] Of course, Britain, and indeed virtually all West European governments have been willing to allow their scientists to take US money for SDI research. But this should not be misinterpreted as political approval.

In sum, the United States risks destroying the edifice of arms control, its own economy, the international economy and the NATO alliance; and for what? To put the best light on it, a (limited) BMD might eventually open the way to a perfect SDI. It might also strain the Soviet economy by forcing it to spend on countermeasures. But that would not end the nuclear threat, for as the conservatives never tire of telling us, you cannot disinvent nuclear weapons.

A more fashionable, but still positive light on BMD suggests that it is only a 'bargaining chip' which was played to bring the Soviet Union back to the negotiating table and will be played again to drive a harder bargain for deep cuts in START. However, a strong counter-argument can be made that it was the United States that took longer to come round to the idea of deep cuts. Then, when both sides favoured such reductions, it became clear that the United States was demanding deeper cuts in precisely the category of weapons where it was weakest, and the Soviet Union strongest—ICBMs. When Moscow adjourned START in 1983, it had more to do with the INF issue and leadership instability; but with the passage of time, both problems were more or less resolved and the Soviet Union returned to the negotiating table. But even if the SDI 'chip' did help bring Moscow back to the table, it is hard to argue that keeping the chip on the table makes an agreement more likely. As already discussed, Moscow has no incentive to cut any offensive forces as long as SDI is not limited.

Seen in its worst light, SDI and the more limited BMD is a sham. For some people in the United States, it is a handy fist of sand that can be thrown into the gears of SALT in order to destroy a long-distrusted mechanism. For others, it is an excuse for an arms race with a Soviet Union that supposedly understands nothing but all-out competition. Moreover, a number of people and industries have an increasing stake in the SDI research billions. Yet, it defies even the most convoluted logic to believe that for the sake of a partial defence against a doubtful threat, the United States should spend billions, when a more obvious solution could be to save money and scrap the vulnerable ICBMs altogether. And if such unilateral security measures do not appeal, then sensible arms control can be used to reduce both sides' land-based forces while encouraging a shift of strategic forces out to sea. What ever happened to that good old common sense American saying: 'if it ain't broke, don't fix it'.

IV.   Eureka . . . or anyone for EDI (European Defence Initiative)?

As if the convoluted logic of SDI and (limited) BMD were not difficult enough, there is another, related idea now floating around the strategic ether—a European Defence Initiative (EDI). The USA's allies, as we have already seen, have ample reason to be concerned about SDI. Militarily, not to mention politically, it increases uncertainty for all those states around the world that rely on the US nuclear umbrella. In addition, because billions of research dollars are being poured into work with an SDI application, the 'free-market' in brains seems to be draining the best and the brightest scientists away from Europe to the United States. As one critic has acidly noted, it gives the Europeans a sense of what it is like to be a Third World country that loses its intelligentsia to the bright lights of the developed world.[11] Even if the problem is not as serious as all that, it is certainly likely to bring up difficult debates in the alliance on technology transfer. The rows over the 'gas-for-pipe' deal in the early years of the Reagan Administration is a not-too-distant reminder of how US claims to extraterritoriality in its business practices can seem like arrogance and clash with the interests of its West European allies.[12]

With this very real fear of SDI's 'picking out the raisins' from European (and other allies') research, some kind of European response was needed. France, ever vigilant about US cultural and intellectual domination, was first to propose (April 1985) that the USA's allies could put together their own research programme that would keep European brains at home.[13] The Eureka project is nominally not a military programme, but rather civilian research which makes use of scientists' skills that would otherwise be directed to SDI's military ends.

If this all sounds very vague, that is because Eureka itself is barely more than a gleam in some Europeans' eyes. On 30 June 1986, 18 European governments agreed to 62 joint development projects worth about £1.4-billion. France, Britain and West Germany are leading the way, and even Iceland was admitted as the nineteenth member.[14] In fact, there seems to be a great deal of speculation that Eureka is intended to be an EDI that will also come to grips with the special problems of strategic defence in Europe. Obviously, the problems are formidable.

On the technical side, the facts of European geography clearly make it more difficult to defend against a Soviet threat. There is even less time to catch a ballistic missile (such as the SS–20) in its boost phase and the time from launch to landing is even shorter. The computer software would need to be even more complex than for SDI. Then there are the different problems of cruise and Pershing-II technology. Cruise offers more warning time, but it is harder to track. Pershing II, like the Soviet SS–21, SS–22 and SS–23, can be tracked, but its flight time is measured in minutes (3–5 minutes for the closest targets). And then there are bombers, a threat that is becoming even more sophisticated with new supersonic and stealth technologies. Nothing, of course, can be done about short-range nuclear weapons, because there are too many and they are deployed too close to the front line to be stopped.[15]

EDI would therefore concentrate on the so-called anti-tactical ballistic missiles (ATBM) as a first stage to developing a European 'peace-shield'. But it is difficult to believe that Europeans, who have enough of a problem joining together to build a Eurofighter or helicopters, will have the political will to begin such a daunting technical task. There has been some glib talk about the model of the Concorde programme, but that is hardly a success story.

Political will is likely to be even harder to come by on simple financial grounds. Most Europeans have not been meeting their 3 per cent real growth targets for defence spending and are hardly likely to spend billions on a highly speculative ATBM system. After one look at Britain, struggling with ways to finance Trident, the British Army on the Rhine (BAOR), a modern navy and the Falklands, the problems of EDI opportunity costs become obvious.

There is also the arms control impact of an EDI to be considered: European governments are the last true believers in arms control. They relied on the process as part of the 'dual-track' policy that allowed INF deployments to go ahead. They need success in arms control to placate peace movements and to reassure the people that Europe is not a dangerous place. Especially for democratic coalition governments, arms control needs to be seen to be done. According to the 1972 ABM Treaty, the superpowers cannot transfer most ABM technology to their allies, so that most work that would be done on an ATBM would have to be done in Europe. It is the Europeans that have held the

United States to a strict reading of the ABM terms (e.g. on exotic technology), and the allies would be unlikely to wreck their own strategy by pushing ahead with their own programme that would punch a European hole in the ABM Treaty.

Finally, and perhaps most cynically, France and Britain are unlikely to want to encourage SDI or EDI because it might hasten the day when their own independent deterrent becomes obsolete. Despite protestations to the contrary, these independent deterrents exist because there may come a time when Americans are not trusted. US interests may diverge sufficiently from those of their European allies that their solidarity in defence cannot be taken for granted. SDI would only enhance that distrust, undermine the twin pillars of NATO and create a greater need for the independent deterrents. It might make more sense for France and Britain to go what appears to be the Chinese route of trying to develop cruise missile technology to swamp an SDI, rather than spend money on EDI. That might also be a way of keeping some of their scientists at home.

V.   Scenarios

To date, SDI, in its various forms, has consisted of a great deal of confused and confusing rhetoric, coupled with minor and a few potentially major research programmes. So far, no arms control agreements have been clearly violated, defence budgets are not yet broken and allies are only mildly worried. The trends towards far more serious problems are clearly apparent, but the entire issue could go the way of the neutron bomb problem in the 1970s—it could quietly be forgotten. Alternately, SDI could do the same sort of damage as the various scares about strategic 'gaps'—boosting the arms spiral. Which way are we likely to go? What follows is obviously only a partial list of scenarios, all of which are necessarily simplistic. The essential purpose of this exercise is merely to suggest that there is a more likely, and for some a more preferable, scenario than is often prophesied.

Pessimist I

Proponents of SDI in the United States fear that the USA's allies will be successful in restraining the US plan. Small-scale research will be carried on, achieving no breakthrough but causing regular rumbles in the alliance as some Americans insist on the right to test rather than just research. US credibility will become undermined, and peace movements will grow because the nuclear threat has not been undone.

Suddenly, just like the shock of 4 October 1957 (the day Sputnik was launched), the United States would wake up to find that the Soviet Union had an SDI programme. While the United States was scrupulously abiding by the ABM accord, Moscow managed to conceal a massive research programme. This Soviet 'break-out' of the nuclear age would give Moscow the opportunity to do what it wanted around the globe, daring the United States to use its nuclear threats. Western Europe and Japan would rapidly become 'Finlandized' and so on.

Not very likely, but then much of the scenario-building in strategic studies is divorced from political and technical reality. SDI itself is a prime example. To imagine that the Soviet Union could overcome the technical and financial problems of a perfect SDI, and then hide it from the United States, beggars the imagination. The Soviet break-out would have to be perfect, because partial protection in SDI is like partial protection from pregnancy—dangerous in practice.

Pessimist II

But let us suppose the US SDI programme proceeds as planned. The research proves promising and the United States decides the ABM accord needs to be 'brought up to date'. US allies protest, but the United States ploughs on regardless. NATO is severely split, but the West Europeans have no option and so bow to US will. The USA's Asian allies are more amenable to playing along and so take an active part in the research programme. The United States shifts its foreign policy focus more clearly across the Pacific.

The Soviet Union of course refuses to talk about a revised ABM Treaty and withdraws from START in order to give it freedom to build countermeasures. Both the Soviet Union and the United States feel the economic pinch of increased spending programmes, but extra sacrifices are called for by the Kremlin. The reformist (mild as they may be) plans of Mikhail Gorbachev are shelved because of the economic crisis. An opportunity to build bridges to the new Soviet technocracy is lost as the hardliners assert themselves.

Yet rumours of the success of the US programme in the 1990s become even more widespread. US tests suggest that a deployable mixed ground and space-based system is not too far off, while the Soviet programme stagnates. The Soviet grip on its allies weakens as it can no longer fund economic support schemes in Eastern Europe. The empire seems to be crumbling, and so the choice is faced starkly in the Kremlin—stop the disintegration, or retreat into fortress Russia. The decision is taken to force the United States into stopping its SDI programme, say, for example, by a demonstration nuclear strike.

Optimist I

The 'opposite' of 'Pessimist II' is the belief that all can go as the USA plans it. Ground-based BMD research goes well and the Soviet Union also makes progress on its own system. No one feels particularly paranoid. Both sides then agree to talk about 'helping history' by a new arms control agreement that would allow BMD, but restrict offensive weapons. The Soviet Union accepts because it wants to move ahead on its own BMD and can trade that off in the Politburo against the need for cuts in offensive weaponry. The superpowers deploy effective ICBM-protecting BMD and then move on to a complete SDI enhanced by limits on offensive forces. Both sides allow extensive verification as part of a comprehensive test ban and agree to police enforcement of similar tough safeguards against any other power that refuses to play by the same rules.

After deep cuts are achieved, the other nuclear powers have to come to the negotiating table. The January 1986 Gorbachev proposal for a non-nuclear world is placed before them and these smaller nuclear powers see the writing on the wall—their offensive systems are becoming obsolete as the superpowers move from (limited) BMD to SDI. They scrap their offensive forces along with the superpowers in the final reductions to a non-nuclear balance of power. The result: the nuclear counter-revolution.

Optimist II

In a less-than-perfect world, however, if we are all lucky, what is most likely is a complex and unco-ordinated scenario. US allies go along with the Reagan Administration, agreeing to carry on research without testing. Testing is strictly defined and the United States becomes increasingly unwilling to break out of the ABM Treaty. The scientists report a number of problems, the US Congressional Budget Office reports funding will have to be cut back, and the computer programmers report that the necessary battle-management software is unobtainable.

In the meantime, the United States agrees that it has plenty to do in the research phase, and so trades a slightly revised ABM agreement against deep cuts in the superpower arsenals at START. Gorbachev accepts that what goes on behind the shutters of laboratories cannot be stopped, and so buys the trade-off. By not breaking out of SALT limits, the Soviet Union gives no 'support' to hardliners in the United States who need evidence of a 'Soviet threat' to drive their own research. The Soviet Union gradually shifts more of its strategic forces from ICBMs to SLBMs and therefore becomes less concerned with BMD of fixed land installations.

A new US Administration is elected and the essential SDI glue—the Reagan charisma—is removed. The new administration is committed of course to a strong US defence, but it defines that defence in terms of enhanced conventional defence in Europe and raising the nuclear threshold. The new administration will tighten up the ABM agreement, but basically confine research to the darker corners of laboratories. The interest groups will get less funding, and as research and research-progress become limited, previously complementary priorities will begin to compete, with the likely result that the original SDI coalition will collapse. Military professionals will take a firmer grip, grabbing what they can of the new spin-off technologies for their own pet projects. If we are lucky, the new technologies will enhance nuclear deterrence by improving mobility of nuclear missiles and make the conventional defence of Europe more effective. SDI will be seen as a 'bargaining chip' after all. Arms control agreements are reached to withdraw all tactical nuclear weapons from

Europe and deterrence will rely on stand-off theatre weapons. Conventional weapons arms control (mutual [balanced] force reduction) will succeed, thereby reducing the expense of maintaining a credible conventional defence against the Soviet threat.

There is an old Israeli proverb that a pessimist is really a well-informed optimist. While it is difficult to be well-informed about such speculative ventures as SDI (despite the scientific jargon that surrounds it), it does seem that an optimist is a well-informed pessimist. After nuclear strategy has just endured a battering from critics on the left, it now appears set to survive an onslaught from critics on the right. The centre appears to be holding out against the 'iron' law of (passing) fads.

In many senses, it is a matter of returning to simple, basic principles of nuclear strategy. The nuclear revolution poses such a credible threat of assured destruction that it is essentially beyond any technical 'fix' that we can devise at present. The advantages of strategic simplicity brings to mind the French folk tale of the Pope of Avignon, a mule and a peasant. The Pope offered vast sums to anyone who could teach his mule to speak. A simple peasant went to the Pope and returned with vast riches, and the mule. When a friend asked the peasant how he won the prize, the peasant replied that he had promised to teach the mule to speak in 10 years time. But, replied his friend: 'Every idiot knows that mules cannot be taught to speak'. 'Ah,' replied the peasant: 'but in ten years time either the Pope will be dead, or I will be dead, and certainly the mule will be dead'. The well-informed pessimist can be confident that the SDI mule will soon be dead.

Notes and references

[1] See generally Slocombe, W., 'An immediate agenda for arms control', *Survival*, vol. 27, no. 5 (Sep.–Oct. 1985).

[2] To name a few of the British believers, Segal, G., Moreton, E., Freedman, L. and Baylis, J., *Nuclear War and Nuclear Peace* (Macmillan: London, 1983); and Freedman, L., *The Evolution of Nuclear Strategy* (Macmillan: London, 1980).

[3] For a more favourable view of SDI, see Jastrow, R., *How to Make Nuclear Weapons Obsolete* (Little Brown & Co.: Boston, 1985); Graham, D., *High Frontier* (TOR Books: New York, 1983); and Perle, R., 'The Strategic Defense Initiative', *Journal of International Affairs*, vol. 39, no. 1 (Summer 1985).

[4] For a deft critique, see Lord Zuckerman 'The wonders of Star Wars', *The New York Review of Books*, vol. 33, no. 1 (30 Jan. 1986), pp. 32–40.

[5] Critics of SDI include: The Office of Technology Assessment, US Congress, *Ballistic Missile Defense Technologies* (US Government Printing Office: Washington, DC, 1985); Union of Concerned Scientists, *The Fallacy of Star Wars* (Vintage: New York, 1984); Freedman, L., 'The Star Wars debate: the Western Alliance and strategic defence: part II', Adelphi Papers, no. 199, International Institute for Strategic Studies, London, Summer 1985; Bethe, H. A., Boutwell, J. and Garwin, R. L., 'BMD technologies and concepts in the 1980s', *Daedalus*, Journal of the American Academy of Arts and Sciences, vol. 114, no. 2 (Spring 1985), pp. 53–72.

[6] Schneiter, G., 'Implications of the SDI for the ABM Treaty', *Survival*, vol. 27, no. 5 (Sep.–Oct. 1985).

[7] On the October 1985 refinement of the US position, see *The Economist*, vol. 297, no. 7418 (2 Nov. 1985), p. 16. According to Agreed Interpretation D in the ABM agreement, systems based on 'other physical principles' could be 'subject to discussion'. Proponents of SDI argue that laser and particle beam weapons come under this heading. They also argue that older style SDI work is not prohibited by the general ban on ABM (article 5) because the products are not components, but rather 'adjuncts' to components of an SDI system. US critics argue that the Soviet 'phased-array' radar at Abalakova near Krasnoyarsk already violates the ABM agreement. Other NATO experts suggest that until the radar is completed, we cannot know for certain. Also, US early warning radars at Thule (Greenland) and Fylingdales (Britain) were tolerated by the Soviet Union in 1972 even though no early warning radar outside the home country is allowed by the ABM agreement. But now, the two facilities are being 'replaced' and Moscow views this as a violation. Whatever the case, none of these actions seem to constitute an unambiguous violation of the 1972 ABM accord. See Smith, R. J., '"Star Wars" tests and the ABM Treaty', *Science*, vol. 229, no. 4708 (5 July 1985), pp. 29–31; Sher, A., 'The languages of arms control', *The Bulletin of the Atomic Scientists*, vol. 41, no. 10 (Nov. 1985), pp. 23–9; and Krepon, M., 'Both sides are hedging', Foreign Policy, no. 56 (Fall 1984), pp. 153–72.

[8] On ASAT, see Stares, P., 'Reagan and the ASAT issue', *Journal of International Affairs*, vol. 39, no. 1 (Summer 1985); and Gottfried, K. and Lebow, R. N., 'Anti-satellite weapons: weighing the risks', *Daedalus*, Journal of the American Academy of Arts and Sciences, vol. 114, no. 2 (Spring 1985), pp. 147–70.

[9] Brown, N., *The Strategic Defense Initiative and European Security*, Rand R–3366 FF (Rand Corp.: Santa Monica, CA, Jan. 1986); and Bertram, C., 'Strategic defence and the Western Alliance', *Daedalus*, Journal of the American Academy of Arts and Sciences, vol. 114, no. 3 (Summer 1985), pp. 279–96; and Dean, J., 'Will NATO survive ballistic missile defense', Journal of *International Affairs*, vol. 39, no. 1 (Summer 1985).

[10] Speech by Sir Geoffrey Howe, *The Times*, London, 16 Mar. 1985.

[11] The ever-acerbic Thompson, E. P., 'Folly's comet', *Star Wars*, ed. E. P. Thompson (Penguin: London, 1985).

[12] Seitz, K., 'SDI: the technological challenge for Europe', *The World Today*, vol. 41, no. 8/9 (Aug.–Sep. 1985), pp. 154–7.

[13] 'On the road certainly, destination unknown', *Financial Times*, 8 Nov. 1985.

[14] *Financial Times*, 1 July 1986. Ten other projects were agreed in Nov. 1985.

[15] Nerlich, U., 'Missile defences: strategic and tactical', *Survival*, vol. 27, no. 3 (May–June 1985), pp. 119–27.

Paper 2.3. Soviet military doctrine and space in the 1980s

DAVID R. JONES

I. Introduction

Recent discussions of US strategic thinking have been dominated by the issues raised by President Reagan's Strategic Defence Initiative (SDI). Many who favour pursuit of a 'Star Wars' capability justify this by pointing to the Soviet Union's existing space weaponry and allegedly static doctrine of 'anti-space defence' (*protivokosmicheskaia oborona* or PKO). Like ABM (anti-ballistic missile) defence (*protivoraketnaia oborona* or PRO), in the mid-1960s this mission was allotted to the more traditional Troops of the Air Defense Forces (*Voiska PVO*). In the eyes of some Western strategists, the PVO already has long presented a growing threat to the air-breathing or bomber leg of the US strategic triad. With alleged capabilities in ballistic missile defence and space being added as well, the Soviet Union seems to possess, or seemed on the verge of possessing, a truly formidable defensive system that will reduce seriously the credibility of the US posture of deterrence through assured retaliation. By the mid-1980s, these analysts saw SDI as imperative if they were 'to preserve our nation and the values it has stood for, so that the course of U.S. history may not end in the smouldering ruin or the emasculated shell of a defeated nation, but in the final triumph of its Judaeo–Christian and democratic ideals'.[1]

Given the long-standing belief in technology in the United States, there has long been a US theoretical interest in the active military uses of space. Many also believe that space inevitably will be the scene of acute military competition. 'Space has become an extension of the Earth battlefield', George L. Keegan, former Chief of US Air Force Intelligence and an early proponent of the use of directed-energy weapons, wrote in 1981: 'Soon it will dominate that battlefield'.[2] In that same year, Herman Kahn, meditating on the successful flight of the US space shuttle Columbia, noted that the new era of space exploitation brought 'the possibility of increased military competition in space', and that the time had come 'to develop the concept of space war'.[3] Not surprisingly, such experts naturally believe that their Soviet counterparts must harbour similar expectations.

It would be absurd to assume that Moscow's specialists are blind to the military possibilities of space, or to the potentialities of the new technologies that eventually could be deployed as weapons there. Indeed, repeated statements demonstrate their concern about US intentions. Thus, in 1981, even before President Reagan launched SDI, Colonel L. Semeiko warned that all the evidence indicated that 'the Pentagon views space as an essentially new sphere for a surprise attack'.[4] None the less, as Paul B. Stares recently noted, to date 'the Soviet Union has not provided a clear exposition of its military doctrine relating to operations in space'. He suggests that this may be a natural result of the USSR's repeated demand that space be reserved for peaceful uses alone, 'and the corollary of avoiding any reference to its military space program'.[5] He also accepts Thomas Wolfe's earlier conclusion that the 'development of a coherent doctrine of space warfare seems to have been inhibited by the necessity to preserve a propaganda image of the Soviet Union as a country interested solely in the exploration of space for peaceful purposes'.[6]

Even so, the 1960s and early 1970s witnessed an increasing interest in both ABM systems and space war in the Soviet military press, as well as an intensification of both the air defence and civil defence (*grazhdanskaia oborona* or GO) programmes, the deployment of the Galosh ballistic missile defence (BMD) system around Moscow and the testing of a Soviet anti-satellite (ASAT) system. Then, throughout the 1970s, Soviet spokesmen warned of US initiatives in both fields, and in the mid-1980s their military journals have shown a renewed interest in space warfare as such. But to date, the articles have been devoted solely to evolving US theories and programmes, and they have made no mention of those of the USSR.[7] In the minds of US analysts like William F. Scott, these references none the less remain significant. He believes that such charges are made largely in 'order to justify what they themselves were probably doing', and argues that complaints about US plans to deploy an ABM system parallel the 'Soviet research, testing and planning that is being carried out in the greatest secrecy'. He also warns that their attacks on SDI may mean 'that this type of system is what the Soviets themselves are seeking'.[8]

To analysts like Scott, since the early 1960s there has been little change in the Soviet Union's doctrinal stance on these issues. He believes that now, as then, Soviet military theoreticians are warning that the correlation between the defence and offence never remains stable, and that all offensive systems will sooner or later be stalemated by defensive ones. From this it logically seems to follow that they must be seeking their own means of negating the power represented by nuclear-tipped ballistic missiles, and that their anti-SDI propaganda is mere camouflage (or *maskirovka*) for their own programme. And this programme, according to the Reagan Administration, is one of alarming proportions.[9]

II.   Soviet strategic defence systems

The *Voiska PVO* emerged as a separate service in 1948. As reorganized in the late 1970s, it was described in 1985 by the US Department of Defense (DoD) as 'a potent and increasingly capable force which would attempt to limit the retaliatory capability of our strategic bombers and cruise missiles'. According to this analysis, the PVO comprises close to 12 000 surface-to-air missile (SAM) launchers at over 1200 locations, over 1200 interceptors devoted exclusively to strategic defence, and some 10 000 air defence early warning (EW) and ground control/intercept (GCI) radars. Impressive as this force is in itself, it reportedly is backed by an additional 2800 interceptors serving with the tactical Air Forces (*Voenno-vozdushhnye sily* or VVS).[10]

In Soviet eyes, the importance of the PVO is indicated by the fact that it ranks third, after the Strategic Rocket and Ground Forces, respectively, in the hierarchy of the five services (that is, ahead of the VVS and the Navy), as well as by its share of the monies allotted to defence in general. While the US Central Intelligence Agency (CIA) estimated that the PVO never received a full fifth of the *totals* invested in overall defence during the 1970s, the agency did argue that the USSR spent roughly half of its *strategic* funds on defence, as compared to a mere 15 per cent of US strategic funding.[11] Further, regular funding of the PVO has meant the continued introduction of new generations of more sophisticated air defence missiles and interceptors. These now may be improving the service's ability to deal with the air-breathing threat at low, as well as medium and high, altitudes. US analysts are even more worried that some upgraded Soviet SAMs (originally the older SA–5, and now the SA–10 and SA–X–12), may have some ABM capabilities that could be converted with relative ease into strategic point defences.[12]

Most Western analysts would agree that the USSR's continuing interest in BMD has resulted in substantial funding for the research and development (R & D) on new ABM missile systems, as well as on investigating the military utility of directed-energy laser and particle beam technologies. But there is less unanimity over space weaponry. Those experts who do insist that 'the Soviet Union is the only nation with a standing space defense capability',[13] support this view by pointing to an existing ASAT system, to one (or two, according to the US DoD) ground-based laser with an alleged capability 'of attacking satellites in various orbits', and to the possible use of the USSR's Galosh ABM system in an anti-satellite role. With this seemingly respectable capability established as an alleged given, these analysts go on to warn of the potential dangers posed by a Soviet ABM research programme that, in the future, may produce space systems employing laser and particle beam weapons, as well as kinetic energy weapons, in space itself.[14]

The reader will note that this view of the PVO's efforts in strategic defence, which largely relies on data released by the US DoD, includes all the weapon systems needed for an SDI programme.[15] So it is hardly surprising that some analysts draw the appropriate conclusions. Citing official US reports, as well as various discussions of space-borne ABM systems in the Soviet military press, they argue that the Soviet Union is preparing to deploy its own Star Wars system. In this, orbital lasers in space supposedly will combine with ground-based lasers to defend Soviet satellites. Meanwhile, the same orbital weapons, as well as ASAT interceptors, will destroy or badly degrade an opponent's space-borne facilities. Success in this last mission in itself would badly hamper any missile strike against the USSR, and so allow the Soviet ABM defences to provide 'a completely leakproof barrier' by using other ground-based lasers and beam weapons.[16] And finally, since some Soviet discussions of such a system precede March 1983, some commentators even suggest 'that the Soviets were thinking about sophisticated multi-layer defences prior to the President's so-called "Star Wars" speech'.[17]

The Reagan Administration has given this vision of Soviet intentions its full blessing. In March 1985 Defense Secretary Weinberger warned that if the Soviet Union alone acquires an effective space-borne ABM and ASAT defence system, deterrence will be doomed 'and we would have no choices between surrender and suicide'.[18] Again, in July 1985, Paul Nitze, arms adviser to the Secretary of State, expressed official concern that in the aggregate, Soviet ABM-related activities could 'provide them the basis for deployment of an ABM defense of their national territory, which would violate the (ABM) treaty' and provide them with their own Star Wars. Another official meanwhile insisted that during the Five-Year Plan 1985–89 the Soviet Government would spend some $26-billion on the necessary technologies, a figure that coincidentally matches the US Government's spending plans over the same period.[19] And finally, in October, the President himself openly charged that the Soviet Government's refusal 'to admit they have any strategic defense program at all' was a 'dangerous deception'. For, he said, they in fact had long been conducting advanced research on their own version of SDI. 'They don't talk about that,' he continued. 'All they say about SDI is that the United States shouldn't have it.'[20]

III.   The technological balance

Such statements obviously are not devoid of special pleading. Even so, given the authority behind them and the awesome potential of the weapons described, they at first sight do seem to provide Western readers with a logical and compelling justification for the US Star Wars programme. None the less, Western discussions of such matters in general often seem to reflect the same 'curious mix of abstract technical fantasy and mirror imaging woven around highly-stylized notions of Soviet military strategy', that Stephen Meyer has discerned in recent conjecture about the Soviet Union's likely responses to SDI in particular.[21] Further, closer scrutiny immediately raises a number of serious reservations about the validity of the judgements above.

Firstly, the Soviet articles cited—as pointed out above—are explicitly discussing the view of 'foreign military specialists', and the implications of presumed US, not Soviet, military programmes. This is true, whether the articles appeared before or after President Reagan's speech of March 1983. And while we may sometimes infer 'a uniquely Soviet doctrine' from such critiques of reported Western plans,[22] this is far from a simple task. Secondly, apart from doubts concerning the accuracy of such inferences, the conclusions of the analysts mentioned rest on a number of other unproven assumptions.

For example, following the US model, they continually link the Soviet space systems, and hence supposed space doctrine, with the USSR's ABM weapons and a perceived doctrine on BMD. Further, many of their contentions about the likely capabilities of any future Soviet space-borne systems reflect an often exaggerated assessment of the ABM and ASAT systems that the Soviet Union possesses at present. So before turning to the problem of doctrine, a few points need to be made about the existing systems, and especially about the techno-logical base that supports them.

As just indicated, such assessments seem fully supported by the Pentagon's public warnings that, in at least some cases, the relevant Soviet programmes of advanced research surpass their US counterparts in size, and possibly in progress. But unfortunately, these well-publicized warnings—in spite of their authoritative sources—are themselves of questionable veracity. Despite admittedly high levels of research funding, cases of Soviet superiority seem few and far between. Further, claims to the contrary contradict other official US assessments of the 'technology balance'. In 1985, for instance, John M. Collins of the US Library of Congress completed an exhaustive analysis of the US–Soviet military balance during 1980–85.[23] With regard to the technologies involved in PRO and PKO, the result is surprisingly modest when viewed next to the warnings of Soviet achievement so often enumerated.

In terms of competence in R & D in the basic technologies involved in BMD, SDI and space systems, Collins admits a US lead in almost every field. Only in those of particle beams and vacuum tubes is the Soviet Union ahead, and only in that of lasers does it tie with the USA. Collins also finds that the Soviet beam lead is only probable, and believes that in any case, 'big breakthroughs' in this and laser technology 'may not occur until AD 2000 or later'. All in all, he concludes that the United States 'still hold(s) strong leads in most respects where "being ahead" really counts, and could eliminate almost all pockets of Soviet superiority in a relatively short order, if decisions were made to do so'.[24]

Other evidence suggests that even Collins's evaluation of Soviet excellence in the field of directed-energy devices may be exaggerated. According to Simon Kassel of Rand, their work on the crystal channelling of charged particle beams gained a substantial impetus from a joint experiment at the Stanford Linear Accelerator Center.[25] Again, their free-electron laser research—an area recently cited by General J. A. Abrahamson, Director of the SDI Organiza-tion, as being perhaps the most significant for BMD—may have been somewhat overrated. Kassel also concludes that the USSR's programme in this field does equal the USA's in 'depth and breadth, as well as in manpower', but he reports that the United States has done twice as many experiments in an effort to verify the basic theory, and that it has had 'significantly' better results.[26]

The most critical area, of course, is that concerning the technologies upon which any BMD or space warfare system must rely for detecting and tracking targets, for sorting out decoys from real targets, and then for aiming sophisti-cated weapons over vast differences in minimal times. Here even US DoD officials feel constrained to admit Soviet deficiencies. Thus, when one recent study turned briefly (one paragraph) to the 'computer and sensor technology' upon which all advanced weapon programmes are 'dependent', it merely remarked that these 'are currently more highly developed in the West than in the Soviet Union'—and added a warning about the dangers posed by continuing Soviet research 'and clandestine access to Western technology'.[27] Collins is more forthright. Concluding that the United States has substantial leads in all the vital areas, he points out that even US 'technologists, who excel at electronics, optics, computer science, sensors of all kinds, telecommunications, and stealth for satellites, cannot accomplish every mission' that a successful SDI would require. He is convinced that they 'lead their Soviet rivals',[28] but admits that despite their own 'sharp tools' and the vast funds now being spent by the Reagan Administration, many US critics remain convinced that in this area the obstacles will remain insurmountable.[29] In which case, the Soviet Union's scientists are even less likely to succeed.

IV.   Existing capabilities

As might be expected, variations in basic technological competence are reflected in the systems employing these technologies. According to Collins, the United States therefore leads in all but one category of command, control, communications, and intelligence (C³I) systems, in unmanned surveillance, reconnaissance and communications satellites, and in BMD warning systems. He believes that the Soviet Union has achieved parity in ASAT systems and in traditional ABM interceptor missile capabilities, and only holds a lead—and a diminishing one at that—with regard to innovative BMD systems (lasers and particle beams).[30] But as just indicated, even this last may be more marginal than he and many others have argued.

Similar technological lags and bottlenecks have long plagued the PVO's efforts to provide an effective defence against the threat posed by air-breathing systems. Despite the large investment in this service, it has little reason to hope that it could beat back a serious assault by modern bombers, even by those lacking the advantages of stealth technologies and air-launched cruise missiles (ALCMs). Having made great efforts to combat possible intruders at high and medium altitudes, in the mid-1970s the PVO command suddenly confronted the possibility of a technologically more advanced enemy entering its air space at levels not far above the tree-tops. Worse still, the spectre of future war no longer entailed the simple interception of aircraft-carrying bombs or short-range attack missiles (SRAMs). Rather, Soviet planners now have to face the possibility that US bombers will launch numerous ALCMs from hundreds of miles off their shores, and that these clever little weapons will penetrate the homeland at such low altitudes that detection will be difficult if not impossible, and the PVO's SAMs and interceptors will prove virtually helpless.[31]

In assessing the measures that the PVO must adopt to deal with the current US bomber force, even one armed only with SRAMs, US analysts list: (a) the replacement of older interceptors with newer MIG–23s, MIG–25s, MIG–29s and MIG–31s, all equipped with look-down/shoot-down radars; (b) the deployment of up to 100 airborne warning and control system (AWACS) air-craft, with capabilities similar to the existing US model; and (c) the re-equip-ping of some 500 SA–1 and SA–2 SAM sites with some 5000 SA–10 SAMs during the 1980s.[32] Further, while the adoption of ALCMs by the US Air Force has been criticized on a number of grounds, few disagree that 'the mixed stand-off penetration force planned for the first phase of cruise missile deployments will present Soviet air defenses with a greater array of problems' than they have faced hitherto.[33] According to US officials, an effective defence against their planned ALCM deployments would upgrade the above estimate by requiring at the very least 50–100 AWACS aircraft, 'several thousand' interceptors with a look-down/shoot-down capability, and 500–1000 SA–10 sites with 10 SAMS each.[34]

If the United States clearly is having developmental difficulties with its ALCM, the Soviet Union is meeting even greater problems in modernizing its air defences to meet this potential threat. True, new interceptors—the MIG–29s and MIG–31s—are entering service, and they do have some look-down/shoot-down capability. None the less, by mid-decade the PVO had only 120 of these modern aircraft, and US technical advances in stealth technologies meanwhile seemed destined to reduce their radar efficacy.[35] In addition, the doubts raised about the PVO's detection, tracking and intercept abilities by incidents in 1978 have seemed tragically confirmed by the Korean Air Lines flight 007 incident of September 1983. Despite constant exhortations about maintaining 'combat readiness', PVO radars once again seem to have proved incapable of consistently tracking, and its pilots of intercepting and identifying, even a relatively slow-moving commercial airliner. Indeed, US charges that the radars must have identified the target's cross-section as a liner (and not an RC–135 reconnaissance aircraft) suggest Soviet technological backwardness as much as perfidy.[36]

More telling yet, despite the much heralded arrival of the new Il–76 Mainstay to replace the old and relatively useless Tu–126 Moss AWACS, only four of the former had entered service (to join nine of the latter) by mid-1985. Indeed, the slowness of the Il–76s' deployment suggests that Moscow is still experiencing grave difficulties in developing successful AWACS.[37] There were also still a mere 520 SA–10s reported in service at 60 sites, only 30 of which seem intended for strategic defence.[38] So the PVO remains manifestly incapable of protecting the Soviet motherland from even the air-breathing systems currently in the West's arsenal, much less against possible future threats. Further, any effort to do so by providing even the minimal requirements just listed will prove extremely expensive, and probably will proceed at a relatively modest rate. In retrospect, the recent reorganization of the PVO and related forces in part may well reflect an attempt to improve the air defence system's low-level capabilities, and thus the military planners' clear recognition of its grave limitations, despite the sums devoted to it.[39] If such is the case, this recognition may have been one of the factors behind the doctrinal reassessment discussed below.

For similar technological reasons, it is not surprising to find that many non-official Western assessments of the existing Soviet PRO/PKO capabilities award them considerably lower marks than has the Pentagon. With regard to BMD, the judgements of Sayre Stevens are a case in point. Noting that the original radars of Moscow's Galosh system 'lacked the sophistication to deal with many targets at one time', he then described how the USSR met 'the radar challenge without a visible flinch'. One result was the transportable, phased-array radar that appeared in the late 1970s. This reportedly could be combined with one or two new types of interceptor missile 'to constitute a BMD system (now designated the ABM–X–3 system) suitable for fairly rapid deployment'. Further, its phased-array engagement radar probably lacks the 'single-target constraint' of those in the Galosh system, and its high-acceleration interceptor presumably allows launches to be postponed until after the atmospheric sorting of penetration aids has been completed. Taken with the USSR's growing system of peripheral missile detection and tracking radars, the ABM–X–3 seems to possess an alarming potential.[40]

By the early 1980s, some Western analysts therefore warned that 'the Soviets may soon deploy a new mobile ABM system in conjunction with the older Galosh system to provide an improved, layered defense complex at least initially in the Moscow area'. They noted that since the new system was mobile, it also 'may hold large potential for concealed stockpiling and rapid deployment (that is, an ABM 'break-out') in a crisis situation'.[41] Yet as Stevens points out, such a 'recitation of theoretically derived implications of the ABM–X–3 is simply that—theoretical'. In the first place, Moscow's plans for its future deployment remain shrouded in secrecy, and a number of arguments exist to suggest that any such 'break-out' would run counter to other Soviet interests. Then secondly, there is no way that Western (or Soviet, for that matter) analysts can ascertain whether or not the new system will perform all, or even most, of the functions some ascribe to it. True, it would likely have significant capabilities if the requisite acquisition data is available, and if the necessary data processing systems are in place. But in Stevens's view, it is improbable 'that a truly transportable radar can do an adequate job of long-range search and acquisition against the very low radar cross sections that characterize newer U.S. ICBM [intercontinental ballistic missiles] reentry vehicles', and doubtful that the older Hen House acquisition systems 'can predict reentry vehicle trajectories with enough precision to make a direct handover of incoming targets' to the ABM–X–3's transportable sets. Even if the newer, large phased-array, very high frequency (VHF) peripheral systems take over this task, they will remain open to neutralization by black-out or destruction. Meanwhile, the true capabilities of the ABM–X–3's data processing system remain obscure so that its ability to perform the functions expected of it by some analysts remains at best an open question.[42]

Analysts like Stevens also believe that the technological factors, among others, provide 'few powerful incentives for them to do it (attempt a 'break-out') in the near term'. Although the Soviet programme has its own momentum and has made considerable progress, 'it really has only now achieved the level of technology that was available to the United States ten years ago'. Meanwhile, the Soviet Government must fear the economic costs of a renewed ABM race, as well as 'the consequences of turning American technology loose, and probably still find the ABM Treaty desirable as a means of constraining the application U.S. prowess to BMD'. For as pointed out, it is precisely in the technologies necessary for developing an advanced BMD, the technologies of high-speed data processing, large-scale integrated circuits, microelectronics in general, and so on, that the 'United States has more or less clear superiority'.[43]

The same is true of space weaponry. This fact may well explain Moscow's recent efforts to gain a diplomatic hedge, such as that provided by the ABM Treaty of 1972, against US military-technological competition in the cosmos. Indeed, the real technological limitations hampering the USSR in such a space race are even more readily apparent than in BMD, and nowhere more so than in their orbital satellite interceptor. Despite the Pentagon's continuing concern over this system, it remains one of the best examples of the extent to which Soviet technology *lags* behind that of the United States. Even the capabilities now ascribed to this system seem almost more a result of upgraded estimates of the US DoD (largely for budgetary purposes), rather than of improvements introduced by Soviet scientists and technicians. For example, US officials now describe the interceptor as having the capability of reaching 'targets orbiting at more than 5,000 kilometres', but estimates in the early 1980s suggested its utility was limited to the much lower altitudes of 160–1600 km (100–1000 miles).[44] Since testing of this system terminated in 1982, it is difficult to comprehend the grounds for the threefold increase in its estimated operational altitudes.

In considering the Soviet ASAT interceptor, we must remember that it too is based on technologies of the 1960s—technologies with which the United States had become fully conversant as part of its similar, but later abandoned, Saint anti-satellite programme. While US interest in that particular weapon waned during the 1970s, between 1959 and 1970 the United States conducted at least 25 tests with other ASAT systems (the Thor and Nike Zeus missiles).[45] The Soviet weapon's kill mechanism therefore is far from sophisticated: passing near its target on its first (if possible) or second orbit, the interceptor is then detonated by ground controllers in an attempt to destroy or damage the target's sensors and other mechanisms by battering them with its fragments. Some call this the 'shotgun' kill method, but the interceptor actually resembles a type of large (*c.* 4500 lbs.) cosmic grenade.[46] Even so, it obviously has some strategic significance and might prove, as Defense Secretary Harold Brown once admitted, 'somewhat troublesome' as far as lower-level US satellites are concerned.[47] None the less, the 19 identified tests of this interceptor, which were staged in three separate periods between 1968 and 1982, suggest that it is anything but reliable. Of the first seven tests (October 1968–December 1971), two clearly failed and US officials later awarded the ASAT only a 50 per cent rate of success. Overall, at least seven trials have been clear failures, including four of the nine conducted between February 1976 and May 1978. Refinements do appear to have improved the system before the five held during the period of 1980 to 1982, but the weapon remains primitive and far from being perfected.[48]

On this basis, one US specialist recently termed the Soviet ASAT's performance as 'abysmal', and blamed this largely on the low quality of the infra-red sensors it uses for passive homing.[49] Similar problems apparently exist with other tracking and homing devices as well. For example, the four tests made with optical sensors in the 1970s apparently all ended in failure, so that the interceptors tested during the years 1981 and 1982 seem to have relied on radar and infra-red systems, despite the former's shortcomings. Other limitations also hinder its utility. Some specialists, for instance, argue that the interceptor's small fuel capacity means that it must be launched when the target's orbit passes near its launching pad at Tiuratam (which occurs every 12 hours).[50] This means that the system is hardly suitable for service as the 'quick reaction' system, which some in the mid-1970s predicted was under development. Further, the Pentagon's recent estimate that several such killer satellites could be launched in a day seems to hark back to similar reports of 1976. Then US sources suggested that the system had launch times of under 90 minutes, and that if stored properly, the ASAT's launch could get under way within an hour of the decision to do so, and in some cases within 10 to 30 minutes.[51] At that time, however, other analysts insisted that its costly and cumbersome technology meant that weeks, and possibly months, are needed to prepare a launch, a possibility which casts still further doubts on its ultimate utility.[52]

V.   A changing view of PKO?

On balance, then, it seems that Moscow's present PRO/PKO inventory is considerably less capable than the Pentagon has suggested, and that its efficiency is not likely to improve dramatically in the foreseeable future. Or so, at least, it must appear to the Soviet leadership. At the same time, it may be equally erroneous to assume that the Soviet military's doctrinal writings of the 1960s and early 1970s still accurately reflect present thinking. This point recently was made by a tale that unofficially surfaced during the arms negotiations in Geneva. According to this, the US negotiators on SDI decided to confront their Soviet opposites with a detailed summary of Moscow's intentions with regard to war in space. The document was carefully prepared with quotations from Marshal V. D. Sokolovskii's *Military Strategy* and other more or less authoritative works of the same vintage. When introduced into the negotiations, it at first seemed to catch the Soviet team completely off guard. Yet the Americans in turn were quickly surprised when their Soviet counterparts announced: 'But we've changed our minds since then.'

Whatever the truth of this story, one thing is clear: official Soviet definitions of anti-space defence do suggest a change in attitude that, significantly, is not reflected in those of ballistic missile defence. In 1965, for example, the official

Dictionary of Basic Military Terms identified both PKO and PRO each as being 'an integral component of anti-air defence (*protivovozdushnaia oborona* or PVO)'. PRO *per se* was charged 'with identifying and destroying enemy ballistic missiles during their flight trajectories and jamming them with radio-electronic interference', and its weaponry divided into anti-missile missiles (*antirakety*) and special jamming stations. PKO, on the other hand, had the 'basic mission . . . of destroying those of the enemy's cosmic means that were used for military purposes in their flight orbits'. The forces devoted to space warfare were to accomplish this with 'special spacecraft and equipment (satellite interceptors) that could be controlled both from the ground or by specially equipped craft (*ekipazhami*)'.[53] A second and only slightly less authoritative source of the same period expanded this definition somewhat. It listed the targets of PKO as those military spacecraft that acted as carriers for nuclear weapons, conducted reconnaissance, and so on, and expanded the description of weaponry to include 'special spacecraft, satellite-interceptors, and other flying devices that are armed with rockets and radio-electronic equipment'.[54]

Before leaving these definitions, one point needs emphasis. In 1965 both PKO and PRO were considered good Soviet and Russian military concepts. But 'space doctrine' (*kosmicheskaia or vozdushno-kosmicheskaia doktrina*), which was defined as a 'doctrine that envisages the conduct of active military operations in the vastness of space, and which regards gaining mastery of space as an important condition for gaining victory in war', was definitely not.[55] Neither, incidentally, were the concepts 'aerospace operations' (*vozdushno-kosmicheskie operatsii*), which referred to active operations directed against targets on earth, or the 'aerospace forces' (*vozdushno-kosmicheskie sily*) conducting these operations. All three terms were definitely branded as 'foreign' (*inostr.*).[56] This perhaps was meant to underline the USSR's peaceful and purely defensive intentions in the cosmos. But it also reflected the fact that any aerospace doctrine was only a component of military doctrine as a whole, as well as the assignation of responsibility for PKO to the *Voiska PVO*—an assignation that prevented the development of a separate doctrinal stance beyond that for air defence in general.

To meet the demand of PKO, by the late 1960s the Soviet military had developed the ASAT interceptor in the late 1960s which it tested during the years 1968 through 1972. These trials suddenly halted, but resumed in 1976. They then seemed to indicate a renewed commitment to maintaining a PKO capability as well. This interpretation seemed confirmed by the attention devoted to this topic in a book entitled *The Development of Anti-Air Defense*, which appeared in that same year. Indeed, its editor—Marshal of Aviation G. V. Ziman—concluded this volume with the warning that the PVO 'must destroy, without exceptions, every warhead that penetrates the depths of the country by air or from space'.[57] But two years later, another work, which admitted the existence of a Soviet ABM system, took a very different course with regard to space weaponry. Allegedly citing 'the opinion of foreign specialists', it warned that the treaty of 1967, which banned the stationing of nuclear and other weapons of mass destruction in space, 'does not prevent the development of weapons with which to launch attacks from outer space'. For this reason, the Soviet Government, with regard to its own security, '. . . cannot afford to ignore the main trends in the development of space systems abroad, nor the possibility of their being used for military purposes'.[58]

When reviewing these and other events at the time, the present writer sadly concluded that while 'American technology can still outdistance them in the foreseeable future, the Soviets' achievements in PKO have increased greatly the likelihood that any future conflict will spread into the cosmos'.[59] Others agreed because, as Stares notes, the Soviets' resumption of ASAT testing, along with allegations about their 'advances in, and even use of, directed-energy weapons such as lasers, added another dimension to the US debate about the Soviet space "threat" during the latter part of the 1970s'.[60] One result of Washington's reappraisal of the vulnerability of its satellites was a US proposal of March 1977 for the creation of a US–Soviet bilateral working group for the discussion of limitations on ASAT systems. Perhaps to the surprise of some, Moscow accepted this offer. Exploratory talks therefore began in June 1978, which led to formal negotiations in the next year. However no agreement was reached before the bilateral meetings were suspended after the Soviet invasion of Afghanistan in December 1979, and then shelved indefinitely by the Reagan Administration.[61]

As might be expected, the USSR has publicly charged that the ASAT talks were 'frozen by the American side', and that 'Washington has made a particularly sharp turn toward the militarization of outer space'.[62] In addition, during August 1980 Moscow also introduced a 'draft treaty on the prohibition of the stationing of weapons of any kind in outer space' into the UN General Assembly. This led to new ASAT talks within the UN Committee on Disarmament, but again, real progress has been minimal.[63] Soviet writers therefore take a certain glee in contrasting their behaviour with that of the US Government in which, they charge, 'on the personal instructions of President Reagan, these matters (i.e., the 'militarization of space') have been repeatedly discussed at the highest level in order to select the most promising ways of developing effective weapons for destroying targets in outer space and targets in the atmosphere and on Earth from space'.[64]

Such accusations, of course, are part and parcel of the continuing propaganda war between Moscow and Washington. But apart from their proposals in the United Nations, other signs existed to suggest that in the meantime, the Soviets too reassessed their position on the active military use of space. During this period, for instance, the military's official discussions of the concept of PKO had undergone a small, but significant, modification. In 1978, when volume 6 of the *Soviet Military Encyclopaedia* appeared, it included a brief entry on PKO that can be usefully compared to those cited above. Firstly, this branch of warfare was no longer defined as an integral part of air defence (PVO) in general. And secondly, unlike ABM or PRO, PKO was completely isolated from any connection with the air defence forces, as well as from PRO *per se*.[65]

PRO was now described as 'the complex of forces and weapons, as well as the measures and combat operations, that are charged with deflecting an enemy's nuclear-missile strike by destroying his ballistic rockets or the armed components of the rockets during the trajectory of their flights', and at least in the cases of the North Atlantic Treaty Organization (NATO), and the navy, was still considered a definite function of PVO.[66] As for space defence, this was confined to the forces, weapons, measures and operations 'charged with the observation and destruction (putting out of commission) of an enemy's spacecraft (*kosmichskie apparaty* or KA)'. This was to be achieved by 'special complexes, equipped to launch automatically piloted satellite-interceptors and to navigate them to the KA designated for destruction, as well as by the fire-control PRO complexes'. But if this last relationship with PRO weapon systems was retained, PKO—unlike PRO—was now demoted to the ranks of foreign terms and doctrinal concepts.[67] That such distinctions were not acciden-tal is clear from entries that appeared five years later in the official *Military Encyclopaedic Dictionary*. These repeated the essentials of the definitions of 1978, and again carefully designated PKO as foreign.[68] This last source, incidentally, ignored completely the other three 'foreign' terms just mentioned.

VI.   A question of doctrine

It might seem easy to dismiss this point as either semantic quibbling, or as further proof of the extent to which Soviet writers will go to mislead Western analysts. None the less, a number of considerations support an opposite interpretation. To begin with, few students of the USSR would disagree that words are used very carefully in the official Soviet press, or that changes (often apparently minor) in language often represent shifts in the official position on a particular issue. Disagreements then usually surface over whether or not a modification in a linguistic formula represents a real change of substance in policy. Thus one school of analysts discerns an ideological continuity that often leads them to treat changes in proclaimed policy as mere tactical shifts of minimal or no serious significance. Another group points out that while tactics may change, literature published within the USSR and intended primarily for Soviet officials and service personnel, can hardly afford to mislead these groups in an effort to confuse the West. Quite simply, as Benjamin Lambeth recently put it, 'the Soviets can scarcely lie to their own officers charged with implemen-ting Soviet defense guidance merely in order to deceive outsiders'.[69]

In addition, the implications of the revised definitions of PKO just con-sidered seem to match changes in other recent pronouncements, the realities of practical policy, and most importantly, a revision in Soviet military doctrine as a whole. To some Western observers, an ongoing analysis of the shifting intricacies of 'doctrine' appears a somewhat arcane exercise. For them it seems to involve sifting through self-evident generalities and well-known Marxist–Leninist axioms to gain minimalist insights that have little to do with the continuing realities of Soviet military power. On this basis, they content themselves with repeating formulations that are based on the now translated, and repeatedly cited, writings of Marshal Sokolovskii and other theoreticians of the 1960s. They thus continue to assert that the Soviet military essentially remains committed to the belief that the development of war-fighting and damage-limiting capabilities provide the best deterrence, that nuclear weapons retain military utility, that any future conflict will inevitably be nuclear, and that they must ensure that the USSR, however mangled, emerges victorious. They also therefore believe that Soviet military planners, given their long-standing commitment to strategic defence, must be striving to create their own capabilities for space warfare and a space-borne BMD system.[70]

None the less, a brief glance at the Soviet military literature underlines the importance of current doctrine for present-day military thought and policy, the changing nature of this doctrine, and hence the need for Western analysts to reassess its content continually. It also makes clear that, as suggested above, any Soviet 'aerospace doctrine' is only one aspect of the larger military doctrine that conditions Soviet military policies in all areas, and which seeks to ensure their overall consistency. And finally, a comparison of military doctrine, as it has evolved over the last decade, with Moscow's announced policy on the uses of space over the same period, indicates that many elements of today's position were developed *before* SDI became an official policy of the United States.

In 1983 the official *Military Encyclopaedic Dictionary* defined 'military doctrine' (*doktrina voennaia*) as that 'system of views, adopted by a state at a given (particular) moment, on the nature, goals and character of a possible future war, on the preparation of the country and the Armed Forces for it, and on the means for waging it'. The entry went on to identify the basic theses of a doctrine as being 'conditioned by the social-political and economic structure of a state, by the level of economic development, and by the means of waging war, as well as by the geographical position of a country, and that of the country (countries) of the presumed enemy'. Beyond this, a doctrine is considered to have 'two closely interrelated and mutually conditioned aspects—the social-political and the military-technical'. The first, which 'embraces questions touching on the methodological, economic, social, and judicial basis for attaining the aims of a future war', is considered to be 'definitive and to possess the greatest stability in as much as it reflects a state's class essence and political goals, which remain relatively constant over a prolonged period of time'. As for the second or 'military-technical' aspect, it includes, 'in conformity with the social-political goals, the questions of the immediate structuring of the military, of the technical equipping and training of the armed forces, and of determining the forms and methods by which the armed forces will conduct operations and the war in general'.[71]

There is nothing novel in this definition. It repeats the essentials of the briefer entry on *voennaia doktrina* of the *Dictionary* of 1965, those of the more extensive article in the *Military Encyclopaedia* of 1977, and it is almost identical to the definitions given by ex-Chief of the General Staff V. V. Ogarkov in his pamphlets of 1982 and 1985.[72] But in 1982 Ogarkov had attempted to define even more precisely the basic questions to which a state's military doctrine should provide firm answers. In his view, these were:

1. How probable is a future war and who is the probably enemy?
2. What is the likely character of the war a nation and its armed forces may have to fight?
3. What goals and missions should be assigned to the armed forces in anticipation of this war, and what forces should the state possess in order to achieve its goals as stated?
4. On the basis of the answers to question 3, what programme of military structuring or building (*stroitel'stvo*) should the state undertake to prepare its forces and the nation for war?
5. If the war does break out, by what methods should it be waged?[73]

In 1982 the Marshal also added a rider that is of special interest here. He pointed out that the 'political and military-political views expressed in a doctrine are changeable. It is periodically refined', he continued, 'in connection with changes in the international situation, and with developments in society and in military affairs'.[74] Or as another writer had put it two decades earlier, the materialistic dialectic of history ensures that military doctrine 'is shaped, developed and changed in the course of the historical development of this or that state and its armed forces. The old military doctrine, which no longer accords with the aims and material-technical possibilities of the state, is replaced by a new one.'[75]

But if all military doctrines must change, that of the USSR and its socialist allies does so differently than did those that preceded it, or than do those of bourgeois states today. Ogarkov explains that at first, military doctrines were 'formed empirically, and not on the foundation of a deep analysis of the laws of war'. Then, as the 'social-political development of society and military affairs' progressed, and especially after the appearance of mass regular armies, military theoreticians began to examine the accumulated experience of military history in an attempt 'to work out and systematize the separate theses and principles for preparing countries and armies for wars, and the means of waging it'. 'Bourgeois military thought' had proven capable of noting 'general tendencies in the development of military affairs', but the Marshal believes that in most cases it has been 'incapable of uncovering and comprehending the objective laws of war, let alone of studying their impact on its conduct'. The reason, he concludes smugly, is that the class essence of bourgeois states means that internally, their military doctrines aimed primarily at preserving the position of their exploiting classes and externally, at 'liquidating, or weakening as much as possible, the world system of socialism, and economically at enslaving other states'.[76]

In contrast, when discussing Soviet doctrine *per se*, Ogarkov repeats the usual formula that it is 'a system of guiding principles and scientifically based views of the CPSU [Communist Party of the Soviet Union] and Soviet government on the essence, character and means of conducting wars that may be unleashed against the Soviet Union, as well as on military structuring and the preparation of the Armed Forces and country for the defeat of an aggressor'.[77] As another theoretician put it earlier, Soviet doctrine thus presents 'a unified system of views and goals, free from individual views and estimates'.[78] Also, as the *Military Encyclopaedic Dictionary* noted, Soviet writers believe that their doctrine is 'by its content . . . radically distinguished from the military doctrine of capitalist states'. This reflects the fact that its 'social-political side is based on the teachings of Marxist-Leninism and emerges from the character of the state and social structure of the USSR, from its Leninist peace-loving policies, from the deep-rooted interests of the Soviet people, and from the objective necessity for a collective defence of the lands of the Socialist Commonwealth from the aggressive aspirations of the forces of imperialism and reaction'.[79]

For Soviet readers, this distinction is more than verbiage. From it, two essential characteristics naturally emerge. In the first place, since socialist states are by nature 'peace-loving', their doctrines must by definition be 'defensive'. And secondly, since their analyses are conducted in conformity with Marxism-Leninism, they must be 'scientific'. Ogarkov thus insists that the content of Soviet military doctrine arises 'from the necessity of defending the Socialist Fatherland', and that it is firmly 'based on the laws and theses of historical and dialectical materialism, on the Marxist-Leninist teachings on war and the armies, and on the conclusions of Soviet military science'.[80]

VII.   Analysing the correlation of forces

Reviewing Western debates in 1980, Derek Leebaert noted that they had centred on the issue of whether or not Soviet doctrinal literature, along with the associated weapon programmes, reflected 'the conviction that nuclear war can be fought and won', or whether Soviet military thinkers had in fact accepted the reality of 'mutual assured destruction (MAD), conceived in essentially the same way as it once was articulated by American academic theorists'.[81] Although debate on this question continues, many now discern a shift of Soviet emphasis away from nuclear to conventional 'war-fighting', at least as far as the initial period of a European war is concerned. Meanwhile, a group of specialists, headed by John Erickson, also argue that the latter 1970s were 'marked by a generally gloomy assessment of the overall strategic situation and of the Soviet/Warsaw Pact capability to conduct the type of warfare the (Soviet) General Staff believes would be necessary to achieve their objectives in a future conflict'.[82]

To appreciate the procedures involved in any doctrinal assessment, or rather reassessment, we must understand the theoretical conception of 'correlation of forces', as well as the 'military' or 'strategic culture' that helps condition the approach of Soviet planners to the problems involved. This culture has emerged from the blending of classical Marxism, largely as transmitted through the often distorting lenses of Marxism-Leninism-Stalinism, with the historical experience of the Great Russians and the traditions of their Imperial Army. Thanks to these last, today's Soviet General Staff partakes of an intellectual heritage that embraces such great European military thinkers as Jomini and Clausewitz, and which somewhat surprisingly often reinforces, rather than contradicts, Marxist-Leninist attitudes and assumptions. Thus, the Great Russians' traditional distrust of foreigners and geographically conditioned sense of insecurity, which to others often seem to border on paranoia, have reinforced Communist concerns about 'capitalist' or 'imperialist' encirclement'.[83]

The resulting mentality often seems more suitable to a garrison state than to a superpower, but it suits full well a Miltonic vision in which the progressive forces of socialism are locked in mortal conflict with the reactionary ones of world imperialism. As Ogarkov explained in 1985, in today's 'dangerously explosive international circumstances', the 'ideology of the bourgeoisie attempts in every way possible to hide the aggressive character of the military doctrines of imperialism, while it constantly crudely falsifies the defensive essence and tendency of Soviet military doctrine'.[84] He insisted that the real danger to peace is not some Soviet military threat, but rather 'the aggressive nature of imperialism' and 'the basic contemporary military doctrines of the leading imperialist powers, and especially of the USA'. These doctrines, he explained, 'consist of sharply expressed anti-Soviet, anti-socialist and anti-democratic tendencies, of the strengthened militarization of the economy, and of direct preparations for a new world war with the aim of gaining world dominance'.[85]

Within this context, Soviet theoreticians obviously regard war as more than the occasional outbreak of armed hostilities between two governments that can be terminated by the legality of a peace treaty. With Clausewitz, they see it as 'the continuation of policy by other (that is, violent) means', and with Lenin they believe it occurs either between competing groups of the same international ruling class for a larger share of the spoils, or between diametrically opposed classes and/or social systems.[86] In today's world, this means that any future global confrontation must be the final clash between socialism and imperialism. Although Soviet theoreticians no longer regard an *armed* clash as inevitable, they do believe the danger is always present that their opponents, faced with the scientifically ordained victory of socialism, will try to stem the tides of history by force of arms. Therefore a responsible Soviet leadership must avoid 'adventuristic' behaviour that might provoke an onslaught against the Socialist motherland. Rather, like their usually prudent tsarist forbears, today's Soviet rulers must seek first and foremost to preserve the motherland, as well as to uphold the USSR's position as a superpower, which in turn often means promoting the cause of anti-imperialist liberation with cautious deliberation.[87]

In assessing the continuously shifting positions of the USSR and its leading imperialist opponents, Soviet planners analyse the overall 'correlation of forces' (*sootnoshenie sil*). Although often translated as the 'balance of power', this term entails a far more extensive set of calculations than is usually denoted by that traditional Western term. In its narrow military sense, it is defined simply as 'the objective review of the military power of the opposing sides which allows one to determine the degree of superiority one has over the other'. Yet it is much more than a 'bean count' of men and *matériel*, since it requires an evaluation of both 'the quantitative and the qualitative character-istics' of the forces involved.[88]

Even in the purely military sense, General Tiushkevich once pointed out, any evaluation of the 'correlation of forces of the contending sides' had to take into account a wide range of factors, including 'the general structure of their military organization, the individual branches of the armed forces and the combat arms, the degree of independence and the capability for efficient cooperation in accomplishing operational-strategic missions'. Other, less easily defined, factors are 'the organizational capabilities and the political, military-technical and operational-tactical training of command personnel', and 'moral-combat qualities' of the troops themselves, as well as such 'qualitat-ive features' of the active operational groupings of forces on each side as their 'organizational structure' and 'the character and degree of their control'. Beyond this, he noted that 'between the military might of a country or a coalition of states there exists a number of intervening links, the numerous rear service organs, the system of rail, motor vehicle, water and air transport, and the signal and transport communications'. And he warned that the high quality of such links 'is a most essential factor in maintaining a given correlation of forces'.[89]

More important for our purpose, such calculations are conceived as having relevance beyond the immediate battlefield. As Tiushkevich himself observed, they also 'are connected with many functions of strategic planning and the military-political leadership both during the prewar period as well as while a war is in progress'.[90] In such cases, an even wider range of factors must be considered. For 'the depth and degree of accuracy in the analysis of the correlation of forces of the sides', Tiushkevich tells us, 'are conditioned not only by the complex of strictly military-technical evaluations, but also by the aggregate of evaluations of economic, socio-political and spiritual factors which play an exceptionally important role'.[91] Among these are the stability of existing alliances, the probable behaviour of neutral states and the rise of new wartime alliances, the technological and economic potential of both sides, and so on. 'Special attention'. Tiushkevich therefore insists, 'should be directed to the character of the international ties of each of the sides, their affiliation with certain military-political groupings, the viability of these groupings, etc.'.[92]

In examining the correlation of forces on this international scale, another Soviet writer cautions that the consideration of 'material factors' is insufficient. There are others which, although they are so 'inseparably linked' to the material factors as to be difficult to treat in isolation, none the less 'do not easily lend themselves to a quantitative calculation'. Even so, they remain vitally important for 'the development of international relations and the balance of world forces'. In addition, 'the international arena has its own type of "wandering values" [e.g., the unpredictable behaviour of nations like Communist China in a general war], which in each concrete case can significantly influence the outcome of events'. So an accurate assessment at this level is even more difficult than in the military sphere.[93]

One other factor—the technological—deserves particular emphasis here. When dealing with the issues of 'military-technical' preparedness and superiority, Soviet writers recall Lenin's dictum that in war, 'he will come out on top who has the greatest technology, organization, and discipline, and the best machines'.[94] They interpret this as meaning 'that superiority over the enemy based on higher technology can bring victory only to those armed forces which are distinguished by the greatest discipline and are best organized'.[95] Even so, the state of technology *per se* must be a major consideration in evaluating the correlation of forces in any given period. As the writer just quoted recognizes, 'military-technical progress invariably leads to a growth in the amount of power and the supply of technical equipment available to the armed forces, increasing thereby their fighting power'. He adds that the 'economic, scientific and engineering-technical aspects are now so great that a high level of training and creative ability of the scientific-technical cadres and workers of industry has become a most important condition for success in such a conflict'.[96]

VIII.   A new revolution in military affairs?

With these strictures in mind, let us return to the reassessment of the correlation of forces conducted by the General Staff in the late 1970s, to its subsequent impact on military doctrine in general, and to its implications for Soviet policy on strategic defence and space.

One major concern was the utility of nuclear, and hence of strategic nuclear weapons. Recognizing the *de facto* nuclear stalemate, the political and military élite obviously saw the need to review the theories adopted in the late 1950s/early 1960s. Then, Soviet military thinkers had concluded that the advent of intercontinental ballistic missiles (ICBMs) with nuclear warheads had ushered in a second 'scientific-technical revolution in military affairs' (the first being heralded by Frunze and later confirmed by the introduction of mechanization and armour during the 1920s–1930s).[97] The immediate result was the creation of the Strategic Rocket Forces (SRF) under Nikita Khrushchev, which displaced the Ground Forces (or army proper) as the senior service in traditional protocol. Further, according to how naval Captain V. Kulakov put it, now 'Soviet military doctrine established the principle of the decisive role of the Strategic Rocket Forces'.[98] The bible for military men of this period, and a text still quoted by many Western analysts, was Sokolovskii's *Military Strategy*, which appeared in three editions during the 1960s. This taught that a future war almost inevitably would be nuclear and unlimited from the first, and that the

SRF would bear the brunt of Soviet offensive operations. Meanwhile, an extensive active PVO system, along with an expanded civil defence network, would seek to limit the effectiveness of enemy strikes against the Soviet homeland.[99]

This doctrinal context spawned the missions of PKO and PRO, which then became the responsibility of the existing strategic air defence forces (PVO). In Moscow's view at least, the 'missile arms race, started by the U.S. in the 1960s, forced the USSR to face the necessity of creating anti-missile defences. They became an important factor in disrupting the imperialists' plans for a surprise rocket strike. . . '. Interestingly enough, and somewhat ironically in view of US claims concerning SDI, this same writer (S. A. Tiushkevich) quotes A. N. Kosygin's assurance to foreign journalists that 'this system is not a means of aggression or attack, but it is a means of defense against an attack . . .'.[100]

Adoption of this doctrine does not mean that the Soviet leaders were blind to the disastrous nature of any future nuclear conflict, that they intended to unleash one, or that they would not be happy to find a conventional alternative to what could only be a catastrophic event in world history. Rather, the doctrine codified in Sokolovskii reflected their perception and fears that world war remained a real possibility, and that if such a conflict came, it was inconceivable without an all-out nuclear exchange. They themselves undoubtedly were 'deterred' by the West's policy of 'mutually assured destruction' (MAD). But, in itself, this stance did not suit the Soviet leaders' own traditional military prejudices, which sought to ensure the motherland's total security, not hold her hostage.[101] Nor did MAD do much to assuage inbred Marxist-Leninist suspicions that the imperialists, if they thought there was the slightest chance of defeating the forces of socialism and surviving themselves, might not be tempted to gamble on 'a cosmic roll of the dice'. Throughout the 1960s and 1970s, Moscow, therefore, trained its forces for war-fighting roles in both nuclear and non-nuclear environments, continued to promote extensive programmes of damage limitation through active and passive strategic defence, and trusted that readiness to wage a nuclear struggle would deter even the most crazed 'imperialist adventurist'.[102]

Many Western politicians and strategists meanwhile spoke of 'educating' Moscow into accepting the premises of mutual deterrence based on MAD. These held that the numbers, survivability and general destructiveness of existing nuclear stockpiles made a disarming strike impossible for either side, so that both therefore would suffer 'unacceptable' levels of damage. All the same, the Soviet planners' continuing interest in damage limitation and war-fighting indicated to many in the West that Moscow still believed nuclear weapons had military utility, and that a nuclear war could be fought and 'won'.[103] However, signs that Moscow too recognized the reality of a nuclear stalemate, and that official policy might be changing, began to emerge tentatively in the late 1970s.

Indeed, Soviet planners' attitudes towards nuclear warfare seem to have begun shifting as early as the late 1960s. On the one hand, the possibility of achieving strategic-nuclear parity with the United States raised the practical problems of just how they would wage a nuclear struggle and still preserve the motherland from catastrophic destruction, especially since their existing strategic defence programmes promised only partial effectiveness at best. As early as 1965 an article in *Pravda* warned that in such a conflict 'the destruction would be so great that this would not speed up the transition to socialism but, on the contrary, would throw mankind a long way back'.[104] Meanwhile, the ongoing rearmament of West Germany in the 1960s, and poor showing of the Group of Soviet Forces in East Germany during surprise exercises in May 1972, refocused the military's, and especially Chief of the General Staff V. G. Kulikov's, attention on conventional issues.[105] Such concerns helped lay the groundwork for the doctrinal revision of the late 1970s. In retrospect, the ABM Treaty of 1972 also appears as evidence of Soviet analysts' increasing gloom about the prospects of developing a reliable strategic defence. But, for the moment, such doubts remained buried in the massive literature devoted to the accepted policies of achieving deterrence through a capability for waging a nuclear war.[106]

The doctrinal re-evaluation as such had begun before Kulikov left the post of Chief of the General Staff. In May 1976 he announced that, thanks to the growing gap between theory and practice, Soviet military policy badly needed a thorough review and complete overhaul. In particular, at a time when many military writers had been concentrating on the implications of the nuclear-missile weaponry brought by this century's second 'scientific-technical revolution in military affairs', Kulikov insisted that they had failed to keep abreast of qualitative improvements in the conventional field. The ground forces, he argued, needed new combined-arms methods at the tactical and operational levels so as to reap the full benefit from improved armaments; troop control must be improved; and so on. Overall, he demonstrated that he himself fully understood the changing conditions of the modern battlefield, but charged his subordinates with having failed to appreciate the 'objective reality'.[107]

Although initially this hardly seemed to signal the beginning of anything as fundamental as a new or third 'revolution in military affairs', the doctrinal reassessment gained momentum after Ogarkov replaced Kulikov in 1977. According to Erickson and his colleagues, at that time there 'seems to have been a shift in Soviet military doctrine which resulted from the rather morbid view which, to judge from their writings, had seized the Soviet military mind and mood'. They see Ogarkov himself, 'a military overlord of some magnitude', as being a central figure, date the shift of 'mind and mood' from his appointment, and argue that the new 'generally gloomy *Soviet view of the strategic environment*' became especially evident in his writings from 1981–82 onwards.[108] Or, as an informed US analyst puts it, since 1977 his influence has been such that he 'clearly emerges as the sole contributor of innovations in Soviet military doctrine, and as the vanguard of the new revolution in Soviet military affairs'.[109]

As for the results of this strategic review, Erickson's group argues persuas-

ively that it brought 'less concern with power projection and greater attentive-
ness . . . to the structure and deployment of forces which will expand the
defensive perimeters of the Soviet Union to meet the threat from whatever
direction it may come'.[110] The main themes of Soviet military thought that
explain this shift include: (a) a recognition that nuclear war is not inevitable,
and that in any case, despite the investments lavished on strategic defence
programmes, the USSR cannot be made invulnerable to nuclear attack; (b) a
conviction that in time, the Soviet Union can still gain its strategic objectives
without having recourse to nuclear weapons, that it therefore has an interest in
preserving the stability of the existing strategic environment, and that the
primary strategic aim is to prevent the outbreak of major hostilities; (c) a belief
that if this last effort fails, the military are responsible for ensuring that the
USSR can gain its objectives by conventional means as quickly as possible and,
in this manner, prevent the West from having recourse to the nuclear option;
(d) a recognition that *time* therefore is crucial in all operations, and that the
command and control procedures and entities must be upgraded accordingly;
and (e) a determination to prepare the Soviet Union to wage a protracted
conflict, be it nuclear or conventional, should this prove necessary.[111]

The suggestion that recent doctrinal and organizational changes have
heralded the 'third revolution' in Soviet military affairs comes from Ogarkov
himself, and in the West from General William Odom, one of the Reagan
Administration's truly perceptive observers of the Soviet military scene. The
latter points to the restructuring of the peacetime composition of the five
branches of the Soviet Armed Forces (especially of the PVO and VVS), and of
the upper chain of wartime command (by the creation of theatre commands
between the front level and general headquarters), as evidence of this revolution. These developments have been well documented in the West and need no
further discussion here. Even so, we should stress that the merging of the SAM
assets of the PVO and ground forces, as well as the assignation of the majority
of the PVO's multi-purpose fighters to the VVS, did signal a marked shift in
military policy. By these measures, Soviet planners may have increased the
PVO's SAM capability against low-level targets. But they simultaneously de-
emphasized the search for a leak-proof defence against US strategic systems in
general, and upgraded the capabilities of the VVS's Frontal Aviation to win air
superiority over a conventional battlefield.[112] Beyond this, the recent doctrinal
changes also reflect Moscow's recognition of the military utility and possibilities of such technologies as micro-circuitry, directed-energy beams and lasers,
and genetic engineering. But most important of all is the fact that the new
revolution appears to confirm the Soviet military's strong shift towards a policy
of waging any future conflict with new high-technology, conventional
weaponry.[113] And as another analyst notes, 'a review of Ogarkov's writings
indicates that he has long been a prophet of this revolution'.[114]

IX.   The 'Tula line'

In the political literature, indications of changing views paralleled the *de facto* revision of military doctrine just described. Yet as Lambeth points out, this was not immediately clear to Western observers. Instead, the emergence of the new political 'line' coincided with 'an abrupt decline in significant public writing on military doctrine that appears too closely matched . . . to be coincidental', and 'the sort of public disclosure on nuclear strategy', such as that found in the 1960s and early 1970s, 'virtually vanished from the pages of *Krasnaia zvezda* and other military periodicals'. While he admits this might simply reflect a pause in military-Party debates thanks to the armed forces' satisfaction with their status, organization and share of resources, he suspects there are other reasons.[115] And indeed, evidence surfaced during Brezhnev's last years of continuing argument that some interpreted as signalling *increased debate*, along with an enlarged role in policy-making for the military in general, and for Ogarkov personally.[116]

Although vastly exaggerated in many Western accounts, such disagreements still might explain an absence of public discussion. In fact, Lambeth himself suspects 'an indefinite moratorium may have been imposed on any open military commentary that does not show seemly obeisance to the current propaganda line', perhaps as a means of depriving vigilant US critics of ammunition for rebutting the sincerity of Moscow's newly expressed intentions.[117] Yet it seems equally arguable that the absence of public commentary simply reflected the fact that the internal revision of the new doctrine remained incomplete, and that its public exposition therefore had to wait. In the end, it seems that the fully revised, new military doctrine, with its reduced emphasis on the military utility of nuclear weaponry, has begun merging openly, unequivocally and explicitly with the Party's revamped political line only in the early to mid-1980s.[118]

In retrospect, the first indication of real doctrinal change was the ABM Treaty and its implicit renunciation of the precept that each offensive system would inevitably spawn a defensive one of equal effectiveness. But the first clear suggestion of an unambiguous shift in the political line came in General Secretary L. I. Brezhnev's speech at Tula in January 1977. Then he openly declared that the USSR accepted strategic parity with the United States, was not pursuing strategic superiority, and that in the near future at least, neither side could expect to achieve a 'first-strike' capability. Along with the usual attacks on 'the aggressive forces of imperialism', he also stated that the Soviet Union's first aim must be to avoid any nuclear conflict, disavowed Soviet military planning for pre-emption, warned that the use of nuclear weapons could not be controlled, laid the basis for a policy of 'no first use', and asserted his belief that such a struggle could have no victors.[119]

The full implications of this speech were not initially realized in the West. In part this was because other Soviet officials and military leaders, like Ogarkov himself in 1978, still repeated the now time-honoured formula that the readiness and power of their strategic forces guaranteed 'an immediate and annihilating retaliation to any aggressor'.[120] Even so, the influence of what has become known as the 'Tula line' is evident in Ogarkov's rejection of the possibility of superiority, his lauding of the existing parity in strategic armaments, and in other statements of his article 'Military Strategy' in the *Soviet Military Encyclopedia* of 1979.[121] Some Western analysts none the less still rejected it as being a propaganda ploy at best, or a subtle piece of *disinformatsiia* ('disinformation') at worst, and charged that as long as the Soviets recognized wars, nuclear included, as a mere 'continuation of policy', their other protestations remained a charade.[122]

Also in this regard, there were signs of change that again dated from the mid-1960s. Then General N. A. Talenskii, among others, had been severely criticized for rejecting nuclear conflict as a means of gaining political ends.[123] Interestingly enough, by 1973 one of Talenskii's earlier critics—Colonel E. Rybkin—also openly stated that 'a total nuclear war is not acceptable as a means of achieving a political goal'.[124] Again, in mid-1980 an article in *Kommunist* noted that nuclear war was no longer a rational means of policy since 'the potential of a retaliatory strike, which would crash down on any aggressor, deprives this choice of any rationality'.[125] But a really authoritative sign of doctrinal revision came only on 22 April 1981. Then, speaking as Brezhnev's presumed heir and the Party's chief propagandist, and from the podium of Lenin's tomb, Konstantin Chernenko explicitly rejected notions that a nuclear war was like any other war, or that a nuclear conflict could be fought in the *rational* 'pursuit of policy by other, that is, violent means'.[126] Once again, subsequent statements by other leading officials and officers generally remained more ambiguous, but it still was obvious that earlier views on nuclear weapons were reappraised.[127]

By this time, military spokesmen too were openly rejecting Sokolovskii's significance for the present era. 'To arrive at a correct evaluation of our doctrine today', M. A. Mil'shteyn, a retired general on the staff of the USA–Canada Institute, said in 1980, 'you must not rely on Sokolovskii's book, but on those quite unambiguous Soviet documents and statements that have appeared in recent years.'[128] While analysts like Lambeth remained sceptical of such claims, these received authoritative confirmation in early 1985. Then a new book appeared on M. V. Frunze. Its author is the noted military historian and theorist, Colonel General M. A. Gareev, who is now a Deputy Chief of the General Staff. His volume, which Odom believes 'can be taken as representing the present official line of military doctrine',[129] presents an extensive critique of Sokolovskii. Gareev both reasserts the contemporary importance of a number of pre-nuclear (that is, conventional) aspects of the 'military art', and simultaneously dismisses Sokolovskii's major arguments as now being obsolete, even if—'given the appearance of nuclear-missile weapons'—they had been valid in their day.[130]

X. Doctrine according to Marshal Ogarkov

As noted, the ongoing revision has been especially evident in the writings of
Ogarkov himself. While he did not immediately embrace Chernenko's rewrit-
ing of the dictum of Clausewitz and Lenin, neither did he refute it in his booklet
of 1982.[131] Further, in 'his writings from 1971–85, in fact, Ogarkov has
increasingly contrasted the stability of *conventional* warfare with the innate
instabilty of nuclear'.[132] In his recent works, both immediately before and since
his sudden transfer from the post of Chief of the General Staff in September
1984, he has stressed three interrelated themes: (*a*) the growing uselessness of
nuclear weaponry; (*b*) the qualitatively new destructive capabilities and usefulness in battle of high-tech conventional systems, along with the possibility of
their even greater future utility thanks to technological advances; and (*c*) the
need to adapt the structure of the Soviet military establishment accordingly to
ensure that Soviet technology can meet the Western challenge in a high-tech
arms race and that the Soviet economy can provide the resulting systems as
demanded by the future battlefield.

   If a full exposition of the Marshal's discussion of these themes is unnecessary
here, a few points do deserve attention. Firstly, Ogarkov has never questioned
the need to maintain 'the approximate equality of nuclear arms between the
US and the USSR', a parity which guarantees the existing reality of MAD.[133]
He defined the preconditions for this doctrine clearly in his important interview
in *Krasnaia zvezda* of May 1984. Then he noted that the 'quantity and diversity
of nuclear weaponry' had made a successful first strike impossible. For, he
explained, an 'annihilating retaliatory strike on the aggressor, even with the
limited number of nuclear weapons left to the defender—that is, a strike that
inflicts unacceptable damage—is inevitable in present-day conditions'.[134]
Although subsequently he replaced this statement with 'a retaliation that
deprives the aggressor of the capability afterwards not only of waging war, but
[of conducting] any kind of serious operations whatsoever', the meaning
remains obvious.[135] When taken with his claim that no nuclear conflict could be
'limited',[136] it is no surprise that Ogarkov did at last openly embrace
Chernenko's revision of Clausewitz and Lenin. By 1985, the Marshal too
argued that 'it is criminal to look on nuclear war as a rational, almost legitimate
means of continuing politics', and warned that a global nuclear struggle would
'threaten the total annihilation of human civilization'.[137]

   Although Soviet thinkers accept that war is not inevitable, they still consider
it remains possible as long as the world remains divided among competing
social systems. In 1982 Ogarkov himself explained that the 'absence of a fatal
inevitability of war, however, does not mean the elimination of the possibility
of its occurring in the present era, the basic conflict of which is the conflict
between socialism and capitalism'.[138] Even so, he now argues that 'the
qualitatively new historical, social-political and military-technical preconditions and circumstances' of today's world are creating a situation in which war
can not only be 'neutralized', but the 'elimination of wars as a social-political

phenomenon, and above all else of world wars', also has become a practical, long-term possibility.[139] And before we dismiss his statement as pure utopianism intended for propagandistic ends, we must remember that for Ogarkov this conclusion is justified 'scientifically' in general by his stated conviction that the 'development of military affairs occurs in strict conformity with the demands of the objective laws of materialistic dialectics',[140] and in particular by 'the law of the negation of the negation—the birth of the new and the extinction of the old'.[141] This same dialectical 'law of negation' had been used by those like Talenskii who, in the mid-1960s, had argued that nuclear war had reached its dialectical limits, and hence 'negated' itself.[142] At that time Rybkin and others had rejected this thesis. Instead, they argued—also dialectically—that every weapon eventually spawned a defence, that nuclear weapons were not qualitatively different in this regard, and that therefore the possibility existed of 'developing and creating new means of waging war, means that can reliably parry an opponent's nuclear strikes'.[143]

At first glance it may seem that Ogarkov and Gareev are merely reasserting the position of Talenskii and his colleagues. But as the Marshal carefully pointed out in 1982, 'the development of each phenomenon of military affairs does not take place in an isolated manner and is not determined by the operation of some single dialectical law, but as a rule by the sum total of laws'.[144] It is this *whole complex* of dialectical forces, and not just that of negation, that he identified in 1982 as being responsible for the 'profound and in the full sense of the word revolutionary, upheaval that in our time is taking place in military affairs in connection with the creation of thermonuclear weapons, the rapid advances in electronics, and the development of new physical principles, as well as in connection with the extensive qualitative improvement of conventional means of armed combat'. Ogarkov then went on to warn that scientific and technological advances demand the renewal of major weapon systems every 10 to 12 years, so that the 'belated updating of views and a stagnation of the development and implementing of new methods of military structuring are fraught with serious consequences'.[145]

While these assertions caused considerable stir in the early 1980s, they seem essentially to be a logical outcome of both Brezhnev's 'Tula line', and of Ogarkov's own concerns over the past decade. In his speech of 1977, the Soviet General Secretary can be said to have introduced two new elements to Soviet military policy. First, 'military superiority' became defined as the capability of launching a first strike. And second, by declaring 'military superiority' to be an impossible goal for either side, Brezhnev was modifying the dialectical 'law of the unity and the struggle of opposites', at least as far as the dialectic of the development of armaments (i.e., defence vs. offence) is concerned.[146] As one Soviet commentator explained later, 'the historical dispute . . . between offensive and defensive weapons will, in the future, apparently tilt in favour of *offensive weapons*', which means that 'the very idea of achieving military superiority has become absurd'. For developments in the potential of nuclear armaments 'has led, in a certain sense, to their beginning to negate themselves'.[147]

In the meantime, Ogarkov had been calling attention to the fact that 'fundamentally new types of weapons and combat technology' would combine with other systems to 'become the decisive means of conducting armed combat' since at least 1971.[148] As Chief of the General Staff from 1977 to 1984, he had an opportunity to inject his views into the doctrine that guides Soviet military planners in recommending future weapon acquisitions and the manner of using them in a future conflict. His writings since 1982 have continually stressed this point, and its repetition suggests that it has had doctrinal impact— even if the Party is unwilling to devote the funds to military expenditure that the Marshal may have wished.[149] Thus in 1983 Ogarkov pointed out that 'the present state of science and technology is facilitating the creation of means of armed combat that are capable even in a non-nuclear war of rapidly destroying all life over enormous areas. This is especially so if one considers the types of weapons that are based on new physical principles which the future clearly holds'.[150]

In his interview of 1984, in what is perhaps the most authoritative, concise exposition of his views, Ogarkov again reiterated that 'the development of conventional means of destruction' was 'making many kinds of weapons global in significance'.[151] Again, in 1985 he warned that US research now sought to make 'conventional weapons approach nuclear ones in the terms of their combat characteristics and effectiveness'.[152] In other words, here Ogarkov suggests that the West too may have recognized the impossibility (or 'negation') of a nuclear war, and so was taking the appropriate steps to once again make the world safe for aggressive, conventional wars. As Lambeth rightly insists, Soviet strategists—given their belief in dialectical progression—cannot accept that peace based on the nuclear stalemate of MAD will be a *permanent* feature of the correlation of international forces, especially if other means of battle become available.[153] For this and other doctrinal reasons, they undoubtedly suspect their Western counterparts are seeking a way out of the nuclear *impasse* so as to make any conflict less of an Armageddon. It therefore seems safe to agree with Odom in concluding that they too have taken the appropriate steps to amend their own doctrine accordingly, and quite possibly—if Ogarkov's fears are taken at face value—along the lines they believe are being adopted by their potential opponents.

XI.   The new doctrine, strategic defence and space

Throughout the doctrinal discussions of Ogarkov and his colleagues, little or nothing is said about strategic defence programmes *per se*, or about the military uses of space. True, their spokesmen have repeatedly attacked foreign (read US) views on this last topic, but no attempt has been made to outline a Soviet doctrine on space warfare. Yet it is inconceivable that any reassessment of military doctrine should have ignored these topics or this potential new battlefield, and Soviet diplomats have been far from silent on the subject of US programmes. Their statements, along with the recent reorganization of the air forces and the revised definitions discussed above, may therefore shed light on Moscow's view of the military possibilities of the cosmos.

The practical implications of the reorganization of the PVO's SAM and air assets have been noted. As might be expected, parallel changes also occurred in the missions envisaged for PRO and PKO. These emerge from an examination of the semantics of the definitions outlined above. Here three things deserve attention:

1. Between 1976 (Ziman's book—see note 57) and 1978 (the *Soviet Military Encyclopaedia*—see note 65), space defence or PKO—unlike ABM or PRO—ceased to be a component of the Troops of Air Defence and was reduced to the status of a foreign concept. The date of this change is intriguing. It corresponds roughly to: (*a*) Ogarkov's appointment as Chief of the General Staff and the presumed acceleration of the process of doctrinal revision; and (*b*) hence to a reassertion of the priority given conventional and, largely, non-strategic, weapon systems. The fact of this second item is evident in data recently presented by Richard Kaufman, who points to a decline in the acquisition of costly strategic systems over this same period.[154] Given the 'lead times' involved in the production schedules of such armaments, the decisions behind such production cuts probably were taken somewhat earlier. None the less, space weaponry surely falls into the strategic category, and it can hardly be coincidental (or accidental) that a change in its conceptual status parallels changes in the status of strategic systems in general.

2. After 1978 PKO is clearly separated from PRO, with the latter retaining its place as a home-grown Soviet (i.e., not a 'foreign') concept. This is clear in both the formal definitions cited, and in Tiushkevich's study of 1978. While he gave implicit approval to the existing PRO system, he simultaneously assigned all intentions of basing weapons in space to the United States.[155] The implications of this distinction are that although Soviet military planners had no qualms about continuing BMD research under the ABM Treaty, they have refrained from tying this practically or doctrinally to space-borne systems. In this they differ radically from their US counterparts, who continue to consider space and ABM systems as interconnected parts of a single strategic whole, and who insist that Moscow does likewise. But just as official US assessments of Soviet capabilities for PRO and PKO may be greatly exaggerated, so it is quite possible that the Pentagon's portrayal of Moscow's space doctrine represents US fears and conceptions rather than the goals of Soviet planners.[156]

3. In practial terms, then, the Soviet distinction between PRO and PKO seems to be one of the mode of basing. In Moscow's eyes, the former seems to concern ground-based and defensive systems only, while PKO involves space-borne systems with possible offensive uses as well. True, US officials worry that Soviet ground-based missiles and lasers may have some ASAT capability. Even so, these systems do seem to have been developed primarily for BMD. But as with possible Soviet designs for the use of exotic weaponry in space, little or no hard evidence is available. Instead, we are left with the Pentagon's

unsubstantiated assumptions of possible Soviet intentions. And, as just suggested, these may tell us more about US perceptions than about concrete Soviet programmes. Indeed, as indicated below, it has only been since the US debate over SDI began in the early 1980s that Soviet spokesmen have *had* to follow Western analysts in lumping PRO with PKO in their comments on the President's plans for a space-borne 'peace shield'.

Of course, the Soviet leaders do fully support an aggressive programme of space research and exploration as a means of maintaining the USSR's prestige, and of reaping possible future economic benefits. They may also consider it a prudent strategic hedge against a future threat from the United States or other space nations. Yet they have consistently insisted that their programme, unlike that of the United States, is mainly civilian and 'peaceful' in intent, and have demanded that steps be taken to prevent 'militarization' of the cosmos. Indeed, this has been a recurring theme since the late 1960s when, interestingly enough, it appeared in discussions about US *land-based ABM* programmes.[157] More recently, Soviet spokesmen have underlined the alleged distinction between military and civilian applications in space in their comments on the newly established US Joint Space Command, and in the declared nature of their own space agencies. While they describe the former as having a broad authority that includes 'theoretical research and planning' and 'the direct use of military space systems', they insist their own institutions are involved in purely peaceful pursuits. Thus the Academy of Sciences Space Research Institute, headed by Academician Roald Sagdeev, centralizes and co-ordinates civil programmes, and the Academy's Intercosmos Council promotes 'international space co-operation'. The same civil aspect has been assumed by the new Main Directorate for the Development and Use of Space Technology for the National Economy and Scientific Research, better known as Glavkosmos SSSR, which was established in October 1985. According to its director, A. I. Dunaev, it too seeks only to further economic and scientific interests, as well as greater international co-operation.[158]

While still stressing its own peaceful intentions, Moscow has officially changed its definition of 'militarization of space'. Nicholas L. Johnson points out that, during the 1950s and 1960s, Soviet officials had insisted on lumping together all military space systems, whether they were active and offensive (i.e., ASATs), or passive (i.e., reconnaissance, navigation and so on). By the 1970s, however, the Soviet Union too had come to rely heavily on its own space-borne early warning, communications and navigation networks, and had accepted the existence of 'national means of verification' as part of the world after the Strategic Arms Limitation Talks (SALT). Since then, Soviet efforts to prevent 'militarization' have focused increasingly on the possible offensive uses of the Space Shuttle, on US plans for new ASAT systems, and finally, on the Joint Space Command and SDI.[159]

This distinction between active and passive space systems also began emerging in the late 1970s. It thus coincided with the ongoing doctrinal review and, perhaps equally important, with plans for testing the US Space Shuttle. Beginning with the first round of ASAT talks that opened in Helsinki in June 1978, Moscow's representatives repeatedly have raised the question of the Shuttle's possible anti-satellite role.[160] Soviet military men obviously were worried that the new US system might be directed against their own spacecraft, as well as a means of deploying new weapon systems for other purposes in the cosmos. In March 1980, one Soviet spokesman insisted in *Literaturnaia gazeta* that at least 25 per cent of the new vehicle's flights would be 'for purely military purposes'.[161] Such suspicions were subsequently fuelled by Western reports that up to one-third of the missions would fall into this category, and by the use of the Shuttle for classified missions.[162] So it is hardly surprising to find commentators like Colonel V. Gorenko insisting that the net result of experiments conducted by these US vehicles will be the development in the future 'of still more powerful means for propelling military payloads into space, and by the turn of the century—for the creation of a new generation of manned spacecraft . . . for direct armed combat'.[163]

Although the USSR has its own 'aerospace plane' programme, lower technological levels mean that it still is far outdistanced by that of the USA.[164] For this reason, renewed testing of the Soviets' own ASAT in 1976, and again in 1980, almost certainly represented their desire to bring Washington into serious negotiations that included the Shuttle in the first instance, and a wish to see these talks resumed in the second. It is inconceivable that they have much faith in their own outmoded system, but it may have appeared to have had diplomatic utility. If such was their reasoning, subsequent US reactions must have sorely disappointed the men in Moscow. Rather than negotiating an end to ASATs in general, Washington instead announced the development of its own, considerably more sophisticated system, and in 1983, the 'Star Wars' programme.[165]

During the early 1980s, Soviet charges about the 'militarization' of space came to focus on the possible stationing of weapons, and increasingly since 1982–83, of 'strike weapons' in space. This position is well expressed in a recent pamphlet on 'Star Wars'—*Zvezdnye voiny*. 'In practice', it notes, '. . . at the moment neither the USSR nor the USA has weapons in the cosmos. But both sides use satellites for communications and navigations, and satellites to give early warning of missile attacks, but they have no other weapons in the proper sense of that word.' That is to say, it explains, 'they create no threat of a direct attack in or from space, they do not "shoot" and they cannot kill'. Equally important, these satellite systems 'support strategic stability' by depriving either side of the possibility of launching a surprise nuclear strike.[166]

When bilateral ASAT talks with the USA remained stalled over inclusion of the Shuttle and other issues, Moscow turned to the United Nations. In October 1982 it presented the General Assembly's First Committee with a draft treaty 'On the Prohibition of the Stationing of Weapons of Any Kind in Outer Space', which was followed in 1983 by a 'Draft Treaty on the Prohibition of the Use of Force in Outer Space and from Outer Space Against the Earth'. Article 1 of this latter draft treaty would prohibit the 'use or threat of force in outer space, in air space, and on the earth, involving the use to that end of space objects in orbit around the earth, on celestial bodies, or stationed in outer space in any other manner as a means of destruction', as well as the threat 'in any other manner' *to* such space objects themselves.[167] Article 2 then called on signatories to pledge: (*a*) 'not to test or deploy, by placing in orbit around the earth, stationing on celestial bodies or in any other manner', any type of 'space-borne weapon for destroying objects on the earth, in air and outer space'; (*b*) 'not to use space objects' in orbit, and so on, 'in any other manner as a means of destroying any target on the earth, in air or outer space'; (*c*) 'not to destroy, damage or disrupt the normal functioning, or modify the flight trajectory of space objects of other States'; (*d*) 'not to develop and test' new ASAT systems, and to 'liquidate' those that already exist; and (*e*) 'not to test or use for military, including anti-satellite, purposes any manned spacecraft'.[168]

In August 1985, the Soviet representatives again officially presented their new formula, this time in a somewhat revised version, in documents that they submitted to the United Nations. These were a set of 'basic guidelines and principles' for the 'Peaceful Exploration of Outer Space Under Conditions of its Nonmilitarization', which were now specifically tied to halting 'plans and actions that aim at creating and developing space offensive weapons to destroy targets in space and from space, in the air, and on earth, including creating a wide-scale ABM system with space-based elements'.[169] In this manner, the Soviet concept of 'strike weapons' has become a central issue in international debates over the future of the cosmos.

XII.   The Soviet Union and SDI

These proposals, of course, must be judged within the context of SDI. On this issue, the line was set initially by Yuri Andropov on 27 March 1983, just four days after President Reagan's famous speech on 'Star Wars'. He told *Pravda* that although many might find Reagan's idea attractive, the facts were that US *'offensive forces will continue to be developed and upgraded at full tilt'* in an effort *'to acquire a first nuclear strike capability'*, and that SDI's missile defences were really aimed at disarming the USSR by 'rendering it incapable of dealing a retaliatory strike'. Andropov also insisted that when Soviet–US talks had begun on strategic arms, the two sides had 'agreed that there is an indissoluble interrelationship between strategic offensive and defensive weapons'. And he argued that it 'was not by chance' that they had signed the SALT I Treaty limiting offensive systems in the same year as the conclusion of the ABM Treaty (1972).[170]

Subsequent Soviet comments need not all be examined here. They have been usefully analysed by Mary C. Fitzgerald, and can be summarized as follows:

1. The Soviet leadership, as Andropov's comments indicate, have no

doubt that SDI is by nature offensive in nature. This is so, in their view, both because it aims at disarming the USSR and making it vulnerable to a first strike, and because the SDI weapon systems in themselves would have a capability against targets in space, and possibly against those on earth.

2.   They also regard SDI as a catalyst for a further strategic arms race, both in space and in terms of ballistic missiles, and predict that even if SDI systems prove technically feasible, new offensive missiles will inevitably be deployed with the capability of penetrating the 'peace shield'.

3.   Since SDI will upset strategic parity and fuel a new arms race, they brand it as essentially destabilizing.[171]

With regard to their own PKO and PRO programmes, Soviet spokesmen recently have made some interesting admissions. To begin with, in announcing a moratorium on their own ASAT testing in 1983, they *tacitly* admitted to that testing, and so to a military space programme. In 1985, General N. Chervov, the General Staff's representative at the Geneva arms talks, also admitted publicly that the USSR possessed an ASAT system of limited operational capability. More interesting still, he seemed to refer not to the co-orbital system described above, but to a direct ascent weapon like the US systems tested on Johnson and Kwajalein Islands in the 1960s. According to Chervov, testing 'against imaginary points outside the atmosphere' had begun in the late 1970s, and ended in 1982.[172] Mention of the co-orbital system was made at the end of 1985 by the Director of the Moscow Space Research Institute. He then admitted its testing between 1968 and 1982.[173] Meanwhile, other Soviet officials openly agreed that Soviet scientists too were engaged in research in the technologies that have become associated with SDI.[174]

At the same time, leading Soviet military figures continue to stress that they are not planning either an ABM break-out, or the deployment of their own SDI system. Defence Minister S. L. Sokolov recently insisted that his government 'is not developing space strike weapons, is not deploying a large-scale ABM defense system, and is not testing weapons for this purpose'.[175] In a similar vein, Chief of the General Staff S. F. Akhromeev has also assured the world that 'no preparation is taking place in the USSR for the creation of a territorial anti-missile system, and that applies also to one based on air defence means'. 'We have no programs', he continued, 'to develop space strike means, and no plans analogous to the American [ones].'[176]

At first sight, these statements might appear to contradict the other admissions just mentioned. Yet laboratory work is far from a firm decision to test and deploy applied systems, and both Soviet ASATs—if two systems do exist— represent outdated technologies. This makes them only of limited use as a bargaining chip, and little else. Official Soviet statements on space warfare therefore are very likely more than just propaganda or semantic sleights of hand. Rather, they appear to represent a logical extension of the new political line and associated military doctrine. In assessing this possibility, the following doctrinal principles must be borne constantly in mind: (*a*) that true military superiority with a first-strike capability are impossible goals for either side in the foreseeable future; (*b*) that, dialectically, throughout history the offensive seems eventually to have overcome the defensive; and (*c*) that since nuclear war is an impossible proposition, it is better to seek to curb the strategic impact of US technological superiority, and to ensure the nuclear parity on which successful deterrence depends, by arms control agreements (SALT I and especially, the ABM Treaty); and to concentrate instead on the conventional alternative.[177]

In this context, recent Soviet statements on space seem more credible. The paradox is that the Soviet Union and the United States have produced very different responses to the nuclear *impasse*. Ogarkov *et al.* have accepted the existing reality of MAD, at least as far as the foreseeable future is concerned, and turned to a conventional alternative alone. The Reagan Administration, on the other hand, is pursuing both that course *and* attempting a strategic end run by seeking a technological escape from the nuclear stalemate. In Soviet eyes, this last avenue can only lead to scrapping the ABM Treaty. And whether by the design of those who signed it in 1972 or not, the principles of this Treaty have become one of the foundations of the Soviet military's newly revised doctrine. As Marshal Sokolov—echoing Andropov—puts it, this pact was based on an agreement 'that an indissoluble interconnection exists between strategic offensive and defensive arms', so that only 'mutual restraint in the sphere of ABM systems can contain the arms race'.[178]

For this reason, Moscow argues that one side's attempt to create an extensive BMD system 'breaks this interconnection, destabilizes the strategic situation, and forces the other side to restore the situation'.[179] In other words, Soviet defence planners clearly see the ABM Treaty as a diplomatic alternative to an accelerated arms race, a race in which they undoubtedly recognize the advantages that superior technology gives the United States. Indeed, despite frequently expressed doubts to the contrary, they may actually fear that the USA may just succeed in developing a workable SDI. But even if the 'peace shield' remains as the 'impossible dream', its pursuit will entail an expensive extension of the existing arms race to space, a major effort to increase the Soviet strategic arsenal still further, and the risk that technological spin-offs from the US programme may increase the West's edge on the conventional battlefield as well. At a time when the USSR's economy already is burdened by heavy defence expenditures, such eventualities can be far from welcome.[180] That US officials—despite their frequent warnings of Soviet technological achievement—are fully aware of their own prowess, and of the validity of Moscow's fears, has recently become abundantly clear. Thus, General James A. Abrahamson and other officials have painted a picture of, as the *Washington Post* describes it, 'decades of competition with the Soviet Union, as the traditional arms race is extended to a costly new game of measures and counter-measures in space'.[181]

Some Soviet spokesmen and Western analysts have suggested that SDI may hold hidden benefits for the USSR. In one sense, it would create a competition in which only the Soviet Union and the United States could at present engage, and thus ensure the Soviet Union's position as one of the two superpowers. Further, the stationing of weapons in space, even at great expense, would at least provide the USSR with its own forward bases, now space-borne, that would match those the USA maintains around the Soviet periphery. In the view of one Soviet writer, space forces would make the Soviet Union a truly global political and military presence by permitting it 'to be present at all times and places, on an equal basis with the USA, where we are now practically absent'. Militarily, they would increase US vulnerability in general; could decrease substantially Soviet naval inferiority, in particular by leaving all Western naval forces open to strikes from the cosmos; and overall; ensure that 'the remaining global [US] advantages come to an end'.[182] And internally, as Jerry Hough has observed, Star Wars—along with the spectre of China's nuclear arsenal—could provide the Soviet military with distant future threats that would justify an immediate diversion of substantial funds into precisely those areas of high technology that they perceive are needed by both their conventional forces and the revamped Soviet economic system necessary to ensure victory in a future conventional war.[183]

In spite of such possible benefits, the prevailing view in Moscow still seems to be that SDI will promote precisely that strategic arms race—which they believe, dialectically, can change very little in the long run—that the revised military doctrine has rejected, and against which economic considerations would argue. But if forced to do so, the Soviet Government will undoubtedly pick up the gauntlet, demand that its citizens tighten their belts and that its soldiers again rewrite their doctrine to meet the changed conditions. As Sayre Stevens notes, faced with an ongoing US programme, the 'Soviets will do what they have done in the past: spend money and allocate scarce resources to the extent that they are required by the military demands they find facing them'.[184] And if forced to do so, Sokolov and other Soviet leaders have made it clear that the necessary steps will be taken, certainly in the form of an increased and more efficient ICBM force, and eventually by the deployment of their own defensive and offensive space-borne system as well.[185] National prestige might force the deployment of a Soviet SDI in the future; Soviet spokesmen suggest that they would expect such a system, along with the appropriate doctrine for its use, to be available by the year 2000. In the interim, they believe existing technology will permit them to develop sufficient numbers of efficient missiles to overwhelm any US defences, and 'low-tech' space systems that will further degrade the space-borne elements of an eventual SDI complex.[186]

But this probably is *not* the preferred option. At the moment, the Soviet leaders seem to accept Stevens's vision of a world with Star Wars, in the years 2000 through 2010, as being one 'in which both the United States and the Soviet Union are actively engaged in the upgrading of both offensive and defensive weapon systems'.[187] They will not, of course, publicly admit that their technology does not allow them to compete in other than terms of complete equality.[188] Even so, they must recognize fully their serious technological handicaps and the likely strategic and economic impact of an SDI-type programme, let alone of a new missile race, on their plans for revitalizing an already sluggish economy. Yet by refusing to follow the US lead, they also take the risk that the ensuing technology race will leave the United States with an even greater edge, the implications of which would hardly be comforting. In SDI, therefore, Washington undoubtedly has a bargaining chip that might wring great concessions from Moscow, if it indeed is a chip the present administration is willing to lay upon the table. From the opposite perspective, SDI might also be considered to be a programme that could force the Soviets to 'spend themselves into the ground'. But although this result seems unlikely in the extreme, the Reagan Administration seems determined to avoid any attempt to use SDI as a means of forcing Moscow into arms agreements in other areas. As a result, strategic defence may again receive unenthusiastic but real support from a Soviet leadership that is determined to maintain strategic parity, whatever the domestic costs, and the Soviet military may find itself in the midst of another doctrinal review.

Notes and references

1 Lockwood, J. S., *The Soviet View of U.S. Strategic Doctrine: Implications for Decision Making* (Transaction Books: New Brunswick, NJ, 1985), pp. 182–3. For a typical worried analysis of the PVO and its place in Soviet strategic defence, see Deane, M. J., *Strategic Defence in Soviet Strategy*, (Advanced International Studies Institute: Washington, DC, 1980), pp. 77–84.

2 Keegan, Jr, G. J., 'Forward', in Baker, D., *The Shape of Wars to Come: The Hidden Facts Behind the Arms Race in Space* (Patrick Stephens: Cambridge, UK, 1981), p. 6.

3 Kahn, H., 'Introduction', in Stine, G. H., *Confrontation in Space* (Prentice-Hall: Englewood Cliffs, NJ, 1981), p. ix.

4 Semeiko, L., 'The US—the source of military danger', *Krasnaia zvezda*, (18 Sep. 1981), p. 3.

5 Stares, P. B., *The Militarization of Space: U.S. Policy, 1945–1984* (Cornell University Press: Ithaca, NY, 1985), p. 148.

6 Wolfe, T. W., *Soviet Strategy at the Crossroads* (Harvard University Press: Cambridge, MA, 1964), pp. 204–5.

7 See the comments in Scott, W. F., 'The Soviets and strategic defense', *Air Force Magazine*, vol. 69, no. 3 (Mar. 1986), pp. 42–3, and such representative articles as Migunov, L., 'Combat with ballistic missiles', *Tekhnika i vooruzhenie* (Technology and Armaments), no. 6 (June 1982); Dvoretskii, A., 'Space in the plans of the Pentagon', *Vestnik protivovozdushnoi oborony*, (The Air Defence Herald), no. 7 (July 1983); Volkogonov, D., 'The strategy of adventurism', *Zarubezhnoe voennoe obozrenie* (Foreign Military Review), no. 8 (May 1984).

8 Scott (note 7), p. 45.

9 Scott (note 7), p. 45.

10 US Departments of Defense and State, *Soviet Strategic Defense Programs* (US Government Printing Office: Washington, DC, 1985), p. 17. Also see the estimates in International Institute for Strategic Studies (IISS), *The Military Balance, 1985–1986*, (IISS: London, 1985), p. 23.

11 US Central Intelligence Agency, National Foreign Assessment Center, *Soviet and US Defense Activities, 1970–79: A Dollar Cost Comparison,* (Washington, DC, Jan. 1980), pp. 7–9, and table 2 in Jones, D. R., 'Air defense forces', *Soviet Armed Forces Review Annual* (hereinafter referred to as SAFRA), 1981, Vol. 5, ed. D. J. Jones (Academic International Press: Gulf Breeze, FL, 1981), p. 115.

12 US Department of Defense, *Soviet Military Power,* 4th ed., (US Government Printing Office: Washington, DC, Apr. 1985), p. 48.

13 Breighner, R. G., 'Air defence forces', SAFRA, 1983–1984, Vol. 8 (Academic International Press: Gulf Breeze, FL, 1984), p. 128.

14 Breighner (note 13), pp. 128–31; Deane (note 1), pp. 104–6; and US Departments of Defense and State (note 10), pp. 12–16. On the Soviet BMD programme, also see Yost, D. S., 'Soviet Ballistic Missile Defense and NATO', *NATO Review,* vol. 33, no. 5 (Oct. 1985), pp. 10–18, and Stevens, S., The Soviet BMD Programme', *Ballistic Missile Defense,* Carter, A. B. and Schwartz, D. N. (eds) (Brookings Institution: Washington, DC, 1984), pp. 182–220. Also Jacobsen (note 188).

15 US Departments of Defense and State (note 10), pp. 12–16.

16 Breighner (note 13), p. 129.

17 Caption to illustration in Yost (note 14), p. 11.

18 Boffey, P. M., '"Star Wars" and mankind: consequences for future', *New York Times,* 8 Mar. 1985, p. A14.

19 Smith, H., 'Nitze details U.S. charges Soviet has own "Star Wars"', *New York Times,* 12 July 1985, p. 5.

20 Boyd, G. M., 'President accuses Soviet over arms', *New York Times,* 13 Oct. 1985, p. A16.

21 Meyer, S. M., 'Soviet strategic programmes and the US SDI', *Survival,* vol. 27, no. 6 (Nov.–Dec. 1985), p. 274.

22 Breighner (note 13), p. 129. Also see comments in Scott (note 7), p. 43, and Yost (note 14), p. 11.

23 Collins, J. M., *U.S.–Soviet Military Balance, 1980–1985,* (Pergamon/Brassey's: New York, 1985).

24 Collins (note 23), p. 36.

25 Kassel, S. *Soviet Research on Crystal Channelling of Charged Particle Beams,* Report No. R–3224–ARPA; (Rand Corporation: Santa Monica, CA, Mar. 1985), pp. 27–8.

26 Kassel, S., *Soviet Free-Electron Laser Research,* Report No. R–3259–ARPA; (Rand Corporation: Santa Monica, CA, May 1985), pp. 38–41; Mohr, C., '"Star Wars" in strategy: the Soviet response', *New York Times,* 17 Dec. 1985, p. 5.

27 US Departments of Defense and State (note 10), p. 16.

28 Collins (note 23), pp. 36–7. Also see the comments and assessments of Meyer (note 21), pp. 275–6, and Schauer, W. H., 'Space Program', SAFRA, 1984–1985, Vol. 9 (Academic International Press: Gulf Breeze, FL, 1985), pp. 222–4.

29 On these problems see Parnas, D. L., 'Software aspects of strategic defence systems', *American Scientist,* vol. 73 (Sep.–Oct. 1985), pp. 432–40; Rensberger, B., 'The software is too hard', *Washington Post,* National Weekly Edition, 11 Nov. 1985, pp. 10–11; and Lin, H., 'The development of software for Ballistic-Missile Defense', *Scientific American,* vol. 253, no. 6 (Dec. 1985), pp. 32–9.

30 Collins (note 23), pp. 38–40.

31 On the dilemma created for Soviet planners by the ALCM see Jones, D. L., 'National air defense forces', SAFRA, 1978, Vol. 2, pp. 109–11; 1979, Vol. 3, pp.

39–40; and 1980, Vol. 4, pp. 147–61; and SAFRA (note 11), Vol. 5, pp. 89–92, 111–12, and 1982, Vol. 6, pp. 170–7 (Academic International Press: Gulf Breeze, FL, 1978, 1979, 1980, 1981 and 1982, respectively). Also see MacDonald, G., Ruina, J. and Balaschak, M., 'Soviet strategic air defense', *Cruise Missiles: Technology, Strategy, Politics*, ed. R. K. Betts (Brookings Institution: Washington, DC, 1981), pp. 53–82.

32 MacDonald, Ruina and Balaschak (note 31), p. 70.

33 Bennett, B. and Foster, J., 'Strategic retaliation against the Soviet homeland', in Betts (note 31), p. 146.

34 SAFRA (note 31), Vol. 4, pp. 148–9; MacDonald, Ruina and Balaschak (note 31), p. 72.

35 IISS (note 10), p. 23.

36 Jones, D. R., 'The military year in review, 1982–1983', SAFRA, 1982–1983, Vol. 7 (Academic International Press: Gulf Breeze, FL, 1983), pp. 26–8; MacDonald, Ruina and Balaschak (note 31), pp. 66–9.

37 IISS (note 10), p. 23. In a paper read to the IUS (Inter-University Seminar) Conference on Air Defense in Calgary, 18 April 1986, A. Karp noted that this delay, which was probably due to technological problems, meant the full deployment of the Il–76 would take at least 15 to 20 years.

38 IISS (note 10), p. 23.

39 SAFRA (note 31), Vol. 6, pp. 170–7.

40 Stevens (note 14), pp. 194–5, 211–13; SAFRA (note 31), Vol. 6, pp. 178–9.

41 Deane (note 1), pp. 112–13.

42 Stevens (note 14), pp. 212–14.

43 Stevens (note 14), pp. 217–18.

44 US Department of Defense (note 12), p. 56; US Congress, Office of Technology Assessment, *Strategic Defenses: Ballistic Missile Defense Technologies, Anti-Satellite Weapons, Countermeasures, and Arms Control. Two Reports*, (Princeton University Press: Princeton, NJ, 1985), pp. 5–6; SAFRA (note 11), Vol. 5, pp. 102–3; and Schauer, W. H., 'Space program', in SAFRA (note 11), Vol. 5, p. 207.

45 Schauer (note 44), pp. 267–8; Stares (note 14), pp. 112ff.

46 SAFRA (note 11), Vol. 5, p. 102; Schauer (note 44), Vol. 6, pp. 268–9.

47 Quoted in SAFRA (note 31), Vol. 2, p. 104.

48 Deane (note 1), pp. 104–5; SAFRA (note 11), Vol. 5, pp. 102–3.

49 Meyer (note 21), p. 276.

50 SAFRA (note 11), Vol. 5, p. 102; Meyer (note 21), p. 276.

51 Stares (note 14), pp. 144–5; SAFRA (note 31), Vol. 2, p. 104.

52 SAFRA (note 11), p. 102. As Bill Keller recently pointed out in his article, 'Imperfect science, important conclusions', *New York Times*, 28 July 1985, p. E–5. US intelligence estimates of Soviet weapon capabilities are often based on inadequate data and often reflect US political considerations as well. This point is documented in impressive detail in Gervasi, T., *The Myth of Soviet Military Superiority* (Harper and Row: Cambridge, UK, 1986).

53 Radzievskii, A. J. (ed.), *Slovar' osnovnykh voennykh terminov* (Dictionary of Basic Military Terms) (*Voenizdat*: Moscow, 1965), pp. 182–4.

54 Skinbeda, P. I. (ed.), *Tolkovyi slovar' voennykh terminov* (Dictionary of Military Terms) (*Voenizdat*: Moscow, 1966), pp. 348–9.

55 Radzievskii (note 53), p. 114.

56 Radzievskii (note 53), pp. 50–1.

57 Ziman, G. V. (ed.), *Razvitie protivovozdushnoi oborony* (Development of Air Defence) (*Voenizdat*: Moscow, 1976), p. 192. On these developments in general, see Stares (note 5), pp. 135–45, and SAFRA (note 31), Vol. 2, pp. 102–5.

58 Tiushkevich, S. A. *et al.*, *Sovetskie Vooruzhennye sily. Istoriia stroitel'stva* (Soviet Armed Forces: A History of their Development) (*Voenizdat*: Moscow, 1978), p. 457.

59 SAFRA (note 31), Vol. 2, p. 105.

60 Stares (note 5), p. 136.

61 Jones, A. M., 'Implications of arms control agreements and negotiations for space-based BMD lasers', *Laser Weapons in Space: Policy and Doctrine*, ed. K. B. Payne (Westview Press: Boulder, CO, 1983), p. 85.

62 *Disarmament: The Main Soviet Proposals* (*Novosti*: Moscow, 1983), p. 16; USSR Ministry of Defence, *Whence the Threat to Peace*, 3rd edn (Military Publishing House: Moscow, 1984), p. 37.

63 Jones (note 61), pp. 85–91; Stares (note 5), pp. 170–1, 180–3, 193–200, and 229–35; Purver, R. G., 'Soviet arms control policy in 1982', in SAFRA (note 36), Vol. 7, pp. 405–7; and Jones, D. L., 'Arms control policy', in SAFRA (note 13), Vol. 8, pp. 318–20.

64 USSR Ministry of Defence (note 62), p. 37.

65 Ogarkov, N. V. *et al.* (eds), *Sovetskaia voennaia entsiklopediia* (Soviet Military Encyclopaedia) (SVE), 8 vols (*Voenizdat*: Moscow, 1976–1980), Vol. 6, pp. 594–5.

66 Ogarkov (note 65), Vol. 6, pp. 603–4.

67 Ogarkov (note 65), Vol. 6, pp. 598–9.

68 Ogarkov, N. V. *et al.* (eds) *Voennyi entsiklopedicheskii slovar'* (Military Encyclopaedia Dictionary) (*Voenizdat*: Moscow, 1983), pp. 598–9.

69 Lambeth, B. S., *The State of Western Research on Soviet Military Strategy and Police*, Report No. N–2230–AF (Rand Corporation: Santa Monica, CA, 1984), p. 51.

70 See, for instance, the views of Deane (note 1) and Lockwood (note 1).

71 '*Doktrina voennaia*' (Military Doctrine), in Ogarkov (note 68), p. 240.

72 Radzievskii (note 53), p. 41; '*Doktrina voennaia*' (Military Doctrine), Ogarkov (note 65), Vol. 7, p. 225; Ogarkov, N. V., *Vsegda v gotovsnosti k zashchite Otechestva* (Always Ready To Defend the Native Land) (*Voenizdat*: Moscow, 1982), pp. 53–4; and Ogarkov, N. V., *Istoriia uchit bditel'nosti* (History Teaches Vigilance) (*Voenizdat*: Moscow, 1985), pp. 57–8.

73 Ogarkov (note 72), *Vsegda*, pp. 53–4.

74 Ogarkov (note 72), *Vsegda*, p. 54.

75 Kozlov, S. N. *et al.*, *O sovetskoi voennoi nauke* (About Soviet Military Science), 2nd edn (*Voenizdat*: Moscow, 1964), pp. 379–80.

76 Ogarkov (note 72), *Vsegda*, pp. 54–5.

77 Ogarkov (note 72), *Istoriia*, p. 73, and *Vsegda*, pp. 55–6.

78 Zheltov, A. S., *Metodologischeskie problemy voennoi teorii i praktiki* (Methodological Problems of Military Theory and Practice) *Voenizdat*: Moscow, 1968), p. 294.

79 Ogarkov (note 68), p. 240.

80 Ogarkov (note 72), *Istoriia*, p. 72, and *Vsegda*, p. 56.

81 Leebaert, D. (ed.), *Soviet Military Thinking* (Allen & Unwin: London, 1981), pp. 13–18.

82 Erickson, J. *et al.*, *Organizing for War: The Soviet Military Establishment Viewed Through the Prism of the Military District*, College Station Papers No. 2, (Center for

Strategic Technology: College Station, TX, Sep. 1983), pp. xxii–xxiii. On the conventional-nuclear issue see, e.g., McConnell, J. M., *The Soviet Shift in Emphasis from Nuclear to Conventional. The Mid-Term Perspective*, Paper CRC–490 (two parts; Center for Naval Analysis: Arlington, VA, June 1983).

[83] Jones, D. R., 'Russian military traditions and the Soviet military establishment', *The Soviet Union: What Lies Ahead? Military-Political Affairs in the 1980s*, eds K. M. Currie and G. Warhall (US Government Printing Office: Washington, DC, 1985), pp. 36–8.

[84] Ogarkov (note 72), *Istoriia*, p. 55.

[85] Ogarkov (note 72), *Istoriia*, pp. 55 and 59–72.

[86] Leebaert (note 81), pp. 36–7; Vigor, P. H., *The Soviet View of War, Peace and Neutrality*, (Routledge & Kegan Paul: London, 1975), pp. 5ff.

[87] Jones (note 83), pp. 39–40; Leebaert (note 81), pp. 22–3.

[88] Raszievskii (note 53), p. 210; Ogarkov (note 65), Vol. 7, p. 445; Ogarkov (note 68), p. 691. For a Western discussion of this concept, see Myer, A. A., 'The balance in Central Europe: reflections through the Soviet prism', *Naval War College Review*, vol. 33, no. 6 (Nov.–Dec. 1980), pp. 15–43.

[89] Tiushkevich (Tyushkevich), S., 'The methodology for the correlation of forces in war', *Selected Readings from Military Thought*, eds J. D. Douglass, Jr and A. M. Hoeber, Vol. 1 (2 volumes) (US Government Printing Office: Washington, DC, n.d.), pp. 62–7.

[90] Tiushkevich (note 89), p. 57.

[91] Tiushkevich (note 89), p. 62.

[92] Tiushkevich (note 89), p. 64.

[93] Sanakoe, S., 'The problem of the correlation of forces in the contemporary world', *Mezhdunarodnaia zhizn'* (International Life), no. 10 (Oct. 1974), pp. 47 and 87.

[94] Cited, e.g., by Kulakov, V., 'Problems of military-technical superiority', in Douglas and Hoeber (note 89), Vol. 2, p. 87.

[95] Kulakov (note 94), p. 89.

[96] Kulakov (note 94), pp. 87 and 89.

[97] Ogarkov (note 72), *Istoriia*, pp. 73–5. For a fuller exposition of the concept of such revolutions see Galkin, M. I., *Nauchno-tekhnicheskii progress i revoliutsiia v voennom dele* (Scientific-Technical Progress and the Revolution in Military Affairs) (*Voenizdat*: Moscow, 1973). Also see Scott, H. F. and Scott, W. F., *The Armed Forces of the USSR*, 3rd edn (Westview Press: Boulder, CO, 1984), pp. 77ff.

[98] Kulakov (note 94), p. 16.

[99] Scott (note 97), pp. 79–87; Sokolovskii, V. D., *Voennaia strategiia* (Military Strategy), 3rd edn (*Voenizdat*: Moscow, 1968), p. 207ff.

[100] Tiuskevich (note 58), p. 463.

[101] Jones, D. R., 'Soviet concepts of security: reflections on flight KAL 007', *Air University Review*, vol. 37, no. 6 (Sep.–Oct. 1986).

[102] See Scott (note 97), chapter 5, for a discussion of the Soviet force posture in the 1970s. On the numerous expressions of Soviet concern about the consequences of a nuclear conflict, see Arnett, R. L., The consequences of World War III: The Soviet perspective, in SAFRA (note 11), pp. 256–65.

[103] See the discussion in Deane (note 1), chapters 5–6; the sources cited in Arnett (note 102), notes 1–6, pp. 262–3; and Prados, J., *The Soviet Estimate: U.S. Intelligence Analysis and Russian Military Strength* (Dial Press: New York, 1982), pp. 248–57.

[104] Glezerman, G., 'The great significance of Leninist ideas on the struggle for democracy and socialism', *Pravda*, 21 Jan. 1965.

[105] Urban, M., 'Red Flag over Germany', *Armed Forces*, no. 2 (Feb. 1985), pp. 72–4.

[106] The growing Soviet doubts about the possibilities of a successful PRO/PKO system are evident from the pessimistic assessment of Anureev, I. I., *Oruzhie protivoraketnoi i protivokosmicheskoi oborony* (Anti-Missile and Anti-Space Weapons), (*Voenizdat*: Moscow, 1971), published on the eve of the ABM Treaty.

[107] Kulikov, V., 'Soviet military science today', *Kommunist* (May 1976), as translated in *Strategic Review*, vol. 5, no. 1 (Winter 1977), pp. 127–34.

[108] Erickson (note 82), pp. xxii–xxiii and 14.

[109] Fitzgerald, M. C., 'Marshal Ogarkov and the new revolution in military affairs', unpublished research paper (Center for Naval Analysis: Arlington, VA, 1985), p. 3.

[110] Erickson (note 82), pp. xxii–xxiii; also see Ogarkov, N. V., '*Strategiia Voennaia*' (Military Strategy) in Ogarkov (note 65), Vol. 7, pp. 563–6.

[111] Erickson (note 82), pp. xxii–xxiii.

[112] On the reorganization of the air services, see the annual reviews of the PVO by Jones (notes 11 and 31) and Breighner (note 13), and of the VVS by Monks, A., along with the numerous sources cited, in Jones, SAFRA (notes 11, 13, 28, 31 and 37).

[113] Odom, W. E. 'Soviet force posture: dilemmas and directions', *Problems of Communism* (July–Aug. 1985), pp. 6–14.

[114] Fitzgerald (note 109), p. 2.

[115] Lambeth (note 69), p. 52.

[116] On this issue, see Jones, D. L., 'The Soviet military year in review, 1983–1984', in SAFRA (note 63), Vol. 8, pp. 1–17, and the comments in the similar surveys in SAFRA (note 36), Vol. 7, pp. 1–8, and SAFRA (note 28) Vol. 9, pp. 2–17.

[117] Lambeth (note 69), pp. 52–3.

[118] This does not mean that these issues were not being discussed in classified journals like *Voennaia mysl'* (Military Thought), which is unavailable to most Western scholars. That such a discussion occurred is suggested by rumours that a new 'Military Strategy' was expected to appear shortly before Chernenko's demise.

[119] Brezhnev, L. I., *Na strazhe mira i sotsializma* (on Guard for Peace and Socialism) (*Politizdat*: Moscow, 1979), pp. 491–2. On the significance of this speech, see the discussion in Holloway, D., *The Soviet Union and the Arms Race* (Yale University Press: New Haven, CT, 1983), pp. 48ff.

[120] Fitzgerald (note 109), pp. 3–4; Jones, D. R., 'Nuclear war and Soviet policy', *International Perspectives* (Nov.–Dec. 1982), p. 18.

[121] Ogarkov (note 110), '*Strategiia Voennaia*' (Military strategy), pp. 563–5.

[122] Lambeth (note 69), pp. 17–18. For an example of those rejecting the reality of the 'Tula Line', see Pipes, R. 'Why the Soviet Union thinks it could fight and win a nuclear war', *Commentary*, vol. 62 (July 1977), pp. 21–34.

[123] On this debate see Arnett (note 102), pp. 257–8.

[124] Rybkin, E., 'The Leninist concept of war and the present', *Kommunist Vooruzhennykh sil* (Communist of the Armed Forces), no. 20 (Oct. 1973), as translated in *Strategic Review*, vol. 2, no. 2 (Spring 1974), pp. 102–3.

[125] Bovin, A., 'The permanent significance of Lenin's ideas', *Kommunist*, no. 10 (July 1980), p. 78.

[126] This speech is quoted and analysed at length in Jones (note 120), pp. 18–19.

[127] Jones (note 120), pp. 18–19; Fitzgerald, M. C., *Marshal Ogarkov and Modern War: 1977–1985*, CNA Professional Paper No. 443, (Center for Naval Analysis: Alexandria, VA, Mar. 1986), pp. 16–17.

[128] Austin,. A. 'Moscow expert says U.S. errs on Soviet war aims', *New York Times*, 25 Aug. 1980.

[129] Odom (note 113), p. 9, note 18.

[130] Gareev, M. A., *Frunze—voennyi teoretik* (Frunze—A Military Theorist), (*Voenizdat*: Moscow, 1985), pp. 239–44; see also McConnell, J. M., 'The irrelevance today of Sokolovskii's book *Military Strategy*', *Defense Analysis*, no. 4 (1985), pp. 243–54.

[131] Jones (note 120), pp. 19–20.

[132] Fitzgerald (note 109), 'New revolution', p. 1.

[133] Ogarkov (note 72), *Istoriia*, p. 88.

[134] An interview with Marshal N. V. Ogarkov on 'Victory Day', entitled 'The defense of socialism: the experience of history and the present day', *Krasnaia zvezda* (Red Star), 9 May 1984, p. 3.

[135] Ogarkov (note 72), *Istoriia*, p. 89; Ogarkov, N. V., 'The unfolding glory of Soviet weapons', *Kommunist Vooruzhennykh sil* (Communist of the Armed Forces), no. 21 (Nov. 1984), pp. 25–6.

[136] See, e.g., Marshal Ogarkov's assertion that it will be 'impossible in practice to confine a nuclear war within some kind of limited framework'; Ogarkov (note 72), *Istoriia* p. 89.

[137] Ogarkov (note 72) *Istoriia*, p. 88.

[138] Ogarkov (note 72), *Vsegda*, p. 45.

[139] Ogarkov (note 135), 'Unfolding glory', p. 26.

[140] Ogarkov (note 72), *Istoriia*, p. 54.

[141] Ogarkov (note 72), *Vsegda*, p. 44.

[142] This point is made in McConnell, J. M., 'Shifts in the Soviet views on the proper focus of military development', *World Politics*, no. 3 (Apr. 1985), pp. 320–4. For Ogarkov's later views on this topic, see Fitzgerald, M. C., 'The Soviet military and SDI', unpublished research paper, Dec. 1985, pp. 26–7.

[143] See, e.g., Bochkarev, K., 'The question of the sociological aspect of the struggle against the forces of aggression and war', *Voennaia mysl'* (Military Thought), no. 9 (Sep. 1968), pp. 10–11.

[144] Ogarkov (note 72), *Vsegda*, p. 44.

[145] Ogarkov (note 72), *Vsegda*, p. 31.

[146] Summarized from the analysis in Fitzgerald (note 142), pp. 19–20.

[147] See the analysis of Zamkovoi, V. I. and Filatov, M. N., *Filosofiia agressii* (Philosophy of Aggression) (Alma-Ata, USSR, 1981), pp. 230, 270–6 and 288.

[148] Ogarkov, Marshal N. V., in *Krasnaia zvezda*, 3 Sep. 1971.

[149] On his 'reassignment' and the funding issue, see Jones, SAFRA (note 63), Vol. 8, pp. 14–17, and SAFRA (note 28), Vol. 9, pp. 8–11.

[150] Ogarkov, Marshal, N. V., 'A reliable defense of peace', *Krasnaia zvezda*, 23 Sep. 1983, p. 2.

[151] Ogarkov (note 134), p. 3. In Ogarkov (note 150), p. 2, Marshal Ogarkov openly equated the developing of 'new conventional means of warfare' with 'precision (-guided) weapons, reconnaissance-strike complexes, and weapons based on new physical principles'.

[152] For a discussion of the trends in recent weapon deployments see Kaufman, R. F.,

'Causes of the slowdown in Soviet defense spending', *Survival*, vol. 27, no. 4 (July–Aug. 1985), pp. 183–92.

[153] Lambeth (note 69), p. 24.

[154] Kaufman (note 152), p. 183.

[155] Tiushkevich, *Sovetskie* (note 58), pp. 457–9 and 463.

[156] On this problem see Prados (note 103), *passim*, and Richardson, J. T., 'U.S. intelligence and Soviet Star Wars', *Bulletin of the Atomic Scientists*, vol. 42, no. 5 (May 1986), pp. 12–14.

[157] See Listvinov, Y., 'Space research, American style', *International Affairs*, no. 11 (Moscow, Nov. 1968), pp. 46–50; Byskovskii, V., 'Who is against using the cosmos for peace?', *Aviatsiia i kosmonavtika* (Aviation and Astronautics), no. 6 (June 1983); and Ponomarev, M., 'What kind of "initiative" is the White House pushing?', *Krasnaia zvezda*, 3 Feb. 1985.

[158] Scott (note 7), p. 42.

[159] Johnson, N. L., *The Soviet Year in Space, 1985*, (Teledyne Brown Engineering: Colorado Springs, CO, 1986), p. 49.

[160] Jones (note 31), Vol. 3, p. 36.

[161] Jones (note 31), Vol. 4, p. 103.

[162] Jones (note 31), Vol. 4, p. 103.

[163] Gorenko, V., 'The "Shuttle" Space System in the Pentagon's plans', *Zarubezhnoe voennoe obozrenie* (Foreign Military Review), no. 4 (Apr. 1985), p. 45; Mikhailov, Y., 'For a cosmos without weapons', *Aviatsiia i kosmonavtika* (Aviation and Astronautics), no. 12 (Dec. 1983), pp. 44–5.

[164] On the Soviet 'Shuttle', see the progress as chronicled in Schauer's annual reviews (note 44).

[165] On these negotiations, see Jasani, B. and Perry, G. E., 'The military use of outer space', *World Armaments and Disarmament: SIPRI Yearbook 1985* (Taylor & Francis: London, 1985), pp. 133–7, and the annual Air Defense and Space Reviews in SAFRA (notes 11, 31 and 44).

[166] 'Zvezdnye voiny'. *Illiuzii i opasnosti* ('Star Wars': Illusions and Dangers), (*Voenizdat*: Moscow, 1985), p. 8; also see Tkachev, L., 'The militaristic ambitions of the USA', *Aviatsiia i kosmonavtika* (Aviation and Astronautics), no. 11 (Nov. 1983), pp. 42–3.

[167] Text as published in Gerasimov, G., *Keep Space Weapon-Free* (*Novosti*: Moscow, 1984), p. 68.

[168] Gerasimov (note 167), pp. 68–9; also see the comments of Purver (note 63), pp. 405–6.

[169] Text as published in Johnson (note 159), p. 87.

[170] 'Yu. V. Andropov's answers to a *Pravda* correspondent's questions', *Pravda*, 27 Mar. 1983, p. 1.

[171] These points are usefully summarized in Fitzgerald (note 142), pp. 3–7.

[172] 'USSR has antisatellite system', *Frankfurter Rundschau*, 30 May 1985, p. 1.

[173] *Frankfurter Rundschau*, 5 Dec. 1985, p. 8.

[174] *Neue AZ*, Vienna, 19–20 Oct. 1985, p. 5.

[175] Sokolov, S. L., 'To preserve what has been achieved in the sphere of strategic arms limitation', *Pravda*, 6 Nov. 1985, p. 4.

[176] Akhromeev, Marshal S. F., 'Washington's assertions and the real facts', *Pravda*, 19 Oct. 1985, p. 5; and 'Excerpts from views of Soviet military chief', *New York Times*, 18 Oct. 1985, p. 6.

[177] Based on analysis of Fitzgerald (note 142), pp. 44–5.

[178] Sokolov (note 175), p. 4.

[179] 'Answers of the USSR Minister of Defense Marshal of the Soviet Union S. L. Sokolov to a TASS correspondent's questions', *Krasnaia zvezda*, 5 May 1985, p. 3; also see 'Excerpts from views', p. 6.

[180] On the Soviet view of US technology, see Meyer (note 21), p. 276. The Soviet statements on the technological feasibility of SDI are presented at length in two reports of the 'Committee of Soviet Scientists for Peace, Against the Nuclear Threat', *Space-Strike Arms and International Security*, (Moscow, Oct. 1985), pp. 9–35; and *The Large-Scale Anti-Missile System and International Security*, (Moscow, Feb. 1986), pp. 9–49. Other Soviet statements on this issue are reviewed in Fitzgerald (note 142), pp. 27–8, an updated version of which will appear in the *Soviet Armed Forces Review Annual*, Vol. 10, 1985–1986 (Academic International Press: Gulf Breeze, FL, forthcoming).

[181] Hiatt, F., 'New SDI scenario: several "generations" of weapons in space', *Washington Post*, 4 May 1986, p. A4.

[182] Off-the-record statements made to this writer by Soviet diplomatic officials; also see Olenev, V., 'The threat from above: the USSR and the militarization of space', *Détente*, no. 5 (Leeds, Mar. 1986), pp. 2–7, which are summarized in Frankland, M., 'Star Wars: Moscow sounds a warning. "Sky's the limit" for Soviet gains in global power', *The Observer*, London, 23 Mar. 1986, p. 5.

[183] Hough, J. H., 'Gorbachev's strategy', *Foreign Affairs*, vol. 64, no. 1, (Fall 1985), pp.48 and 53.

[184] Stevens as quoted by Hiatt (note 181), p. A4. Soviet accusations of the possible *offensive* utility of SDI systems recently was echoed in Tirman, J., 'Star Wars technology threatens satellites', *Bulletin of the Atomic Scientists*, vol. 42, no. 5 (May 1986), pp. 28–32.

[185] Taubman, P., 'Soviet vows to match U.S. space arms', *New York Times*, 23 Oct. 1985, p. 3; Sokolov (note 175), p. 4; Akhromeev (note 176), p. 5; 'Our May Day', editorial in *Krasnaia zvezda*, 30 Apr. 1985, p. 1. These and numerous other statements are discussed in Fitzgerald (note 14), pp. 38–44.

[186] 'Olenev', as quoted by Frankland (note 182), p. 5. The countermeasures that could be taken to degrade the US systems are outlined in *Space-Strike Arms* (note 180), pp. 36–46, and *Large-Scale Anti-Missile System* (note 180), pp. 50–60. Many of these already had been envisaged by I. I. Anureev in 1971.

[187] Stevens as quoted by Hiatt (note 181), p. A4.

[188] See, e.g., Arbatov, A. G., 'Limiting anti-missile defense systems: problems, lessons, and prospects', *SShA; Ekonomika, Politika, Ideologiia* (USA: Economy, Politics, Ideology), no. 12, (Dec. 1984), p. 26; and Sokolov's comments in 'Answers', p. 3. *Note*: For further background information on Soviet BMD views and programmes, see Jacobsen, C. G., *Soviet Strategy—Soviet Foriegn Policy* (Glasgow University Press: Glasgow, 1972), pp. 99–109, and Jacobsen, C. G., 'From American nuclear dominance to US–Soviet strategic equivalence', *The Nuclear Era* (Oelgeschlager, Gunn & Hain, Publishers, Inc.; and Spokesman: Cambridge, MA; and Nottingham, respectively, 1982), chapter 2.

Paper 2.4. Conventional force modernization and the asymmetries of military doctrine: historical reflections on Air/Land Battle and the Operational Manoeuvre Group[1]

JACOB W. KIPP

I. Introduction

One of the paradoxes of the superpower rivalry over the past four decades has been the trend towards the militarization of a political-ideological competition and the simultaneous exercise of restraint in the employment of expanding and increasingly sophisticated arsenals. An evolving deterrence theory, which sees the post-war environment shaped by the reality of weapons of mass destruction, has dominated Western international security studies.[2] In part, this may be the result of the fact that within the context of superpower relations such weapons of mass destruction have exercised a restraint upon a trend towards systemic war, evident over the preceding century as combat became more industrial; involved the mobilization of larger numbers of the population; took on greater geographic extent, intensity and lethality; and obliterated the distinctions between combatant and non-combatant. War in this systemic form reached its apogee during the years 1941 through 1945 on the Eastern Front, where it assumed the character of a *Vernichtungskrieg, voina na unichtozhenie*, or war of annihilation.[3]

Deterrence theory has identified a number of factors in the post-war international environment that have contributed to this check upon the all-out employment of military power by one of the superpowers and its allies against the other. In addition to the acquisition of arsenals of weapons of mass destruction and effective intercontinental delivery systems, these include the emergence and continuation of a bipolar international environment and a shared assumption within the policies of both coalitions that no matter how intense the ideological and political competition between the powers, systemic war would result in mutual annihilation, making a *Vernichtungskrieg* a suicide pact.[4]

At the same time, the pace of technological change has accelerated the process of military modernization, reduced the life cycle of weapon systems, and forced military institutions to adapt their force structures, organizations

and missions to new circumstances. Recent developments in military technologies have brought about increased interest in war-fighting capabilities and
conventional force modernization. Conventional deterrence has become a
topic of scholarly research.[5] These developments have complicated deterrence
and should stimulate comparative studies of the respective national security
systems, military institutions and doctrines. The interactions and interconnec-
tions between those systems, institutions and concepts are complex and can
best be grasped within their historical context. This essay will employ a
historical approach to analyse the evolution of US and Soviet military doctrines, particularly in connection with their respective ground forces, over the
past four decades.

The acquisition of atomic weapons and the subsequent expansion of those
arsenals in the immediate post-war period did not negate conventional military
power. The new weapons did, however, place old means into a new context. As
late as 1949 Vannevar Bush, Director of the US Office of Scientific Research
and Development during World War II, could argue that the atomic bomb had
not fundamentally reshaped the nature of total war, nor were such weapons
likely to do so in the immediate future.[6] The pace of scientific-technical
development was, however, much more rapid than expected, and since the
early 1950s military planners and statesmen in the West and East have been
struggling to come to grips with this process of innovation as it affects the
development, procurement, deployment and doctrinal use of their respective
arsenals. In the US and Soviet militaries, this has been a process of adapting
distinctive national military doctrines to military-political and military-technological changes.

In Western usage, military doctrine, as Barry Posen has pointed out, is a sub-
system of national grand strategy dealing with the construction, organization
and employment of military means.[7] In Anglo-American usage, military
doctrine describes the armed forces', or a single service's, understanding of the
nature, theory and practice of war. As officially established views, military
doctrine prescribes the general principles and methods by which units fight in
concert with other services and allies. Military doctrine lays the foundation of
subordinate doctrine, *matériel* development, training and professional education. In the West, the political leadership sets national strategy, and military
doctrine is subordinated to those missions and constraints, which arise from
national strategy, set within a democratic polity. Thus, military doctrine has a
political and societal context. This leads to the conclusion that military doctrine
and *voennaia doktrina* are not cognates.

Voennaia doktrina is, in fact, much broader in its implications. Reflecting the
application of Marxism–Leninism to the laws of war and guided by the military
policy of the Communist Party, *voennaia doktrina* is nothing less than 'the
nation's officially accepted system of scientifically founded views on the nature
of modern wars and the use of the armed forces in them, as well as the
requirements arising from these views regarding the country and its armed
forces being made ready for war'.[8] Soviet military doctrine has two mutually

interconnected sides: the military-political and the military-technical, with the dominance of the former over the latter. Seen through the prism of Marxism–Leninism, the basic tenets of *voennaia doktrina* are set by the nation's socio-political system, level of economic, scientific and technological development and the armed forces' combat *matériel*, with due regard to the conclusions of military science and the nature of the threat posed by the probable enemy. *Voennaia doktrina* stands above and shapes strategy, which is the highest level of military art.

Voennoe iskusstvo (military art), which embraces strategy, operational art and tactics comes much closer to the Western meaning of military doctrine as applied to the general principles and methods by which units fight in concert with other services and allies. However, in the Soviet case *voennaia doktrina* is unified, embracing both civil and military preparations for war, and imposing upon *voennoe iskusstvo* much greater unity among the branches of the armed forces.

The Soviet General Staff, which Marshal Shaposhnikov called 'the brain of the army', provides both the institutional and intellectual unification through its efforts to use military science to determine the nature of future war and guide the preparations and combat readiness of the armed forces towards that end. The General Staff is thus at the very heart of the Soviet military system. This situation has its roots in Russian military history. The combination of an autocratic political culture, social instability and the emergence of industrial war led some Russian General Staff Officers (*genshtabisty*) to call for a unified military doctrine (*edinaia voennaia doktrina*) in the wake of defeat and revolution during the Russo–Japanese War. The experience of World War I and the Civil War reinforced such calls, while the Great Patriotic War as a *Vernichtungskrieg* confirmed the necessity of such a centralized system.[9] Marxism–Leninism with its emphasis upon ideological struggle between an emerging socialist world order and a dying capitalist one reinforced this logic. This has encouraged a militarization of society but not militarism, which might challenge the political hegemony of the Communist Party.[10]

In the four decades since the end of World War II, these very different military systems have had to manage major doctrinal shifts at roughly 10-year intervals. In each case the systems dealt with change by a process of adaptation within its particular societal and institutional context, while at the same time responding to what it perceived to be the salient features of the threat, that is, the other superpower's military system. In each case, new concepts, which would shape doctrine in the next era, made their appearance in the military literature. The current debate regarding the military-political implications of Operational Manoeuvre Groups (OMGs), Air/Land Battle and Follow-On-Forces-Attack (FOFA) marks the beginning of another doctrinal era, defined by a resurgent interest in conventional forces.

II.   The post-war era, 1945–1953

In the immediate post-war period the US and Soviet Armies each engaged in assessing the lessons of World War II. Their very distinct socio-political orders, economic capabilities, geostrategic concerns, historical experiences and ideological assumptions assured that the lessons learned would be radically different. Soviet territorial gains and political advances did not alter the reality of the Soviet Union's geostrategic situation as a Eurasian continental power. The considerable destruction suffered by the national economy made demobilization an imperative. For Stalin, Soviet acquisition of nuclear weapons and the means of delivery was a national priority. Thus, the Soviet Army had to confront a scarcity of resources during the period of economic recovery. These developments had not, however, called into question the logic of a large conventional military force. For the Soviet Army, the hard-won campaigns in Eastern Europe and the Far East had set an agenda for the further mechanization of Soviet ground forces, the improvement of their tactical and operational mobility, and the augmentation of the combat power of their combined arms formations.[11]

For the US Army, the lessons were not so clear and the problems of combat organization not so easily addressed. While US society emerged from World War II as an unchallenged industrial giant, the new globalism which shaped US foreign policy did not immediately translate into a new national grand strategy. The US atomic monopoly, the prestige of strategic airpower and the geostrategic realities of the United States as a maritime power did not provide a definite role for ground combat power. The creation of the Department of Defense and the emergence of the Air Force as an independent service left the issue of joint operations, especially air-ground co-operation, unresolved at the service level. Rapid demobilization and a lack of clarity as to where and under what circumstances US ground forces would be committed to combat made it difficult for the Army to address lessons learned above the tactical level. The outbreak of the Korean War and the commitment of US forces did lead US commanders to conclude that US forces would fight outnumbered and would have to rely upon firepower to destroy enemy forces.[12] Following the onset of the Cold War and the organization of the North Atlantic Treaty Organization (NATO) in 1949, General Dwight D. Eisenhower, its first Supreme Commander, proposed a force of 96 divisions and 9000 aircraft for the defence of Central Europe. NATO's ministers, however, rejected such a posture as infeasible and too costly.

III.   The scientific-technical revolution in military affairs

From the early 1950s, when both powers almost simultaneously acquired the ability to produce nuclear weapons, military planners in both countries turned their attention to the integration of nuclear weapons and conventional forces. Following the death of Stalin, Soviet military theorists began to address the problem of future war, in which such means of mass destruction were employed. In the past doctrinal change in response to new weapon systems had begun at the tactical level and gradually extended until it embraced strategic adjustments. Nuclear weapons and their delivery systems seemed to negate that process. Discussions in *Voennaia mysl'* and within study groups at the Voroshilov General Staff Academy led to the conclusion that a future war would be a global, thermonuclear contest between socialism and capitalism. Its salient features would be radically different from those of the Great Patriotic War and would put a premium upon integrated national leadership at the strategic level prior to and following the initiation of hostilities.[13] In retrospect, it would appear that Soviet military planners overestimated the extent to which nuclear weapons had caused a break with the past. Colonel General M. A. Gareev has argued that in evaluating the impact of nuclear weapons the theorists went to extremes in dismissing the relevance of existing military theory.[14]

Soviet military planners approached this future war with a realistic assessment of the military-political and military-technical correlation of forces during the next decade. US strategic capabilities far exceeded those of the USSR. At the same time the political leadership emphasized that socio-political changes were affecting the military-political correlation of forces in favour of socialism, so that systemic war was not fatally inevitable. Soviet military planners thus faced a situation where the long-range trends affecting the political competition between the camps were seen to be shifting in their favour, although the military-technical situation clearly favoured the West. This situation promoted both prudence and confidence.[15]

During this period of strategic inferiority, Soviet military planners assumed that deterrence (*sderzhivanie*) of such a systemic conflict went hand in hand with war-fighting capabilities under the assumption that the risks of deterrence failure demanded a viable defence. This has been called 'deterrence by punishment' and contained a good measure of Clausewitzian military-political realism, revised in light of Marxism–Leninism's vision of war as a social phenomenon.[16] A state led by men who had fought through the disasters of 1941 could hardly assume anything else. These war-fighting capabilities were, however, shaped by the scientific-technical revolution in military affairs. The Soviet Armed Forces underwent substantial changes in structure and missions.

Soviet ground forces were seriously challenged for pre-eminence within the military establishment. Under Khrushchev, the revolution in military affairs was narrowly focused upon the new nuclear-tipped rockets and interpreted to mean that conventional forces were of declining value. The budgetary requirements of those branches which were to play a decisive role in strategic operations, that is, the newly formed Strategic Rocket Forces and the National Air Defense Forces (*PVO Strany*) received top priority. Long-Range Aviation, which had received substantial attention in the post-war decade, found its strategic role pre-empted. Soviet naval forces under Admiral Sergei Gorshkov were reconfigured to support such strategic operations, and large-scale shipbuilding programmes for surface combatants were cancelled. The Soviet Army faced cut-backs in manpower, as the government struggled with a demographic crisis, which affected the work-force by the early 1960s.[17]

The Soviet General Staff, although led by *front* and army commanders, oversaw this transition. A collection of authors led by Marshal V. D. Sokolovskii, Chief of the General Staff from 1952 to 1960, produced a work, which broke new ground. *Voennaia strategiia*, which appeared in 1962, was the first work on strategy by a Soviet officer since A. A. Svechin had addressed the topic in 1926. The Sokolovskii volume radically redefined the nature of future war. Since the development of the theory of consecutive deep operations in the late 1920s, Soviet military theory had assumed that systemic war over large theatres of military action would require a succession of deep operations to destroy the enemy's forces in the field and eliminate his will to resist. Arsenals of nuclear weapons and ballistic missiles seemed to negate this assumption of a long war.[18]

Some General Staff Officers, as *The Penkovsky Papers* suggest, were uneasy with this one-sided emphasis on strategic capabilities and called for a reshaping of tactics and operational art in the light of nuclear weapons.[19] The fact that *Voennaia strategiia* went through three editions between 1962 and 1968 suggests the amount of ferment affecting Soviet military circles during the period.[20] The appointment, removal and then reappointment of Marshal M. V. Zakharov as Chief of the General Staff during Khrushchev's last years in power strengthens this impression. During Zakharov's second tenure, that is, after the Cuban missile crisis, the Soviet military press turned its attention to the architects of the theory of deep operations, including the victims of Stalin's purge of the military.[21] This and other events signalled an end to the Khrushchevian definition of the scientific-technical revolution in military affairs as narrowly confined within the bounds of strategic nuclear weapon systems.

On the US side, in the aftermath of Korea, national grand strategy shifted towards the threat of the use of nuclear weapons for general deterrence. The adoption of 'massive retaliation' as a defence posture drove military procurement towards the acquisition of strategic delivery systems and fostered inter-service competition for a role in this central area of national military policy.[22] The Eisenhower Administration sensed that public opinion would not accept the large-scale commitment of ground forces in another limited war and so emphasized the acquisition of strategic and tactical nuclear weapons. Within NATO, the administration accepted an alliance posture of 26 divisions, 1400 combat aircraft and 15 000 tactical nuclear weapons. US ground forces were reorganized for the nuclear battlefield. The Pentomic Division of 1956 represented the US Army's attempt to create a tactical formation with cellular structure, based on five battle groups, using improved firepower, mobility, and command and control to defeat a numerically superior foe. This shift, like that in the Soviet Union, inaugurated a period of doctrinal ferment, precisely at a time, 1956–59, when the size of the standing army was being reduced.[23]

Global security concerns and a recognition of the possibility of the engagement of forces across the spectrum of conflict led to internal criticism of the Pentomic concept. Even prior to the Kennedy Administration, proponents of a shift away from the nuclear battlefield as the standard form of future combat had made flexibility their watchword. These concerns fit in well with the Kennedy Administration's desire to separate strategic nuclear warfare from other kinds of combat on the assumption that strategic nuclear forces could not provide extended deterrence against the broad range of threats around the globe. At the same time Secretary of Defense McNamara was critical of efforts to substitute tactical nuclear weapons for conventional military power.[24]

By the early 1960s, US and Soviet ground forces had both passed through a period when strategic nuclear weapons had seemed about to transform them beyond recognition, bringing about a radical break with past doctrine. The paths taken by each army in the following period were, however, radically different. In the Soviet case, historical experience drawn from the Great Patriotic War was employed to recast the tactics and operational art of the Soviet Armed Forces on the modern battlefield. In the US Army, the Vietnamese experience refocused doctrinal concerns for a decade. In the Soviet case, this process embodied an integration of military theory with the rich practical experience of the Great Patriotic War and a reassertion of the claims of continuity in the face of radical technological developments. For the US Army, the present demands of combat in a distant guerrilla war absorbed its energy, resources and intellectual capital.

IV.   The resurgence of conventional military forces, 1963–1973

As originally envisioned, 'flexible response' was intended to provide a range of military options which would fit an expanding set of global security requirements. Much attention went to unconventional warfare and special forces.[25] The cornerstone of 'flexible response' in the US Army was, however, the Reorganized Objectives Army Division (ROAD 1965), which was first presented as a concept in the spring of 1961. ROAD was designed to fight in both a nuclear and conventional environment. Mobility and dispersion dominated tactics, while infantry forces were further mechanized. These improvements were designed to permit the ROAD to function conventionally on a battlefield where nuclear weapons might be used at any time.[26]

In 1967 the Johnson Administration was successful in getting NATO to adopt 'flexible response' as alliance strategy. In the European context, however, the concept took on a particular meaning. The US assumption had been that 'flexible response' would promote the acquisition of additional conventional forces to make conventional deterrence a viable alternative for the alliance. As adopted, 'flexible response' translated into the possession of sufficient conventional military power to mount a forward defence along the inter-German border to meet a Soviet/Warsaw Pact offensive without immediate recourse to tactical-theatre nuclear weapons. Inter-Allied discussions, which highlighted distinct, national defence requirements and budgetary constraints, resulted in this compromise solution. So long as US strategic superiority was not open to question, the issue of conventional sufficiency remained one of buying time for political manoeuvring after the initiation of hostilities. NATO, as a defensive alliance and coalition of sovereign states, could agree upon the need for sufficient military power to deter aggression, but was intentionally unclear regarding its war-fighting role, should deterrence fail. Should hostilities be imposed upon the alliance, its members were agreed upon modest military objectives, that is, the restoration of the inter-German border.[27] In the 1960s, Gaullist reservations aside, the dominant assumption for US and NATO planners was that US strategic superiority made linkage between conventional, theatre-nuclear and strategic nuclear forces into a credible deterrent.[28]

A number of trends over the next decade undermined that assumption. US involvement in and commitments to the war in Viet Nam shifted the US defence posture, leading to an imbalance of budgetary expenditures and resource allocations in support of the effort in Southeast Asia but at the expense of commitments elsewhere. Internal divisions within the US polity eroded the post-war consensus supporting US global security commitments and undercut support for defence. The political fall-out of Viet Nam strained US–European relations, while the expansion of the Soviet strategic arsenal in the second half of the decade to a level approaching parity contributed to a growing unease by the first years of the next decade regarding the viability of linkage as it had been understood in NATO.

The Viet Nam War brought its own impulse for doctrinal change to the US Army. The non-linear nature of the conflict, the difficulty of identifying and fixing the opponent, the peculiarities of the theatre, its distance from the United States, and the nature of Vietnamese society prompted changes in doctrine. The war was fought at the small unit level. Firepower, attrition and the desire to keep US combat losses as low as possible dominated US tactics. Although large-scale operations were mounted in support of the pacification programme, US commanders found it difficult to identify and attack the enemy's centre of gravity, and as a result the war lacked operational coherence. New types of operation based upon the use of air-mobile forces emerged: 'search and destroy, clearing and securing'.[29]

The USA's longest war had a profound impact upon the army that fought the conflict. By the early 1970s army leadership recognized that there were substantial problems with morale, leadership and training. Military reformers were particularly concerned about the impact which Viet Nam was having on the place of the military in US society. A painful process of deep introspection and adjustment began. The shift from a conscript to an all-volunteer military marked one of the most profound changes in the US military establishment to emerge as a result of Viet Nam.[30]

After a decade of intense preoccupation with tactical and doctrinal concerns shaped by the fighting in Viet Nam, the US Army returned its attention to the problem of mechanized combat in Europe. The Vietnamese experience provided the sub-text to the Army's approach to its role in NATO. Although a conflict between NATO and the Warsaw Treaty Organization (WTO) was considered much less likely than another peripheral war fought against insurgents, Army leadership decided to address the doctrinal requirements of such a conflict on the grounds that such a war would represent the gravest threat to US national security.[31]

While their US counterparts were caught up in Viet Nam, Soviet Army Officers were in the process of shifting their paradigm of future war from one dominated by the immediate and massive use of nuclear weapons to one, which included the possibility of an initial non-nuclear phase. The Soviet military press began to address the problem of combined-arms combat on a nuclear battlefield. Historical experience from the Great Patriotic War was emphasized in the adaption of Soviet ground forces to the demands of combat and operations. Soviet officers turned their attention to the conduct of offensive operations in the initial period of war. Surprise figured prominently in the recasting of operational art and tactics to make possible deep, swift offensives, which relied upon the exploitation of nuclear fires. As Chief Marshal of Tank Forces P. Rotmistrov pointed out: 'In the initial period of a nuclear-rocket war the role of tank forces will be quite significant'. Modern tank forces possessed much greater combat capabilities than those of World War II and could be employed on the main axes of land theatres of military action (TVD). Tank forces were well suited for rapid advances through regions subjected to weapons of mass destruction and so could be employed decisively in offensive operations in conjunction with rocket troops, aviation and airborne landings in order to seize key objectives (regions) in the enemy's deep rear, making possible the rapid achievement of the most immediate strategic objectives.[32]

Soviet military art responded rather quickly to the US shift to 'flexible response' and began to address the problem of combat across a spectrum of alternatives, ranging from general nuclear war to include theatres where nuclear weapons would not be used initially and local wars where nuclear weapons might not be employed at all.[33] The presence of enemy nuclear weapon systems in a theatre demanded the application of combined arms forces against them. The high-speed advance of tank and motorized forces, the application of airpower and the use of airborne landings were intended 'to limit to some extent the defender's opportunities to employ nuclear weapons'.[34] Soviet authors addressed command and control of combined arms formations as a problem of time and sought the means by which to gain relative advantage over a probable opponent through the application of cybernetics to the decision-cycle. The advantage gained in the planning and execution of staff and command actions, Soviet authors termed 'critical time'.[35] In 1968, the third edition of *Voennaia strategiia* addressed the problem of an initial period of non-nuclear combat during a general war, when conventional means might be employed to achieve immediate strategic objectives.[36]

The potential use of nuclear weapons still dominated the requirements for deployment of combat formations, making dispersal and mobility crucial to success, but now Soviet officers sought the means to make conventional forces more effective at the tactical and operations level during the initial period of war. Mechanization extended not only to motorized rifle divisions but also to the growing number of airborne divisions.[37] The possession of a broad spectrum of nuclear weapons by both sides made it apparent to Soviet commanders that they could not count upon a massing of forces to achieve a breakthrough as the Red Army had done during the Great Patriotic War. On the other hand, the need of the enemy to disperse his forces under the threat of nuclear fire precluded massing for the defence and thus made penetration easier if the attacker had sufficient manoeuvrability in both forces and fire-power. One conspicuous result of the Soviet search for greater mobility over the next decade was the mechanization of Soviet artillery—a shift from towed tubes to tracked vehicles.[38]

Gradually the Soviet Army emerged from a decade of reform with a dual-track capability to fight either nuclear or conventional. These doctrinal requirements radically exceeded what Soviet force planners could deliver in the 1960s, but they provided an agenda to guide the modernization of Soviet combat arms and support services into the next decade.[39]

V.   Détente and the era of 'realistic deterrence'

The period of the late 1960s and early 1970s represented a watershed for both the US and Soviet military systems. In a highly contradictory and fluid international environment, the two superpowers embarked upon a decade of negotiations designed to reduce the risks of war, manage the arms race and secure a mutually agreed-upon set of principles to structure their continuing competition. On the Soviet side, it was a period marked by growing confidence in the USSR's status as a great power and in the shift in the correlation of forces in favour of the USSR. US global strategy was seen as in a process of collapse under the weight of defeat in Southeast Asia and an internal crisis within the ruling élite.[40] At the same time, a growing unease in the United States over the expansion of Soviet military power and the ability to project that power during the same period contributed to the gradual deterioration and final collapse of détente and 'realistic deterrence'. The superpowers' competition during this period was shaped by a host of other factors which influenced their domestic political situations and international positions; these factors influenced directly and indirectly the assumptions of actors in both polities regarding the relevance and utility of military power in their bilateral relations.[41]

During this period, radical changes in military-political and military-techni-cal affairs began to affect the paradigms of future war held by planners on both sides. On the Soviet side, the deterioration of relations with the People's Republic of China, which degenerated to border clashes along the Ussuri in 1969, created a different threat environment. On the one hand, the possibilities of hostilities with the PRC imposed upon the USSR the need to enhance its military capabilities in the Far East and to create a command structure to direct such forces.[42] At the same time, the Soviet employment of WTO military forces against Czechoslovakia in 1968 highlighted a growing capability to execute large-scale operations and achieve surprise.[43] In the wake of the Israeli successes against the Soviet Union's Arab allies in 1967, major problems of air defence and combined arms tactics received renewed attention. Soviet involvement in the air defence battles over Sinai during this period brought valuable practical insights into modern air defence, as did the experiences of their Vietnamese allies in countering the US air offensive over Southeast Asia. Surprise in all its manifestations figured even more prominently in Soviet military studies, especially those devoted to the initial period of war.[44] How much these concerns have been shaped by the Soviet General Staff assessment of the risks of a war on two fronts and the need to use surprise to resolve conflict decisively in one theatre so as to avoid a widening, protracted struggle or to bring about a radical shift of the correlation of forces in other theatres is unclear.

By 1977 the Soviet Union possessed sufficient confidence to make no first use of nuclear weapons its declaratory policy, and by the early 1980s, Chief of the General Staff Marshal N. V. Ogarkov in his writings on military art and force posture addressed the conduct of high-speed, multi-*front*, strategic operations.[45] Ogarkov emphasized the capabilities of Soviet forces and other objective factors as decisive elements in the struggle to prevent the imperialists from unleashing a world war. Should such a conflict begin, Ogarkov and other Soviet officers pictured it as a struggle between coalitions, which would encompass all continents and involve the use of the entire arsenal of means of armed struggle.[46] More recently Marshal Ogarkov has pointed to the paradox of current massive strategic offensive arsenals as negating the logic of Western theories on the employment of nuclear weapons in a limited nuclear war option. At the same time, Ogarkov has emphasized the need to modernize conventional forces in the wake of technological developments associated with the appearance of precision-guided munitions (PGMs), the infusion of aviation into combined-arms combat and the development of more advanced command and control systems.[47]

For both US and Soviet military planners, the practical experience of combat in recent local wars began to reshape perceptions of tactics and operational art. Many Western commentators addressed these changes as a shift in the balance between offence and defence on the modern battlefield. In retrospect, these authors saw the 1967 Arab–Israeli War as the last hurrah of the conventional combined-arms mechanized offensive, for its fighting still resembled that of the Western Desert during the period of 1941 through 1943. Those Israeli lightning victories on several fronts had seemed to confirm that a modern mechanized force employed in conjunction with a devastating pre-emptive air attack still dominated the battlefield. However, the October 1973 conflict called this assumption into question. Some saw the mass use of PGMs in their anti-tank and anti-air roles as radically shifting the balance towards the defence. John Mearsheimer, writing on conventional deterrence, has gone so far as to assert that the PGM had drawn down the curtain on an era of warfare which began with the German Blitzkrieg of 1940.[48] Others have not been so certain, although all would agree that new conventional technologies were clearly pointing the way towards new tactical and operational possibilities.[49]

In US military circles what emerged out of the events of October 1973 was a deepening concern for the role of conventional forces in the initial period of war and the problem of surprise in all its forms and complexity.[50] In the wake of the October War, the US Army refocused its attention upon large-scale conventional warfare within the context of 'realistic deterrence'. The lessons of the October War raised questions regarding the structure of US ground forces. General William E. Dupuy, who assumed command of the US Army Training and Doctrine Command in July 1973, played a leading role in redirecting Army doctrine towards NATO concerns over the next three years. This effort culminated in a new set of field regulations which emphasized active defence and the initial period of hostilities. The section devoted to operations stated: 'Today the US Army must, above all else, *prepare to win the first battle of the next war*'.[51] The difficulties of fighting outnumbered in a situation where the adversary held the initiatives were formidable. The new doctrine rested upon the assumption of an initial conventional phase to such a conflict. It proposed that US forces would by means of fire and attrition along the forward edge of battle (FEBA) be able to inflict such losses upon Soviet/WTO forces that the enemy's offensive plans would be frustrated and the political leadership would have to face the risks of theatre escalation or stalemate. Theatre nuclear weapons were to be used against the second echelon, by which US planners meant those forces concentrated and deployed behind the initial attack force for the purpose of exploiting a breakthrough. The interdiction of strategic reserves, or strategic second echelon, which referred to the forces mobilized, concentrated and deployed from the western military districts of the USSR to support the development of a Soviet/WTO offensive, did not receive Army attention since they were outside the realm of corps concerns.[52] Active defence with its European orientation was designed to be in keeping with NATO requirements associated with 'flexible response' and 'forward defence'.

Some critical problems with 'active defence' emerged in the debates that followed the publication of the field manual (FM) in 1976. In its emphasis upon firepower and lethality in the close battle, it seemed to subordinate manoeuvre and depth to forward defence. Critics were quick to point out difficulties in conducting such a defence. For one thing, FM 100–5 (1976) seemed to postulate a Soviet attack based upon set-piece breakthrough operations like those executed during the final period of the Great Patriotic War, that is, the massing of forces in a very narrow sector with deep echeloning to create the penetration and exploitation of the breakthrough.

In its emphasis upon winning the first battle, FM 100–5 did not take into account the conclusions drawn by Soviet military science regarding the nature of combat in the initial period of war. On the basis of these conclusions, Soviet military art emphasized that initial combat would be dominated by the meeting engagement (*vstrechnyi boi*) fought by combined arms units under circumstances which would maximize the effectiveness of armour. In such meeting engagements, Soviet theorists posited a situation where both sides would enter into combat from the march and seek to gain the initiative and carry out their missions by offensive actions. Thus, the first battles of the next war were not, in the Soviet view, a series of set-piece general battles but a series of meeting engagements in which Soviet combined arms commanders would use forward detachments and advanced guards to penetrate, outflank and envelop enemy forces, making it impossible for those units to conduct an organized defence. The commanders of combined-arms and tank armies were expected to provide direction and coherence to these meeting engagements according to the *Front* commander's operational plan. By directing the development of the various meeting engagements into an operational encounter battle (*vstrechnoe srazhenie*), he would achieve his objectives and bring about the destruction of the opposing forces throughout their depth. Depending upon his mission, the enemy force, terrain, his own forces and the time available, he might decide to unleash one or several forward detachments on key axes to strike into the enemy's operational depth and by high-speed march, avoiding combat, seize some crucial objective.[53]

The Soviet concept of the meeting engagement posed a major dilemma for active defence because FM 100–5 had changed a basic assumption regarding the ratio of forces in contact to those in reserve. In place of the traditional idea of two units up to one back, active defence presupposed that all forces not irrevocably committed formed a reserve in being, thus reducing, if not eliminating, the need for tactical reserves.[54] Some critics worried that the doctrine was too intent upon a linear defence and that this, when combined with efforts to achieve concentration at critical points along the FEBA, would create opportunities for enemy forces to penetrate weakly defended areas and achieve encirclements. Winning the first battle depended upon concentration tactics, but these required freedom of lateral movement not easily achieved by engaged forces. Soviet manoeuvre and friction appeared likely to make such redeployment by engaged battalions most difficult.[55]

These and other issues stimulated a debate within the Army which created a climate for the consideration of a wide range of new concepts relating to central battle, future force requirements, placing the second echelon at risk, and world-wide contingencies. Over the next five years, the US Army began to shift its doctrinal focus from the division and tactics towards those measures which would link together the close, rear and deep battles into an operational whole, thereby setting the stage for the emergency of the corps as a focal point of combat power and the articulation of operational art as the expression of that idea.[56]

In 1981 Army doctrine writers coined a new term, Air/Land Battle, to emphasize a combined-arms approach to include deep operations, and in August 1982, with the publication of a new FM 100–5, Air/Land Battle became Army doctrine.[57] Although some proponents initially presented Air/Land

Battle as a radical break with the past, the new doctrine was evolutionary, adding depth to the battle, underscoring the need for commanders to forge tactical successes according to an operational plan to bring about success in a theatre, and presenting an integrated battlefield where circumstances might dictate the use of nuclear and/or chemical weapons. Air/Land Battle reflected an Army concern for a doctrine which would fit conditions in other probable theatres where US forces might engage Soviet or Soviet-surrogate forces just as well as those found in Europe.[58]

VI.   Renewed cold war and conventional military power

The articulation of new Army doctrine had over the preceding post-war decades stimulated discussion within the military and to a lesser extent without. Air/Land Battle, however, came at a time when the political climate and foreign policy concerns were giving shape to a new strategy. The years between 1976 and 1982 had witnessed a steady erosion of public support for détente and a growing hostility towards the Soviet Union. A consensus had emerged that defence had been neglected after Viet Nam and that there were real external interests which required military power for their protection. The growth of Soviet military power and Moscow's ability and willingness to project that power into the Third World received increased public attention. The debate surrounding the ratification of the Strategic Arms Limitation Talks (SALT) II turned into the consideration of a strategic window of vulnerability in the mid-1980s when the US strategic arsenal was supposed to be vulnerable to a disarming first strike. The combination of the national humiliation in Iran and the Soviet coup and military intervention in Afghanistan were taken as proof of the need for an expanded commitment to national defence. In the final years of the Carter Administration and under President Reagan, the level of defence spending increased.

Questions concerning the character of that defence effort also received greater attention. Critics, especially those associated with the military reform movement, which had close bipartisan ties to Congress, criticized the command structure, debated the force posture, and questioned the procurement and acquisition of various weapon systems. These circumstances alone would have guaranteed broad attention to Air/Land Battle.

The formulation of Air/Land Battle coincided with an intense debate within NATO over the role of theatre-nuclear forces in 'flexible response'. The modernization of Soviet theatre-nuclear forces, which began in 1977 with the introduction of the SS–20, had prompted an alliance decision to respond with its own force modernization. The deployment of Pershing II intermediate-range ballistic missiles (IRBMs) and ground-launched cruise missiles (GLCMs), when no negotiated solution appeared possible, created a political climate conducive to efforts to raise the theatre-nuclear threshold through the improvement of conventional forces. In the past, the costs of matching Soviet/WTO conventional forces had seemed beyond the realm of political-economic reality. Now, however, emerging technologies, especially those that extended the range, accuracy and lethality of smart conventional weapons, held out the prospect of negating Soviet/WTO numerical superiorities by permitting their engagement and destruction at great distance from the line of contact. Upon assuming command of NATO in 1979, General Bernard Rogers, former Army Chief of Staff, supported efforts to acquire such weapon systems and to integrate them into NATO doctrine.[59]

Such views gained broad public attention thanks to a volume published under the auspices of the American Academy of Arts and Sciences by the Steering Group of the European Security Study (ESECS). Composed of 26 leading civilian and military figures from four NATO-member countries and with an invited observer from Supreme Headquarters Allied Powers Europe attending, the Steering Group formed three workshops to address aspects of the problem: the estimation of the Soviet threat; the requirements for conventional defence; and the contributions that emerging technologies could make to conventional defence.[60] The document, when it appeared in the summer of 1983, quickly became identified as the Rogers Plan for the application of emerging technologies to the engagement and destruction of Soviet/WTO forces of the strategic second echelon, or Follow-On Forces Attack (FOFA).[61]

The core of the workshop report on the Soviet threat was Christopher Donnelly's analysis of an emerging Soviet capability to engage in deep, sustained raiding actions from the initiation of hostilities as part of a theatre-strategic operation. Donnelly identified such combined-arms raiding forces as had been seen during the exercise 'ZAPAD–81' as Operational Manoeuvre Groups (OMGs), a term found in Polish military periodicals, describing a modernized 'mobile group' (*podvizhnaia gruppa*) from the Great Patriotic War.[62] Donnelly and his colleague, Peter Vigor, had already pointed to the multi-front offensive executed by Soviet forces in Manchuria against the Kwantung Army in August 1945 as a model for such a deep, high-speed, theatre-strategic operation.[63] Vigor later described this as 'Soviet blitzkrieg theory', by which he meant the utilization of surprise, shock and deep operations by conventional forces to achieve victory quickly over NATO.[64]

Philip Petersen and John Hines have added to the picture of this theatre-strategic operation and the role of an initial air operation, airborne and airmobile landings, and the high-speed advance of tank and combined-arms formations led by OMGs.[65] These authors were not arguing that the Soviet military had, in fact, achieved such capabilities, but only that troop norms were being revised to be in keeping with operational objectives. Soviet military periodicals had called attention to serious problems in command and control, air defence and logistical support for such high-speed operations. Wider use of automated systems of troop control, which was seen as a means of maintaining centralized operational direction of an increasingly complex battle while permitting greater tactical initiative to junior commanders, has been touted as an answer to the command and control problem. Greater logistic support and a more streamlined command organization for rear services have been introduced. The entire structure of Soviet air defence forces has undergone a sweeping reorganization to provide more airpower to theatre, front and army commanders.[66]

None of these developments were revolutionary. They reflected a greater emphasis on theatre-scale operations and the need to exercise effective operational control of the forces committed, but this was a not a radical break with the past. The OMG created such a stir because of the confidence it seemed to demonstrate in the Soviet Union's ability to use conventional forces in a decisive manner at the operational-strategic level. To some extent the surprise was the result of the poverty of Western analysis of Soviet military art. Intelligence communities, pressed by current requirements for immediate assessments of the order of battle, seldom had the time or opportunity to address intentions.[67]

Open-source Soviet military publications received little attention outside a very narrow circle of specialists, and few of these devoted much attention to the history of the Soviet, much less Russian, military. With the exception of John Erickson, few Western scholars could make any claim to having mined the mountains of publications devoted to every aspect of the Great Patriotic War.[68] Until very recently, Western scholarship, relying heavily upon the memoirs of German commanders, took for granted Field Marshal von Manstein's notion that the East was a realm of 'lost victories', taken from the Wehrmacht by 'Corporal Hitler and Generals Mud and Winter'.[69] On closer examination, the Red Army emerges as a much more formidable opponent. Learning from mistakes in the initial period of the war, Soviet forces during the second and third phases of the war, that is, from the Stalingrad Counter-Offensive, demonstrated a growing mastery of the operational level of war. German tactical successes, which could be found until very late in the fighting, drowned in a sea of operational disasters.[70]

Such a reappraisal of Soviet military art raises serious issues regarding the search for tactical solutions for NATO's problems of fighting conventionally and outnumbered. Some analysts have argued that the Wehrmacht's tactical experience confirms the wisdom of training commanders in mission-oriented tactics (Auftragtaktik).[76] However, some recent commentators have questioned whether Soviet tactics were or are as stereotyped as the advocates of mission-oriented tactics assume.[72] The attention to the development of Soviet operational art has led to a better appreciation of the Soviet way of war and from this a more realistic appreciation of the threat than that provided by aggregate counts of formations, men-under-arms, or weapon systems.

Turning to the improvement of NATO conventional forces, the ESECS report addressed a wide range of reforms designed to enhance existing NATO strategy. 'Flexible response' and 'forward defence' were taken to be entirely adequate to meet the WTO threat. Raising the nuclear threshold would permit the alliance to deter more effectively and in case of hostilities allow NATO forces to fulfil required missions without early resort to nuclear weapons.[73] While the study addressed a number of issues relating to improved conventional forces, the topic that received the greatest attention was a set of proposals designed to use emerging technologies to obtain accurate and real-time target acquisition and to employ precision-guided munitions delivered by stand-off air platforms or by ground-based missiles in deep strikes. The targets of the new conventional weapons were to be Soviet/WTO command and control, air power infrastructure, interdiction of logistical support, and direct attack upon elements of the strategic second echelon. The execution of these deep-strike missions would depend upon the costs, rate of acquisition, and net advantage gained through the development of such emerging technologies. The workshop promised rapid procurement and low costs; the entire pro-gramme outlined by the ESECS was to cost less than $10 billion.[74] This proposal to enhance conventional deep-strike capabilities became known as Follow-On Forces Attack (FOFA).

While the report contained a number of valuable proposals, which addressed the improvement of NATO intelligence capabilities and increased inter-operability of alliance forces, FOFA received the greatest public attention. In Europe, critics feared that FOFA was an attempt to shift NATO strategy to fit Air/Land Battle, and some worried that it would worsen East–West relations.[75] The Rogers Plan, as it became known in the press, was either a radical strategic departure or a modest reform, depending upon the viewer's perspective.

Some supporters of FOFA certainly presented it as a major first step to a new NATO strategy. Professor Samuel Huntingdon outlined one variant of this new strategy in an article for *International Security*. Based upon a paper presented to a conference at the US Army War College, the article called for improved conventional capabilities to provide for conventional, in place of nuclear, retaliation.[76] Huntington began with the problem of the erosion of credibility of extended nuclear deterrence and proposed to substitute conven-tional retaliation in the form of a prompt NATO counter-offensive into WTO territory. He argued that the threat of such an attack would force Soviet political leaders to think twice before undertaking an attack upon NATO because it would apply military power against their political vulnerabilities, that is, their uncertain allies in Eastern Europe.[77] Such a conventional counter-offensive would frustrate Soviet hopes for a short war without necessarily invoking suicide.

Controversial on military grounds because it proposed an offensive action for which there did exist an effective command structure to bring about its timely execution by the various national corps, the proposal had severe liabilities when it treated the military vulnerabilities of Soviet forces to such an attack. Huntington based his counter-offensive on the oft-repeated assertion that Soviet forces are configured for the offensive and so would be particularly vulnerable to a NATO counter-blow.[78] The historical record, and it is the only evidence that we have in this area, does not confirm such an assessment of Soviet vulnerability to counter-attacks. The most outstanding successes by opponents against Soviet offensives have come when they outran their supplies and air support, their lead elements were badly attritioned and friction had undermined operational command and control. An early case of this was Marshal Pilsudski's counter-offensive before Warsaw and the best known case fom World War II was Manstein's counterstroke before Kharkov in 1943.

The Soviet ability to recover from unexpected attacks has been less well studied, but strategic echeloning is designed to provide front and theatre commanders with the necessary forces to engage in operational adjustments. A particularly effective Soviet counter-offensive was that launched against the 6th *SS Panzerarmee* in the Lake Balaton region of Hungary in 1945.[79]

Huntington specifically associated his proposal with an attempt to escape from a 'Maginot Line' mentality, calling to mind the tragic consequences when prudent measures become a substitute for effective strategy. Nuclear retaliation had become such a 'Maginot Line', and Huntington was purposing a shift in strategy that would recreate a credible deterrence. But like the French shift to manoeuvre when her army had no effective tank divisions and insufficient manoeuvre battalions to engage in mobile warfare, Huntington's proposal placed the cart before the horse. As General Donn A. Starry pointed out, Air/Land Battle and FOFA represent efforts to restore manoeuvre to the corps battle by linking together close, deep and rear battle. Its fundamental objectives are '(1) politically to collapse the Warsaw Pact's will to pursue military action; and (2) to avoid, if at all possible, the use of nuclear weapons—theater nuclear forces to be sure, but more importantly strategic or central nuclear systems, the intercontinental ballistic and submarine launched ballistic systems'.[80] Air/Land Battle and FOFA addressed how to defeat the enemy operationally at the corps level, not how to send army groups rushing into Eastern Europe seeking to use a counter-offensive by conventional forces to force a strategic political decision in the theatre.

Even the limited manoeuvre capabilities required in FOFA will not spring from wishful thinking in one or two capitals, but depend, as does the alliance's entire edifice, upon the members' collective willingness to sustain the joint effort in the face of a commonly agreed-upon threat. Men and *matériel* to conduct a viable defence are the product of political will. Huntington's underlying assumption is that the conventional counter-offensive will not tax NATO resources.[81] That is, in fact, open to question.

Most supporters of FOFA were more willing to build and sustain consensus than remake strategy; they presented the improved deep-strike capabilities as the acquisition of a real conventional interdiction capability, a mission to which NATO had paid lip-service in the past.[82] They pointed to the need to adjust doctrine to a changing threat and then seek to match the doctrine with relevant force capabilities.[83] Following the approval of the FOFA concept in November 1984, General Rogers himself stressed the tactical aspects of FOFA and affirmed that it was in no way incompatible with 'flexible response' or 'forward defence'.[84]

Another area of dispute between proponents and critics of FOFA has been the issue of whether the emerging technologies solution did, indeed, address NATO's dilemma effectively. Supporters claimed that the new weapon systems' promise and low costs justified the investment. James A. Tegnelia, Assistant Under-Secretary of Defense for Conventional Initiatives, made the case for this solution as a necessary augmentation to NATO's nuclear deterrence capabilities, which would allow NATO to sustain 'forward defence'. Tegnelia underscored the application of the emerging technologies to the deep battle which he defined as at a depth of 100 kilometres from the Forward Line of Troops (FLOT). While noting the progress in the development of the necessary weapon systems and their integration into an operational concept, Tegnelia pointed to a cost that was on the order of $20 to $30 billion dollars.[85]

Critics were much less optimistic and denied these claims, judging FOFA of bad deterrence and poor war-fighting.[86] Steven Canby has argued that NATO's central problem is, in fact, a shortage of operational reserves. NATO in this argument has been outgunned and not outmanned.[87] Canby asserted that FOFA advocates were wrong-headed in attempting to deal with a shortage of NATO reserves by eliminating Soviet/WTO follow-on forces before they reached the battlefield. He pictured the commitment to emerging technologies and deep strike as the latest in numerable attempts to achieve technological fixes to doctrinal and force structure problems within the alliance.[88] Canby doubted that the various emerging technologies, that is, sensors, command and control capabilities, delivery systems and munitions would have the synergetic effect that proponents claimed. He saw the cost estimates as still too low, the lead-times too short and the countermeasures too cheap to justify the hopes. He reminded his readers that technology is neutral, it favours neither offence nor defence, only the force which has mastered its application at all levels of war. Technological leads always seemed longer and more decisive in the development stage of weapon systems than they did in practice. Any truly radical advances in NATO capabilities were likely to instigate a vigorous and simultaneous effort by the Soviets to obtain the capabilities, integrate them into existing doctrine, reform doctrine to optimize their application and develop effective countermeasures to enemy employment.[89] Canby also underscored the distinction between a political solution to a strategic problem and a realistic military one by pointing to the reality of war in which friction would play havoc with doctrinal assumptions from the initiation of hostilities. He cited Michael Howard's sound counsel that the best doctrine did not provide ready-made solutions to such complex situations but only the framework and mental agility for commanders and their staffs at all levels to adapt to new and unanticipated situations.[90] As Howard himself pointed out, the historical record is not one to sustain great optimism in this area.

V. Conclusion

For all the ink spilled and all the passion expended, we return to those doctrinal asymmetries with which we began. The increased interest in a new generation of smart weapons has not brought a radical break in military doctrine on either side. Political factors loom much larger in setting the context of doctrinal change than do wonder weapons. Efforts to seize and hold the technological initiative in key areas have influenced each side's threat perception. Within NATO, technological innovations have often been recommended in lieu of military-political reforms, which carry much higher socio-political costs. Nor have conventional weapons become a substitute for nuclear weapons, although some of them are approaching the area effectiveness of tactical nuclear systems. No clear lines have been drawn between the use of conventional forces and nuclear weapons for that matter, and the appearance of more cruise missiles and tactical ballistic missiles with conventional warheads will make discrimination of the threat more difficult. The best that may be achieved is the raising of the nuclear threshold while sustaining deterrence; the worst is a blurring of the distinction.

One of the most intriguing aspects of these doctrinal asymmetries lies in the realm of language. Advocates and opponents of improved NATO conventional forces are united in their use of one term to describe the threat posed by a WTO conventional offensive: blitzkrieg. They disagree regarding the meaning of the term. All associate it with a short war and the use of surprise. But some link it to the employment of mechanized forces and tactical aviation to achieve victory on the model of the Wehrmacht in 1940.[91] Others would define it as an attempt to win quickly before an economically more powerful opponent can mobilize and shift the correlation of forces against the attacker as the Schlieffen Plan set out to do against France.[92]

Blitzkrieg, however, does not carry these meanings in Soviet usage. Soviet military theorists before, during and after the Great Patriotic War have shared a continuing hostility to blitzkrieg, which they identify with German militarism and categorize as the embodiment of an adventuristic strategy. This strategy took grave risks in trying to use limited means to achieve expansionist goals. The Soviets indict the German Government and military for making the same mistake in both world wars. The Germans' willingness to take high-level military risks in the hope of achieving quick and overwhelming success culminated in the planning and executive of Operation Barbarossa, a task for which Hitler's Germany was totally unprepared politically, economically and militarily. The correlation of forces scarcely favoured any German success, much less one achieved in five weeks.[93] Soviet authors criticized blitzkrieg because of this disconnect between military means and political objectives.

Soviet authors have used the term 'lightning operation' (*molnienosnaia operatsiia*) with approval, applying it to the Jassy-Kishinev Operation, where two Soviet fronts achieved the destruction of Army Group South Ukraine, Romania's withdrawal and then re-entry into the conflict on the Soviet side and a rapid Soviet penetration of the Balkans.[94] Marshal Zakharov, then Chief of the General Staff, thus used Jassy-Kishinev as an example of what Soviet forces should expect to achieve in a modern offensive operation. The Soviet destruction of the Kwantung Army and the occupation of Manchuria and northern Korea in August 1945 can also be classed as a lightning operation.[95] From a Soviet perspective, one of the crucial distinctions between lightning operations and blitzkrieg lies in the level of risk involved. Jassy-Kishinev and Manchuria were not high-risk military ventures. Soviet military power and foreign policy worked hand in hand to create a situation where the military risks were low, the possibilities of foreign complications minimized and the potential political gains high. These operations were Clausewitzian in the highest sense of that term. Surprise, mobile groups, concentration of effort in key sectors, the exploitation of terrain that the opponent saw as impossible, the echeloning of the attacks, and the effective use of *maskirovka* to conceal the extent and timing of the action were practiced in many other operations on the Eastern Front—operations which covered more ground, destroyed more enemy forces and had a more decisive impact upon the enemy's centre of gravity. But I have found no record where Soviet military analysts have used the term lightning operation to refer to any of these.

The conclusion follows that lightning operations are exceptional opportunities to be exploited when the chance arises but not the expected form of combat, and certainly not the one which would begin a systemic war between NATO and WTO. Vigor is certainly right in his assertion that the Soviets would like to avoid escalation by bringing about a quick and decisive victory in the theatre. But Soviet doctrine must assume that the option of escalation will be exercised by NATO forces should the Soviets seem likely to achieve such results. As Benjamin Lambeth has pointed out, the Soviet High Command would face so many uncertainties that no decision to attack would come easily.[96] This underscores a certain prudence in the Soviet use of military power. NATO solidarity and an effective commitment to conventional deterrence thus can serve to reinforce such prudence. Soviet society may be militarized, but the Soviet regime, as Michael Howard has pointed out, is not bellicose.[97] Howard further argues that Western prudence consists of maintaining a viable military posture, secure alliance system and general economic prosperity, while at the same time making certain that Western actions never confront the Soviet leadership with the appalling dilemma of choosing between systemic collapse and systemic war.

Soviet declarations about the nature of future war remain remarkably clear and consistent. Such a conflict is not inevitable; the forces of peace are growing, and Soviet military power can deter Western adventurism. Should that deterrence fail, then war would be systemic, involve coalitions of powers, take on global dimensions, witness the employment of the full arsenals of both sides and be historically decisive.[98] Such statements are always couched in terms of imperialism's aggressive nature, but they emphasize the Soviet willingness to use military power to threaten the adversary's social system. This is deterrence by threat of war of annihilation, which may seem reassuring because it leaves little room for adventurism, but must raise anxieties because of the ideological hostility upon which it is based and the possibility that miscalculation, misperception and simple accident could transform a political struggle into a general war in which there would be little room for limitation once deterrence failed.

The modernization of conventional force doctrine must be viewed within this context. A conventional force option has become part of the military doctrines on both sides. Yet, as an option to initiate hostilities with some notion of political gains in keeping with the risks involved, it remains an option in theory, not in practice. War is too complex, chaotic and uncertain for any commander to believe that the engagement of the major forces of each coalition in the vital central region could be kept conventional for anything but a short period of time. The OMG, as Donnelly has pointed out, fits both conventional and nuclear operations. Successful penetration in the former could make it very difficult for NATO to exercise a nuclear option against it. The recent edition of Reznichenko's *Tactics* underscores the impact of nuclear weapons on the battlefield while exploring the ways in which conventional forces might be employed to negate them in the initial period of war.[99] Air/Land Battle and FOFA, likewise, are extensions of a conventional option to an integrated battle. Indeed, as Soviet observers point out, the recce-strike complexes, which are the heart of deep strike's emerging technology, are an attempt to create smart conventional weapons, which can be more lethal against certain types of target than the tactical nuclear weapons they replace.[100]

The world of deterrence has become more complex and the need for doctrinal clarity more compelling. Among the many proposals that have addressed the military-political context of the superpower competition, those confidence-building measures that provide for greater opportunities for the study and exchange of information regarding military doctrine have substantial promise. The proposals put forward by Senators Nunn and Levin in March 1983, which called for exchange visits between senior US and Soviet military leaders, deserve serious attention. The Soviets may object to wider exchanges of military information as a form of 'legal espionage', but such exchanges offer opportunities for a much more accurate appraisal of those factors which shape doctrine. A more realistic assessment of the threat is in the interest of both sides. Such exchanges were developing under the Carter Administration, but died with Afghanistan. They will not flower in a time of superpower confrontation. But, in a more relaxed period, when the competition is less strident, they could serve to reinforce greater confidence in the political arena by drawing greater attention to the problem of political-military intentions and doctrinal change.[101] In a more favourable climate, they could serve as a means of addressing the problem of surprise in the threat perception of both sides and make possible more effective arms control measures for reducing the risk of surprise in the central region and other potential theatres of military action.

If some military forecasters are correct, there are even more compelling reasons for such exchanges. In a provocative book, Brigadier Richard E. Simkin argues that military affairs have reached a turning point analogous to that of 50 years ago when mechanized warfare emerged. Simkin sees a qualitative shift in air-mobile operations, which until now have supported a tank-dominated battle. Air-mobile operations may become the 'rotary wing revolution'. He has linked this trend to another, a shift to special forces as the most usable form of military power left to states in the late twentieth century. This combination is conditioned by greater emphasis upon strategic surprise in the employment of combat power.[102] Marshal Ogarkov's comments on the expanding role of aviation in all its forms as part of theatre-strategic operations lends some support to the rotary revolution.[103] His attention to the idea of the unity and struggle of opposites and the negation of the negation as elements of the dialectic relevant to contemporary military affairs suggests that he too sees the current period as one of revolutionary change.[104] These indications of radical changes in military affairs point towards a greater role for conventional forces within the military postures of each state. The need to grasp the significance of these doctrinal asymmetries has become more than a matter of military policy.

Notes and references

[1] The opinions expressed in this essay are solely those of the author and should in no way be construed to represent the opinions of the US Department of the Army or the US Department of Defense.
Jervis, R., 'Deterrence theory revisited', *World Politics*, vol. 21, no. 2 (Jan. 1979), pp. 289–324.

[3] On the problem of the war in the East as a *Vernichtungskrieg*, see: Messerschmidt, M., '*Der Kampf der Wehrmacht im Osten als Traditionsproblem*', *Unternehman Barbarossa*': *Der Ueberfall auf die Sowjetunion 1941*, eds G. Ueberscharl and W. Wette (*Schoningh*: Paderborn, 1984), pp. 253–70.

[4] Howard, M. (ed.), *Restraints on war: Studies in the Limitation of Armed Conflict* (Oxford University Press: Oxford, 1979), pp. 1–17. See also essays in this volume by J. G. Garnett on conventional war in the nuclear era (pp. 79–102) and L. Martin on limited nuclear war (pp. 103–22). Howard argues that war is instrumental and not elemental, its only legitimate purpose is a better peace. This argument is very close to the Soviet idea that the defence of socialism, first of all, should prevent attack; once hostilities have begun, however, the end of conflict must involve the termination of the root of war. In this case, the source of potential hostilities and the root of war is ideologically defined to be militarized capitalism. See: Kipp, J. W., 'Lenin and Clausewitz: the militarization of Marxism', *Military Affairs*, vol. 49, no. 4 (Oct. 1985), pp. 184–90.

[5] Mearsheimer, J. J., *Conventional Deterrence* (Cornell University Press: Ithaca, NY, 1983).

[6] Bush, V., *Modern Arms and Free Men: A Discussion of the Role of Science in Preserving Democracy* (Simon and Schuster: New York, 1949), pp. 113–36.

[7] Posen, B., *The Sources of Military Doctrine: France, Britain, and Germany between the World Wars* (Cornell University Press: Ithaca, NY, 1984), pp. 1–33.

[8] *Sovetskaia voennaia entsiklopediia* (Soviet military encyclopaedia), Vol. III (*Voenizdat*: Moscow, 1976–1980), pp. 225–6.

[9] Zhilin, P. A., *Problemy voennoi istorii* (Problems of military history) (*Voenizdat*: Moscow, 1975), pp. 135–41.

[10] Howard, M., 'The future of deterrence', *Journal of the Royal United Service Institution*, no. 6 (June 1986), pp. 3–10.

[11] Kir'ian, M. M. (ed.), *Voenno-tekhnicheskii progress i Vooruzhennye Sily SSSR*

160   THE UNCERTAIN COURSE

(Military-technological progress and the armed Forces of the USSR). (*Voenizdat:* Moscow, 1982), pp. 218–55; and Dunnin, A., *'Razvitie sukhoputnykh voisk v poslevoennyi period'* (The development of land forces during the post-war period), *Voenno-istoricheskii zhurnal* (Military history journal), no. 5 (May 1978), pp. 33–40.

12 Doughty, R., 'The evolution of US Army tactical doctrine, 1945–1976', *Leavenworth Papers No. 1* (Combat Studies Institute, US Army Command and General Staff College: Ft Leavenworth, KS, 1979), pp. 2–7.
13 Holloway, D., *The Soviet Union and the Arms Race* (Yale University Press: New Haven, CT, 1983), pp. 29–39.
14 Gareev, M. A., *M. V. Frunze—voennyi teoretik* (M. V. Frunze—military theorist) (*Voenizdat*: Moscow, 1985), pp. 238–9.
15 Gareev (note 14), pp. 39–43.
16 Erickson, J., 'The Soviet view of deterrence: a general survey', *The Soviet Union: Security Policies and Constraints*, ed. J. Alford (St Martin's Press: New York, 1985), pp. 136–45.
17 Khrushchev, N., *Khrushchev Remembers: The Last Testament* (Bantam Books: New York, 1976), pp. 16–29, 44–56 and 250–62.
18 Korotkov, I., 'On the basic factors determining the course and outcome of war', *Sovetskaia aviatsiia* (Soviet aviation), no. 8 (Aug. 1958) in Horelick, A., *Some Soviet Views on the Nature of Future War and the Factors Determining Its Course and Outcome* (Rand Corporation: Santa Monica, CA, 1958), p. 32.
19 Penkovsky, O., *The Penkovsky Papers* (Doubleday & Company: New York, 1965), pp. 252–7.
20 Kulikov, V. G. (ed.), *Akademiia General'nogo Shtaba* (General Staff Academy), (*Voenizdat:* Moscow, 1976), pp. 141–59; and Sokolovskii, V. D., *Soviet Military Strategy*, ed. and trans. H. Scott (Crane Russack: New York, 1984).
21 Isserson, G., *'Zapiski sovremennika o M. N. Tukhachevskom'* (Contemporary notes about M. I. Tukhachevskij), *Voeinno-istoricheskii zhurnal* (Military history journal), no. 4 (Apr. 1964), pp. 65–7.
22 George, A. L. and Smoke, R., *Deterrence in American Foreign Policy: Theory and Practice* (Columbia University Press: New York, 1974), pp. 26ff.
23 Doughty (note 12), pp. 12–18.
24 McNamara, R. S., *The Essence of Security: Reflections in Office* (Harper & Row: New York, 1968), p. 69.
25 Doughty (note 12), pp. 25–32.
26 Doughty (note 12), pp. 22–5.
27 NATO, *The North Atlantic Treaty Organization: Facts and Figures* (NATO Information Service: Brussels, 1981), pp. 139–40.
28 Graebner, N. A., 'The United States and NATO, 1953–1969', *NATO after Thirty Years*, eds L. S. Kaplan and K. W. Clawson (Scholarly Resources: Wilmington, DE, 1981), pp. 31–47.
29 Doughty (note 12), pp. 31–2.
30 Janowitz, M., 'The impact of a volunteer force on strategic affairs', *National Security and American Society: Theory, Process and Policy*, eds F. N. Trager and P. S. Kronenberg (The University Press of Kansas: Lawrence, KS, 1973), pp. 579–93.
31 Starry, D. A., 'A tactical evolution—FM 100–5', *Military Review*, vol. 58, no. 8 (Aug. 1978), pp. 3–4.
32 Rotmistrov, P., *'Boevoe ispol'zovanie bronetankovykh voisk v nachal'nyi period*

voiny' (The use of armoured troops in battle during the initial period of war), *Voennaia mysl'* (Military thought), no. 7 (July 1964), p. 70.

[33] Reznichenko, V., *'Voprosy sovremennogo obshchevoiskovogo boia'* (About the integrated all-arms battle of today), *Voennaia mysl'* (Military thought), no. 3 (Mar. 1964), p. 21.

[34] Reznichenko (note 33), p. 25. See also Savkin, V. E., *Tempy nastupleniia* (Momentum of attack) (*Voenizdat*: Moscow, 1965), pp. 7–15.

[35] Tatarchenko, A., *'Kriticheskoe vremia i operativnost' upravleniia voiskami'* (Critical time and efficiency of the control of troops), *Voennaia mysl'* (Military thought), no. 7 (July 1965), pp. 27–32.

[36] Sokolovskii, V. D., *Voennaia strategiia* (Military strategy) (*Voenizdat*: Moscow, 1968), pp. 240–1 and 335–7.

[37] Kir'ian (note 11), pp. 301–4. Soviet airborne divisions, which now number seven, were transformed into light mechanized forces with sufficient mobility and firepower to create a serious threat in the enemy tactical zone, if dropped as battalions or regiments, and at operational depth, if dropped as regiments or a division. Their potential utility for a military-political *coup de main* against a capital city was first demonstrated against Prague and then in 1979 against Kabul. On Soviet airborne forces, see Turbeville, G., 'Airborne forces', *Soviet Armed Forces Review Annual*, vol. 9 (Academic International Press: Gulf Breeze, FL, 1986), pp. 161ff.

[38] Isby, D., *Weapons and Tactics of the Soviet Army* (Jane's: London, 1981), pp. 161ff.

[39] Erickson, J., 'The Soviet military system: doctrine, technology and "style"', *Soviet Military Power and Performance*, eds J. Erickson and E. J. Feuchtwanger (Shoe String Press: Hamden Court, CT, 1979), pp. 18–23.

[40] Kulish, V. M., *Voennaia sila i mezhdunarodnye otnosheniia* (Military power and international relations) (*Izdatel'stvo 'Mezhdunarodnye Othnosheniia'*: Moscow, 1972), pp. 3ff.

[41] Kipp, J. W., 'US–USSR military balance' *Dimensions of Detente*, ed. D. Sheldon (Praeger: New York, 1978), pp. 196–216.

[42] Kulikov, V., *'Strategicheskoe rukovodstvo vooruzhennymi silami'* (Strategic leadership of armed forces), *Voenno-istoricheskii zhurnal* (Military history journal), no. 6 (June 1975).

[43] Littell, R. (ed.), *The Czech Black Book: Prepared by the Institute of History of the Czechoslovak Academy of Sciences* (Praeger: New York, 1969), pp. 5–71.

[44] Ivanov, S. V. (ed.) *Nachal'nyi period voiny (po opytu kampanii i operatsii Vtoroi Mirovoi voiny* (The initial period of war—after the experience of World War II) (*Voenizdat*: Moscow, 1974), pp. 4–22; Shavrov, I., *'Lokal'nye voiny i ikh mesto v global'noi strategii imperializma'* (Local wars and their place in the global strategy of imperialism), *Voenno-istoricheskii zhurnal* (Military history journal), no. 3 (Mar. 1975), pp. 24–38 and no. 4 (Apr. 1975), pp. 90–7; Shavrov, I. (ed.), *Lokal'nye voiny: Istoriia i sovremennost'* (Local wars: history and the present) (*Voenizdat*: Moscow, 1981); and Kir'ian, M. M., *Vnezapost' v operatsiiakh vooruzhennykh sil SShA* (The surprise in the operations of the US armed forces) (*Voenizdat*: Moscow, 1982).

[45] Ogarkov, N. V., *Vsegda v gotovnosti k zashchite otechestva* (Always ready to defend the native land) (*Voenizdat:* Moscow, 1982), pp. 34–9.

[46] Altukhov, P., *'Osobennosti upravleniia ob'edineniiami i soedineniiami koalitsionnogo sostava po opytu voiny* (1939–1945 gg.)' (Special features in the control of the formations and groupings within coalition troops), *Voenno-istoricheskii zhurnal*, no. 3 (Mar. 1982), pp. 45 and 52.

47 Ogarkov, N. V., *Istoriia uchit bditel'nosti* (History teaches vigilance) (*Voenizdat*: Moscow, 1985), pp. 76–90.

48 Mearsheimer, J. J., 'Why the Soviets can't win quickly in central Europe', *International Security*, vol. 7, no. 1 (1982), pp. 3–39.

49 *FM 100–5: Operations, 1 July 1976* (Field Manual), US Department of the Army, Washington, DC; pp. 2–1 to 2–4.

50 Handel, M., 'Crisis and surprise in three Arab–Israeli wars', *Strategic Military Surprise: Incentives and Opportunities*, eds K. Knorr and P. Morgan (Transaction Books: New Brunswick, NJ, 1983), pp. 111–46; Betts, R., *Surprise Attack: Lessons for Defense Planning* (The Brookings Institution: Washington, DC, 1982); and Betts, R., 'Surprise attack and preemption', *Hawks, Doves, and Owls: An Agenda for Avoiding Nuclear War*, eds G. Allison, A. Carnesale and J. S. Nye, Jr, (W. W. Norton & Company: New York, 1985), pp. 54–79.

51 *FM 100–5* (note 49), p. 1–1.

52 Romjue, J. L., *From Active Defense to AirLand Battle: The Development of Army Doctrine, 1973–1982* (Historical Office, United States Army Training and Doctrine Command: Fort Monroe, VA, 1984), pp. 33–9. While the 1976 edition of *FM 100–5* had posited the use of nuclear weapons in an interdiction role, the targets had been close behind the FEBA. In 1979, the argument emerged that improved technology in target acquisition, command and control, and long-range strike capabilities made it possible to engage in deep strikes with corps taking on the responsibility for such a mission.

53 On the development of meeting engagement (*vstrechnyi boi*) and the operational encounter battle (*vstrechnoe srazhenie*), see Iamanov, A. A., *Vstrechnyi boi: Operativno-takticheskoe issledovanie na voenno-istoricheskoi osnove* (Meeting engagement: operative-tactical research on military-historical grounds) (*Voenizdat*: Moscow, 1959); Reznichenko, V. G. (ed.), *Taktika* (Tactics), 1st edn., (*Voenizdat*: Moscow, 1966), pp. 137 ff; Babadzhanian, A. Kh. *et al.*, *Tanki i tankovye voiska* (Tanks and tank troops), 2nd edn. (*Voenizdat*: Moscow, 1980), pp. 269–304; and Reznichenko, V. G. (ed.), *Taktika* (Tactics), 2nd edn. (*Voenizdat*: Moscow, 1984), pp. 152–73.

54 Romjue (note 52), pp. 14–18.

55 Romjue (note 52), pp. 19–21.

56 US Army Training and Doctrine Command (Tradoc), *US Army Operational Concepts for the AirLand Battle and Corps '86*, Tradoc Pam 525–5, 25 Mar. 1981; and Romjue, J., 'The evolution of the AirLand Battle concept', *Air University Review*, vol. 35, no. 4 (May/June 1984), pp. 11–15.

57 *FM 100–5: Operations 20 August 1982* (Field Manual), US Department of the Army, Washington, DC; pp. 2–1 to 2–3.

58 FM 100–5 (note 57), US Army, pp. 17–1 to 17–13. On the question of whether this manual was revolutionary or evolutionary, see Jones, A., 'FM 100–5: view from the ivory tower', *Military Review*, vol. 64, no. 5 (May 1984), pp. 17–22. Professor Jones had reviewed the 1976 edition of FM 100–5 for *Military Review* in 1978. While expressing some doubts about the manual's rhetoric concerning the strength of the offence over the defence, he found it an extension of the 1976 publication, rather than its negation.

59 Rogers, B., 'Enhancing deterrence—raising the nuclear threshold', *NATO Review*, vol. 30, no. 6 (Dec. 1982), pp. 6ff.

60 *Strengthening Conventional Deterrence in Europe: Proposals for the 1980s*, Report

of the European Security Group (St Martin's Press: New York, 1983), pp. 7–36.

[61] Bonnart, F., 'Follow-on Forces Attack', *NATO's 16 Nations*, vol. 29, no. 7 (Nov.–Dec. 1984), pp. 49–51.

[62] Donnelly, C. S., 'The Soviet Operational Manoeuvre Group: a new challenge for NATO', *Military Review*, vol. 63, no. 3 (Mar. 1983), pp. 43–60. On ZAPAD 81 and the OMG, see Simon, J., *Warsaw Pact Forces: Problems of Command and Control* (Westview Press: Boulder, CO, 1985), pp. 192–4.

[63] Vigor, P. H. and Donnelly, C., 'The Manchurian campaign and its relevance to modern strategy', *Comparative Strategy*, vol. 2, no. 2 (1980), pp. 159–78. For an informed treatment of the OMG issue and its historical antecedents, see Bellamy, C., 'Antecedents of the modern Soviet Operational Manoeuvre Group (OMG)', *Journal of the Royal United Service Institution*, no. 3 (Sep. 1984), pp. 50–8.

[64] Vigor, P. H., *Soviet Blitzkrieg Theory* (Macmillan: London, 1983), pp. 1ff.

[65] Petersen, P. A. and Hines, J. G., 'The conventional offensive in Soviet theater strategy', *Orbis*, vol. 27, no. 3 (Fall 1983), pp. 695–739.

[66] Hemsley, J., *Soviet Troop Control: The Role of Command Technology in the Soviet Military System* (Oxford University Press: Oxford, 1982); Ivanov, D. A., Savel'ev, V. P. and Shemansky, P. V., *Osnovy upravleniia voiskami v boiu* (Principles of troop control during battle) (*Voenizdat*: Moscow, 1977); and Erickson, J. and Hanson, L. M., *Soviet Combined Arms: Past and Present* (Center for Strategic Technology, Texas A & M University: College Station, TX, 1981).

[67] For an appreciation of the problem of assessing Soviet military capabilities and intentions, see Prados, J., *The Soviet Estimate: US Intelligence Analysis and Soviet Strategic Forces*, 2nd edn. (Princeton University Press: Princeton, NJ, 1986). Problems relating to the structure of the intelligence system, its tasking and bureaucratic politics reinforce a tendency towards immediate concerns at the expense of context and perspective. Ethnocentricism can reinforce a bias towards capability analysis by promoting stereotyped assumptions regarding intentions, interests and mirror-image assessments of the relevance of numbers of units and weapon systems. On the impact of ethnocentricism on military analysis, see Booth, K., *Strategy and Ethnocentricism* (Croom Helm: London, 1979) and paper 1.3 (pages 39–66).

[68] Erickson's three volumes—*The Soviet High Command; The Road to Stalingrad; and The Road to Berlin*—form the classics of Soviet military studies in the West. Much has happened in the past decade to add depth and variety to those studies, including the publication of supporting bibliographies, specialized studies, an annual and an ambitious encyclopaedia project. Soviet publications have also become more forthcoming as well. For more details on these developments, see Kipp, J. W., 'Studies in Soviet aviation and air power', *Aerospace Historian*, vol. 31, no. 1 (Spring/Mar. 1984), pp. 43–4.

[69] Recent works have interpreted the Wehrmacht's Eastern War in a very different light. See Boog, H. *et al.*, '*Der Angriff auf die Sowjetunion*', Vol. IV, *Das Deutsche Reich und der Zweite Weltkrieg*, (Deutsche Verlag-Anstalt: Stuttgart, 1983). The most controversial recent work on the initial phase of the Great Patriotic War is B. Fugate's volume on Operation Barbarossa. Fugate offers the thesis that the Soviet High Command did, indeed, have a realistic plan or operational concept for dealing with the German attack. See Fugate, B., *Operation Barbarossa* (Presidio Press: San Francisco, CA, 1984). On this issue and the debate surrounding Soviet doctrine and operational plans on the eve of the invasion, see Watts, B. D. and Murray, W.,

'Inventing history: Soviet military genius revealed', *Air University Review*, vol. 26, no. 3 (Mar.–Apr. 1985), pp. 102ff; Fugate, B., 'On inventing history', *Air University Review*, vol. 26, no. 6 (Sep.–Oct. 1985), pp. 121–5; and Kipp, J. W., 'Barbarossa, Soviet covering forces and the initial period of war: military history and AirLand Battle', *Air University Review* (forthcoming).

70 Glantz, D. M., 'The nature of Soviet operational art', *Parameters*, vol. 15, no. 1 (1985), pp. 2–12; and US Army War College, *1984 Art of War Symposium; A Transcript of Proceedings* (Center for Land Warfare, US Army War College: Carlisle Barracks, PA, 1984).

71 Von Mellenthin, F. W. and Stolfi, R. H. S. with Sobik, E., *NATO under Attack: Why the Western Alliance Can Fight Outnumbered and Win in Central Europe without Nuclear Weapons* (Duke University Press: Durham, NC, 1984). Von Mellenthin, a respected German officer and author on mechanized warfare with his co-authors argues that German success with *Auftragtaktik* can be repeated against the Soviet Army because Soviet tactics, based upon battle drills, are inflexible and stifle the initiative of company, battalion and regimental commanders. That NATO does not have one tactical doctrine but many—as many as there are distinct national corps—and that these doctrines are quite different raise some reservations regarding the applicability of mission-oriented tactics. Put bluntly, one can imagine any number of tactical successes, which in their sum, amount to operational defeat. The more fundamental problem, which cannot be resolved by tactical innovations, is NATO's focus on war at the corps level and below. NATO's problem at the operational level of war is to forge unity from diversity. For a look at the NATO and Soviet approaches to theatre war, see Hines, J. G. and Petersen, P. A., 'Is NATO thinking too small? A comparison of command structures', *International Defense Review*, vol. 19, no. 5 (May 1986), pp. 563–72.

72 Baxter, W. P., *Soviet AirLand Battle Tactics* (Presidio Press: San Francisco, CA, 1986), pp. 28–32.

73 *Strengthening Conventional Deterrence in Europe* (note 60), pp. 7–12.

74 *Strengthening Conventional Deterrence in Europe* (note 60), pp. 243–52. For an assessment of the various weapon systems, see Berg, P. and Herolf, G., '"Deep Strike": new technologies for conventional interdiction', *World Armaments and Disarmament: SIPRI Yearbook 1984* (Taylor & Francis: London, 1984), pp. 291–318.

75 Van der Vlis, A., 'AirLand Battle in NATO', *Parameters*, vol. 14, no. 2 (Summer 1984), pp. 10–14; Coolsaet, R., 'NATO strategy under different influences', *ADIU Report*, vol. 6, no. 6 (Nov.–Dec. 1984), pp. 4–8; and Plesch, D. T., 'AirLand Battle & NATO's military posture', *ADIU Report*, vol. 7, no. 2 (Mar.–Apr. 1985), pp. 7–11.

76 Huntington, S. P., 'Conventional deterrence and conventional retaliation in Europe', *International Security*, vol. 8, no. 3 (1983/1984), pp. 32–56. Huntington's article received quick attention from *The New York Times*, when the paper's military correspondent, Drew Middleton, devoted an article to it as part of efforts to change NATO strategy. See *The New York Times*, 5 Feb. 1984, p. 18. In the summer of 1983, at least one author identified the Rogers Plan, as opposed to AirLand Battle, with deep strikes by ground forces, either a specially tailored brigade in each corps or a high-technology, light division, across the Inter-German border. See Schepe, G., 'The Rogers Plan and the concept of "deep battle" on the Central Front', *Canadian Defence Quarterly*, vol. 13, no. 1 (Summer 1983), pp. 30–3.

77 Huntington (note 76), pp. 32–5.

[78] Huntington (note 76), pp. 47–50.

[79] Erickson, J., *The Road to Berlin* (Westview Press: Boulder, CO, 1983), pp. 508–17.

[80] Starry, D. A., 'The evolution of US Army operational doctrine—active defence, AirLand Battle, and future trends', *Proceedings of a Symposium on Military Doctrine for Central Europe (Stockholm, June 5–6, 1984)*, ed. L. B. Wallin (The Swedish National Defence Research Institute: Stockholm, 1986), p. 55.

[81] Huntington (note 76), p. 50.

[82] The New York Times, 14 Nov. 1984, p. 3.

[83] Starry (note 80), p. 60.

[84] Rogers, B., 'Follow-On Forces Attack (FOFA): myths and realities', *NATO Review*, vol. 32, no. 6 (Dec. 1984), pp. 1–9.

[85] Tegnelia, J. A., 'Emerging technology for conventional deterrence', *International Defense Review*, vol. 18, no. 5 (May 1985), pp. 647–52.

[86] Goure, D. and Cooper, J. R., 'Conventional deep strike: a critical look', *Comparative Strategy*, vol. 4, no. 3, (1984) pp. 215–48; Hampson, F. O., 'Groping for technical panaceas: the European conventional balance and nuclear stability', *International Security*, vol. 8, no. 3 (1984), pp. 57–82; and Garrett, J. M., 'Conventional force deterrence in the presence of theater nuclear weapons', *Armed Forces and Society*, vol. 11, no. 1 (Fall 1984), pp. 59–84.

[87] Canby, S. L., 'The conventional defense of Europe. Part I: the solution is operational reserves' in Wallin (note 80), pp. 96–105.

[88] Canby, S. L., 'The operational limits of emerging technology', *International Defense Review*, vol. 18, no. 6 (June 1985), pp. 875–81.

[89] Canby (note 88), pp. 880–1.

[90] Canby (note 88), pp. 881. See also Howard, M., 'Men against fire: expectations of war in 1914', *International Security*, vol. 9, no. 1 (Summer 1984), pp. 41–57.

[91] Mearsheimer (note 5), pp. 2–36.

[92] Vigor (note 64), pp. 1–62.

[93] *Voennyi entsiklopedicheskii slovar'* (Military encyclopaedic dictionary) (*Voenizdat*: Moscow, 1983), p. 455. Regarding Soviet views on the connections between military doctrine and strategic adventurism, see also Ogarkov (note 47), pp. 59–71.

[95] Zakharov, M., '*Molnienosnaia operatsiia (Iz opyta 2-go Ukrainskogo fronta v Iassko-Kishinevskoi operatsii*' (Lightning operation—experience of Ukrainian front, operation Yassy-Kishinev), *Voenno-istoricheskii zhurnal* (Military history journal), no. 8 (Aug. 1964), pp. 15–28.

[95] Glantz, D. M., *August Storm: The Soviet Strategic Offensive in Manchuria, 1945* in *Leavenworth Paper No. 7* (Combat Studies Institute, US Army Command and General Staff College: Ft Leavenworth, KS, 1983); and *August Storm: The Soviet Tactical and Operational Combat in Manchuria, 1945* in *Leavenworth Paper No. 8* (Combat Studies Institute, US Army Command and General Staff College: Ft Leavenworth, KS, 1983).

[96] Lambeth, B., 'Uncertainties for the Soviet war planners' *Conventional Forces and American Defense Policy*, ed. S. E. Miller (Princeton University Press: Princeton, NJ, 1986), pp. 159–86. On the contradictions affecting the WTO as a political alliance, see *The Warsaw Pact: Alliance in Transition*, eds D. Holloway and J. M. O. Sharp (Cornell University Press: Ithaca, NY, 1984). For a prudent assessment of Soviet efforts to adapt the Warsaw Pact to bring about greater military-political cohesion through pact institutions and exercises, see Simon (note 62).

[97] Howard (note 10), p. 4.

[98] Ogarkov (note 47), pp. 68–95.

[99] Reznichenko, V. G. (ed.), *Taktika* (Tactics) (*Voenizdat*: Moscow, 1984).

[100] Belov, M. and Shchukin, V., *'Razvedyvatel'no-porazhaiushchie kompleksy armii SShA'* (Reconnaissance-destroying complexes in the US Army), *Voennyi vestnik* (Military survey), no. 1 (Jan. 1985), pp. 86–90; and Grishin, S. V. and Tsalenko, N. N. *Soedineniia i chasti v boiu* (*Voenizdat*: Moscow, 1985), pp. 32–40 and 45–50.

[101] For a discussion of the need for expanded discussions between US and Soviet military leaders, see Williams, W. J., 'Expanding the US–USSR military dialogue', *Preventing Nuclear War: A Realistic Approach*, ed. B. M. Blechman (Indiana University Press: Bloomington, IN, 1985), pp. 145–60.

[102] Simkin, R. E., *Race to the Swift: Thoughts on Twenty-First Century Warfare* (Brassey's Defense Publishers: London, 1985).

[103] Ogarkov (note 45), p. 44.

[104] Ogarkov (note 47), pp. 40–54.

Paper 2.5.   US naval strategy and nuclear weapons

RICHARD W. FIELDHOUSE

I.   Introduction

Under the Reagan Administration, US naval strategy, forces and activities have become increasingly provocative, as evidenced both by actions and words. Although much of the strategy rhetoric coming from senior naval officials seems exaggerated and intended for political purposes, it is clear that significant developments are occurring. The US Navy has been propounding a maritime strategy that features offensive and controversial elements, including attacks against Soviet territory. While it is unclear to what degree this emerging naval strategy has been adopted as US national strategy (and by whom), many of its features are being implemented, especially regarding force structure, operations and exercises, thus exacerbating a dynamic and dangerous aspect of the military competition between the two superpowers: the naval arms race. New tactics, objectives and weapon systems, particularly nuclear weapons, all combine to make naval warfare appear more likely and more risky than in previous years. The fact that both the US and Soviet Navies are heavily armed with nuclear weapons and increasing their nuclear capabilities makes naval warfare particularly dangerous.

Naval forces armed with nuclear weapons pose special risks for the outbreak of war and for the escalation of naval war to a nuclear war. Nuclear war may be more likely to start at sea than on land for several reasons. Both the USA and the USSR regularly deploy nuclear weapons with their naval forces; the great majority of their combatants are nuclear-capable. More important, neither navy can rule out the possibility that the other may use nuclear weapons (possibly early) in battle, so there is a desire to be able to defend oneself against nuclear attack with any means available, including nuclear weapons. However, since defence against nuclear weapons is still a tenuous venture at best, both sides acquire new weapons to threaten the other and to dissuade them from using nuclear weapons in the first place. In addition, it is possible that nuclear navies and political leaders might believe that using nuclear weapons at sea would be less escalatory than on land, or could be contained to the seas, because it would result in little obvious collateral damage and no direct strikes against enemy territory. According to the US Navy, 'in a limited war at sea arising from attempts to hinder or sever lines of communication, both parties to the conflict might be reluctant to extend the war to land or to use nuclear weapons except at sea'.[1] Current US and Soviet naval developments do nothing to diminish this danger; instead they heighten it.

One disturbing feature of the US–Soviet naval nuclear competition is that it has received little attention from the arms control, peace research and security studies communities, much less the general public and news media, and thus has not been subjected to the same scrutiny as other nuclear forces. Aside from the submarine-launched ballistic missile (SLBM) launcher limitations imposed by the Strategic Arms Limitation Talks (SALT) agreements, there have been no arms control limitations or considerations for other naval nuclear weapons. Thus, although it may be the most likely avenue to a nuclear war, the naval nuclear arms race has gone essentially unchecked.

The impact of superpower naval developments needs to be considered, especially given the dangerous and escalatory potential of naval nuclear forces and activities. Accordingly, this paper contains an examination of US naval nuclear weapons, strategy and operations with a nuclear perspective. It presents the nature and extent of nuclearization of the US Navy, and considers what this means for the evolving US naval strategy and the prospects for naval confrontation. The paper also contains a discussion of the naval operations and exercises that have characterized the new Navy thinking. It does not treat similar Soviet developments except to provide necessary comparisons. It concludes with an assessment of the impact of these developments and some ideas for improving the situation.

The nature of superpower naval activities

Before delving into questions of US naval nuclear weapons, strategy or deployments, it is important to consider a few salient features of superpower navies that make them particularly worth studying. This prelude will provide the necessary context for the larger issues. To begin with, warships have the right under international law to sail in any international waters, generally agreed to mean those waters not recognized as territorial waters of a nation, but including the exclusive economic and similar zones. This fact is not only fundamental to naval operations, it forms the basis of the central goal of naval forces: unimpeded access to and freedom of action on the high seas. Disputes concerning the right of innocent passage or the right of free navigation may serve as one catalyst for armed conflict, as has happened in the Gulf of Sidra. Naval forces can quickly arrive on the scene of a crisis, or contribute to one by their presence or activities. Thus, any place a superpower navy sails could become a centre of crisis that erupts into a war.

The fact that navies can operate in virtually any ocean area beyond national jurisdiction has other implications as well. Most importantly, it means that the US and Soviet Navies can, and do, operate in the same locations, playing a non-stop game of cat-and-mouse under, on and above the oceans. As US Secretary of the Navy John Lehman put it: 'From the Baltic to the Caribbean to the South China Sea, our ships and men pass within yards of Soviet naval forces every day.'[2] They do more than just pass; they conduct exercises that are meant to demonstrate their capabilities and their 'resolve' to each other. They constantly jockey for the best tactical position and often harass each other. Occasionally they even collide.[3] They practice what appear to be mock attacks against one another, gather intelligence, try to find and follow each other's submarines and otherwise keep a close eye on each other's moves.

Another feature of the two superpower navies is that they maintain high combat readiness because they assume they may be called into combat at a moment's notice, and because the forward deployed forces will have no chance to return to port for resupply. This is especially important considering the intermingling of US and Soviet nuclear-armed naval forces. As Secretary Lehman told Congress in 1983: 'Unlike land warfare, should deterrence break down and conflict begin between the navies of the United States and the Soviet Union, it will be instantaneously a global naval conflict'.[4] The transition from peace to war can take minutes with naval forces, not weeks. This puts a premium on quick decision-making, loosened rules of engagement (under what conditions one can shoot) and keeping good tactical positioning for the first shots of the next war. This is especially important to the US Navy because of the 'one-shot' character (what is often called the 'first salvo') of the Soviet Navy, its desire to shoot first in a war because of its limited supply of weapons aboard ships and the inability to resupply forces at sea. It should be noted that this feature of the Soviet Navy is changing.

The most important feature of modern superpower navies is the fact that they are heavily armed with nuclear weapons. Both the US and Soviet Navies routinely carry nuclear weapons in their naval forces around the world. Some 12 000 nuclear weapons, roughly one quarter of all the world's stockpiles, are intended for use by naval forces.[5] The US and Soviet Navies have nuclear weapons for all their combat missions: strategic intercontinental attack, 'theatre' land attack, attacks against surface naval forces (anti-surface warfare), anti-submarine warfare and attacks against airborne forces (anti-air warfare). Both navies have introduced or are introducing new 'tactical' nuclear weapons into their naval arsenals without any arms control restraint. Both navies are, *inter alia*, increasing their capabilities to wage nuclear warfare with naval forces, not only against each other's navies but against land targets as well. This thorough nuclearization of the two navies decreases the likelihood that any naval war between them could remain non-nuclear.

All these features make superpower naval activities particularly dangerous and difficult to control. In order to consider the relevant issues of the emerging US naval strategy, one should first have an understanding of the nature and extent of the US Navy's nuclearization. For, although even a conventional war between the superpower navies could escalate to nuclear war, it is the nuclear dimension of this naval picture that is the most dangerous and yet the most ignored by the current US naval leadership.

II.   Nuclear weapons and naval warfare

The US Navy maintains some 9000 nuclear weapons for nearly 300 ships and submarines, and over 1300 nuclear-capable naval aircraft.[6] Some 5600 'strategic' warheads are deployed on SLBMs, the remainder are considered 'tactical' weapons although some are assigned strategic roles. Many of the weapons are carried aboard those vessels, the rest are at storage depots on land. Nuclear weapons are important to the US Navy because they are so destructive. Defense Secretary Weinberger reported that, in addition to their deterrent value, naval nuclear weapons possess 'unique capabilities that serve as a backup for [US] conventional systems'; a euphemistic reference to their destructive capacity.[7] Conventional weapons are not capable of destroying some targets; only nuclear weapons can assure the destruction of certain high priority targets.

To understand the role of nuclear weapons in the US Navy, it is necessary to consider briefly the wartime functions of the Navy and their associated nuclear weapons. The US Navy has three wartime combat missions: strategic nuclear operations; 'sea control'; and 'power projection'. Nuclear weapons exist for all three of these missions:

1.   *Strategic nuclear operations* are those involving the nuclear ballistic missile submarines, which are exclusively for nuclear weapons.

2.   '*Sea control*' is the term for those actions that permit unrestricted use of the ocean, including fighting (and destroying) adversary naval forces at sea: ships; submarines; and aircraft. The three tasks of sea control are: 'anti-surface warfare' (ASUW); anti-submarine warfare (ASW); and anti-air warfare (AAW), respectively. The US Navy deploys nuclear weapons for all three of these tasks, primarily for ASW.

3.   '*Power projection*' is the term used to describe naval attacks against land targets, mainly by carrier-borne aircraft but including everything from battleship artillery barrages to amphibious invasions and to nuclear attacks against the Soviet Union. Secretary of Defense Weinberger wrote in January 1986 that 'A primary objective of the naval expansion program has been to strengthen the power projection forces. These are the forces that would seize the initiative in wartime by carrying the battle to the enemy', and would 'conduct counter-offensive operations against the enemy's areas of greatest vulnerability'.[8] The nuclear elements of the 'power projection' forces are the aircraft carriers and the ships and submarines equipped with Tomahawk sea-launched cruise missles (SLCMs).

Nuclear weapons for the two latter missions, and their roles, are as follows:

•   *Sea control*. The US Navy maintains a large arsenal of nuclear weapons for sea control tasks, primarily for ASW and AAW. (Although the United States does not deploy nuclear weapons exclusively for anti-surface warfare, carrier-based nuclear-armed aircraft 'continue to provide the United States with a flexible nuclear land attack and antiship capability'.)[9] ASW provides the best example of *de facto* reliance on nuclear weapons. There are some 1700 ASW warheads in the US arsenal, including 900 depth bombs for ASW aircraft and roughly 800 warheads for missiles launched by surface ships (ASROC) and submarines (SUBROC).[10] Although the Navy stocks conventional torpedoes for ASW, nuclear weapons are kept for situations when conventional ones cannot guarantee the destruction of an enemy submarine. The fact that the USA has five nuclear weapons for every Soviet submarine (not just the modern ballistic missile-equipped, nuclear-powered submarines—SSBNs) demonstrates that the United States has the ability to use nuclear weapons massively against those submarines in war. US contingency plans exist to deploy hundreds of nuclear depth bombs to foreign coastal bases in a crisis or war, further demonstrating the important role of nuclear weapons for ASW. The US Navy has tried to develop new nuclear warheads for a new 'series' of ASW weapons to augment and eventually to replace those currently in the stockpile. These efforts have run into difficulty in the US Congress, and it remains to be seen to what degree the Navy will receive the funding it has requested for a thorough nuclear modernization.[11] If the stated Navy goal of destroying Soviet SSBNs proves infeasible with conventional weapons, the Navy has its nuclear 'back-up' ready.

Nuclear weapons have been components of the Navy's anti-air warfare arsenal since the early 1950s, but only recently has it become apparent that the Navy is renewing its interest in nuclear weapons for AAW. The currently deployed weapon system is the Terrier surface-to-air missile. The primary purpose of these weapons is to shoot down approaching enemy aircraft or incoming anti-ship missiles, 'especially those aboard Backfire and Badger bombers'.[12] Since Backfire and other Soviet naval bombers can be armed with nuclear anti-ship cruise missiles, and new Soviet nuclear sea-launched cruise missiles pose an increasing danger to US surface forces, the premium on destroying air and missile forces is increasing. Defense Secretary Weinberger noted that 'because they are difficult to intercept, the missiles can best be countered by detecting and engaging the aircraft and vessels that carry them.'[13] The Navy has been trying to get congressional funding for a new nuclear warhead for the Standard surface-to-air missile and has been considering a new warhead for the Phoenix air-to-air missile.

• *Power projection.* The Navy has historically relied on its aircraft carriers as its primary power projection force, as well as the core of its fleet. The aircraft aboard these ships are able to fly conventional or nuclear bombs up to a radius of more than 800 kilometres. Given the large and nuclear-armed Soviet naval bomber force, it is inconceivable that US aircraft carriers would be able to launch bombing attacks against the Soviet homeland without coming under intense submarine and land-based air attack. Yet the forward offensive strategy relies heavily on the US ability to conduct global attacks against Soviet land targets (power projection). Numerous critics of the Navy's traditional dependence on one dozen carriers maintain that they are vulnerable to Soviet anti-ship forces. But the Navy began deploying a new generation of weapons in 1984 that will radically alter its ability to attack Soviet land targets: SLCMs. These new weapons are the key to the Navy's power projection mission and will give the Navy over 200 new platforms for launching land attacks from greater distances than carriers and with greater chance of succeeding, thus increasing by an order of magnitude the Navy's capability to launch such attacks. The most important characteristics of the SLCMs follow.

The sea-launched cruise missile is the most versatile and flexible weapon system in the US arsenal—conventional and nuclear. It serves strategic, theatre and tactical roles and will be the mainstay of the US 'strategic reserve' force, the nuclear weapons that would be held back in a nuclear war so that 'the United States would, in any post-nuclear exchange environment, retain a measure of coercive power'.[14] SLCMs can be installed on and fired from ships or submarines, given the proper launching equipment. Thus, according to the head of the US cruise missile programme, the SLCM 'will allow virtually all Navy combatants, not just the carrier battle groups, to go on the offensive whenever necessary and from any corner of the globe'.[15] The Navy plans to build 3994 SLCMs, 758 of which will be nuclear-armed for land attack, 2643 will be conventionally armed for land attack and 593 will be anti-ship missiles with conventional warheads. The nuclear land-attack variant will have a range of 2500 kilometres. More than 200 ships and submarines are expected to be armed with SLCMs, thus vastly increasing the Navy's 'power projection' capabilities.

Since nuclear SLCMs will have more than twice the range of aircraft from carriers, they will augment the carriers in land-attack missions. According to the Navy, SLCMs will be assigned to targets that aircraft carriers cannot strike, including 'targets deep inside enemy territory, currently outside the combat radius of tactical aircraft, point targets of extreme hardness, previously unable to be attacked with a high kill probability, and targets close to the FEBA [forward edge of the battle area] that are so heavily defended as to cause excessively high levels of aircraft attrition.'[16] One Navy official told Congress that the longer range of SLCMs deployed on 'a larger number of surface platforms operating under carrier air cover and independent, covert, forward-deployed submarines presents the Soviets [with] a formidable threat' that assures that 'Soviet firepower cannot concentrate on the carrier alone' and provides 'an increase in the range of escalation control options available to the nation [US] without resort to central strategic systems'.[17]

Although the nuclear SLCM has 'strategic', 'theatre' and tactical roles assigned to it, the USA has never suggested that it should be considered in any arms control regime or agreement, quite the contrary. While theatre nuclear forces on land are the central focus of US–Soviet arms control efforts, SLCMs are promoted. The USA has conspicuously avoided including SLCMs in any of its arms control proposals. This is somewhat typical of the general pattern for naval nuclear weapons: actively resist including them in the arms control process. Between the Navy's institutional urge to maintain its variety of nuclear weapons (more for reasons of nuclear prestige than of necessity) and the habit of excluding its tactical nuclear weapons from arms control, the US Navy has become a thoroughly nuclearized force—as has the Soviet Navy.

III. New naval strategy

Since 1980, the US Navy has spent more time and effort examining its strategy than its sister services. From this effort the Navy has proposed a new maritime strategy, the forward offensive strategy. Simply put, the strategy emphasizes deploying offensive naval forces as close to the Soviet Union as possible in peacetime and being prepared either to bottle up Soviet naval forces in their ports (if need be, destroy them before they can get into the open ocean) or destroy their support bases on land, without which they cannot sustain lengthy operations. This strategy is based upon a set of US Navy assumptions:

- the US Navy is fundamentally superior to the Soviet Navy;
- a major naval conflict between them could be waged entirely without nuclear weapons;
- naval forces can make a decisive difference in a US–Soviet war by exploiting certain Soviet disadvantages and vulnerabilities (especially geographic) and thus add a new dimension to dissuading any Soviet attack on the Central European Front;
- offensive, pre-emptive actions near Soviet territory are the most efficient and most effective way to defeat the Soviet Navy once the conflict has begun;
- such destructive goals can be achieved without undue risk of nuclear escalation; and
- the US Navy can defeat the Soviet Navy before the Soviets have a chance to cause unacceptable destruction.

US naval forces today play a far different role than even 10 years ago, largely because of the thinking of the current naval leadership and the Reagan Administration goal of confronting the Soviet Union around the globe with US military might. Although US and Soviet military forces are both capable of massive destruction, the Reagan Administration appears to believe US naval forces to be uniquely capable of maintaining meaningful military advantage over the USSR. Naval forces are extremely flexible and usable in virtually any situation—unlike land armies or air forces—and the US Navy actually has the component capabilities of these other forces when operating with the US Marines. The US Navy leadership suggests that only naval forces can fully exploit Soviet weaknesses, vulnerabilities and its general preoccupation with land warfare. Thus, many Navy professionals consider the US Navy an important actor in US military efforts to raise the stakes should the Soviets contemplate any military adventurism in Western Europe.

But, there are important political reasons that US naval forces have been given such a prominent role. Some members of the Navy leadership have long suggested an expanded role for their forces; the seeds of the current strategy debate were planted before Secretary Lehman started flying in Navy aircraft. Only since the Reagan Administration came into office have these advocates had a sympathetic ear in the White House. In earlier administrations, it was recognized that there are fundamental differences between the political and military considerations of such plans. What may be militarily advisable (or desirable) is often politically unacceptable. The Reagan Administration has given the political 'green light' to the Navy because it serves the political interests of the administration, including a desire to exert as much military and political pressure as possible on the USSR. The Lehman Navy is the best service to execute the plan.

Forward deployment

The Navy argues that in order to fulfil its missions it must train in the manner it expects to fight and where it expects to fight—which means being deployed as close as possible to Soviet home waters. Two considerations come into play here. First, despite its rhetoric about the global reach of the Soviet Navy, the US Navy is well aware that the Soviet Navy is both unable and unwilling to operate all over the globe. The Soviet naval posture is essentially defensive, that is, structured to defend against naval attacks near or against Soviet territory. Thus, Admiral James Watkins, the US Chief of Naval Operations (CNO), wrote that 'initially the bulk of Soviet naval forces will deploy in areas near the Soviet Union, with only a small fraction deployed forward'.[18] Second, by operating in Soviet territorial waters and near Soviet territory, the US Navy hopes to force the Soviet Navy to keep its traditional defensive posture.

One of the important motivations for the forward strategy concerns Soviet ballistic missile submarines. The US Navy now states publicly that it plans to sink Soviet SSBNs if a war breaks out. Before the USSR began operating its current Delta Class and Typhoon Class submarines, Soviet Yankee Class SSBNs had to approach the USA in order to be within range of their targets. At that time, US naval forces could conduct ASW operations against those Soviet SSBNs far from Soviet home waters. Since Soviet SSBNs can now fire their missiles from or near their home waters, the US Navy is determined to be able to conduct strategic ASW operations near the USSR. Such operations would require the US Navy to establish sea control and air superiority where the SSBNs are—which would require massive US naval presence in those same locations. Although the US Navy does not offer this controversial plan as a primary justification for its forward strategy, it helps drive that strategy.

In order to understand the stated reasoning behind the US strategy, it is necessary to consider briefly the US Navy view of Soviet military and naval strategy. The view, as elaborated by Admiral Watkins in his January 1986 strategy exposition,[19] is that the 'Soviets appear to assume a future war with the West will be global in scope, violent and decisive', and that 'the probable centerpiece of Soviet strategy in global war would be a combined-arms assault against Europe'. This presumes that 'the Soviets would prefer to concentrate on a single theater', rather than on several fronts. 'A central premise of US strategy', wrote Watkins, 'is to deny them such an option.' 'While Soviet ground and air forces conduct a massive offensive', he explained, 'a critical Soviet Navy role in a future conflict would be to protect the Soviet homeland and their ballistic missile submarines.' Thus, by increasing the threat to the Soviet Navy and territory, the US Navy claims a crucial role for itelf in diverting any Soviet effort to concentrate entirely on central Europe in a war. The US naval leadership speaks as though it wants primary responsibility for 'turning NATO's flanks' and pressuring the Soviet Pacific Fleet and land forces in order to defeat any Soviet war aims.

Previous strategy

Before the Reagan Administration, US naval strategy was oriented more towards redeploying some portion of the Navy to the crisis area (the so-called 'swing strategy') and to protecting the 'sea lines of communication' (or SLOCs) where ships would transport troops, supplies or commerce through potentially hostile waters to reinforce the war effort. The idea was that, if a war erupted in one theatre (Europe), ships from another theatre (Pacific) would be dispatched to support naval operations in the war theatre. SLOC protection evolved from the World War II practice of protecting shipping with convoys under escort and with barrrier operations against adversary naval forces. The US Navy planned to prevent opposing forces, especially Soviet attack submarines, from entering into sea areas where allied shipping would be heavy, such as the North Atlantic Ocean, particularly to prevent Soviet naval forces from threatening US/allied ships south of an imaginary line extending from Greenland to Iceland to the UK (known as the GIUK 'gap').

During the mid- to late-1970s, there was much discussion in the US national security community about the need for the ability to fight several conflicts at once, either 'one-and-a-half' or two wars, generally assumed to be a US–Soviet war simultaneously with a smaller conflict. Upon entering office, Secretary of the Navy Lehman claimed that this strategy stretched thin the notion of swinging the Navy around: what if naval forces had to remain in place? His answer was the 600-ship navy, one that can operate independently in all of its theatres without depending on outside assistance from the other US Fleets. In 1986, Secretary Lehman said: 'We must have forces available to deploy not only to the Atlantic theater . . . but also simultaneously to the Pacific as well as the Mideast Force', citing US 'commitments in the Indian Ocean, East Africa and Southwest and Southeast Asia'.[20] Lehman decried the previous SLOC protection idea as inefficient, ineffective and impossible without a huge naval expansion. He stated that a 'GIUK gap' defensive posture 'would lead to almost certain defeat in a war of attrition in the North Atlantic and subsequent defeat on the Central European Front'.[21] But this is a misleading statement, since it supposes that the pre-Lehman strategy relied entirely on using naval escorts for convoys, which was not the case. The strategy was based on the priority of assuring that allied shipping could transit the North Atlantic to resupply Europe during a war, and thus on preventing Soviet anti-ship forces from getting close to the North Atlantic Treaty Organization (NATO) shipping lanes below the 'GIUK gap'. Anti-submarine warfare and barrier operations in the GIUK gap were the primary implements of the strategy.

The idea now is to prevent the Soviet Navy from ever getting into the open ocean, let alone near the sea lines. According to Admiral Watkins, 'Aggressive forward movement of [US] anti-submarine warfare forces . . . will force Soviet submarines to retreat into defensive bastions to protect their ballistic missile submarines. This both denies the Soviets the option of a massive, early attempt to interdict our sea lines of communication and counters such operations against them [SLOCs] that the Soviets undertake'.[22]

Horizontal escalation and land attack

One of the major elements of the forward offensive naval strategy is its implementation of 'horizontal escalation'. Briefly stated, the idea is that in a superpower war, the US Navy would try to keep the Soviet Navy permanently on the defensive by initiating attacks where and when it chose in order to keep the Soviets off-balance and reacting. This is intended to force the Soviet Navy to divert its forces from planned theatres and operations, thus preventing them from 'engaging in hostilities on their terms' or from waging a short, intense war in one theatre (Europe). As Admiral Watkins put it: 'We must dilute their effort, divert their attention, and force them to divide their forces. We must control the type and tempo of conflict, making sure the Soviets understand that they can take no area for granted.'[23]

One of the main stated objectives is to make the war global, which the US Navy believes puts the Soviets at a great disadvantage. Watkins cites the example of forward deployments to the Western Pacific, stating that in a war 'such deployments tie down Soviet forces, especially strike aircraft, limiting the Soviet's ability to concentrate their forces on Central Europe'.[24] However, it is doubtful whether the USA would (or could) indeed escalate a limited conflict into a global one without running the strong risk of fighting an uncontrolled war that threatens to involve nuclear weapons. This is one element of the new strategy that lacks credibility.

Another US Navy goal is to make the war protracted, since the Soviet Navy is not equipped to fight a long naval war. Some US naval officials posit that if the US Navy can survive the initial battles of a naval war with the USSR that the USA will have a decisive advantage because the Soviet Navy is at present simply unable to fight for more than a brief period. This assumes that a protracted (and global) war between the USA and the USSR would remain conventional. This is one of the most doubtful aspects of the proposed strategy.

The option of attacking Soviet land targets is considered especially import-ant to the US Navy. The Navy seems to be of two minds—one conventional and the other nuclear—on the subject of attacking (or threatening) land targets. In the untested event that a global war with the USSR could remain conventional, the Navy would contemplate striking targets on Soviet territory with conventional weapons to destroy ships in port, destroy aircraft at their bases and cut off naval command, control and communications (C^3), supply and logistics.

In order to dissuade the Soviets from initiating the use of nuclear weapons in a naval war, the US Navy threatens to attack Soviet land targets with nuclear weapons (SLCMs) in retaliation. According to various reports, the secret US Defense Guidance document for 1984–88 states: 'It will be US policy that a nuclear war beginning with Soviet nuclear attacks at sea will not necessarily remain limited to the sea.. . . The prospect of losing their fleet to US naval theater forces may not be sufficient to deter the Soviets from initiating a nuclear campaign at sea.'[25] Secretary Lehman stated that 'the objective of this policy is to tell the Soviets that the bases from which an attack on US naval forces might be initiated may not necessarily be sanctuaries'. He explained that 'it would be unwise to adopt a policy which would by default allow the Soviets to believe they could neutralize the US fleet through the use of nuclear weapons and not risk attacks in the bases which initiated and/or supported those attacks'.[26] Although this US policy (to consider nuclear land attacks) is explained in terms of US concern about Soviet nuclear capabilities and prospects for escalation, the US forward offensive strategy logically increases the Soviet incentives to use nuclear weapons. If the USA were not planning to conduct offensive missions near Soviet territory, the USSR would have less reason to consider resorting to nuclear weapons. Although US naval officials have defended the new US strategy by saying that it is considered unlikely that the USSR would initiate the use of nuclear weapons at sea in response to some US action at sea, there is reason to believe otherwise. The USA is willing to initiate the use of nuclear weapons in Europe in response to Soviet conventional attacks. Why would the USSR be any less willing to use nuclear weapons at sea, away from other countries and populations, in a situation where its naval forces were being overwhelmed by US naval forces?

Until recently, the US Navy had to rely entirely on its aircraft carriers to carry out its 'power projection' mission of attacking land targets. In peacetime, the US Navy deploys an average of four carriers in four forward ocean areas (Atlantic, Pacific, Mediterranean and Indian), and the Soviet Navy keeps close tabs on the precise location of each carrier. Such a force is not sufficient to threaten or carry out attacks against Soviet land targets; Soviet land-based aircraft, like Backfire and Bear bombers, would prevent carriers from operating within striking range of Soviet territory. Admiral Watkins stated that 'the main threat to our fleets during [war] are the "Backfires" and other missile-carrying aircraft of Soviet Naval Aviation'.[27] While aircraft carriers are indeed heavily defended and relatively hard to sink, they might not survive the entire Soviet Naval Aviation (SNA) land-based nuclear-armed bomber force. Land-based bombers that can fire missiles at ranges greater than 300 kilometres need not sink an aircraft carrier to disable it, they need only start a serious fire or cripple the aircraft catapults or arresting gear to prevent the aircraft fom flying.

The intense firepower that the USSR could muster to attack approaching aircraft carriers would likely be more than the carriers could manage.

Nuclear schizophrenia

It is important to note the disparity between the schizophrenic Navy thinking about nuclear weapon issues and the nuclear reality of superpower naval competition. The Navy seems to have multiple outlooks when dealing with nuclear weapons; it stresses the many and ominous Soviet naval nuclear capabilities when talking about 'the threat', but tends to remain reticent about US naval nuclear weapons, almost as though they did not exist. Proponents present the naval strategy as though they believe that a global naval war can be fought against the USSR without either side ever using a nuclear weapon, while espousing plans for the destruction of Soviet naval forces, including ballistic missile submarines. Admiral Watkins suggests 'changing the nuclear balance' so as to dissuade the Soviets further from escalating to using nuclear weapons, because the United States will have the nuclear advantage:

The Soviets place great weight on the nuclear correlation of forces, even during the time before nuclear weapons have been used. Maritime forces can influence that nuclear correlation, both by destroying Soviet ballistic missile submarines and by improving our own nuclear posture, through deployment of carriers and Tomahawk platforms around the periphery of the Soviet Union. Some argue that such steps will lead to immediate escalation, but escalation solely as a result of actions at sea seems improbable, given the Soviet land orientation. Escalation in response to maritime pressure would serve no useful purpose for the Soviets since their [nuclear] reserve forces would be degraded and the United States retaliatory posture would be enhanced.[28]

Perhaps this statement is evidence of a perception within certain circles of the US Navy that the USSR is more afraid of nuclear escalation than is the USA, and that this situation can be exploited. However, if in a war the USA succeeded in sinking a number of Soviet SSBNs, it could not exclude the possibility that the USSR would choose to attack a US aircraft carrier with nuclear weapons in response.

The Navy does not appear able to support its own argument. In discussing Soviet naval war goals, Admiral Watkins wrote that 'Soviet doctrine gives a high priority to locating and destroying Western sea-based nuclear assets, including aircraft carriers, ballistic missile submarines, and Tomahawk-equipped platforms. The Soviets would particularly like to be able to destroy our ballistic missile submarines, but lack the antisubmarine warfare capability to implement such a mission'.[29] If the Navy believes this to be true, then it should be extremely circumspect about any strategy that advocates sinking Soviet SSBNs; the Soviets might only be more inclined to use nuclear weapons and would be left less choice than before by the current US plans.

US proponents claim that the forward offensive strategy is a strategy for conventional war and thus an alternative to a nuclear war. According to Francis West, a former Assistant Secretary of Defense and one of the pioneers of the strategy, 'its fundamental concept, that dwarfs any other concept, is that it looks at a conventional war, not a nuclear war'.[30] Given the facts that nuclear weapons are spread throughout both navies and that both navies are increasing their capacity to attack each other's territory with nuclear weapons, one cannot simply remove the nuclear equation from strategy and hope that any war will remain conventional. On the contrary, the new strategy may increase the probability that a superpower naval war, or any war that involves US and Soviet naval forces, will lead to the use of nuclear weapons.

IV.   New deployments and exercises

During peacetime, the US Navy conducts scores of exercises every year that are meant to test its war plans and strategy. In recent years these exercises have taken on a new offensive and provocative cast. One element of the current US naval strategy is to practise forward offensive operations that are similar to those expected in wartime. After all, one of the primary purposes of conducting these exercises is to send a 'signal' to the Soviet Union and to pressure the Soviet Navy. Admiral Watkins wrote that 'we have begun emphasizing exercises with multiple carrier battle forces, which would be required in a major war. We have increased our exercises in the Northern Pacific and Norwegian Sea, to build our base of experience in these key areas. We have begun exercising our submarines in Arctic waters', where, according to the USA, Soviet SSBNs patrol. These peacetime exercises may provide a path for hostilities to erupt; they are certainly provocative on a regular basis. Several good examples of the more provocative exercises are:

• In early 1985, for the first time, the US Navy conducted a '24-hour notice surge deployment exercise' that sent 44 nuclear-powered attack submarines (SSNs) sailing from Atlantic ports fully loaded with their weapons.[31] This kind of surge of the majority of SSNs from the Atlantic coast could potentially be misinterpreted by the Soviet Union, especially since it is not a routine US practice and because the US Navy admits it would be one of its aggressive moves in a crisis. Admiral Watkins told Congress that 'The Soviets expect us on warning to surge SSNs. They know we are going to the bastions.'[32] Speaking of a larger exercise, Watkins also told Congress that the USA was considering alerting the USSR before a planned surge from all ports, 'because we have not done it for about 30 years'.[33] Analogous actions on land would be so provocative that they are prohibited in Europe by agreement.
• During the largest NATO Atlantic Ocean exercise of 1985—Ocean Safari '85—the Striking Fleet Atlantic command sent carrier battle groups into the Norwegian Sea and into Norwegian fjords to practise offensive operations close to the Soviet naval stronghold on the Kola Peninsula.[34] Although the idea of the exercise was to practise 'sea lane defence' and defence of convoys, the method practised was that of striking far northern forces before they could get far from their home ports.

- In May 1985 the nuclear-powered guided missile cruiser *Mississippi* was given 20 hours to sail alone from Norfolk, Virginia to the Norwegian Sea for operation 'Snap Lock' to intercept and conduct surveillance operations against a Soviet task force. Roughly one quarter of the crew was left behind in the haste to leave port. When the *Mississippi* intercepted the Soviet ships, she approached to within 30 kilometres and 'conducted appropriate simulated strikes' before assuming surveillance duties into the Barents Sea.[35]
- In the Pacific Ocean exercise—'Fleet Ex-85'—the United States operated two carrier battle groups simultaneously in the Sea of Japan, where the bulk of the Soviet Pacific Fleet is based. The last such carrier operations in the Sea of Japan had not been held since 1969, during the height of US–Soviet naval incidents.[36]
- Two US ships, the destroyer *Caron* and the cruiser *Yorktown*, operating in the Black Sea, crossed 11 kilometres into Soviet territorial waters and stayed there for some hours in mid-March 1986. The USSR filed a formal protest to the USA, which responded by claiming that the ships were exercising their right of innocent passage. One must stop to ask: passage to what destination from what point? Although the USA has regularly operated ships in the Black Sea on presence missions—to prove the right to operate there—the ships have not entered inside territorial waters unless permitted for a port call.

These are only some recent examples. There have been notable examples in previous years as well, including the first-ever exercises in the Sea of Okhotsk, where US submarines now operate routinely. In September 1982, a two-carrier battle group exercise was conducted off the western Aleutian Islands (the first such operations since World War II) within 800 kilometres of the Soviet coast.[37] One year later a similar exercise with three carriers was held to practise co-ordinating attacks with the US Air Force against the Soviet bases of Petropavlovsk and Alekseyevka.[38]

The Soviet Navy has responded to the new US exercises with ominous moves. In 1982, for the first time, the Soviets used Backfire bombers to fly simulated bombing missions against a two-carrier battle group off the Aleutian Islands in the North Pacific. The USSR has used Backfire bombers in similar exercises since 1982, which indicates a Soviet interest in sending their own 'message' back to the United States. Soviet attack submarines also operate in US–NATO exercise areas; in March 1984 a Victor-class submarine collided with the US aircraft carrier *Kitty Hawk* in the Sea of Japan. In addition, Soviet naval exercises in both the Atlantic and Pacific Oceans have grown larger and more offensive in recent years. According to Secretary Lehman, Soviet attack submarines are regularly present off the major US naval and submarine bases. Soviet naval forces routinely shadow and harass US forces operating near the USSR, especially in the Black Sea and the Sea of Japan.

Atlantic and Pacific

Since the current US naval strategy stresses far forward deployment, we should consider the two primary regions where these deployments are taking place: the North Atlantic and the western Pacific Oceans. These are the two areas that the US Navy considers most important for winning the naval war and for defeating Soviet military objectives, although for entirely different reasons. In the North Atlantic, the US Navy sees an opportunity to prevent the massive Soviet Northern Fleet from ever getting into the open ocean and also to provide the decisive element to any battle for NATO's northern flank. In the Pacific, the US Navy sees great geographic vulnerabilities for the Soviet Navy as the primary attraction for US offensive actions. Each region is considered below.

Since 1981, the main characteristic of US surface naval operations in the North Atlantic has been that they have advanced much farther north, closer to the Soviet Union, than previous practice. Instead of conducting exercises in the 'GIUK gap' area, US and NATO naval forces are operating in the Norwegian and Barents Seas and increasingly in the Arctic—where, according to the USA, Soviet ballistic missile submarines operate. The central justification for these naval operations is twofold. First, by crippling the Soviet Navy and mounting attacks against Soviet armed forces in the region, the US and NATO forces could prevent the Soviets from invading Norway and from attacking any of the allied territories in the North Atlantic, thus diverting any Soviet effort to overwhelm central Europe. Second, by attacking the Soviet Navy close to home, the US Navy could prevent it from getting into the ocean to cause trouble for NATO shipping, thus obviating the need for defending the SLOCs. This thinking was summed up by the Commander of NATO's Striking Fleet Atlantic, the naval forces responsible for the region:

The best means of protecting the sea lines of communications and bolstering the full alliance is by the conduct of offensive sea control operations far forward. The key to winning the battle of the Atlantic is winning the battle of the Norwegian Sea; it is no accident that the Soviets have constructed their navy to fight the critical battle in the high north. NATO's maritime objectives in the Norwegian Sea are to repel a Warsaw Pact amphibious assault on north Norway, to support the defense of Norway against land threats, to prevent Soviet use of facilities in Norway, and to contain the Soviet Northern Fleet or destroy it at sea.[39]

This is not merely some theoretical discussion of what the Navy would like to do, it is their plan: 'The Striking Fleet is charged formally by [a] NATO mission to conduct offensive operations to contain and neutralize the Soviet maritime threat, and these operations include destroying the threat at its source.'[40]

Although there is some logic to this thinking, it is both flawed and distorted. Protecting NATO's sea lines does not require pre-emptive attacks against the Soviet Navy in Soviet waters; the requirement was suitably met before the advent of the 600-ship navy and without nearly the risks assumed by the Lehman Navy. The fact that the Soviet Navy is best suited to fighting close to home is considered one of its major disadvantages. An objective account of this situation would admit that the Soviet Navy is simply incapable of operating in force outside the range of its land-based aircraft; it is essentially a defensive navy by choice, design and geography. NATO traditionally is considered to be fortunate to have considerable maritime advantages over the USSR, and thus does not have to go looking for a fight to defend its maritime areas. Although the efficiency argument—that it is easiest to mop up the Soviet Navy while it lies in or near port—may be correct in theory, it would be different in practice since such a campaign would likely compel the USSR to fight with every available means, including nuclear weapons if necessary. If the US Navy begins sinking Soviet SSBNs in a battle, it is wholly conceivable that the USSR could choose to destroy at least one US aircraft carrier with nuclear weapons, exactly the opposite of the reaction the strategy is supposed to draw.

The US naval posture and practices in the Pacific focus on Soviet geographic and military weaknesses: all but one of their ports are ice-bound most of the year; the major ports—Vladivostok and Petropavlovsk—suffer from differing degrees of logistic and supply problems caused by their isolated locations; except for Petropavlovsk, all Soviet Pacific naval forces must pass through 'choke points' to get to the open ocean, and US allies (Japan and Korea) sit astride those choke points.[41] In a war, Japan would be the major launching pad of intensive US and allied ASW and ASUW campaigns in the Sea of Japan and the Sea of Okhotsk. US exercises in the region have taken place increasingly closer to Soviet territory since 1981, including a massive submarine 'barrier' exercise in April 1983 off the coast of Petropavlovsk that involved six layers of ASW forces.[42] US naval forces in the Pacific are normally deployed far forward, especially in Japan, Guam, the Philippines and Hawaii; that is the geographic structure of the Pacific. It permits the US Navy to operate close to the Soviet Union and to prepare for wartime operations that would quickly take advantage of Soviet vulnerabilities.

Perhaps the most ironic point about the Pacific is that the US justification for its naval buildup, operations and strategy—the Soviet naval threat and buildup—may have a self-fulfilling effect. Despite US discussions of the massive Soviet buildup in the Pacific region, the Soviet Union's primary regional security concern is China, not the distant islands of the Pacific. Soviet actions and reactions in the Pacific show increasing concern with the US naval presence and strategy. The Soviet naval base at Cam Ranh Bay, Viet Nam, is an example of efforts to overcome some of its geographic deficiencies. Soviet efforts to build a large aircraft carrier and to operate naval forces further from home waters may reflect Soviet ambitions to rival the US Navy—and thus imitiate US naval practices.

V.   Conclusion

What do these numerous developments mean? The impact of US naval activities suggested by the preceding discussion can be briefly summarized. These activities are increasing the probability of conflict by their provocative nature and, should conflict erupt, increasing the risk of nuclear escalation. These developments complicate efforts to control naval nuclear weapons and naval activities. They are spurring an intensified naval competition with the Soviet Union which may contribute to several undesirable Soviet actions, including:

- increasing Soviet incentives to use nuclear weapons in a major naval conflict between the superpowers, since nuclear weapons alone may be able to stop or defeat the pre-emptive US strategy;
- developing new Soviet naval nuclear weapons, such as the most recent generation of SLCMs and anti-ship air-to-surface missiles (ASMs), that make naval conflict more dangerous and arms control efforts more difficult;
- adopting tactics that will increase the tensions between the two navies, for example operating further from Soviet home waters to avoid being hemmed in by US forces, and seeking increased access to foreign bases, or by adopting offensive measures meant to counter the US forward strategy, such as increased deployments in waters near the USA (on both coasts and in the Caribbean or Gulf areas); and
- resuming dangerous tactics at sea that increase incidents and confrontations with the US Navy, such as those in effect before the Incidents at Sea Agreement.

Many of these actions are already taking place, more will follow. The emerging US naval posture has been taking shape for more than five years, and the Soviet Union has seen such developments coming for an even longer time. Although nobody should suggest that Soviet military decision-making is based largely on reactions to US plans and activities, such factors do play a part in Soviet military and resource planning.

In most fields of their military competition, the superpowers have agreed at least to discuss measures to limit arms, restrain provocative actions, prevent unintended war and seek common ground on ways to build confidence that neither side intends to start a war. Generally, the two sides have avoided discussing naval arms control measures. The one exception to this rule is the Incidents at Sea Agreement, which was born out of the realization that naval forces are particularly prone to stumble into a war arising from unintended, misinterpreted or ambiguous circumstances. The Incidents at Sea regime has been very useful and serves as a precedent and a model for continued efforts to assure that US and Soviet naval forces do not provoke a war inadvertently. However, the US forward offensive naval strategy is intentionally provocative, for military and political reasons. Consequently, the Incidents at Sea Agreement should be reinforced and expanded. Several subjects were intentionally omitted from the agreement at the time it was signed, for example submarine operations and the question of establishing a minimum distance formula to separate US and Soviet naval vessels operating near one another. These items could logically be discussed again.[43] Additionally, other nations could be invited to join the agreement or enter into similar agreements with adversary navies, particularly NATO and Warsaw Treaty Organization (WTO) Navies. In July 1986, Great Britain and the USSR signed a bilateral agreement on preventing incidents at sea. It is an important step and other countries could do the same.

Naval nuclear arms control is considered to be a particularly complex venture with nightmarish verification problems. But the naval nuclear arms race is far too dangerous to ignore simply because it would be difficult to control or stop. If the current nuclearization of naval forces is allowed to continue unabated, it may make moot the other efforts to control or reduce nuclear arms; two confrontational, nuclear-laden navies possessing thousands of SLCMs and every manner of tactical weapon might present a more dangerous situation than the current nuclear stand-off. If the USA and the USSR ever take seriously their statements about ridding the world of nuclear weapons, they will have to include naval nuclear weapons in that process. Denuclearizing naval forces should be a vital part of any serious arms control and disarmament process.

There are some measures that are suitable for discussion as naval arms control goals, including: efforts to halt and eliminate nuclear SLCMs, nuclear surface-to-air missiles and nuclear air-to-surface missiles deployed with naval forces. These are among the weapons that most increase the pressures to use nuclear weapons in a superpower naval conflict. The US and Soviet Navies have agreed to limit some actions that they find mutually unsuitable at sea; they should be able to agree on others, including efforts to control the weapons and the operations they believe most dangerous. However, both countries feel compelled to continue deploying weapons and pursuing actions that are meant to pose increasing risks to the other. As long as this zero-sum game mentality is in effect, it is doubtful that either side will have the courage or confidence to change the historical pattern. It should be clear to both nations that strategies for fighting prolonged global wars are inherently incompatible with the reality of nuclearized militaries, especially navies.

The preceding discussion of US naval developments is meant to demonstrate that current ideas, actions and weapon systems are already having a serious (if unappreciated) impact on international security and the prospects for conflict. These developments must be considered in the context of arms control and war prevention efforts. Weapons—especially nuclear weapons—are being developed without any arms control considerations, and naval operations and strategies are increasing the likelihood of conflict while increasing the risk of nuclear escalation in a naval war. The time to assess the impact of such developments should be before they reach their current stage of affairs. It is thus past the time to recognize the provocative and nuclear nature of superpower naval developments and to begin to remedy the situation.

Notes and references

[1] US Navy, *Nuclear Warfare Operations*, Naval Warfare Publication 28, Revision D, Change 1, Nov. 1980 (secret, partially declassified), p. 1–2.

[2] Lehman, J., 'The 600-ship navy', US Naval Institute *Proceedings* (Jan. 1986), supplement, p. 32.

[3] Collisions are relatively rare today largely because of an agreement between the USA and the USSR on the conduct of naval manoeuvres, the 'Agreement between the United States of America and the Union of Soviet Socialist Republics on the prevention of incidents on or above the high seas', commonly referred to as the 'Incidents at Sea Agreement', signed in May 1972.

[4] US Congress, Senate Armed Services Committee (SASC), Hearings on Department of Defense (DoD) Authorizations for FY 1983, Part 2, p. 1059 (herinafter referred to as SASC, FY 1983 DoD). The other three regular congressional hearing series on DoD are abbreviated similarly—HAC: House Appropriations Committee; HASC: House Armed Services Committee; and SAC: Senate Appropriations Committee.

[5] See Arkin, W., Burrows, A., Fieldhouse, R. and Sands, J., 'Nuclearization of the oceans', Background Paper for the Symposium on the Denuclearization of the Oceans, Norrtälje, Sweden, May 1984; also in *Denuclearisation of the Oceans*, ed. R. Byers (Croom Helm: London, 1986).

[6] See Arkin *et al.* (note 5).

[7] US Department of Defense, *Annual Report to the Congress Fiscal Year 1987* (US Government Printing Office: Washington, DC, annual) (hereinafter referred to as DoD, FY 1987), p. 228.

[8] DoD Fry 1987 (see note 7), p. 181.

[9] The Organization of the Joint Chiefs of Staff, *United States Military Posture for FY 1987* (US Government Printing Office: Washington, DC, annual) (hereinafter referred to as JCS, FY 1987), p. 35.

[10] See Arkin *et al.* (note 4), and Cochran, T., Arkin, W. and Hoenig, M., *Nuclear Weapons Databook, Volume 1: US Nuclear Forces and Capabilities* (Ballinger: Cambridge, MA, 1984).

[11] See Morrison, D. M., 'The Navy's vanishing nuclear arsenal', *National Journal*, vol. 18 (13 Sep. 1986), pp. 2184–5.

[12] DoD, FY 1987 (see note 7), p. 228.

[13] DoD, FY 1987 (see note 7), p. 185.

[14] US Congress, Senate Armed Services Committee, *Strategic Force Modernization Programs*, Hearings, 97th Congress, 1st Session (US Government Printing Office: Washington, DC, 1981), p. 203.

[15] SASC, FY 1984, DoD, Part 6 (see note 4), p. 3211.

[16] HAC, FY 1980 DoD, Part 3 (see note 4), p. 755.

[17] Statement of Commodore Roger Bacon to Senate Armed Services Committee, 13 Mar. 1984.

[18] Watkins, Adm., J. (USN), 'The maritime strategy', US Naval Institute *Proceedings* (Jan. 1986), supplement, p. 7.

[19] Watkins (note 18). This is the most complete public airing of US naval strategy in many years. Other valuable sources on this subject are found in the annual Navy posture statement, the JCS annual report (see note 9) and the DoD annual report (see note 7), as well as numerous volumes of the annual congressional budget hearings (see note 4).

[20] Interview with Lehman in *Naval Forces*, vol. 7, no. 1 (1986), p. 21.

[21] Lehman (note 20), p. 18.

[22] Watkins (note 18), p. 9.

[23] Watkins (note 18), p. 11.

[24] Watkins (note 18), p. 10.

[25] See, e.g., Halloran, R., 'New Weinberger directive refines military policy', *New York Times*, 22 Mar. 1983, p. 1.

[26] SASC, FY 1984 DoD, Part 2 (see note 4), p. 1134.

[27] Watkins (note 18), p. 12.

[28] Watkins (note 18), p. 14.

[29] Watkins (note 18), p. 7.

[30] *The Maritime Strategy*, US Naval Institute Professional Seminar Series, 29 May 1986 (US Naval Institute: Annapolis, MD, 1986), p. 6.

[31] Wright, C., 'US naval operations in 1985', US Naval Institute *Proceedings* (May 1986), annual review edition, p. 34.

[32] Arkin, W. M., 'Provocations at sea', *Bulletin of the Atomic Scientists*, vol. 41, no. 10 (Nov. 1985), p. 7.

[33] Arkin (note 32).

[34] Wright (note 31), p. 34.

[35] Lt Michael Ruth quoted in Wright (note 31), p. 284.

[36] This period of naval incidents led to the 1972 Incidents at Sea Agreement between the USA and the USSR. For a good account of this period see Lynn-Jones, S. M., 'A quiet success for arms control: preventing incidents at sea', *International Security*, vol. 9, no. 4 (Spring 1985), pp. 154–84.

[37] See Arkin (note 32), p. 6.

[38] See Arkin (note 32), p. 6.

[39] Mustin, VAdm. H. C., 'The role of the Navy and Marines in the Norwegian Sea', *Naval War College Review*, vol. 39, no. 2 (Mar./Apr. 1986), pp. 4–5.

[40] Mustin (note 37), p. 5.

[41] For a good discussion of these issues and US naval strategy in the Pacific, see Arkin, W. M. and Chappell, D., 'Forward offensive strategy: raising the stakes in the Pacific', *World Policy Journal*, vol. 2, no. 3 (Summer 1985); and their forthcoming book (tentatively titled) *Naked as a Jaybird*.

[42] See Arkin, W. M. and Fieldhouse, R. W., *Nuclear Battlefields: Global Links in the Arms Race* (Ballinger: Cambridge, MA, 1985), p. 124 and chapter 7, 'The Pacific'.

[43] For a good discussion of these issues see Lynn-Jones (note 36).

Paper 2.6.   Soviet strategy: the naval dimension

CARL G. JACOBSEN

I.   Introduction

Geopolitics, the geographical fact of location in the heart of the Eur-Asian land mass and the political fact of contiguous threats and enemies, dictated that Muscovy focus first and foremost on land power. Naval and, later, air capabilities were developed to complement that power and to integrate with it, not to challenge or supplant it. During World War II limited-reach naval and air elements acted as tactical adjuncts to land formations. Today, the Soviet Union's more potent, part-global navy and new-found strategic air power serve as integral components of evolving combined-arms continental and supra-continental Theatres of Strategic Military Operations (TVDs).

II.   The Soviet Navy in historical perspective

The emergence of expanding Soviet naval power in the 1960s has been likened to the buildup of the tsarist fleet after the Crimean War (during which, typically, naval guns were used as land cannon, and marines as infantry).[1] The analogy is useful. It reminds us that Russian sea power and presence in distant oceans is not novel, but a response to situations in which narrow reliance on land formations has proved dangerous and/or unduly restricting. It also reminds us that fiscal pressures and more urgent land priorities have in the past always aborted or at least reigned in the aspirations of the admiralty. This pattern threatened 'Gorshkov's Navy', too, in the late 1970s. Circumstance and naval perspicacity, in disavowing independent aspirations and adopting, moulding and pursuing the banner of combined arms, may now have broken the pattern and established a more enduring basis for Soviet naval power.

The post-Crimean expansion typified traditional overreach. In the West, the Russian navy placed major warship orders with French and US union ship-yards, accepted an offer from Louis Napoleon and Cavour for a base at Villafranca, now Villefranche, in 1858, and in 1863 sent naval squadrons to New York and San Francisco, in the midst of the Civil War, to bolster anti-British potentials. In the East, the first 'independent squadron for the Eastern Ocean' was formed; in 1861, with the permission of the local Prince, Russia's fleet established a *de facto* base in the Strait of Tsu Shima. But the Tsar was ultimately persuaded that the danger of provoking Austro-Hungary and

Britain in the West and of antagonizing Japan and British interests in the East outweighed the advantage of overseas possession. The Villafranca and Tsu Shima initiatives were rescinded. The US venture did gain his approval, as a response to the threat of British and French meddling in Poland. The principle that naval reach can be a useful instrument of power was affirmed; so also, however, was the dictum that it must not precipitate or commit power.

There was one other legacy. The fleet landing in Vladivostok Bay in 1860 prodded Chinese agreement to the Treaty of Peking, which ceded the territories east of the Ussuri. But the navy scarcely benefited. The naval response to war with Japan in 1904 had to draw on the Baltic Fleet. Its attack on British North Sea fishing boats, mistaken for Japanese warships, nearly sparked another war, exposed abominable judgement and foretold the odyssey's ignominious end.

The Spanish Civil War, and Italy's blockade of Soviet sea supplies to anti-Franco government forces, spawned another naval revival. Stalin ordered the building of a fleet that could challenge Western command of the seas. But World War II loomed and other priorities intervened.

In 1948, the Greek Civil War saw a repeat. Stalin acknowledged the effectiveness of the US blockade and Soviet impotence. Again, he directed that the USSR build a high-seas fleet to protect distant interests and clients. Again, the ambition was thwarted and sidetracked by the demands of reconstruction, Stalin's death, the move towards a relaxation of East–West tensions and his successors' domestic needs.

Some capital ships were procured, however. Distant ambitions were put aside. But changing strategic realities brought new naval purpose. The nuclear threat from US carriers compelled emergence from coastal waters. The navy was also an early beneficiary of the search for a means of delivery for Soviet nuclear warheads. The 1950s brought nuclear-armed torpedoes and the pioneering deployment of limited-range missiles on submarines.

It was a harbinger of things to come. Yet in the late 1950s the moves were aborted because of: technical difficulties; problems of command and control, and the need to traverse hostile seas; and, more importantly, the advent of intercontinental ballistic missiles (ICBMs) and the Soviet Union's rather naive and euphoric assessment of their import.

ICBMs appeared, finally, to have given the Soviet Union a secure deterrent: a certain and devastating retaliatory capability. Moscow embraced the thesis that contemporary war would be nuclear and would inevitably escalate to all-out cataclysm. Naval potentials appeared redundant and, like the cavalry, a relic of earlier times. But, the navy did not long remain on the dustbin of history (to paraphrase Trotsky). 1961 brought renewed purpose.

III.   Geographic constraints and the USSR response

Russian and Soviet naval power have also faced daunting geographic challenge.[2] The Oresund exit from the Baltic—the old capital and the naval-industrial heartland—is easily blocked. The Dardanelles exit from the Black Sea's southern industrial regions (to which much of the Baltic Fleet could redeploy through interconnecting canal and river systems) is also narrow and easily blocked.

The degree of constraint felt, and the compulsion to circumvent it, was dramatized by World War I. The British–French promise that the Dardanelles would be hers kept Russia in the war. Assaults in the East may well have saved the West, but doomed the Tsar. The liberal-conservative governments that succeeded him, after February 1917, were equally dazzled by the lure. Again, Russia attacked, sucking German troops from the West at a crucial juncture. Again, the carnage doomed the regime. Bolshevik slogans—peace now, bread now, and all power to the (then democratically elected) Soviets—swept it away.

When naval expansion returned to the agenda, attention focused on the remaining alternatives—the Kola Peninsula in the far northwest, and the Far East. Neither was ideal. Both lay far from the heartland, connected to it only by a solitary, exposed railway. Both promised improved access to open seas, but neither is free from geographic constraints.

At its maximum extension the polar ice cap sweeps south of Svalbard, north of Norway, curves eastward, paralleling the Kola coastline at a mean distance of 180 miles, and swings south, to land-lock at Mys Svjatoy Nos, 240 nautical miles from the Norwegian border. In other words, ice forms the northern shore of a wide, yet constricting, fiord that funnels surface traffic to and from the Kola.

In the Far East the maximum ice limit runs outside Kamchatka and the Kuriles, down to Japan's northern Hokkaido Island, and then west, south of Sakhalin and across the mouth of Vladivostok Bay. Vladivostok averages 85 days of fog a year, and freezes for three months. Sovetskaya Gavan, the Trans-Siberian railway's eastern terminal, across from Sakhalin Island, is even more prone to fog, and ice-bound from December to March. Petropavlovsk, on the Kamchatka, is protected from winds and fog by volcanic mountain ranges, but freezes in December, and remains frozen for three to four months. All can be kept open with ice-breakers. The result, however, is that surface traffic from all is restricted in winter. From Vladivostok, Sovetskaya Gavan and later-built bases along the Sea of Okhotsk's shores, surface traffic is furthermore funnelled by the need to pass through relatively narrow and exposed straits in order to get by Japan and to open waters.

The Barents was nearer. Its ports and and infrastructure received a boost from World War II, when Murmansk served as gateway for allied convoys. After the war, Finnish neutrality provided a protective buffer-zone for the umbilical railway. The initial buildup of Soviet naval strategic potentials centred on Murmansk and on the Kola's maze of fiords and natural harbours.

The main problem concerned the limited range of early submarine-launched missiles. Targeting the USA demanded proximity to US shores. Exit into the Norwegian Sea was not then challenged by the North Atlantic Treaty Organization (NATO). And, Soviet Naval Commander-in-Chief, Admiral of the Fleet Gorshkov, evinced little respect for the bottling-up capacity of NATO anti-submarine warfare efforts across the Greenland–Iceland–UK (GIUK) gap. But he respected the US Navy's underwater acoustic listening systems (SOSUS) and the attrition probabilities associated with traverse through thousands of miles dominated by NATO surface, sub-surface and air units.

Gorshkov ordered exploration of under-ice Arctic transit routes and priority development of intercontinental-range submarine-launched ballistic missiles (SLBMs).[3] By 1967 the Soviet Union had published tectonic (structural) maps of the Arctic Ocean floor right up to Canada's northern islands that were more accurate and had better discrimination than the best analogous Canadian maps of these islands' land surfaces.

The first intercontinental-range Delta Class SLBMs, arriving after 1972, promised relief from the need to transit the Atlantic Ocean. Missiles could be fired from the northern bastion, protected by concentrated surface elements and naval and land-based aircraft cover. Pioneering Arctic expertise was subsequently incorporated into new hull and superstructure designs that allowed ballistic missile submarines to break through the ice cap. Adjacent Arctic regions became extensions of the home fortress.

The incorporation of Arctic expanses was forced by Norway's creeping integration into US naval operational designs. Loran C navigational facilities in the early 1960s provided 'fixed launch surveillance' for the Polaris. The subsequent installation of a SOSUS listening network off northern Norway furthered the trend. The 1970s and early 1980s brought pre-positioning for the US Marine Corps, a Collocated Operating Base (COB) agreement to prepare airfields to host US Air Force squadrons, and the INVICTUS accord, which allows a US aircraft-carrier's up to 100 fighter-bombers and other aircraft to use Oerland airfield, north of Trondheim. Peacetime training patterns routinized procedures intended for war or 'crisis'. The strike and range potential of Norwegian access provided crucial underpinning to the US Navy's ambition of the 1980s to penetrate into and challenge Soviet control of the Barents.[4] The Norwegian anchor was complemented by a pattern of increasing US attack submarine activity under the polar ice.

The under-ice threat was manageable. The absence of a comprehensive Arctic SOSUS and of supporting surface and air anti-submarine warfare components provided good survival odds for Soviet SLBMs, especially in view of their greater familiarity with Arctic conditions and phenomena. And core Norwegian facilities—first-priority targets (subject to pre-emption if fully employed)—could be crippled.

Nevertheless, the trend towards greater exposure in the northwest may have contributed to the mid-to-late 1970s decision to develop a second 'home bastion' for SLBMs, in the Sea of Okhotsk—although the decision may merely have reflected the confluence of intercontinental range, a much-improved maritime-industrial infrastructure and the coming of a second, more northerly trans-Siberian railway. The geography of the Okhotsk is extraordinarily favourable for the purpose. Soviet land-based aircraft dominance over at least its inner reaches appears assured. The multiple but narrow straits that constrain exit are ideal to defend against entry. Some underwater penetration may occur, but shallow regions give peculiar advantage to Moscow's new diesel-electric submarines. Supporting surface and carrier-air penetration is not likely.

The complementary development of The Northern Sea Route proceeded apace. Ever-increasing ice-breaker capabilities, both nuclear and conventional, gradually extended the season for surface navigation. Obvious civilian and commercial benefits dominated the official rationale. Yet military ramifications are evident. Submarines could transit before. But now surface warships could also redeploy, under cover of land-based air power, far more quickly than before and far quicker than US fleets.

IV. Naval buildup

The emergence of the new Soviet Navy dates from 1961.[5] Disdained as a relic a few years before, it became, instead, crucial to the future. The transformation mirrored a more sober understanding of ICBMs. Experience, tests and increasingly caustic US appraisals (particularly scathing in 1961) revealed a whole series of problems, covering missile design, reliability and accuracy, and command and control. Early fuels could not be stored aboard. It would take days to prepare them for firing. They were stationary, above ground, and extremely vulnerable.

The decision to put some to sea, and to upgrade the navy, was part of the response. Other elements of the drive for survivability and availability ranged from silo construction to experiments with mobile missiles, missile defence and space basing. But silo-hardening prospects constituted an uncertain race against improving accuracies; and mobility, defence and space aspirations foundered against both technological and operational obstacles. The navy grew.

Its primary task was to ensure Soviet strategic might. The Yankee nuclear (theatre-range) ballistic missile submarine was developed. The strategic priority was reflected in efforts to ensure its viability. The preparation of the Arctic transit option has been mentioned. It was also accompanied by an array of surface vessels designed to provide a protective anti-submarine warfare screen. The defensive strategic task of engaging carrier and later Polaris nuclear threats was also reaffirmed. New classes of surface combatants with nuclear-tipped torpedoes and cruise missiles were procured. As numbers increased, exercises established a regular operating pattern in the Norwegian Sea, then extended the presumed engagement perimeter westward, to beyond the GIUK gap. A Mediterranean squadron was established, and then a (less permanent) Indian Ocean squadron and an intermittent Caribbean presence. By 1970 Moscow was able to stage its first truly global exercise, Okean.

The Soviet Union's oceanographic research and fishing fleets—the largest in the world—and the rapidly expanding Merchant Marine provided scientific, intelligence and other support. The Soviet Navy acquired its own acoustic listening systems, though less advanced than the USA's. Satellites revolutionized navigation and over-the-horizon targeting prospects.

Distant power projection capabilities brought peacetime and low-intensity options. Naval squadrons were positioned to dissuade US intervention in Angola, Bangladesh and elsewhere. Fleet presence was employed to secure the release of Soviet fishing trawlers in West Africa, to shore up morale in Havana, Tripoli and Mogadishu, and help Viet Nam resist and counter Chinese attack. The navy embraced the role of protector of State interests abroad, agent and defender of Soviet politico-economic initiatives in the Third World, and used its new mantle to press for a larger share of defence resources.

The navy was in danger of overreaching, again. Its primary purpose was embodied in its design. The navy was then predominantly nuclear, one-shot, with little or no reload capability. It was designed in accordance with prevailing doctrine: war would be nuclear, sudden and cataclysmic. Its new ambitions suggested more general challenge for command of the seas—an infinitely more demanding task, in terms of quantity, and sustainability.

The navy of the mid-late 1970s could control home seas, with a high degree of confidence; intercontinental-range missiles dispensed with the offensive requirement to extend domination and break-out support westward. More powerful cruisers with longer range and larger yield anti-ship and better air defence missiles signalled greater potency against carrier task forces. And in peacetime the navy could now support clients and also protect and to a limited degree further overseas interests. The latter was a major accomplishment, with profound international ramifications. Distant interventionary-type potential, however, was still marginal, effective only where US interest was slight, or where the balance on the ground was particularly favourable, as in Angola, Ethiopia and Viet Nam.

But the climate no longer favoured naval advocacy. Economic growth slowed. Soviet military procurement growth ended, in 1976 (according to US Central Intelligence Agency (CIA) reports of 1983, and 1986).[6] Domestic needs were pressing.

V.   New Soviet strategy: new naval purpose

Strategic building programmes sanctioned by Strategic Arms Limitation Talks (SALT) I appeared to confirm parity, secured and buttressed by survivability and redundancy, that is, the judgement that neither side could circumvent or negate the other's capacity for devastating retaliation. Nuclear pre-emption no longer made sense, nor did strikes against the other's homeland.

By 1977 Moscow embraced a second postulate. Nuclear weapons and probable escalatory dynamics defy control and threaten holocaust. Nuclear capabilities were not discarded. They remained the ultimate deterrent. Nuclear war-fighting was to be avoided because of escalatory dangers; the 'friction' of real combat is likely to defy control, whether horizontal or vertical.

If unleashed, however, the only distinction that can possibly be maintained is the ultimate one—between other areas and the superpowers' own homelands (because of the profusion of nuclear-capable systems at sea, and because nuclear capabilities remain a central theme of US naval expansion, nuclear avoidance may not be feasible in this arena; on the other hand, and notwithstanding US naval doctrine to the contrary, this is perhaps also the arena that can most easily be 'quarantined'). Nuclear pre-emption against the USA or, conversely, against the USSR, is no longer viable. This means that strategic reserves must be able to survive a lengthy period of threat.

The Reagan Administration's apparent espousal of nuclear war-fighting tenets in the 1980s caused no change in Soviet posture.[7] Soviet nuclear strike forces were modernized. But the strategic component's share of the defence budget was reduced (again, according to the CIA).[8] Soviet funds were diverted, to new conventional, 'smart' and exotic weapon technologies that promise nuclear-type efficiency, without the nuclear albatross of loss of control and purpose.

The navy, also, retooled. Priority efforts were directed to the development of long-range conventional sea- and air-launched cruise missiles. Systems were designed for reload. The new doctrine required sustainability on land and at sea. First-salvo nuclear engagement expectations were replaced by scenarios that put a premium on conventional options. Naval journals evinced new interest in the 'operational level of war'.[9]

Naval strategic forces were also affected. They no longer provided sole insurance. Firstly, by the 1970s Soviet strategists had become far more sanguine than their US counterparts about the impact of new accuracies on land missile survival odds (a decade later, three quarters of their strategic arsenal remained land-based, as opposed to less than one-quarter of the USA's). They appreciated the fact that pro forma accuracies reflected the calibration of gyroscopes and accelerometers over peacetime test ranges. Wartime trajectories entailed different atmospheric and gravitational phenomena, and, while satellite readings can correct for many of these, theoretical accuracies are not likely to be fully realized. In view also of improved silo-hardening techniques, a significant proportion of land-based missiles is likely to survive attack, and be available for response. Secondly, ballistic missile defence remained a hope. Early technologies proved inadequate, but substantial investments in research reflected continuing aspirations. Finally, missile mobility problems were overcome. The mid-1980s saw deployment of a new generation of mobile intercontinental-range ballistic missiles .

The fear that new accuracies and counterforce dynamics imperilled land missile survival gave special status to the SLBM force; as the perhaps sole future guarantor of Soviet retaliatory might, its survival prospects appeared sacrosanct. The sinking of a single Soviet SLBM might then have sparked an all-out exchange. The emergence of complementary insurance elements— redundant second-strike potentials—changed the equation. It suggests that a portion of the SLBM force may now conceivably be released for other theatre and sea combat (anti-carrier) operations. It also suggests that at least limited SLBM attrition can be tolerated and that it will be answered by action against analogous high-value, strategic, yet off-shore, targets—enemy SLBMs or carriers. This interpretation is reinforced by, and is in fact a compelling and logical corollary of, the new doctrinal dictum that strikes against superpower homelands must be avoided.[10]

The navy's relative eminence was also threatened by the new doctrine's increased emphasis on combined-arms integration and sustained mobility, and on combined-arms support for deep penetration and forward drive. Wartime Theatres of Strategic Military Operations (TVDs) were redefined.[11] The wartime practice of Supreme Command representatives taking direct charge of these multi-front all-arms composites was institutionalized; Marshal Ogarkov's 1984 assignment to direct the crucial Western TVD (incorporating Soviet and Warsaw Pact forces aimed at the central front), after seven and a half years as Chief of the General Staff responsible for the doctrine's adoption and implementation, underlined the seriousness of purpose. Military book-store display prominence and other indicators confirmed Ogarkov's continuing stature as the Soviet Union's most influential strategist. In the Soviet military, the stature of the man reflects the stature of the post.

The navy stood, once again, as an adjunct to a land and army-dominated whole. Naval interventionary-type potentials were accorded low priority. The first genuine carrier, still smaller than the USA's 15, would not be fully operational until the 1990s. The navy's procurement of specialized underway replenishment and amphibious assault vessels was set aside (after one Berezina Class and two Ivan Rogov Class ships); landings would employ civilian transport and the roll-on roll-off (ro-ro) ships. The combined-arms approach and the co-option of civilian resources re-emphasized tradition, and the fact and purpose of a unified, integrated command structure.

But whereas Gorshkov, the 'Father of the Red Navy', may have fought the new doctrine, his successor as Naval Commander-in-Chief, Vladimir Chernavin, anticipated and embraced it. Chernavin's embrace of the integrative approach went beyond mere acceptance of historical inevitability and fiscal circumstance.[12] His prior experience as a submariner and later as the Commander of the Northern Fleet suggests appreciation of the role and efficacy of land-based air support (50 per cent of the 4000-kilometre-range Backfire bombers, now armed with stand-off missiles, have been assigned to naval aviation); PVO (air defence) forces provide multiple interceptor and surface-to-air missile screens for naval bases and facilities.[13]

The greatly extended range of maritime stand-off missile threats against land targets furthermore meant that naval flank protection for European theatre operations must be correspondingly extended; land defence requirements demand command of adjacent seas, or at least sea denial. In the North and the Far East, the absence of a land buffer adds a crucial defensive dimension to the argument—a dimension reinforced by the US Navy's declared readiness to hit land targets in response to loss at sea (Soviet strategists might doubt the logic, rationality and hence likelihood of retaliation against the homeland, but contingency planners must perforce prepare for contrary mind-sets, and other eventualities). Land security demands a naval buffer; a modern naval buffer must have high seas potency.

The Soviet Union is not likely to add to its embryonic carrier fleet, however. The existing carrier, when operational, is likely to be assigned primarily to fleet protection, not power projection. The traditional Soviet view of carriers, as 'sitting ducks', was reinforced by the Falklands War: the British Navy owed its survival to the extraordinary failure rate of Argentine munitions. Argentine Exocets served notice that power projection against missile-equipped adversaries is becoming increasingly hazardous. The point applies to distant interventionary designs; it also applies to the far more potent and sophisticated air defence screen that envelops the Barents Sea.

By adopting the combined-arms approach as his own, Chernavin appears to have broken the traditional pattern of naval rise and fall, and in the process established a niche of perhaps greater substance, and permanence.

In the mid-1980s a Soviet commentary assigned national territorial sectors to five Theatres of Strategic Military Operations (in war 'they may stretch to several continents . . . over the whole globe—including . . . space') but identified commanders for only four.[14] The exception was the northwestern, which encompassed Leningrad and the Kola, and projected out over northern Scandinavia. The 1983 Soviet *Military Encyclopaedic Dictionary* notes that TVDs include 'the coastal waters of the oceans . . . and the contiguous coastlines of continents and the airspace above them'.[15] Two contiguous oceanic TVDs were also identified—the Arctic and the Pacific—also without publicly designated commanders.

The formulas assign Baltic and Black Sea Fleets to continental TVDs. In the Arctic and Pacific, however, the overlap in continental/oceanic TVD responsibilities and acknowledgement that TVD boundaries may be 'variable' suggest different constellations, especially in the context of all-arms integration.[16] Fleets may be subordinated to continental TVDs; but divisions, armies and even fronts may also be subordinated to oceanic TVDs. In the northwest the navy is dominant. In a war, the Arctic commander is likely to be the naval commander-in-chief, acting as designated representative of the Supreme High Command. As senior combined-arms commander in the region, his authority will extend to its *de facto* rear, namely the northwestern TVD. In the Far East, the fact that the Pacific Fleet is not explicitly assigned to the continental TVD suggests that it may, in war, act as a separate oceanic TVD, with responsibility extended to include air and land support forces, or, alternatively, that it could be assigned to the (presumably senior) Arctic TVD commander.

VI.   Conclusion

The independent navy was vulnerable, beholden to fate and to circumstances over which it had little control or influence. Its moments of glory were transient. The new Soviet combined-arms navy, on the other hand, is integral to Soviet power.

The USA's new 600-ship navy, configured according to forward strategy precepts, with attack submarines penetrating close to Soviet base complexes, a doctrine that calls for strikes on Soviet land targets in response to clashes at sea and cruise missiles that can be launched from afar, serves the cause of Soviet naval advocacy. In earlier eras coastal defence scarcely had an impact on homeland survival, while naval power projection was a luxury, useful if you could afford it, but not necessary. Today's US naval posture and emerging long-range strike capabilities directly affect the core concerns of the Red Army. Distinctions between periphery and heartland are erased. Technological and adversarial dynamics have compelled the Red Army to adopt and integrate naval potentials. The navy has become crucial to heartland defence—and to the deterrence-task of ensuring that the adversary faces the same dilemma, the same threat. During the 1960s, 1970s and early 1980s only the SLBM forces were essential to Soviet deterrence. In the new threat environment long-range naval surface and land/naval air-strike technologies also become vital. Previously their import could be dismissed as marginal. Today they are of the essence.

Finally, the Soviet Union's official position on long-range (dual-purpose) cruise missile developments is the same as its position on the weaponization of space: that both dynamics threaten to make verification (and hence arms control) impossible, and that neither can alter the fundamental underpinnings of the strategic equilibrium, yet both will inevitably increase jitteriness and instability. If these dynamics do proceed, however, the relative advantage may be the USSR's (though not one commensurate with the cost of greater instability). Today, the USA's allies and its forward-based systems encircle the USSR. Advanced cruise missile capabilities deployed on civilian as well as on military carriers, and space-basing will allow Soviet forward-based systems to encircle the United States.

Notes and references

[1] Kipp, J. W., 'Russian naval reformers and imperial expansion 1856–1863', *Soviet Armed Forces Review Annual*, Vol. 1, ed. D. R. Jones (Academic International Press: Gulf Breeze, FL, 1977), pp. 118–48.

[2] Jacobsen, C. G., *Soviet Strategy—Soviet Foreign Policy* (Robert MacLehose & Co., Ltd; University Press: Glasgow, 1972), pp. 142–60.

[3] Jacobsen, C. G., *Soviet Strategic Initiatives* (Praeger: New York, 1979), pp. 73–117. On Soviet Arctic exploration, note, for example, *Tektonicheskaya Karta Arktiki i Subarktiki* (The Tectonic Map of the Arctic and Subarctic) (Institute for the Study of the Arctic and Antarctic: Leningrad, 1967).

⁴ Watkins, J. D., 'The maritime strategy', *The Maritime Strategy*, US Naval Institute Proceedings, Supplement, Jan. 1986, pp. 3–17.

⁵ MccGwire, M., 'Naval power and Soviet oceans policy'; McConnel, J. M., 'Military-political tasks of the Soviet Navy in war and peace'; and Jacobsen, C. G., 'The civilian fleets', *Soviet Oceans Development* (US Government Printing Office: Washington, DC, Oct. 1977), pp. 80–183, 184–210 and 257–86. For the larger strategic context, see Jacobsen, C. G., *The Nuclear Era* (Spokesman: Nottingham; and Oelgeschlager, Gunn & Hain: Cambridge, MA, 1982).

⁶ Jacobsen, C. G., 'Soviet military expenditures and the Soviet defence burden', *World Armaments and Disarmament: SIPRI Yearbrook 1986* (Oxford University Press: Oxford, 1986), pp. 263–74.

⁷ Ogarkov, N. V., *Istoria Uchit Bditelnosti* (History Teaches Vigilance) (*Voenizdat*: Moscow, 1985), pp. 24, 47 and 88.

⁸ Jacobsen (note 6).

⁹ New Soviet naval designs reflect the doctrinal emphasis on surface-to-surface sustainability: see, e.g., Jordan, J., 'The Soviet surface fleet in 1985—Part One—A review of current trends and capabilities', *Defence*, vol. 17, no. 6 (1986), pp. 265–70. In *Morskoi Sbornik*, no. 9 (1986), Admiral Chernavin pioneers discussion of a purely *conventional* 'first salvo'.

¹⁰ MccGwire, M., *Soviet Military Objectives* (The Brookings Institution: Washington, DC, 1987), see chapters 1, 5 and 7.

¹¹ Hines, J. G. and Petersen, P. A., 'Changing the Soviet system of control: focus on theatre warfare', *International Defence Review*, vol. 19, no. 3 (1986), pp. 281–9; see also Ogarkov (note 7); and Gareyev, M. V., *M. V. Frunze—Voyennyy Teoretik* (M. V. Frunze—Military Theorist) (*Voenizdat*: Moscow, 1985), pp. 239–41 and 380–1.

¹² 'Chernavin—the new C-in-C of the Soviet Navy', *Jane's Defence Weekly*, vol. 5, no. 2 (1986), pp. 61–2. See also Chernavin, V. N., '*O teorii voenno-morskogo flota*' ('About naval theory') in *Morskoi Sbornik* (Naval Review), no. 1 (Jan. 1982), pp. 20–4, 'there are no purely independent spheres of armed struggle . . . (victory) is attained by the joint effort of all combat arms'. Shlomin, R. V., '*Voennaya nauka i voenno-morskoi flot*' ('Military science and the navy') in *Morskoi Sbornik* (Naval Review), no. 4 (Apr. 1983), pp. 20–7, notes 'the objective requirements . . . of mutual penetration of combat arms to the sphere of activities of the other combat arms'.

¹³ Analogous trends began to affect US dispositions: *Memorandum of Agreement on Joint USN/USAF Efforts for Enhancement of Joint Co-operation* (US Government Printing Office: Washington, DC, 1982); see also *Basic Aerospace Doctrine of the United States Air Force* (US Government Printing Office: Washington, DC, 1984) (this upgrades the 'maritime role' to the status of 'major mission').

¹⁴ Hines and Petersen (note 11), quoting from Binieda, Z., 'Ogolne pojecie teatru dzialan wojennych' (The general concept of a theatre of strategic military action), *Prezeglad Morski* (Polish Naval Review), no. 12 (1981), p. 4.

¹⁵ *Voennyi Entsiklopedicheskij Slovar* (Military Encyclopaedic Dictionary) (*Voenizdat*: Moscow, 1983).

¹⁶ Hines and Petersen (note 11); also Ogarkov (note 7), p. 47.

Paper 2.7.   Future cruise missiles: nature and impact

WILLIAM H. KINCADE

I.   Introduction

This essay examines the future of the cruise missile with particular attention to its implications for both military and political strategy and for security. The focus is primarily on nuclear-armed cruise missiles. Yet the nature of this versatile weapon requires discussion of non-nuclear variants.

Projecting the future of the cruise missile requires, first, an understanding of how the weapon is likely to evolve given past trends, current programmes and technical opportunities, cost considerations, doctrinal developments, the effect of the offence–defence interaction and the broader superpower competition, and the relationship of the cruise missile to other weapons, especially those contending for similar missions.

The last of this paper surveys the effects of projected developments on security and security policy, including arms limitation. It involves consideration of factors more problematic and speculative than those addressed in the earlier sections.

II.   Advanced cruise missiles

Among the factors obscuring a full appreciation of the future of cruise missile technology is the fact that such weapons have been around a long time. And, the concept has existed far longer. But technological problems and, later, service (especially air force) bias retarded development. Technological limitations were overcome during the 1970s. Service doubt and bias were overcome during the 1980s.[1]

The advantageous characteristics of today's advanced cruise missile are relatively well known. They are highly reliable, increasingly accurate, relatively inexpensive and extremely versatile weapons that can be fired from virtually any platform (ship, submarine, aircraft, ground vehicle or fixed site). In currently deployed models, they can attain ranges up to nearly 2000 miles and achieve supersonic speeds (above the speed of sound). They can carry nuclear or conventional warheads, including conventional warheads with specialized submunitions.[2]

Moreover, they are small, which gives them logistical advantages, especially in sea-borne and airborne versions. Essentially the same airframe can be used for sea-launched, air-launched and ground-launched versions. They can be adapted for use in vertical, horizontal, angled and rotating launchers. And they can be employed in tactical, theatre or strategic roles.

In addition, the cruise missile is ideally suited to take advantage of advances in sensor, target identification and acquisition, and related technologies. Unlike the original heavy bomber, the cruise missile arrives at a time when its intrinsic characteristics can be thoroughly exploited owing to the state of supporting technologies. The cruise, furthermore, is not only especially suited to certain kinds of target normally difficult for aircraft to destroy at acceptable sortie and loss rates (bridges, dams, power stations, airfields, etc.), it is effective or can be made to be effective against a variety of less specialized targets—another reflection of its adaptability and versatility.

III. Projectile-platform synergism

The performance achievements of current-generation cruise missiles would, by themselves, make them an important new military capability. However, this new capability becomes even more dramatic owing to the flexibility and the versatility of advanced cruise missiles, which makes them highly compatible with existing and projected launch platforms. The importance of this synergistic interaction is often neglected.

Yet it means that advanced cruise missiles can be readily incorporated in the weapon suites of a variety of sea-borne and airborne platforms largely without the great expense and engineering problems associated with the development of purpose-built platforms. Even the ground-launched cruise missile, which did require the development of a special-purpose launcher, was able to take advantage of highly evolved ground-vehicle technology for transporting and launching small- to medium-sized missiles.

In short, the cruise missile is ideally suited for use with platforms which are themselves in a highly mature state of development, especially with surface vessels, submarines and aircraft. This is no small advantage when it is recalled that certain innovations, such as those associated with post-Dreadnought classes of superbattleships or with new aircraft engines, required the costly design and development of entirely new platforms to accommodate the changes. As a result of its compatibility, the cruise missile can take advantage of the particular strengths of available platforms. For example, it can benefit from the relative invulnerability of modern submarines and from the specific advantages of different types of aircraft, such as their manoeuvrability.

It is these features of versatility and compatibility that account for the rapid and comprehensive programme of the US Navy for integrating advanced cruise missiles in the fleet. Current plans call for production of nearly 4000 *Tomahawk* sea-launched cruise missiles (SLCMs). Of these, 758 will carry nuclear warheads for attacking land targets, while 593 are for anti-ship missions, and 2643 have conventional warheads for land-attack purposes. Within five years, the

US Navy will have over 2500 ship and submarine launchers capable of firing either the nuclear or conventional cruise missile.[3]

While the addition of 758 nuclear warheads to the existing US nuclear arsenal will not amount to a significant increase, it has been estimated that, if desired, as many as 3310 nuclear *Tomahawks* could be deployed on US vessels by the year 1995 and, further, that if the US decided to equip surface ships and submarines with cruise missiles alone (displacing other offensive and defensive weapons), it could develop a total 'break-out potential' of just over 10 000 *Tomahawk* cruise missiles—the equivalent of the current US strategic arsenal.[4]

This is not likely to prove a realistic scenario, of course, violating as it does the requirement for other capabilities on ships and submarines, thus revealing the self-limiting factor of usable hull space that may constrain future cruise missile deployments. However, such projections do illustrate the potential for growth in cruise missile arsenals in the event of a major competition in this new technological capability.

Emulating the US revival and improvement of the cruise missile, the Soviet Union began in the late 1970s to modernize its cruise missiles for ground, air and naval forces. By the mid-1980s, the USSR had in development or in early deployment long-range, nuclear-tipped cruise missiles analogous to US types, including the AS–15 air-launched cruise missile, the SSC–X–4 ground-launched cruise missile, and the SS–N–21 sea-launched cruise missile, similar to the US *Tomahawk*, although first developed in fewer variations.[5]

These missiles, when deployed in quantity, will not only help to equalize the US numerical advantage, but will give the Soviet Union for the first time a long-range naval offensive attack capability similar to that previously enjoyed only by the United States because of its attack aircraft carriers. Cruise missiles will also give added capability to Soviet Naval Aviation in its primary role against US naval forces.

The synergism between launch platform and projectile that is seen in the case of the sea-launched cruise missile is repeated in the air-launched versions. Indeed, the combination of the air-launched cruise missile and the improved bomber or cruise missile carrier is leading to the revitalization and diversification of the air-breathing leg of strategic nuclear forces. This was scarcely thought possible a decade ago. At that time, the bomber appeared to many to be so anachronistic in the ballistic missile age that public sentiment in the United States helped lead to the termination of the B–1 programme. This meant continued reliance on the 20-year-old B–52.

However, the bomber proved to have unappreciated potential for improvement, partly through incorporation of first-generation signature-reducing or 'stealth' technology and partly through the development of greater speed and agility in such aircraft as the B–1B bomber. And this potential will be further expanded by the even harder-to-detect advanced technology bomber (ATB), a high-altitude penetrating aircraft. Hence the aerodynamic or air-breathing portion of strategic nuclear forces is being vastly improved by developments in both platforms and projectiles.[6]

Efforts to improve the performance and protection of intercontinental ballistic missiles (ICBMs), meanwhile, are bogged down in engineering difficulties associated either with their mobility or with their hardening. The ICBM has proved to be a victim of its own virtuosity. It is so effective as a hard-target killer (perhaps approaching perfect accuracy) that it cannot be readily protected from its counterparts in adversary arsenals. On the other hand, the aerodynamic team of the bomber and the cruise missile has a new and promising lease on life.

IV.   Technology projections and possibilities

Although recognized by some officers, officials and analysts, the still unexhausted potential of the advanced cruise missile in combination with various types of firing platform has been remarkably neglected. Fascination amounting to fixation with the steady technical progress of ICBMs has contributed to this neglect, along with the strong interest in the application of embryonic and emerging technologies to other conventional and nuclear missions. Finally, the dominant role played in the evolution of contemporary nuclear strategy by sea-launched and land-launched ballistic missiles has also obscured the seemingly pedestrian aerodynamic portion of strategic nuclear forces.

The net effect of these influences has been to cause a certain kind of myopia, wherein developments in the foreground (such as the virtuosity of the ballistic missile) and the intriguing potential of technology on the farther horizon (for deep-strike missions or ballistic missile defence) have meant that the middle ground of the strategic picture has been overlooked. Yet it is in this area that the developments determining the environment of the 1990s are likely to occur.

To take an example at hand, the penetration potential of pilotless, aerodynamic vehicles—cruise missiles, drones and remotely piloted vehicles (RPVs)—to deliver attacks against heavily defended rear areas and to conduct battlefield or rear-area reconnaissance has been well remarked. Less well examined currently is the capability of these same systems and other emerging technologies for damage limitation and for electronic warfare, that is, protective missions.[7]

Adopting a command technology approach to military-technological innovation (MTI), the Reagan Administration has, on the one hand, pitted embryonic or newly emerging technological possibilities against the very mature ballistic missile system, while, on the other hand, it has substantially increased the developmental momentum of the rapidly evolving aerodynamic weapons. The consequences of this mixed, and indeed contradictory, approach, are likely to be quite different from the administration's expectations and forecasts. The exploitation of the technologies with the most promise in the near term—offensive aerodynamic weapons—will alter the future technological environment and therefore provide a different context for eventual decisions about the technologies with only more distant exploitability, that is, those associated with the Strategic Defense Initiative (SDI).

In the immediate future, the most significant development in strategic weapon technology will be the continued improvement of the cruise missile. Although its specific characteristics will be determined by the missions to which it is assigned, the cruise missile has the potential to become smaller, to attain supersonic and perhaps hypersonic speed, to gain greater accuracy, and to acquire greater penetration capability from signature-reducing technology and other evasive or deceptive measures. The ability to tailor it to a variety of specific missions through interchangeable nuclear and conventional warheads (including variable-yield nuclear warheads and special-purpose conventional warheads)—combined with its suitability to a variety of launching platforms—will lead to the widespread integration of cruise missiles throughout the military forces of the East and the West.

This development will be accompanied by significant improvements in aircraft in terms of speed, penetration capability and other performance characteristics, whether or not these aircraft are intended to serve as cruise missile carriers. The programmes to develop a stealth-configured fighter plane, 'fly-by-wire' and 'wing-in-ground' aircraft, and a hypersonic aircraft or transatmospheric vehicle (TAV)—even if not immediately successful in their own right—will considerably advance military aircraft capability, especially deep-strike aircraft.

In brief, then, techno-strategic development of the most profound significance from now to the end of the century will not be in the area of ballistic missile defence but in the comparatively more prosaic area of advanced aerodynamic weapons.

V.   Impact on forces and warfare

The changes which will likely be created by the superpower acquisition of large numbers of variously launched cruise missiles in the early to middle 1990s have scarcely been appreciated. The magnitude of such change can best be understood in terms of the nature of strategic nuclear forces in the past. Until the advent of modern cruise missiles, the distinguishing characteristics of long-range nuclear weapons were that they were large; employed identifiable, limited-purpose delivery vehicles or platforms (such as heavy bombers or special-purpose submarines); could operate only from a relatively small number of special missile fields, bomber bases or submarine ports; and the delivery vehicles or launchers could not be readily reloaded.

The cruise missile represents a relaxation of virtually all of these constraints. Current transporter-erector-launchers (TELs) for ground-launched cruise missiles remain somewhat restricted in their basing and mobility, of course. Yet improvements in cruise missile technology generally allow long-range, nuclear models to be deployed with considerable freedom. Launching platforms can be easily reloaded, if modest logistical efforts are made to provide for this capacity. Air and naval platforms for cruise missiles can be operated from standard air and naval bases throughout the world. The penalties imposed by trading off other ordnance for cruise missiles are tolerable.

The pace and direction of this process of cruise missile integration will be influenced by such factors as absolute and relative costs, national strategic traditions and service preferences, and competition with other systems that have already been acquired for similar roles. The Soviet Union, for example, may prove reluctant to deploy nuclear cruise missiles as broadly as the United States is now planning to do, owing to its greater concern for central control of nuclear forces. Future US administrations might likewise restrain nuclear deployments out of concern for accidents.

However, these factors are likely to have their effect at the margins. The versatility, effectiveness and reliability of the cruise missile and its low cost compared to other weapons make it an extremely attractive system. In the 1990s, therefore, steadily improving models are likely to be produced and deployed in large numbers, although nuclear warheads may be retained in depots for issue when needed. At the same time, cruise missiles will also increasingly appear in conventional versions in the inventories of other nations.

In considering the impact of cruise missiles on warfare, five possibly related roles stand out in particular: (a) the *deep-strike mission*, especially against hardened, heavily defended, or high-value targets (such as depots, bridges, dams, command centres, airfields, etc.); (b) the *defence-suppression mission* against surface-to-air missile batteries and associated equipment or similar facilities; (c) the *pre-emptive mission* against targets deemed crucial to the successful launching of a conventional or nuclear attack; (d) the *anti-ship mission* in conflict at sea; and (e) the '*horizontal escalation*' mission against targets outside the primary zone of engagement. The cruise missile has been touted for each of these roles, explicitly or by implication.[8]

Far more speculative, of course, is the question of the employment of advanced cruise missiles in conventional or nuclear conflict involving both of the superpowers or their coalitions. For 40 years, the United States and the Soviet Union have generally been quite careful—with some notable lapses—to avoid conditions leading towards direct conflict. This situation may endure, although the occurrence of notable lapses (e.g., the Cuban missile crisis, the recurring Berlin crises, and various incidents at sea) and the record of history militate against it.

Furthermore, cruise missiles are being deployed by both superpowers primarily or exclusively for use against one another. The ground-launched cruise missiles deployed for the North Atlantic Treaty Organization (NATO) in England and Sicily are for use against the Warsaw Pact. Horizontal escalation against Soviet and Warsaw Pact forces is one mission anticipated for US cruise missiles. And the primary targets of cruise missiles deployed by Soviet Naval Aviation are US and allied surface vessels.

Finally, the very versatility and broad-scale deployment of the cruise missile, with attendant ambiguity about the purpose and character of the deployed warheads, provide new opportunities for escalation from low-level regional warfare to direct superpower conflict, whether intended or inadvertent. In this connection, it must be remembered that escalation is primarily a product of the value of the targets hit (or that can be hit) and of the speed with which operations unfold, perhaps preventing political control. Widespread integration of multi-mission cruise missiles in superpower forces means, in technical terms at least, the proliferation of possibilities for conflict expansion and intensification.

A confident forecast about the use of advanced cruise missiles in superpower conflict is not possible. Yet the early experience, the assigned or potential missions, and the capabilities of the cruise missile are highly suggestive. Should there be a breakdown in the inhibitions that have thus far prevented direct military conflict between the United States and the Soviet Union, it seems clear that the cruise missile will be used early, often and in a variety of modes. Whether its use can be restricted to conventional variants is, at best, problematic, since the stakes in any such warfare will presumably be perceived as very high indeed and since the integration and versatility of the weapon argue against achieving such distinctions operationally.

In combination, improvements in aerodynamic weapons will also stimulate even further the already growing interest in air defence systems. The design of these air defence systems will have to be responsive to the fact that future aircraft and cruise missiles—separately or in combination—will be able to perform in tactical, theatre and intercontinental roles. That is, air defences will have to contend with deep-strike aerodynamic threats, whether the objective of such deep strikes is tactical or strategic.

Furthermore, the mobility of cruise missiles and their launching platforms further suggests the need for a flexible, modular approach to air defence. Defences utilizing permanent installations along static borders and oriented to predictable azimuths of attack—such as characterized strategic air defence and ballistic missile early warning systems in the 1950s and 1960s—will have to be substantially augmented by mobile but powerful air defence weaponry so as to be better able to cope with less predictable flight paths and raids of varying intensity or size.

While satellite and ground-based wide-area early warning facilities will be appropriate for many scenarios, space-based and stationary facilities adequate to cover potential target areas fully may prove prohibitively costly. Furthermore, such facilities will be subject to pre-emptive and defence-suppression attacks. Thus, mobile acquisition, tracking and firing units may be required in numbers and types not contemplated in current air defence programmes, depending on the extent of the growth in the advanced aerodynamic weapons.

Technologies under development for the SDI may be of help in the air defence area, especially in terms of target acquisition and tracking, and command and control. Given the time normally required for embryonic technologies to mature, even in forced-draft development programmes, it is unlikely, however, that any of the more exotic missile killers themselves will be available in the 1990s to deal with the rejuvenated and proliferating aerodynamic threats. Thus, air defence systems will continue to rely on projectile weapons rather than on directed-energy beams.

At the same time, however, these projectile weapons will have a growing capability not only against aerodynamic offensive arms but also under certain conditions, against ballistic missiles. For example, it is increasingly regarded as feasible to defend against ballistic missiles with ground-based defences, so long as the attack is limited, its targets can be identified precisely beforehand, or the incoming ballistic missiles are tactical ones. It would not be at all surprising, therefore, to see the deployment of multi-purpose, mobile defence systems that are designed to cope with cruise missiles and aircraft but possess some capability against a constrained ballistic missile attack. Such systems could be suitable for deployment around missile fields, strategic bomber bases, missile submarine ports and similar high-value strategic targets.

Currently, of course, such high-value targets are vulnerable to recent-generation ballistic missiles, and this is unlikely to change much over the next 10 to 15 years. However, one consequence of the steady improvement and proliferation of aerodynamic attack weapons is that these targets will now be vulnerable to a different kind of attack. This diversification of attack options amounts to an increase in vulnerability.

As a response to the deepening vulnerability of targets to contemporary weapons, hardening faces severe limitations in the case of some targets and is impossible in others. Various techniques for evasion—such as mobility, dispersal, proliferation and deception—are additional responses to target vulnerability. Interest in these approaches has grown considerably as vulnerability has deepened.

Thus, given the additional vulnerability occurring as a result of the improved aerodynamic weapons and given their dependence on electronic guidance packages, the defence can also be expected to make more creative use of electronic warfare to blunt or foil an attack by scrambling the electronic environment in which these weapons operate. Selective and general jamming, electronic decoys and other measures designed to foil the avionics, guidance and homing mechanisms of aerodynamic weapons will probably be more intensively developed and deployed.

This would only be reflective of a large underlying trend in MTI; that is, the replacement of energy efficiency by information efficiency as the primary determinant of weapon system effectiveness. Indeed, as information technology has steadily revolutionized weaponry and combat, it is to be expected that more attention will be accorded to thwarting an adversary's information capacity, whether it resides in a tactical display system, a data link or a missile guidance system. Information warfare may thus be another distinguishing feature of future military planning and conflict.

VI. Impact on planning, strategy and the military balance

Planning and strategy for warfare depend on images, images of warfare in the abstract, of previous wars and of future conflict. In the case of nuclear or, more likely, conventional and nuclear warfare, abstractions and recent wars may be unreliable guideposts in many respects, so that our image of future general war is based to a very considerable extent on well-worn but untested hypotheses, arguable scenarios and rebuttable presumptions. The very strategy of 'flexible response' is to some degree an admission of the manifold uncertainties involved in the onset and conduct of future warfare between the dominant coalitions.

In their political dimension, Western military planning and strategy are based on an elaborate, but ultimately only partly proven, theory about the efficacy of deterrent and compellent threats in terms of influencing adversary decision-making and behaviour in peacetime. This theory is also thought to be applicable to nuclear warfare, during which the escalation of violence or the threat to escalate the violence may discourage one side or both from prolonging the conflict and produce initiatives for its termination. In this respect, the theory is entirely unproven, although there are modern cases of limited war that suggest its possible relevance.

The strategies that may be possible or employed in future warfare are thus highly conjectural and may prove quite different fom the current image or from the image that will likely replace it as advancing technology has its inevitable impact on strategic thinking. Nevertheless, taking into account the lines along which peacetime nuclear strategy has thus far evolved and the technological environment of the future, some of the directions and problems of future strategy-making can be divined.

As to the technological setting, it seems reasonably safe to say that the advanced aerodynamic forces of bombers and cruise missiles will not replace or significantly displace any of the weapon systems that are now in inventory, at least over the next 15 years or so. That is, ICBMs, SLBMs and bombers that do not carry cruise missiles will remain a part of the picture. Likewise, at the conventional level, cruise missiles will assume some of the roles of other anti-ship weapons, such as torpedoes, or of manned fighter aircraft, but they will not replace them. Instead, these improved aerodynamic systems will be more complementary to existing weapons than competitive with them, sharing missions rather than seizing them.

The ICBMs, SLBMs and non-cruise-missile bombers will be retained because they are more suitable for missions of last resort, that is, destroying urban-industrial or economic targets and heavily hardened or highly mobile counteract forces. They are also considered to weigh more heavily in the calculations of adversary leaders and thus to have a greater deterrent or compellent effect. And, despite hopes for effective, wide-arca shields against these weapons, there is no reason to think that the embryonic technologies now being explored will be able to produce anything more than a stimulus for better and more numerous ballistic missiles in the period with which this analysis is concerned.

The future technological environment, then, includes rejuvenated aerodynamic forces alongside improving ballistic missile forces. And it involves more capable, but far from insurmountable, air defences, together with new and improved information warfare systems and techniques. But it does not include effective ballistic missile defences, nor the equally long-sought breakthrough in anti-submarine warfare technology. Instead, the protective technologies with the greatest promise in the next decade and a half are those relating to evasion, deception and mobility.

In terms of direct East–West conflict, improved aerodynamic strategic weapons are most suitable for missions in the area at the upper end of the scale of conventional warfare and the middle range of the spectrum of nuclear conflict. That is, their capacity for carrying out deep-strike missions without putting costly aircraft and air crews at risk fits them best for high-intensity conflict above the level of tactical manoeuvres and weapons but below the threshold of intercontinental ballistic missile exchanges against strategic forces or economic assets. This suggests that they will find their niche in the already varied panoply of modern weapons in the region that involves theatre warfare and, for example, limited strikes on superpower homelands or adjacent operating areas.

Whether a zone in the spectrum of conflict could or will exist *in reality* between conventional operations limited to the theatre and full-scale ballistic missile exchanges is a proposition that remains open to much doubt. Yet the tendency of Western strategists to define conflict in terms of rather finely calculated gradations of violence and the character of the missions being considered for or assigned to the emerging aerodynamic force of the future suggest that this is where peacetime strategy-making will locate them.

And once again, the political justification for this development will involve the circular rationale that these forces are needed to deter the equivalent capability of the Soviet Union, so that there are no gaps across 'the full spectrum of deterrence'. Indeed, one of the signal aspects of the cruise missile is that it is well suited to a variety of 'limited nuclear options' or 'counter-military options' envisaged by former US Defense Secretaries James Schlesinger and Harold Brown, options that lie above theatre conventional warfare but below strategic counter-force strikes.

This is not to suggest that fighting a nuclear war necessarily will make any more political or military sense than it ever has. After all, the new capability represented by strategic cruise missiles will complement, not replace, ICBMs and sea-launched ballistic missiles (SLBMs). Thus, the overwhelming destructive power of these nuclear behemoths will remain available to the powers possessing them and *should* serve as a strong disincentive to crossing the nuclear threshold by any route.

Nevertheless, the existence of this new cruise capability will require planners to consider the opportunities it offers, as well as the threats it poses in the hands of adversaries. Prominent among those opportunities (and threats) is the growing possibility of tactical or theatre nuclear-conventional war or strategic nuclear conflict fought below the level of ballistic missile exchanges.

Contrarily, the very proliferation of air-launched and sea-launched, land-attack, nuclear-tipped cruise missiles throughout superpower air forces and fleets increases the likelihood of their use and of their serving as a powder train for escalation. This is even more the case since control of such multi-role or multi-purpose weapons will necessarily be more decentralized than the control of the 'dedicated' or single-purpose ballistic missiles and heavy bombers. Moreover, improvements in conventional weapons arising from the same or similar technological innovations are making them more and more suitable for some missions now dominated by nuclear weapons.[9] Thus, innovation is generally obscuring or obliterating the conventional-nuclear distinction rather than raising the nuclear threshold.

The kind of nuclear warfare, or combined nuclear and conventional warfare, that is thereby made possible short of ICBM exchanges would not, probably, be short, sharp precision or surgical warfare, as is often imagined. Rather, it would have a character somewhat akin to what the British in the 1950s termed 'broken-backed warfare', albeit for different reasons. That is, such warfare could involve prolonged or sporadic low-level but deep strikes with advanced cruise missiles—nuclear and conventional—as each side sought to gain a decisive advantage without resorting to ballistic missiles or attacks on central strategic forces, command and control facilities, or economic targets.

The consequences of fundamental change in the character of strategic nuclear weapons have been, to a degree, recognized in terms of the difficulties it imposes on the monitoring of arms control agreements. But they will also have important, probably decisive, consequences for strategic and tactical intelligence, and for nuclear strategy and tactics. Heretofore, military intelligence, arms control classification and verification, and nuclear doctrine have been shaped by the particular characteristics of weaponry essentially devel oped in the 1950s. All will be altered by the changes in the weapons of the 1990s.

Firstly, the ability, not only to multiply strategic cruise missiles (SCMs), but to multiply their storage and operating sites many times over and to give them a variety of launching modes will change the complexion of vulnerability. In the past, when heavy bomber bases, ballistic missile submarine operating bases and ICBM silos were easily detected and targeted, strategic force survivability was primarily a matter of the size of the alert portion of the arsenal, of early warning and of reaction time. Soon SCMs could be widely deployed or stored in widely dispersed depots in the homelands of the superpowers and prepared for rapid transfer by air transport, if necessary, to airfields and ports throughout the world to replenish depleted supplies aboard ships and aircraft. Pre-launch survivability of larger portions of the total forces could thus be better guaranteed, yet the vulnerability of other targets—those that are centralized, stationary and visible—will grow still greater.

Secondly, as we have seen in the case of the ballistic-missile-dominated forces, there is a 'ratchet' effect that results from counterforce targeting, so that an increase in the number of weapons on one side begets growth in the forces of the other in order to carry out counterforce missions. This ratchet effect may be somewhat dampened in the case of cruise missiles by the sheer magnitude of the difficulties involved in keeping track of them, their launching platforms and their depots. This is the kind of situation that causes planners to consider more economical uses of weapons, as in attacks on command and control systems. But this option may be of limited utility in view of the anticipated decentralization of politico-military control over cruise missiles.

In any event, there is sure to be some, probably significant, upward pressure on cruise missile inventories as they are assigned missions against counterpart cruise missile platforms, depots or transfer points. At the same time, consideration will have to be given to providing air defences for these potential targets. If cruise missiles become smaller, more capable and less expensive (in either relative or absolute terms)—as this study projects—then current land-based or naval systems for air defence, such as the US Navy's *Aegis* anti-air warfare cruisers, will have to be substantially upgraded to cope with the potential for system saturation.

Thirdly, the capacity for reloading weapons provides significantly more flexibility in planning their use. Less stringently required to contemplate large-scale salvos of ballistic missiles or bomber-delivered weapons—because of the vulnerability of their bases and pressures to 'use them or lose them'—nuclear war planners can more effectively withhold weapons and thus consider protracted nuclear war scenarios. While command and control systems remain vulnerable and their long-term *durability*, if not immediate *survivability*, is seriously in question, strategic cruise missiles could be deployed in a manner that would make them far less dependent on the elaborate command and control links now associated with ballistic missiles.[10]

These developments might, to some degree, add stability to the superpower balance. As George Quester has suggested, when cruise missiles are widely deployed and fully integrated in future forces yet difficult to detect and define, they will impart a certain stability in the sense that they will not be a cause of deep concern about disarming strikes.[11] In particular, so-called arms race stability might be enhanced because neither side would have quite the same incentives or reliable data on adversary forces to stimulate a force-matching or force-trumping competition. And, it might further eventuate, the already low possibility of East–West conflict would be reduced even further because of the high probability that it would be nuclear and at least theatre-wide almost from the outset, owing to the nature of cruise missiles.

However, the purchase price for this kind of cruise missile stability could be high indeed. And there are reasons for thinking that instabilities of other kinds will be even greater with the large-scale deployment of the cruise. For one thing, the stability thus engendered might well be more sensitive to smaller shocks than the kind of equilibrium that has so far persisted. That is, with the nuclear threshold presumably lower, command of nuclear forces pre-delegated

to lower echelons, and the powder trains running from conventional engagements at the tactical level to large-scale nuclear 'throws' more numerous and
fast-burning, less consequential incidents might ignite a conflagration more
easily. Recognizing this possibility, there may be more temptation, not less, to
use the 'big ones', rather than take chances with an ambiguous escalatory trail.

In the Western strategic lexicon, moreover, the notion of stability has been
very narrowly defined, both as regards crisis stability and arms race stability.
What may happen is not that cruise missiles will stabilize the balance in terms of
competition or crisis, but that our definitions or understandings of stability will
change. Stability is, after all, partly psychological and an extremely crude and
elastic concept. It resides, ultimately, not so much in the nature of weapons or
forces, as it does in levels of uncertainty, competing fears, and perceptions of
greater and lesser evils. Political stability could be upset by measures that
appear to enhance the technical stability of nuclear forces.

Cruise missiles, and their varied platforms, furthermore, will not fit neatly
into the hierarchy of forces associated with flexible response strategy in the
past. They are too versatile for such neat pigeonholing. Instead, like other
multi-purpose systems, only more so, they will blur or break down the
distinctions on which graduated response and inter-war deterrence have
formerly depended. The incorporation of dual-use (nuclear or conventional)
and variable-yield nuclear warheads will considerably aggravate this trend.

Thus, while cruise missiles appear to fit a conceptual niche in peacetime
strategic thinking, their effect in general warfare will be to bridge the 'firebreaks' in the imaginary escalatory ladder on which Western strategy has been
founded. The problem for future strategy, then, is to find ways to make the use
of cruise missiles plausible without their fuelling escalation rather than retarding it through escalation control or escalation dominance. In other words, can
systems like the cruise be reconciled with flexible response? This problem,
certainly formidable enough in itself, is further complicated by the increasing
capability of advanced conventional weapons, including conventionally armed
cruise missiles, which make deep-strike attacks on many military targets just as
damaging and therefore as escalatory as attacks with nuclear warheads.

From a larger perspective, cruise missiles represent part of a trend towards
the proliferation of nuclear weapons among conventional forces and the
contemplation of their use in situations where the stakes may not warrant the
risk of escalation to ICBMs or SLBMs. The pressures in the United States for
the pre-delegation of nuclear release authority to lower-level commanders and
for semi-automatic response systems to compensate for shorter warning times
are reinforced and are further stimulated by this trend. The aggravated
vulnerability of command and control systems owing to an improved cruise
missile threat, in turn, fuels pressures for decentralization of command and
control and pre-delegation of authority. An indiscriminate approach to technological opportunities has made this slippery slope towards 'warfighting' easier
and seemingly more necessary.

In terms of political strategy, it might be assumed that a more 'seamless' web of nuclear contingencies would strengthen deterrent threats by making their activation more automatic. While this might be so in terms of responding to acts that menaced core national values, a seamless escalatory web would be less believable as the basis for a deterrent or compellent threat in situations of lesser import. And the situations where the threat to use nuclear weapons is most common have been just these cases involving lower stakes.

The easy hybridization of military forces made possible by the modern cruise missile and future generations of them will also have implications for US strategy regarding regional conflicts. Showing the flag by deploying naval or air force units to actual or potential hot spots and crisis zones will have quite a different impact in these areas, at home, and in Eastern and Western capitals if these units are equipped, or thought to be equipped with a variety of nuclear weapons suitable for tactical, theatre or strategic use. In a world made more jittery by the prevalence and versatility of nuclear weapons, the implications will be more than those involved in a few nuclear-capable planes on an attack aircraft carrier, formerly the only means of moving nuclear forces quickly into an area distant from US-controlled air bases.

Nuclear neuralgia may also hamper the ability of presumptively nuclear-capable naval or air units to make port calls or use air corridors necessary to their regional missions. Yet, separating nuclear-equipped vessels or aircraft from non-nuclear ones so as to avoid these problems may impose unwanted operational limitations and still not satisfy other governments. Meanwhile, the eventual incorporation of conventional variants of advanced cruise missiles in the arsenals of other nations will give them a potent weapon against US naval forces. It is not that the United States will not be able to sail and predominate at sea wherever it wishes, but that smaller powers will be able to exact a higher price if they feel their own national values are at stake.

The risks of inadvertent or miscalculated use of nuclear weapons necessarily increase with ubiquitousness and socialization to nuclear war-fighting doctrines. Planners and strategists will have to be ingenious to cope with this and with its political repercussions at home and abroad. And, making the perhaps optimistic assumption that the vertical and horizontal spread of cruise missiles reduces the incentive to resort to traditional armed violence (i.e., between regular military forces), decision-makers may have to cope with a more inventive application of other violent techniques, such as terrorism, sabotage, forceful subversion, irregular warfare, and so on. When blocked in one form of expression, the resort to violence as a means of change tends to shift to other modalities, if the basic grievances are strong enough.

Looming over, but importantly affecting the terrestrial environment, will be developments in space weaponry, where the likely outcome of current technological opportunities and momentum will be the development, principally, of increasingly effective anti-satellite and satellite-protection weapons. This will place in doubt the effectiveness, in the event of a general East–West conflict, of many of the communications and intelligence resources on which weapons and the conduct of battle will so greatly depend in the future.

Portrayed intentionally in bleak shades, the foregoing picture of future possibilities and problems remains highly speculative. Addressing the political implications of these developments would be even more hazardous. It does suggest, however, that many of the problems implied by MTI in general, and advanced aerodynamic weapons in particular, have only been superficially considered or not addressed at all. There remains the oft-encountered but dangerous perspective that technological change can be entirely comprehended in terms of old ideas, when the record indicates that new technological conditions require equally ingenious thinking.

How much opportunity there will be for innovative thinking depends, in part, on the pace of the technological developments prefigured in this analysis. If the projected changes are telescoped, the probability of miscalculation and error is higher. The forecast, then, depends partly on the resolution of engineering problems (which are generally far greater than expected), partly on the willingness and ability of governments to intervene in the process of change, and partly on the wisdom of their intervention.

VII.   Impact on security and arms control

In the narrow sense that it brings certain classes of target under additional or more effective fire, the cruise missile will increase target vulnerability and therefore physical insecurity. Security, or insecurity, however, is to a large extent a matter of perception. Hence the security impact of the widespread integration of cruise missiles into future forces projected above may not greatly alter how people feel about their security. Such a development, for example, may have an influence on perceptions quite different from, even less dramatic than, that of intercontinental ballistic missiles.

The previous analysis, moreover, is based on the assumption that the future development of cruise missiles will not be limited by arms control agreements. Given the well-known difficulties of developing constraints, counting rules and verification measures suitable to this eminently 'grey' weapon, such an assumption seems plausible. But it is not necessarily valid. Given adequate determination on the part of the superpowers, human ingenuity may be capable of finding more or less acceptable ways of constraining the developments suggested earlier. Thus, estimating the security impact of future cruise missiles is complicated still further by the need to forecast the possibility and likely influence of efforts to constrain their deployment.

Attacking this question presents formidable difficulties. Various ways of controlling cruise missiles can be conceived, although even the authors of such conceptions concede that they contain many practical flaws. Typically, moreover, force posture and modernization decisions are made on their own terms, without reference to what might be desirable from the standpoint of grand schemes for weapon limitation. Arms control is therefore truly the art of the possible, with very little manoeuvring room left for the practice of this art.

Yet assuming that cruise missiles will be quite difficult to constrain in arms control regimes—owing to their overall attractiveness for military missions and their ability to confound present or future monitoring techniques—may in itself suggest an arms control approach. That is, how can the very drive to deploy cruise missiles be harnessed to some positive arms control objective? Can an increase in cruise missile deployments, which now seem inevitable, be exchanged for a decrease in weapon systems that are viewed as more dangerous or destabilizing? And, if some such trade-off can be imagined and arranged, would it actually have a positive effect on security and the balance of nuclear terror?

Two related premises are necessary to facilitate analysis. First, it must be assumed that there is adequate superpower willingness to constrain cruise missile deployments politically and reciprocally. Second, it must also be presumed that the superpowers perceive that the consequences of such constraints are preferable to those of some alternative force posture outcome. At present, both postulates are open to serious doubt. But, without them, there is no point in considering the question.

On the side of accepting these premises is the US need to consider its relatively greater vulnerability to cruise missiles, especially land-attack variants, given its long coastlines and lack of territorial air defence. US planners may also see a virtue in reducing nuclear cruise missile deployments on aircraft and vessels that would encroach on their conventional capability and make them presumptive strategic targets. For the Soviet Union, there is the consideration that it will likely remain relatively disadvantaged technically and economically in pursuing this option. In general terms, then, the *desirability* of limiting cruise missiles can be imagined, if not realized. It remains to consider the *possibility*.

If George Quester is right in asserting that a world dominated by cruise missiles is more stable than one dominated by ballistic missiles, both parties might elect to trade more of the former for less of the latter.[12] Since the Soviet Union has rarely accepted all of the niceties of the Western strategic view about stability, however, it seems slightly more realistic to assume that agreement on limits could be reached if each side were permitted to pursue its programme of perceived advantage under common ceilings on overall force strength.

There is a precedent for this approach in the treatment of ICBMs with multiple, independently targetable re-entry vehicles (MIRVs) and air-launched cruise missiles (ALCMs) in the SALT II Treaty. In this instance, each side was willing to include its own preferred system under a ceiling that also constrained the weapon it most wanted to limit in the other's forces. Whether this principle can be pushed much further is open to question. Nevertheless, it probably represents the most effective way to achieve mutual arms limitation.

Recognizing that this analysis of arms control possibilities rests on a series of assumptions almost as heroic and fragile as those that govern nuclear war planning itself, we at least have a basis for thinking about what might be accomplished. The underlying assumption, of course, is that each side has an interest in limiting the opponent's forces sufficient to make it give up some portion of what it wants for itself.

If this is true or, more importantly, accepted, then the United States should desire to constrain both the MIRVed ICBMs of the Soviet Union (which has certainly been the case in the past), as well as its potential for deploying land-attack nuclear cruise missiles on naval platforms. And it should be willing to give up something in return for this limitation by the USSR, something that is meaningful to the Kremlin. At the present moment, it would seem that the Soviet Union is most anxious about SDI, although this may not last once the programme enters or gets well along in the test phase.

For now, however, it seems that a package of additional limitations on ballistic missile defence and limitations on land-attack nuclear cruise missiles offered by the United States could purchase from the Soviet Union reductions on their 'heavy' (highly MIRVed) ballistic missiles and Soviet potential for proliferating their own advanced land-attack nuclear cruise missiles—the system that could be useful for sudden strikes against critical US targets, such as command and control systems. While this is not technically balanced, in terms of Western strategic nuclear theorizing, it may nevertheless prove appealing on other grounds more important to the USSR.

The question, then, is how to make limits on cruise missiles seem plausible from the standpoint of their monitoring. Most analysts are in agreement that such limits can only constitute what Joel Wit has called a 'loose constraint regime'.[13] That is, the characteristics of the cruise missile are such that it cannot be encompassed in controls as rigid as those which have been developed for ballistic missiles and heavy bombers.

Here it is important to remind ourselves that the superpowers have made an effort to stay within the limits of the Strategic Arms Limitation Talks (SALT) regime on ballistic missiles and bombers, including those with cruise missiles, while letting sea- and ground-launched cruise missiles, more or less, run free. It is unlikely that this situation will persist much longer, however. (In fact, the USA has now contravened the SALT limit on strategic delivery vehicles.)

What these factors suggest, though, is that an enduring arms limitation regime must eventually encompass all forces deemed 'strategic', but could do so in a scheme that involves tight constraints on some systems and looser ones on others. In other words, while it might offend the aesthetics or canons of symmetry so esteemed by many Western analysts, it is not politically, or even militarily, repugnant to contemplate an overall regime which included some highly restrictive and quite verifiable limits with some less restrictive and less verifiable ones, so long as the mix seemed to satisfy most of each party's core security interests.

Coming to specifics, what the control of cruise missiles would involve is finding a way to isolate those with theatre and strategic potential and nuclear capability from other variants. This is the difficulty on which cruise missile arms control is expected to, and may well, founder. If there is a way to resolve this conundrum, it probably involves limiting the deployment of the most objectionable forms of cruise missile to recognizable platforms and, eventually, to designing cruise missiles so that they make this distinction easier to detect. For the present, at least, this has not proven a problem in the case of air-launched and ground-launched cruise missiles, but, as every arms control analyst recognizes, the sea-launched versions pose significant difficulties.[14]

Limiting nuclear land-attack cruise missiles to certain classes of vessel and counting each vessel in the designated classes as a highly MIRVed ICBM or a bomber with ALCMs provides, conceptually, a means of integrating this capability in a regime with a common ceiling on nuclear forces. Under this ceiling, each side would be allowed to develop the force posture appropriate to its strategic situation by stressing the weapons it favours, but an increase in one category would require reductions in another.

Ideally, such a regime would, like SALT II, also involve sub-ceilings that would further constrain weapons viewed as the most undesirable from the point of view of crisis stability or other criteria. Borrowing from the 'build-down' principle, it would be still more advantageous if the freedom-to-mix under the ceiling and sub-ceilings were so arranged that it provided incentives for reducing still further the least desirable weapons, which would probably be the land-attack nuclear cruise missiles and the highly MIRVed ballistic missiles. This concept could also be applied in such a way as to penalize modernization, so that cruise missiles or other systems of higher performance could only be introduced by eliminating from a force a large number of older weapons.

Again taking a cue from the analysis of Joel Wit,[15] the most ideal agreement imaginable would include provisions for incorporating detectable features in future cruise missiles to facilitate the differentiation of nuclear and conventional models, as well as, perhaps, to distinguish other pertinent features, such as range or dual-capability.

Other measures that might be considered for the purpose of constraining some of the less desirable effects of cruise missiles are: (a) the designation of restricted areas, such as in coastal waters, where vessels or aircraft with nuclear cruise missiles would be banned, thus facilitating patrol and early warning tasks; and (b) the development of rules of the road, roughly analogous to those in the successful Incidents at Sea Agreement of 1972, so as to minimize the possibility of nuclear conflict arising from this quarter. Finally, ship visits by the parties to an agreement or by a third party on an unannounced basis but limited to a definite number of such visits per year and to ships *not* designated as land-attack nuclear cruise missile carriers could facilitate monitoring of this aspect of a comprehensive arms agreement.

If all such measures could be agreed on, the result would be a fairly stringent limitation on nuclear-capable naval cruise missiles. Yet it would still be a 'loose' regime because either party could readily manufacture and warehouse missiles and launchers for rapid installation on platforms not designated under the agreement to receive them, thus gaining a significant 'break-out' capacity.

Platform segregation, moreover, is not the principle of current deployment plans, at least in the United States, nor is detectable differentiation the direction in which cruise missile technology is running. Though constraints on cruise missiles could well be in the joint and separate interests of the superpowers, the MIRV case is a familiar example of how the desirability of limiting a new technology goes unrecognized until its control is exceedingly difficult or virtually impossible. The initial euphoria about a new military capability often blinds planners to its full implications when deployed by the adversary.

The achievement of even the loosest kinds of constraint on the most worrisome types of cruise missile would thus seem to require an enormous and simultaneous act of political will on the part of the two superpowers. Even if their mutual interest in preventing the rise of new nuclear powers should cause them to work together to prevent the exploitation of cruise missiles as a nuclear delivery system for potential proliferators, precedent suggests that this would be outside the framework of their own competition in this technology.[16]

The arms control implications of cruise missiles must be calculated therefore under two scenarios. In the first, and bleakest, the superpowers prove unequal to the challenge of imposing constraints on naval cruise missiles and this leads to the progressive deterioration of the existing offensive arms control regime, including limits on existing systems such as bombers, bombers with ALCMs, ICBMs and submarine-launched ballistic missiles (SLBMs) and on potentially limitable weapons such as ground-launched cruise missiles (GLCMs). Meanwhile, the limits on defensive systems in the Anti-Ballistic Missile (ABM) Treaty would also be eroded, not by the prospect of an SDI shield, but by the expansion of air defence systems with a presumptive capacity against constrained ballistic missile attacks.

In the more optimistic scenario, a loose constraint regime on naval cruise missiles is contrived which does not limit their total numbers but controls their deployed numbers to tolerable levels and which relates these systems to other weapons so as to permit freedom-to-mix. (Such a regime might also encompass theatre-range and intercontinental-range nuclear weapons under sub-ceilings that would allow some flexibility to transfer units from one category to another and back, as a means of both dealing with the versatility of the cruise missile and of resolving the more general theatre-strategic arms control problem.) This would preserve and build on the existing regime, although it would probably also require a new treaty governing the ABM potential of advanced air defence systems designed primarily against aerodynamic weapons. This situation, if achieved, would not only limit the physical threat but could help keep uncertainty and other factors contributing to the onset of war to more manageable levels.

Under the pessimistic scenario, the physical security of nations and peoples would decrease as a function of the large-scale deployment of an additional, accurate and increasingly speedy nuclear weapon not restricted to targets of ultimate importance. However, the contribution of the cruise missile to this decline in physical security might not be particularly salient, as a variety of other weapons, such as advanced conventional systems or future-generation ballistic missiles, received relatively more attention.

Furthermore, the difficulties encountered by technical arms control—that which is reflected in most of the measures described above—is already pushing interest in the direction of confidence-building measures and risk-reduction or crisis-management centres. This trend, which seeks to attack the nuclear problem in a more political rather than technical way, would likely be stimulated in a world that saw the present, tattered limitation regime unravelling completely and no chance of saving or extending it. Adequate progress in this direction could, to some indeterminate degree, lessen the threat to security from the growth in uncertainty, unpredictability, and opportunities for accident and miscalculation that cruise missiles and other new weaponry will foster. But it would not be as effective as an approach that combined *both* weapon restrictions and reductions and confidence-building measures.

The leading characteristics of what journalist James Meacham has called the 'second nuclear age' will be heightened vulnerability and growing uncertainty, both products of trends in the human exploitation of military-technological innovation.[17] The cruise missile will be a major contributor to the increase in vulnerability and uncertainty in the techno-strategic environment and thus to an overall decline in physical security, with perhaps similar implications for economic and political security.

Whether that overall decline can be kept to tolerable levels depends on many variables, including some of which we may not even be aware. It may depend on whether the superpowers can find and agree on an alternative to a relationship so heavily reliant on nuclear deterrent and compellent threats. But it will also depend on how well arms limitation and confidence-building measures can—either as interim expedients or long-term measures—constrain the many sources of vulnerability and uncertainty. And that, in turn, hinges on how effective we are in making arms control restrain the specific impact of cruise missiles, for some versions of this weapon, almost by themselves, have the ability to end the very structure and process of arms control. Should that occur, the security implications of the cruise missile will have proven grave indeed.

Notes and references

[1] Werrell, K. P., *The Evolution of the Cruise Missile* (Air University Press: Maxwell Air Force Base, AL, 1985), chapters 2, 4, 5 and 6; see also Fitzsimmons, B. (ed.), *The Illustrated Encyclopedia of 20th Century Weapons and Warfare* (Phoebus Publishing Company: New York, 1978); and Hall, S. L., *Weapons Choices and Advanced Technology: The RPV,* Occasional Paper No. 10 (Cornell University Peace Studies Program: Ithaca, NY, 1978).

[2] For these and the other characteristics of current or projected cruise missiles, see Cochran, T. B., Arkin, W. M. and Hoenig, M. H., *Nuclear Weapons Databook*, Vol. I, *U.S. Nuclear Force and Capabilities* (Ballinger Publishing Co.: Cambridge, MA, 1984), chapter 6; Arkin, W. M., Burrows, A. S., Fieldhouse, R. W., Cochran, T. B.,

Norris, R. S. and Sands, J. I., 'Nuclear weapons', *World Armaments and Disarmament, SIPRI Yearbook 1985* (Taylor & Francis: London, 1985), pp. 41–74; and Clausen, P., Krass, A. and Zirkle, R., *In Search of Stability: An Assessment of New U.S. Nuclear Forces* (Union of Concerned Scientists: Cambridge, MA, 1965), chapter 5.

[3] These deployment plans are taken from official US sources and may be found in the works cited in Note 5. See also: Sloan, S. R., Bowen, Jr, A. M. and O'Rourke, R., 'The implications for strategic arms control of nuclear armed sea launched cruise missiles' (US Government Printing Office: Washington, DC, 10 Dec. 1985).

[4] This is the estimate of Sloan *et al.* (note 3), appendix B.

[5] Cochran, T. B., Arkin, W. M., Norris, R. S. and Sands, J. I., *Nuclear Weapons Databook*, Vol. III, *Soviet Nuclear Weapons* (Ballinger Publishing Co.: Cambridge, MA, forthcoming), chapter 10; see also Arkin *et al.* (note 2).

[6] For a useful summary of bomber developments, see Clausen *et al.* (note 2), chapter 4.

[7] Current US programmes for such vehicles and their potential for both offensive and defensive use are outlined in John Morocco, 'Military designing "Kamikaze" drones', *Defense News*, vol. 1, no. 13 (14 Apr. 1986), p. 1.

[8] See the sources cited in notes 5 and 6 for official statements regarding the roles of cruise missiles; see also the extensive discussion in Sorrels, C. A., *U.S. Cruise Missile Programs: Development, Deployment, and Implications for Arms Control* (McGraw-Hill, Inc.: New York, 1983), and the more limited treatment in Pfaltzgraff, Jr, R. L. and Davis, J. K., *The Cruise Missile: Bargaining Chip or Defense Bargain?* (Institute for Foreign Policy Analysis: Cambridge, MA, 1977).

[9] The increasing capability of conventional weapons to perform in roles formerly reserved to nuclear weapons is analysed in Builder, C. H., *The Prospects and Implications of Non-Nuclear Means for Strategic Conflict*, Adelphi Paper No. 200, International Institute for Strategic Studies: London, Summer 1986.

[10] For the vulnerability of strategic command and control systems, see Steinbruner, J. D., 'Nuclear decapitation', *Foreign Policy* no. 45 (Winter 1981–82), and Blair, B. D., *Strategic Command and Control: Redefining the Nuclear Threat* (The Brookings Institution: Washington, DC, 1985). Command and control systems below the strategic level suffer from similar vulnerabilities.

[11] Quester's analysis appears in Quester, G., 'Arms control: toward informal solutions', *Cruise Missiles: Technology, Strategy, Politics*, ed. R. K. Betts, (The Brookings Institution: Washington, DC, 1981).

[12] Quester (note 11).

[13] Wit has elaborated his ideas on naval cruise missile arms control in 'Dealing with sea-launched cruise missiles: a U.S. strategy for the future', unpublished paper, and in conversations with the author, both of which have provided information for the present analysis. A summary presentation of potential arms control problems and techniques relevant to naval cruise missiles appears in Sloan *et al.* (note 3).

[14] Arms control measures applicable to air-launched and ground-launched cruise missiles are discussed in Kincade, W. H., 'Arms control: negotiated solutions', in Betts (note 11).

[15] Wit (note 13).

[16] Delivery vehicle options for potential proliferators are discussed in Jones, R. W., *Proliferation of Small Nuclear Forces* (Georgetown Center for Strategic and International Studies: Washington, DC, 1983) and Spector, L. S., 'Foreign-supplied

combat aircraft: will they drop the Third World bomb?', *Journal of International Affairs*, Columbia University, New York, forthcoming.

[17] Meacham, J., 'The technology of nuclear weapons', *The Economist*, vol. 292, no. 7357, special supplement (1 Sep. 1984).

Paper 2.8. The implications of increased mobility, force diversification, and counterforce capabilities for strategic arms control

MICHAEL KREPON

1. Introduction

Three growth trends in Soviet and US nuclear forces—the mobility and diversification of nuclear weapon launchers, and the continued accumulation of counterforce capabilties—have generated widespread concerns over strategic stability and the future of nuclear arms control. Mobile deployments of solid-fuelled missiles generate concerns over force reconstitution (the reload/refire issue), while mobility and diversification pose added verification concerns—perennial problems for arms control sceptics that must now be given added credence. At the same time, growing counterforce capabilities raise questions about the utility of past agreements and the feasibility of new accords to provide for a more stable balance of nuclear forces at lower levels.

All three trends took root in the Strategic Arms Limitation Talks (SALT) decade, and all are connected centrally to the seminal decision by US and Soviet political leaders early in the negotiations not to pursue in any serious way a ban or strict limits on multiple independently targetable re-entry vehicles (MIRVs). The proliferation of MIRVed systems with refined accuracies and high weapon yields provided much of the subsequent impulse for mobility and force diversification. Political, bureaucratic and technological factors were undoubtedly involved as well (such as the Nixon Administration's push to develop modern cruise missiles for bargaining leverage going into the SALT II negotiations), but these innovative weapon systems would not have been so well received by tradition-minded military commands if MIRVs had not called into question the survivability of central strategic systems. Nor is it likely that both superpowers would have absorbed the economic costs and military complications imposed by mobile land-based missiles were it not for the threat posed by opposing prompt counterforce capabilities.

The three growth trends of mobility, diversification and counterforce capabilities have therefore been closely interconnected, despite their inherent tension. This complex dynamic will continue as long as both superpowers feel compelled to keep their adversary's nuclear forces 'at risk'. Secretary of

Defense Caspar Weinberger reaffirmed the Reagan Administration's intentions in this regard in his Fiscal Year 1987 Posture Statement by asserting: 'The ability of land-based missiles to put time-urgent, hardened targets at risk is essential for strategic deterrence.'[1] The US pre-occupation with prompt hard-target-kill capabilities follows a path well-worn by the Soviet SS–18 and SS–19, although US efforts have been rather tentative by comparison. Thus, Reagan Administration officials continue their efforts to persuade the Congress to deploy more than 50 MX missiles, even as considerable resources are devoted to the advanced development of the mobile Midgetman missile. For its part, the Kremlin is firmly embarked along both paths, proceeding to deploy the mobile, single warhead SS–25 while preparing to deploy a new, 10-warhead missile, the SS–X–24, that can be housed in silos or on specially equipped trains. A silo-based follow-on to the SS–18 is also expected.

While the trend lines for mobility, diversification and counterforce capabilities are decidedly up, their implications for the future are difficult to assess. Mobility and diversification suggest greater survivability, while growing counterforce capabilities work in the opposite direction. Virtually all new strategic systems will have some counterforce capabilities, although the ability to strike opposing targets quickly raises the most serious concerns over strategic stability. Mobile land-based systems can continue to provide such prompt counterforce capabilities, although not without complications for combat readiness and command and control. New air-breathing and sea-based nuclear forces can also provide prompt counterforce options, but only if deployed in forward areas where they can increase warning of an impending attack.

Both sceptics and proponents of strategic modernization programmes share a dim view of the net effect of current trends, emphasizing the dynamic growth of counterforce capabilities, even while acknowledging the trends towards mobility and force diversification. For example, a 1986 study by the Union of Concerned Scientists foresees currently programmed US counterforce efforts causing 'a dramatic reduction in crisis stability' because 'Soviet tendencies toward massive preemption are likely to be increased'. Yet the same report concludes that US counterforce initiatives have 'prompted the Soviets to make their own counterforce weapons more secure'.[2] Similarly, Secretary of Defense Weinberger and his like-minded colleagues within the Reagan Administration assert that the buildup in Soviet counterforce capabilities threatens effective deterrence, while acknowledging that US forces 'are now far more capable of absorbing a Soviet strike and retaliating in a flexible and controlled way'.[3]

In this curious way, supporters and sceptics of strategic arms control reinforce each other's threat inflation by downplaying the trends towards mobility and diversification. Beyond this, of course, the analyses of nuclear weapon and arms control strategists diverge sharply. Western supporters of arms control assume that the Kremlin will not respond sensibly to the accumulation of US nuclear war-fighting capabilities, with the prospects for a stable arms control regime suffering as a result. Nuclear weapon strategists in the West fear that their own political leaders will not respond effectively to the Soviet counterforce syndrome. They, too, are concerned about strategic stability, but their remedies usually bear little resemblance to those proposed by the arms control community.

Throughout the SALT decade, both sides of this strategic divide within the United States coalesced uneasily around modest agreements that permitted the deployment of weapon systems having strong institutional support and few technological impediments—basic criteria far different from those suggested in the classic arms control texts. Over time, this loose domestic coalition supporting the SALT process broke down as a result of accumulated grievances with each other and with the Kremlin.[4] Each domestic constituency supporting SALT (with reservations, of course) had something to show for its efforts— agreed limitations for arms controllers, and strategic modernization programmes for nuclear weapon strategists. The specific mix that was patched together, however, contained the seeds of its own demise. Again, the inclusion of MIRVs was central, undermining agreed SALT restraints on both offences and defences at one and the same time.

The SALT II ratification debate in the United States became a testing ground for nihilistic arguments about the value of negotiated agreements with the Soviet Union. The subsequent presidential election of Ronald Reagan allowed proponents of this zero-sum view of strategic arms control to act out their concerns within key positions of the Executive Branch—a novel experience for them, and for a sclerotic Kremlin leadership about to undergo an unprecedented turnover.

In subsequent negotiations, both superpowers talked about major reductions in nuclear forces and visionary alternatives to nuclear deterrence, but hard political realities suggested otherwise. The SALT process postponed far too many critical issues to a time when political leaderships in both Washington and Moscow were particularly ill-suited to resolve them satisfactorily. In the years immediately following the abortive SALT II debate in the United States, the operative question was not whether this 'modest but useful' agreement would be superceded by another of significantly greater value, but whether its terms would remain tenuously in effect.

The 1980s may well be a lost decade for strategic arms control, during which time conservative elements in the USA exercised a veto over new agreements while a new managerial élite consolidated power in the Soviet Union. Throughout this period, substantive problems carried over from prior years have been exacerbated, while newer problem areas have risen to the fore, particularly those dealing with verification and compliance as well as a growing interest in the military exploitation of space. Meanwhile, strategic modernization programmes and deployments continued apace, prompting a bipartisan group of past practitioners of nuclear arms control to be pessimistic about the prospect for new agreements.[5] More optimistic appraisals have come from active members of the arms control community, although their prescriptions are long on 'political will' and short on specific remedies.

This essay will survey the strategic landscape facing US and Soviet political leaders as the lost decade of the 1980s comes to a close. An assessment of the trends towards greater counterforce capabilities, mobility and diversification will be provided, followed by the critical choices these trends pose for political officials who may want to pursue arms control agreements in the future. What follows is by no means a net assessment extrapolating from current trends; this task is well beyond the scope of this essay and the competence of the author. (Indeed, US intelligence agencies do not now engage in net assessments correlating US and Soviet nuclear forces, owing in part to the political sensitivity of these analyses and the degree to which they are dependent on the assumptions used.)[6] One need not carry out a comprehensive net assessment, however, to derive useful insights about prospective US and Soviet decisions that can either improve or further harm the likelihood of nuclear arms control in the 1990s.

II. Strategic modernization programmes

The profusion of new nuclear weapon-carrying platforms continues to confound estimates that the strategic arms competition will lose its intensity over time as offensive nuclear options rise. In actuality, strategic 'modernization' programmes continue unabated as both the Soviet Union and the United States replace (or supplement, if SALT limits on offensive forces are not reinstated) central strategic systems with newer and more capable models. According to US Government publications,[7] the Kremlin will proceed to test three new intercontinental ballistic missiles (ICBMs) over the next four years (the SS–18 follow-on, SS–X–24 follow-on and SS–25 follow-on), two new submarine-launched ballistic missiles (SLBMs) (the SS–N–20 follow-on and SS–NX–23 follow-on), a new ballistic missile-equipped, nuclear-powered submarine (SSBN), as well as the deployment of a new bomber, the Blackjack. During this period, the USA will proceed to test another new ICBM (the Midgetman) and SLBM (the Trident II), along with a new stealth bomber. In the interim, the Soviets can be expected to deploy SS–25s and SS–24s, Delta IV and Typhoon SSBNs carrying SS–N–23 and SS–N–20 SLBMs respectively and air-launched cruise missile (ALCM)-carrying Bear-H bombers. The United States will continue to deploy Trident submarines, perhaps additional MX missiles, and air-, land- and sea-launched cruise missile variants.

These new ICBMs and SLBMs can be expected to provide both sides with a wide range of flexible nuclear options. The US Central Intelligence Agency (CIA) projects a net Soviet increase of approximately 3000 deployed nuclear warheads by 1990, assuming SALT controls remain in place. By the mid-1990s, the Soviets could deploy almost 16 000 nuclear warheads within existing SALT constraints. If SALT limits are breached, this number could rise to a high of 21 000 by 1994.[8]

Counterforce capabilities will also rise appreciably with the introduction of new generations of cruise missiles. In addition to the AS–15 air-launched cruise missile to be deployed on BEAR-H and Blackjack bombers, the United States is awaiting Soviet deployments of the SS–NX–21 submarine-launched cruise missile (SLCM) and the SSC–X–4 ground-launched cruise missile (GLCM), as well as the SS–NX–24, either on a new, cruise-missile carrying submarine or on ground-based launchers. The SS–NX–21 has been flight tested on a modified Victor III, and could be deployed on the Victor III, Yankee, Sierra, Mike and/or Akula SSN classes.[9] In all, the CIA projects a deployment of 2000 to 3000 nuclear-armed Soviet cruise missiles of all types over the next 10 years.

For its part, the United States plans to procure 758 nuclear-armed SLCMs which can be deployed on 91 surface ships and 106 submarines: 4 battleships, 5 nuclear-guided missile cruisers, 22 guided-missile cruisers, 31 destroyers, 29 guided-missile destroyers, 67 Los Angeles Class and 39 Sturgeon Class submarines. The new SSN–21 class will also be capable of launching nuclear-armed, land-attack cruise missiles.[10] The USA has no plans to deploy more than the 464 GLCMs approved by the North Atlantic Treaty Organization (NATO). In contrast, ALCM deployments are expected to rise considerably: a force mix of approximately 3000 ALCMs will be procured, almost half of which will utilize stealth technologies.[11] ALCMs initially will be deployed on B–52G and H models. In all, approximately 4225 nuclear-armed cruise missiles will be deployed by the USA by the early 1990s, unless accelerated further by the demise of SALT.

Despite these projected increases in counterforce capabilities, neither superpower seems inclined to diminish reliance on its ICBM forces. Instead, mobile ICBMs gradually will assume an increasing share of ICBM launchers and deployed warheads, while SSBN force levels will drop as ageing Yankee and Poseidon boats are phased out of existing inventories in the early 1990s. Drawing from CIA testimony, SIPRI estimates that by 1994, approximately 41 per cent of Soviet ICBM launchers and 22 per cent of their deployed ICBM warheads will no longer reside in silos.[12] US totals are more difficult to project because of turbulence in the Midgetman programme and the uncertainty surrounding MX-basing. However, planning studies assume initial deployments of 500 Midgetmen, and Congress has made deployment of additional MX missiles contingent on an approved, non-silo-basing mode.

Mobility is essential to compensate for projected growth in counterforce capabilities. For example, a March 1986 report of the Defense Science Board suggests that peacetime Midgetman deployments would require barrage attacks over 5500 square miles, consuming approximately one-quarter of current Soviet ICBM and SLBM throw-weight.[13] Six minutes of dispersal movement time would require barraging 11 000 square miles, consuming one-half of current Soviet missile throw-weight. If enough warning time is available to disperse mobile missiles off-base, targeting problems consume extraordinary levels of throw-weight: barrage attacks over 22 000 square miles, for example, would require virtually the entire current Soviet inventory of ICBMs and SLBMs to achieve a 90 per cent damage expectancy. A corresponding Executive Branch analysis projecting US throw-weight against Soviet mobile missile deployments is not available, but a clear inference can be drawn from the Defense Science Board's assessment: US strategic missiles possessing approximately one-third the throw-weight would have extreme problems placing Soviet mobile missiles at risk.

III.   Survivability and the counterforce mind-set

One conclusion that appears unavoidable from the concurrent trendline growth in counterforce capabilities, mobility and launch-platform diversification is that US nuclear forces able to survive a pre-emptive Soviet attack are growing, despite concerted Soviet efforts to place these forces at risk. Using data from the US Department of Defense and the International Institute for Strategic Studies, Jack Ruina calculates an increase in US retaliatory nuclear capabilities over the next decade from 4930 re-entry vehicles (RVs) and 1450 equivalent megatons (EMT) in 1985 to 5380 RVs and 2120 EMT, by 1995.[14]

Testimony by US Government officials suggests that Ruina's projections are understated. Former Air Force Secretary Verne Orr and Chief of Staff General Charles A. Gabriel estimated that US forces able to survive a pre-emptive strike should roughly double by 1990.[15] In addition, Secretary of Defense Weinberger noted that, primarily as a result of Trident submarine deployments, the USA had in FY 1985 'almost 20 per cent more weapons able to retaliate after absorbing a Soviet first strike than in FY 1980. Over the same time period, and largely resulting from the deployment of ALCMs on B–52s, we achieved almost a 75 per cent increase over FY 1980 in surviving "hard-target-kill" capability'.[16]

The assumptions behind these assertions remain hidden from view and could, of course, be subject to challenge in individual cases. Soviet actions, however, appear to confirm the conclusion that US counterforce capabilities, whether calculated before or after a postulated Soviet first strike, continue to climb. Soviet political and military authorities are engaged in costly efforts to improve the survivability of their own nuclear forces—as a matter of simple prudence and sound military planning, if not as a confirmation of the action-reaction theory of nuclear arms competition. As noted above, Soviet efforts to deploy mobile ICBMs are already well advanced, as are programmes to increase the hardness of ICBMs based in silos. The construction of tunnels for SSBN protection and the belated rejuvenation of Soviet air-breathing strategic forces also attest to the Kremlin's firm commitment to protect and expand investments in its strategic forces.

Even if one questions official assessments on this issue, the targeting difficulties and command, control, communications and intelligence (C³I) requirements for locating the profusion of mobile ICBM and cruise missile launch platforms pose indisputable complications for US and Soviet military planners. While decapitation strikes will continue to be less demanding than pre-emptive strikes against opposing nuclear forces, they, too are becoming increasingly difficult as plans are implemented to guard against this eventuality. In sum, the uncertainties involved in carrying out a pre-emptive nuclear attack have never been greater, and they are growing steadily.

The growth of US and Soviet retaliatory capabilities has not, however, ameliorated either side's requirements for new strategic modernization programmes. Indeed, the reverse appears to be true: with nuclear war-fighting strategies of deterrence firmly in place, an unending array of new counterforce systems and ever-more sophisticated C^3I targeting strategies appear to be in the offing: there is no other way for the superpowers to place at risk opposing strategic forces that are increasingly mobile and diversified. Only the deployment of space-based strategic defences can provide some hope to alter the progressive growth of ballistic missile retaliatory capabilities. Even so, enlarged cruise missile inventories will continue to be a source of grave concern. Moreover, based on past superpower performance, the prospect of space-based systems is likely to spur still greater growth in opposing ballistic missile capabilities.

Thus, if present trends continue, the nuclear arms competition is likely to become even more energized than during its previous stages, despite the steady growth of retaliatory capabilities on both sides. Unless targeting requirements are relaxed, Washington and Moscow will feel compelled to add to their arsenals to cover expanding target sets, while seeking additional relief in mobility and diversification. This, in circular fashion, places a premium on ballistic missiles with significant counterforce potential that either can be fractionated for use against a multiplicity of targets or whose equivalent megatonnage can be gainfully employed in barrage attacks. A premium will also be placed on air-breathing forces that can employ 'look-shoot-look' tactics against mobile targets on the nuclear battlefield.

Successful arms reduction accords therefore hinge on the willingness of US and Soviet political leaders to alter deeply embedded counterforce mind-sets, particularly with respect to the premium placed on prompt hard-target-kill capabilities. For a stable strategic environment to evolve, growth levels in counterforce capabilities must be held well below the growth in rataliatory capabilities due to mobility and diversification. The necessity for restraining counterforce capabilities lies not so much in the threat of pre-emption: while this threat will remain a concern to US and Soviet political leaders—especially if space-based strategic defences are deployed—both can be expected to accelerate current trends by taking steps to guard against this eventuality. The need for mutual restraint in counterforce capabilities is more broadly based. Without it, the prospects for a marked expansion of strategic force requirements, with all of the attendant political and military complications, are extremely high.

The first critical choice for US and Soviet political leaders is, therefore, whether they are prepared to place their nuclear war-fighting plans in greater conformity with their public statements about the inherent unwinnability of a nuclear war. Given prevailing trends, some relaxation of targeting requirements appears inevitable, since some military targets are becoming more elusive despite the best efforts of planners on both sides. But until national leaders in Washington and Moscow agree not to buck this trend—and indeed, to accelerate it—the prospect for significant arms reduction accords that also enhance strategic stability will be remote. A political agreement in principle to widen the disparity between prompt counterforce capabilities and military targets in favour of greater survivability can open up a wide range of arms reduction possibilities, while relieving pressures to deploy strategic forces in non-co-operative and non-verifiable ways. In contrast, planning to proceed with deployments of space-based strategic defences will likely have the reverse effect, further accelerating counterforce, diversification and survivability measures.

If US and Soviet political leaders can agree to accentuate the disparity between counterforce capabilities and targeting requirements, the officially stated negotiating objective of both sides—deep reductions in superpower arsenals—can be achieved through a wide range of stabilizing agreements. The scope of future accords largely will be defined by how US and Soviet officials choose to handle two by-products of the counterforce syndrome: mobile land-based missiles and sea-launched cruise missiles. Comprehensive agreements in the future must include both under their umbrella.

IV. Limitations on mobile missiles

Comprehensive agreements limiting deployed forces were fairly easy to devise in the past, when ICBMs were based in silos and when concerns over verification dictated a readily observable unit of account in the SALT negotiations—missile launchers, rather than missiles. Even so, the prospect of cold-launched ICBMs and reloadable silos caused considerable concern among SALT critics, notwithstanding agreed prohibitions on storage of excess missiles at launch sites.

With the deployment of mobile, solid-fuelled missiles, concerns over launcher reloading and refiring have far more relevance, leading some analysts to suggest agreements limiting total missile inventories in addition to deployed launchers and warheads. Expanding the scope of agreements in this way, however, raises considerable verification difficulties, especially for those who found prior SALT limits on strategic nuclear delivery vehicles not 'adequately' verifiable. Future agreements limiting total missile inventories will be even more difficult to verify, unless, at the very least, far-reaching co-operative monitoring arrangements are in place before missile production has begun.

If such arrangements can be worked out prior to mobile missile deployments, the two sides need only concern themselves with a direct count of key missile components (such as solid rocket motors for ICBMs and intermediate-range ballistic missiles (IRBMs) and missiles leaving the final assembly facility). This direct count can be rendered by means of continuous inspections of production facilities or by *in-situ* monitoring by technical devices that work in conjunction with existing security perimeters around production facilities.

Portal monitoring schemes along these lines need not be deeply intrusive to provide information on key items entering and leaving production facilities. Even then, sceptics of the agreements under consideration will be uneasy about the possibility of covert production facilities.

The issue of limiting missile inventories may be moot—at least according to the most exacting verification standards—since superpower negotiations have not yielded agreed procedures to monitor production facilities and since new missiles have begun their production runs. A more relaxed verification standard can still be employed—after all, yearly production runs are routinely estimated in US Government publications[17]—but data exchanges providing declared inventories will be suspect, and there is little prospect of either side allowing unlimited access to search for hidden missiles over and above declared inventories.

For all of these reasons, the political choice of seeking limits on total missile inventories for mobile systems with warm production lines appears to raise insuperable negotiating difficulties. As a practical matter, US and Soviet political leaders face the narrower choice of continuing to focus on deployment limitations or forgoing limits altogether for mobile missiles, due to the unique problems they pose for force reconstitution and verification.

If, for whatever reason, political leaders opt not to conclude limitations on mobile, solid-fuelled systems, useful agreements could still be pursued in other worthwhile areas—such as reductions in MIRVed, silo-based missiles. The more, however, one is concerned about the threat posed by mobile ICBMs and IRBMs, the more it makes sense to seek agreed limitations on their deployment, tied to wide-ranging collateral constraints and co-operative measures that make force reconstitution difficult. Although domestic political concerns in the United States over the resulting agreements would by no means be alleviated, political leaders who seek limits on mobile missile deployments will at least be able to argue that their solution, drawing on a wide variety of collateral constraints and co-operative measures, is better than none at all. Alternatively, if concerns over force reconstitution are considered to be overdrawn—perhaps because of the difficulty in maintaining operationally ready missile stockpiles over time, or the difficulty in carrying out missile reloads and refires in the fog of nuclear war—deployment limitations appear a less risky course. Thus, whether one believes that the force reconstitution problem is extremely serious or seriously overdrawn, limitations on mobile missile deployments appear desirable, even if total missile inventory limits are not feasible.

The unratified SALT II Treaty provides a baseline from which to elaborate an interlocking set of collateral constraints and co-operative measures to alleviate concerns over verification and force reconstitution. These could include designation of key missile production facilities and constraints against rapid reload exercises, in addition to prohibitions against storage of excess missiles near deployment areas. Concerns over break-out can also be alleviated somewhat by data exchanges on missile production rates that could be confirmed by mildly intrusive production-monitoring procedures. Decisions by US and Soviet leaders to pursue accords along these lines would reflect political decisions that the benefits accruing from agreed limitations on mobile missile deployments are worth their associated risks, especially the risk of non-compliance with and break-out from agreed limitations.

Limitations on mobile missile deployments will depend also on basing schemes meeting agreed criteria, along with consultative mechanisms to redress concerns or grievances over basing practices through private channels. One model for mobile missile-basing meeting stringent verification criteria was the MX/horizontal dash system considered during the Carter Administration. It featured designated deployment areas, openable roof parts for missile shelters, final missile assembly facilities adjacent to mobile missile deployment areas, unique missile assembly buildings that would be removed once full system operational capability had been attained, physical barriers blocking access to deployment areas, and unique design features for mobile missile transporter-erector-launchers.[18] While actual Soviet deployment practices for the SS–20 and SS–25 have not gone to such elaborate lengths to simplify monitoring, they have enabled US officials to maintain a precise count of deployed forces.

Of course, mobile missile deployment practices could be altered at any time, either within the context of agreed limitations or especially in the absence of mutually agreed procedures. If, however, both sides wish to maintain limitations on mobile missile deployments—or, at least not undermine the prospects for such limits in the future—they will refrain from engaging in altered deployment practices that seriously impede verification. The political repercussions resulting from difficulties in keeping an accurate count of deployed forces would be great, particularly for Western political leaders who are perceived to be too eager for new accords. The Kremlin, therefore, has an important choice to make: it can continue to deploy the SS–25 in ways that simplify monitoring, or it can alter SS–25 deployment practices in ways that raise barriers to subsequent agreements.

The burden of decision falls initially on the Kremlin, since Moscow's mobile ICBM programmes are moving on a faster track than comparable programmes in the United States. Planning in the USA for mobile missile-basing for the MX and small ICBM should nevertheless set high standards against which to judge Soviet basing schemes. Soviet deployment practices for the mobile SS–X–24 are particularly critical, since the USA has no experience in monitoring rail-mobile nuclear forces. The procedures established by Soviet officials for rail-mobiles can be roughly analogous to those established for ground-mobiles, or they can result in large monitoring uncertainties. Again, the near-term choice the Kremlin makes will have long-term consequences.

V.   Limitations on cruise missiles

Modern cruise missiles pose some of the same negotiating problems as mobile ICBMs and IRBMs: mobile cruise missile launchers also can be reloaded and refired, raising difficult verification and force reconstitution concerns. Soviet basing practices for ground-launched cruise missiles are extremely important in this regard. As with mobile SS–X–24 deployments, Soviet GLCMs can either help or hinder the prospects of future accords. If deployed in ways comparable to shorter range nuclear forces, Soviet GLCMs can deeply complicate the prospects for future intermediate nuclear force (INF) agreements; if deployed in ways comparable to US ground-launched cruise missiles or Soviet SS–20s, they need not raise new impediments to nuclear arms accords. The negotiating problems with SLCMs run particularly deep. Any agreement that attempts to be comprehensive must find a way to deal with the modular design, multiple missions, variable payloads and variety of naval platforms on which SLCMs can be deployed.

Other categories of modern, long-range cruise missiles do not pose such difficult problems. Ground-launched cruise missile deployments can be monitored successfully with appropriate basing modes and co-operative arrangements. Methods for dealing with air-launched cruise missile-carrying platforms were considered and approved in the SALT II negotiations. Co-operative measures and counting rules to allow an extension of these provisions can be envisioned, such as providing advance notification of cruise missile flight test activities from designated test areas, and prohibiting such tests elsewhere.

Despite the formidable problems posed by SLCMs, US and Soviet political leaders may wish to limit their number due to the national security complications they present, especially future generations of stealthy and/or high-speed cruise missiles.[19] The potential growth of nuclear-armed SLCM deployments may also be of concern to political leaders. While such growth is unlikely to double existing nuclear arsenals—the worst case projected by independent analysts[20]—past experience suggests an increased level of effort in SLCM deployments if limitations are placed on other aspects of the strategic arms competition.

Several alternative approaches could be utilized for SLCM limitations, although none are without serious difficulties. One choice for political leaders is to attempt to negotiate direct limitations on SLCM production: since cruise missiles are so difficult to count once they are deployed, the focus of negotiating effort would be to devise mechanisms to allow counting during the production phase. In this sense, SLCM-monitoring would become similar to, but far more extensive than, current monitoring practices for SSBNs. Production-monitoring capabilities could alleviate concerns over opposing military capabilities and simplify military planning. Co-operative arrangements to monitor compliance with declared production rates at declared production facilities would have to be negotiated, as would provisions to address compliance questions, including those relating to the possibility of covert production.

An alternative approach would be to focus on limitations of SLCM deployments, with or without agreed procedures to monitor production. Deployment limitations could take several forms. If carried out in conjunction with production-monitoring, tagging schemes could conceivably be arranged for all SLCMs leaving declared production facilities. Alternatively, tagging schemes could be employed only for those SLCMs that are mated with nuclear warheads at designated facilities.[21] At selected intervals, tagged items could be interrogated, with the response time-delayed to protect the location of SLCM-carrying platforms.

If SLCM production-monitoring is not desirable or feasible, deployment limitations could conceivably be monitored in other ways. SLCM deployments could be monitored when ordnance is being loaded onto surface ships and submarines prior to their patrols.[22] For surface ships, spot checks to verify compliance with agreed limitations could be devised. For example, either side could designate a ship at sea to be inspected, which must not be approached by other naval vessels until a thorough inspection is carried out. Agreed inspection procedures would need to be worked out, including the number of inspections and classes of ships to be covered.

Deployment limitations could also be based on agreed counting rules. The simplest rule would be to count every modern SLCM-carrying surface ship and submarine as a MIRVed launcher, to be included within agreed aggregates. Type-rules might be required, similar to those devised for ICBM launchers in the SALT II Treaty: if an SLCM meeting certain characteristics is flight-tested from a ship, then all ships of that class would be designated as SLCM-launchers. Co-operative arrangements necessarily would be required to assist in the monitoring of SLCM test flights.

Counting rules could also be applied to deployed nuclear-armed SLCMs permitted on certain classes of ships. One method for doing so would be derived from ongoing production programmes: since the United States will be producing approximately one nuclear-armed SLCM for every five purchased, arbitrary TLAM/N force loadings could be calculated for various classes of surface ships based on the number of Tomahawk launchers they will carry.[23] Still another alternative has been proposed by the Soviet Union—prohibiting nuclear-armed SLCMs entirely from surface ships. Appropriate verification procedures would be required.[24]

Even if intrusive verification measures can be negotiated for SLCM deployments, the potential for evasion or circumvention of agreed limitations remains great. Co-operative arrangements on cruise missile production and basing have not been agreed to, and there is little prospect for doing so in the near future. An endless array of verification and compliance concerns are therefore unavoidable with agreed limitations on SLCMs already in production. In other words, what has long been predicted has come true: the deployment of modern SLCMs has conferred a certain degree of military flexibility, but at a direct cost to the prospects for effective arms control. Political leaders in the USA therefore must judge whether the political costs associated with tight controls over current generation SLCMs—domestic disputes over verification and compliance as well as negotiated trade-offs for intrusive co-operative measures—are worth the associated military benefits.

If political leaders decide to forgo SLCM limits in the near future because of these considerations, the burden of avoiding an intensified competition in advanced SLCM deployments will fall on their successors, if and when reductions are belatedly carried out on more verifiable nuclear launch platforms. Sound naval judgement concerning the disutility of nuclear-armed SLCMs, the opportunity costs of deploying them in still greater profusion and modest forms of production monitoring might well be the best checks against an intensified competition in this uncontrolled area. There is still time, however, to devise firm controls over future generations of SLCMs that will intensify concerns over vulnerability of bomber and land-based systems due to their stealth and speed. Alternative approaches to ease concerns over future SLCMs include outright bans, production-monitoring and the incorporation of functionally observable differences for various SLCM types. Confidence-building measures, such as SLCM-free zones, might also be important substitutes for or complements to more formal controls over future generations of stealthy and/or high-speed cruise missiles.

VI.   Conclusion

A brief survey of this kind raises far more questions than answers about future national security policy choices in the United States and the Soviet Union. An entire decade is in danger of being lost for strategic arms control, leaving a legacy of confusion and an enterprise badly in need of repair. To further complicate matters, basic questions have been raised at the highest political level concerning strategies of deterrence, while US–Soviet relations remain in a state of flux, symbolized by the uncertain status of the SALT accords.

Within this political context, prediction is a hazardous enterprise. The arms control implications of the upward trends in counterforce capabilities, mobility and launch-platform diversification clearly complicate future negotiations and present greater opportunities to those opposed to new agreements to question their worth. Mobile missiles and diversified launch platforms raise new problems of accurately counting deployed forces, while at the same time raising the spectre of break-out from agreed limitations. New agreements must therefore be accompanied by more intrusive verification procedures, particularly in the production of those platforms that are hard to count once deployed. Because perceptions of the risks associated with new agreements will seem to be great in some quarters—East as well as West—robust safeguards no doubt will accompany new accords. Even then, political concerns over verification and compliance will continue to swirl around political leaders in the USA who wish to advance the arms control process.

The picture is not entirely bleak, however. Each superpower has managed to increase its retaliatory capabilities over the past decade, despite concerted efforts by its adversary to place opposing nuclear forces at risk. This has lent a degree of stability to the strategic competition, although it has not moderated requirements for new strategic modernization programmes.

The framework of SALT limitations, while permissive, kept the nuclear arms competition within important bounds. Arms control agreements can play a similarly useful role in stabilizing the strategic competition in the years ahead by reinforcing the trend towards increased survivability and ameliorating new force requirements. Even if the prospects for agreements are not good at the present time, both sides may still have the wisdom not to foreclose future possibilities for new accords that sharply reduce nuclear forces of primary concern and that easy concerns over verification and compliance in path-breaking ways.

The United States and the Soviet Union can succeed at nuclear arms control despite all of their competitive pursuits as long as neither side seeks unilateral advantage at the expense of the other's central strategic concerns. Gerard C. Smith, Chief United States SALT I negotiator, understood this political fact of life at the outset of the negotiations, when he wrote to Secretary of State William Rogers: 'If either side is striving for or appears to be striving for an effective counterforce first strike capability, then there is no hope for strategic arms control.'[25]

Currently, the deployment of space-based strategic defences together with the growth of counterforce capabilities lends new credence to these fears. Strategic arms control can withstand the upward trends of mobility and diversification. Progress is still possible with growing counterforce capabilities, as long as these are outpaced by measures to improve the survivability of strategic deterrent forces. Strategic arms control cannot succeed in the future, however, in the face of concerted efforts to procure the combined offensive and defensive forces geared to implement war-fighting strategies of deterrence.

Notes and references

[1] *Report of the Secretary of Defense Caspar W. Weinberger to the Congress on the FY 1987 Budget, FY 1988 Authorization Request and FY 1987–1991 Defense Programs*, (US Government Printing Office: Washington, DC, 5 Feb. 1986), p. 214.
[2] Clausen, P., Krass, A. and Zirkle, R., *In Search of Stability: An Assessment of New U.S. Nuclear Forces*, A Report of the Union of Concerned Scientists, Mar. 1986, pp. vii–viii and p. 63.
[3] Weinberger (note 1), p. 46.
[4] For a thematic treatment of these differences, see Krepon, M., *Strategic Stalemate, Nuclear Weapons and Arms Control in American Politics* (St Martins Press: New York, 1984).
[5] For example, Zbigniew Brzezinski, President Jimmy Carter's national security adviser, notes that 'the verification problem is becoming increasingly acute, given the mobility of the new systems and the opportunities for rapid reloading and covert deployment. As a consequence, it is realistic to conclude that for both political and technological reasons, the chances of a truly comprehensive agreement, which can be reliably verified, are rapidly fading'. *Wall Street Journal*, 10 July 1984. Helmut Sonnenfeld, an official in the Nixon and Ford Administrations has come to a similar

conclusion: 'I don't think broad, verifiable arms control agreements are "doable", but that doesn't mean we shouldn't try to do useful things at the margins'. *Los Angeles Times*, 27 May 1984.

[6] See testimony of US Central Intelligence Agency officials Robert M. Gates and Lawrence K. Gershwin in *Soviet Strategic Force Developments*, Joint Hearing Before the Subcommittee on Strategic and Theater Nuclear Forces of the Committee on Armed Services and the Subcommittee on Defense of the Committee on Appropriations, United States Senate, 99th Congress, 1st Session, 26 June 1985 (US Government Printing Office: Washington, DC, 1985), pp. 5, 26.

[7] Unless otherwise indicated, this discussion draws from 'Soviet Strategic Force Developments', *Soviet Military Power—1986,* and the *Fiscal Year 1987 Posture Statements* prepared by the Secretary of Defense, the Organization of the Joint Chiefs, and the Under Secretary of Defense, Research and Engineering.

[8] *Soviet Strategic Force Developments*, Joint Hearing Before the Subcommittee on Strategic and Theater Nuclear Forces of the Committee on Armed Services and the Subcommittee on Defense of the Committee on Appropriations, United States Senate, 99th Congress, 1st Session, 26 June 1985 (US Government Printing Office: Washington, DC, 1985), p. 14.

[9] *Department of Defense Appropriations for 1986*, Hearings Before a Sub-Committee of the Committee on Appropriations, 99th Congress, First Session (US Government Printing Office: Washington, DC, 1986), Part 2, p. 914, and *Defense Department Authorization and Oversight*, Hearings on H.R. 1872, Department of Defense, Authorization of Appropriations for Fiscal Year 1986 and Oversight of Previously Authorized Programs, Before the Committee on Armed Services, House of Representatives, Ninety-Ninth Congress, First Session (US Government Printing Office: Washington, DC, 1986), Part 3, p. 4.

[10] *Department of Defense Appropriations for 1986* (US Government Printing Office: Washington, DC, 1986), Part 4, p. 322, and Part 2, p. 914.

[11] *Department of Defense Authorization for Appropriations for Fiscal Year 1986*, Hearings Before the Committee on Armed Services, United States Senate, Ninety-Ninth Congress, First Session (US Government Printing Office: Washington, DC, 1986), Part 7, p. 3670, and *Defense Department Authorization and Oversight*, Hearings on H.R. 1872, Department of Defense Authorization of Appropriations for Fiscal Year 1986 and Oversight of Previously Authorized Programs, before the Committee on Armed Services, House of Representatives, Ninety-Ninth Congress, First Session (US Government Printing Office: Washington, DC, 1986), Part 4, p. 1061.

[12] *World Armaments and Disarmament, SIPRI Yearbook 1986* (Oxford University Press: Oxford, 1986), p. 54.

[13] *Report of the Defense Science Board Task Force on Small Intercontinental Ballistic Missile Modernization*, Office of the Under Secretary of Defense for Research and Engineering (US Government Printing Office: Washington, DC, Mar. 1986), p. 14. The report assumes Midgetman deployments at four base complexes on hard mobile launchers with at least 30 p.s.i. hardness. All calculations are based on a 90 per cent damage expectancy.

[14] 'Perspectives on hard-site defense', *Issues on Science and Technology*, vol. 2, no. 2 (Winter 1986), pp. 131–3.

[15] *Defense Department Authorization and Oversight*, Hearings on H.R. 2287, Department of Defense Authorization of Appropriations for Fiscal Year 1984 and Over-

sight of Previously Authorized Programs Before the Committee on Armed Services, House of Representatives, 98th Congress, 1st Session (US Government Printing Office: Washington, DC, 1984), Part 1, p. 1047.

[16] Weinberger (note 1), p. 46.

[17] For example, the FY 1987 US Department of Defense Program for Research and Development lists the approximate production level for Soviet ICBMs and SLBMs in 1985 at 100 each. *Statement by the Under Secretary of Defense, Research and Engineering to the 99th Congress, Second Session, 1986* (US Government Printing Office: Washington, DC, 1986), p. III–3. Soviet yearly SLCM production levels have also been publicized in the past. The Defense Intelligence Agency estimated an annual SLCM production rate of 600 in 1977–1978, rising to 700 in 1979 and 1980, and rising again to 750 in 1981. *Allocation of Resources in the Soviet Union and China—1982*, Hearings before the Subcommittee on International Trade, Finance, and Security Economics of the Joint Economic Committee, 97th Congress, 2nd Session (US Government Printing Office: Washington, DC, 1982), Part 8, p. 36.

[18] See *Fiscal Year 1981 Arms Control Impact Statements*, Joint Committee Print, 96th Congress, 2nd Session, May 1980 (US Government Printing Office: Washington, DC, 1980), pp. 8–12 and 60–3.

[19] See Wit, J. S., 'Dealing with Sea-Launched Cruise Missiles: A U.S. Strategy for the Future', unpublished manuscript, pp. 18–34; and Sloan, S. R., Bowen, Jr., A. M. and O'Rourke, R., *The Implications for Strategic Arms Control of Nuclear Armed Sea Launched Cruise Missiles*, Congressional Research Service, The Library of Congress, 10 Dec. 1985 (US Government Printing Office: Washington, DC, 1985), pp. 13–14.

[20] Sloan, Bowen and O'Rourke (note 19), pp. 18–23.

[21] See Garwin, T., *Tagging Systems for Arms Control Verification* (Analytical Assessments Corporations: Marina Del Ray, CA, Feb. 1980).

[22] See Lin, H., 'Technology for co-operative verification of nuclear weapons', *Arms Control Today*, vol. 16, no. 3 (Apr. 1986), pp. 10–11.

[23] See Lin, H., 'Nuclear SLCMs: Strategic and Arms Control Implications' (Center for International Studies, Massachusetts Institute of Technology: Cambridge, MA, unpublished manuscript), pp. 10–14.

[24] See Wit (note 19), pp. 18–34.

[25] Smith, G. C., *Doubletalk, The Story of the First Strategic Arms Limitation Talks* (Doubleday & Co.: Garden City, NY, 1980), p. 24.

Part 3. New complications for international security

Paper 3.1. Modernization of British and French nuclear forces: arms control and security dimensions

EDWARD A. KOLODZIEJ

I. Introduction

The British and French nuclear modernization programmes, projected for completion in the 1990s, pose serious arms control and security problems for the superpowers. Neither superpower can remain indifferent to enlarging British and French nuclear capabilities. Each will deploy near-invulnerable submarine-based systems capable of destroying Soviet population and industrial centres and of attacking key military installations. The operational strategies pursued by both European states also raise questions about the maintenance of a stable nuclear deterrent regime. The first part of the discussion below outlines British and French nuclear modernization plans and the problems which both systems present for the superpowers. Part two evaluates British–French pre-conditions for their participation in superpower arms negotiations and examines how these might be relaxed to encourage arms control co-operation among the nuclear powers in the Western Alliance and between them and the Soviet Union.

II. British–French modernization

British capabilities and operational doctrine

Britain and France are planning major increases in their nuclear-strike forces in the 1990s. Britain will acquire the US Trident system. Four nuclear-powered Trident submarines will be deployed, each with 16 D–5 missiles (in contrast to 24 in US Tridents). Once hidden below the sea, these submarines are almost invulnerable to destruction.

The Trident runs quieter and dives deeper than the Polaris system that it replaces. Its payload will also have greater range and destructive power than Britain's current submarine force composed of 64 Polaris A3TK missiles. The latter are armed with the British-designed Chevaline multiple re-entry vehicles (MRVs), each with two and possibly three 200-kiloton (kt) warheads and penetration aids.[1] The Trident D–5 missile has a range of approximately 7000 kilometres (km) and can carry one of two types of delivery vehicle: either the

US Navy's newly designed M–K5/W88 with eight 475-kt independently targeted re-entry vehicles (MIRVs) or the older Mk4/W76 carried on US Trident C–4 missiles, each with 12–14 100-kt MIRVs.[2]

Since the British Government, as a unilateral arms control initiative, has announced that it will restrict its D–5 missiles to eight warheads, each Trident submarine is expected to carry 128 warheads for a total of 512 for the entire system. This number is at least two-and-a-half times larger than the current Polaris–Chevaline force estimated at 192 warheads at the outside. Each Trident system warhead will be somewhere in the neighbourhood of two-and-a-half times more powerful than those now carried by Chevaline and will permit multiple targeting. The Chevaline can only hit a single target. Its superiority over the one-megaton Polaris A3 warhead that it replaced derives from the larger footprint that it leaves and from its enhanced capability to penetrate enemy defences. The D–5, with its M–K5/W88 features, surpasses Chevaline in all these respects. Its greater range and the Trident's improved performance capabilities also multiply Soviet tracking problems, already taxed beyond their limits by the Polaris system. According to British sources, the Polaris has successfully evaded detection by Soviet anti-submarine warfare (ASW) forces.[3]

The Trident system, even if confined to the self-imposed eight warhead limit, significantly enlarges the targeting options previously available to British planners. British submarines will be able to hit targets from greater distances with accuracies approaching land-based systems. The larger number of more powerful warheads available to London also raises the possibility of targeting both military and civilian centres. The 'Moscow Standard' previously guiding British planning as the minimal level of damage needed for a credible deterrent[4] (and one of the reasons why the Chevaline was developed, namely, to counter the anti-ballistic system (ABM) around Moscow)[5] has been superseded by the embarrassment of warhead riches that Britain will enjoy before the close of the century.

The availability of so many warheads raises temptations to increase targets to the number of disposable warheads. British deterrence policy may be re-defined by rising capabilities rather than by a strategic doctrine based on minimum deterrence standards as a guide for weapon and target acquisition. The eight-warhead limitation was partly motivated by an attempt to quiet domestic critics of the government's decision to expand the number of warheads in Britain's arsenal and to adopt the D–5, with potential silo-busting capability, rather than by the less accurate C–4 missile currently carried by US Poseidon submarines. The attraction of improved number and warhead technology and harmonization between US and British forces—not to mention alleged long-term cost benefits of a system that is to remain in the US inventory for another generation—proved too compelling. How these more powerful warheads will be used, on whose authority and under what circumstances are now critical questions. No Soviet planner can be indifferent to these issues, nor can US policy-makers who are interested in reducing the risk of war, in preventing escalation to nuclear levels if war should erupt, and in bringing hostilities to a quick close.

Approximately 100 Soviet metropolitan cities with a population of 250 000 contain roughly half of the Soviet population.[6] These centres also contain most of the Soviet Union's industrial plants. It might be remembered that in the early 1960s, the United States equated stable deterrence with a standard of assured destruction defined as the capacity of the United States to destroy approximately one-third of the Soviet population and 75 per cent of its industrial plants after being struck first.[7] It has been estimated that a nuclear strike of approximately 400 equivalent megatons meets this standard.[8] The British force in the 1990s, armed with 8 warheads for each D–5 missile, each rated at 475 kilotons, can be roughly estimated at 300 equivalent megatons distributed over 512 warheads. This force approaches the US assured destruction standard of the 1960s. The US standard was itself four times the amount that was estimated to be needed if one did not correct for the reliability, survivability, penetrability of missiles and warheads, and for other complicating factors that might defeat a second-strike attack.

The great accuracy of the D–5 missile and MIRVing which increases target options will increase the area that can be destroyed, measured simply by the prompt effects—principally blast and fire—caused by the initial explosion of nuclear weapons. Widespread radiation and the degrading synergistic effects of large-scale devastation will doubtless increase the casualties and deaths as well as the material of Soviet territory. The British force of the 1990s places the Soviet Union at risk as a viable functioning society. Even the pre-Chevaline Polaris force of 64 Polaris A3 missiles has been estimated to kill 20-million people and destroy 25 per cent of the Soviet Union's industrial capacity.[9]

The British approach to nuclear deterrence and what appears to be the operational code guiding British planning for the use of nuclear weapons is both quieting and disconcerting. A case can be made that, in principle, a British nuclear force can add to European and global deterrence stability. From the start of the British nuclear programme during World War II, when British and US scientists worked closely together on the Manhattan Project, to the present, British planners conceived their efforts within a framework defined by continued close US–British collaboration. British nuclear requirements were largely defined as a supplement to stipulated levels of US nuclear-strike capacity despite Britain's exclusion for over a decade after World War II from US nuclear planning and technology.[10] With the amendment of the MacMahon Act in the 1950s, Britain acquired access to the US nuclear policy process and know-how. Relaxation of US prohibitions was restricted to allies who had reached a level of nuclear development justifying closer co-operation. But only Britain was deemed by US officials to have met these political and technical standards in the mid-1950s.

With the purchase by Britain of the Polaris system in the early 1960s, the United States underscored the privileged role assigned to Britain in US and NATO (North Atlantic Treaty Organization) nuclear planning, partially justifying the expectation widely held in British policy circles that British influence over US policy hinged critically on its own possession of nuclear weapons. These nuclear ties are central to the maintenance of what remains of the special US–British relations forged during World War II. Britain's purchase of Trident reaffirmed the decision of the 1960s to underwrite an independent nuclear deterrent for Britain.

Those concerned about the erosion of extended deterrence, with the development of superpower nuclear parity and the linkage of US global and European planning, are assured by US–British nuclear co-operation. Since the 1960s British nuclear forces have been integrated into NATO planning. British and US specialists consult about targeting priorities and the responsibilities of both national systems for the destruction of enemy targets. This bilateral process links both states to NATO planning and to the concerns and needs of their allies. Britain thus acts as a nuclear bridge between the United States and Europe by means of which European security and arms control concerns are introduced into US thinking, planning and policy debates.

Beyond the Trident system, there are other critical roles played by Britain in US nuclear planning. Britain is second only to West Germany in the number of weapons deployed on its territory. It also provides key air, naval and space command, communications and surveillance bases which are important for nuclear defence as well as facilities for the stationing of 170 F–111 fighter-bombers, US Poseidon and Trident submarines, and ground-based cruise missiles (GLCMs).[11] These tangible elements of British nuclear assistance link US and European security interests in fundamental ways. As long as Britain's security is considered a vital US interest—expressed in the multiple forms of nuclear co-operation that have been developed and nurtured over decades— and as long as Britain remains closely identified with Europe, principally as a member of the European Community, Europeans are given assurance that their defence needs will not be ignored. Nor will the Soviet Union be encouraged to believe that an attack on Europe will spare it from a US military response including the possibility of nuclear weapons.

The prominent role played by Britain in NATO's nuclear modernization of medium-range nuclear systems further enhances its contribution to European security. It seems worth mentioning that former German Chancellor Helmut Schmidt initiated the debate over NATO's response to the modernization of Soviet nuclear forces in Europe, principally SS–20s, Backfire bombers, and short-range nuclear systems, in his Alastair Buchan address of 1977, sponsored by the London-based International Institute for Strategic Studies.[12] NATO's response assumed the form of a so-called two-track decision in December 1979. It was decided that the United States would deploy 108 Pershing-II missiles and 464 ground-based cruise missiles in several European countries (West Germany, Britain, Italy, Belgium and the Netherlands) unless progress could be made in arms control accords with the Soviet Union to eliminate or reduce sharply its theatre nuclear forces. Britain's willingness to accept 160 cruise missiles and the determination of the Thatcher Government to weather some of the strongest domestic pressures from the peace movement since the 1950s solidified allied cohesion and forged still another link between US and European security interests.

British participation in NATO nuclear modernization was assuring on several fronts to its European partners, though with differing and differential impact. First, it entangled NATO and British nuclear modernization with US nuclear policy, transforming a bilateral process into a multilateral process of negotiations and consultation. German concerns for allied nuclear support were specifically addressed. France's withdrawal from NATO and its refusal to participate in NATO's nuclear modernization programme precluded its ability to play Britain's nuclear bridge-building role. Besides British commitment of its strategic forces to NATO, it also assigns its theatre nuclear forces to SACEUR (NATO's US Supreme Allied Commander, Europe). All British Tornado aircraft, equipped for deep nuclear strikes against Warsaw Pact forces in Europe, are integrated into NATO planning and are presumably under SACEUR's control during a crisis. These forces support over 50 000 British conventional forces stationed in West Germany.

Conversely, European states anxious about West German predominance in conventional forces look to Britain as counterweight within Europe. As one close student of British defence concluded, in assessing the increased import-ance of Britain for Europe in the 1980s over the 1960s (when its application for entry into the European Community was vetoed by France): 'What dis-tinguished 1962 from 1980 was the inarticulated recognition that independent British forces were militarily useful in an era of strategic parity and politically essential in a time of growing West German power.'[13]

Third, Britain has been traditionally closer to Europe than to the United States on arms control and détente issues. Its support for the two-track strategy in NATO, which gave Europe leverage over US arms control policy and partial entry into superpower strategic arms talks, testified to Britain's usefulness in pressing European concerns,[14] focused alternatively on strengthening the US nuclear guarantee while holding it in check to suit European interest in arms control, confidence-building measures and détente. Britain's announced policy of minimum deterrence in contrast to a war-fighting strategy was also consistent with the priority assigned to arms control. The record of British Governments over the past generation in prodding superpower arms accord is evidenced by its prominent roles in signing the Partial Test Ban and Non-Proliferation Treaties in the 1960s.

Finally, there was the assurance of an independent British nuclear capability as a contribution to stable deterrence in Europe. As a European power, many Europeans feel that British nuclear forces provide additional insurance against the temptation that the Soviet Union might successfully attack Western Europe with conventional forces. The United States has officially abandoned its hostility to autonomous European nuclear forces, expressed by Secretary of Defense Robert McNamara's characterization of these forces as 'dangerous, expensive, prone to obsolescence and lacking in credibility as a deterrent'.[15] At the NATO meeting in Ottawa in 1974, NATO ministers agreed that independent European systems contributed to stability by strengthening deterrence. The Trident sale was partially justified as a move to strengthen deterrence.

There are significant disquieting features about British modernization that raise doubts about its contribution to stability. London remains ambiguous about its likely response in a crisis. It is not at all clear whether it will act independently or permit its nuclear decisions to be delegated to SACEUR and, by extension, to a US planner in a crisis. As Lawrence Freedman suggests in his careful analysis of British targeting: 'Despite the assignation of Britain's nuclear forces to NATO, the assumptions and dominant plans surrounding their targeting do not, as far as can be gathered from the public record, naturally fit in with any NATO plans. The trend in British public pronouncements suggests that the "standing alone" hypothesis is the underlying rationale for the nuclear force.'[16] The possibility that British forces might be used independently, without consulting US officials, is a distinct possibility. Whatever the uncertainty created by this prospect on Soviet decision-makers, it also complicates the control of a crisis, particularly incentives for pre-emption. If hostilities erupt, added problems in controlling escalation and damage arise. Bringing hostilities to a swift and timely close is also more difficult.

On the other hand, even if British assurance of participation in NATO operations are taken at face value, questions still arise whether there will be enough time to consult with British forces in a crisis to have these nuclear assets available. Or, London may simply withdraw its forces from NATO when they are most needed in an effort to stand apart from a crisis and shelter Britain from attack.

These concerns are deepened from an alternate and contradictory perspective. To the degree that British forces are integrally tied to US planning and operations, their arms control impact may be seriously eroded. The evolution of US strategic thinking and nuclear force posture development has progressively moved in the direction of being able to fight a limited nuclear war. Beginning with the Schlesinger doctrine in 1974 to the publication of Presidential Directive-59 under the Carter Administration through the Reagan years, with its accent on developing greater offensive nuclear capabilities and nuclear defensive systems, the trend in US policy has been towards creating nuclear options through a larger number of sophisticated nuclear capabilities. This trend can well be traced to the 1960s when the USA adopted an announced strategy of mutual assured destruction (MAD). This strategy, while implying the priority targeting of civilian targets, was actually pursued with the intention of delaying such strikes as long as possible, of suppressing Soviet nuclear forces to limit damage, and of maintaining an ascendant position during hostilities to control escalation and to bring the conflict to a swift close on terms favourable to the West in general and to the United States in particular.[17] Viewed from this perspective, the British Trident can be seen as an addition to US strike capabilities and as a dubious means by which to observe the letter but not the spirit of SALT-II limitation.

Britain's acquisition of D–5 missiles goes beyond minimal deterrent requirements. The Thatcher Government's self-limitation of eight warheads for each missile can be abrogated at any time. Since it is difficult to conceive of the British deterrent apart from substantial US assistance in all phases and levels of its development, including financial support through low-cost buy-ins, Soviet planners have some basis for worry that the British force is an integral, if not integrated, part of the US nuclear arsenal. As one analyst suggests in looking at the D–5 through US lenses: 'Trident advocates choose to see the missile in isolation, whereas in fact it will be integrated in war plans with the MX, Pershing II, Midgetman, stealth, cruise missiles, and bombers, and eventually British Trident II forces.'[18] The issue may well not be British independent use of its forces but its too close integration into US limited war planning.

Finally, the deep divisions within British politics and public opinion over the future composition and role of the British deterrent are potentially destabilizing elements. The Labour Party is on record favouring a unilateral abandonment of British nuclear forces. The Social Democrats and Liberals are more ambivalent with opinions ranging from unilateralism to the maintenance of an independent nuclear force whose composition would be negotiable through Britain's active participation in superpower strategic talks on European security.[19] Unilateral abandonment would quickly unravel the pattern of expectations held in important segments of European and US policy circles that Britain play a critical bridging role in NATO. The position of the Social-Democratic and Liberal Parties, while less extreme, do not resolve the issues of the composition of the force and its relation to US, NATO or future European nuclear co-operation.

British nuclear policy appears to be in contest with itself, simultaneously assuring and unsettling allies and adversaries. These conflicting messages are reinforced by the dissonance of the British political debate over nuclear policy and the fundamental divisions between and within the parties over nuclear weapons. What is clear is that neither superpower can be indifferent to British nuclear modernization, nor can Britain's European allies.

French nuclear modernization

French nuclear modernization poses the same problems for the superpowers as the British force. The Soviet Union will confront a formidable adversary capable of placing the Soviet population and society at risk. France's allies in NATO also have cause for concern since the independence of French nuclear forces creates uncertainty about how and when they might be used. This uncertainty is given a deeper dimension in the French than in the British case because France has no formal ties to NATO and the history of the French nuclear programme has underscored its autonomous development. Unlike Britain, whose indebtedness to the United States for two generations of weapon systems—Polaris and Trident—is firmly established, the French have created a deterrent force largely through their own efforts. They have carefully avoided entanglement in alliance commitments and have kept their distance from both superpowers. The internal cohesion within France on the issue of retaining an independent *force de dissuasion* (deterrent force), ranging across the political spectrum from the Communist and Socialist Parties on the Left to the centrist and Gaullist Parties on the Right, insulates France from outside influence and reduces the leverage that can be brought to bear by other governments or the peace movement to pressure the French Government to participate in arms talks.

In the 1990s the French are expected to have a triad of nuclear forces composed of six nuclear submarines, 18 intermediate-range ballistic missiles (IRBMs), and (until 1992–94), 15 Mirage–IV aircraft. Five of the six submarines will carry 16 M–4 missiles, armed with six warheads of approximately 150 kilotons each. The sixth submarine, carrying 16 M–20 missiles, each with a one-megaton charge, is scheduled for retirement in the late 1990s at about the time that it will be replaced by a new submarine, with M–4 missiles or an advanced-design system yet to be developed. The 18 IRBMs on the Albion Plateau in southeastern France already in place are expected to be operative through this century. Unlike the submarine force which is near invulnerable, the IRBM squadrons are susceptible to destruction by Soviet theatre forces, principally the SS–20. The announced aim of the IRBMs has shifted from deterrence to a trigger of France's nuclear forces. If attached, the *force de dissuasion* (deterrent force) would become a *force de frappe* (striking force). As one Frenchman observed: 'The *signature* of such an attack would . . . justify the use of the strategic nuclear forces against the aggressor.'[20]

The future of the airborne component of the triad is uncertain. The Mirage IVs will carry medium-range air-to-ground missiles (*air-sol-moyenne portée*, ASMP) with a range variously calculated from 100 to 300 km at twice the speed of sound. The Mirage IV must be refuelled in flight by US-supplied KC–135 tankers. The Mirage 2000 may replace the Mirage IV, but this follow-on is subject to revision in light of the rising cost associated with maintaining independent nuclear forces and the capability of Warsaw Pact and Soviet air defences to defeat the Mirage force.

The warheads that will be available to France when modernization is complete, with six submarines armed with M–4 missiles, vastly exceeds current capabilities. The 576 warheads of the French fleet of the 1990s will exceed the number of long-range warheads that Britain is expected to deploy, although its equivalent megatonnage will be roughly half. It will have the advantage of having three submarines on station at all times—more during a crisis. Three British submarines on patrol is likely to be the exception, not the rule, with only four submarines available. The shorter range of the M–4 (4000 km) relative to the D–5 (7000 km) will restrict French manoeuvrability, but the size of the area to be surveyed by Soviet ASW forces still appears sufficiently daunting to ensure the invulnerability of the French force for the foreseeable future.

France's independent stance, reaffirmed repeatedly by Fifth Republic leaders, poses several problems for allies and adversaries. The French insist on the principles of national autonomy in threatening or using nuclear weapons. Any integration, operational co-ordination or co-operation in planning with allies is unequivocally ruled out. At a meeting in the Kremlin, Socialist President François Mitterand told his Soviet listeners that 'if . . . we belong to a defensive alliance, . . . the Atlantic Alliance, we are no less deprived, outside as we are to the integrated command of this alliance, of our decisional autonomy'.[21] He went on to underline the point that 'only the President of the French Republic can use them. These are not words devoid of reality. We know in all certitude that our fate, our independence, our very survival, depends on our autonomy'.[22]

Under what conditions, for what purpose, in response to what provocation, and in what form might French nuclear forces be used? On these key questions French statements and public debate about nuclear policy are contradictory and ambiguous. First, there is the question of what is to be protected. Is it only the French territory? Or, does modern warfare, based on manoeuvre and long-range firepower, necessarily expand a nation's effective line of defence beyond its legal, territorial borders. French opinion remains divided on this key question. After much debate, dominant thinking today apparently identifies French security with that of its allies, particularly West Germany, which is in the first line of alliance defence. This means that French security extends to the Elbe River. The thinking of French officials who have adopted this view,[23] while roundly criticized initially for their alleged abandonment of French autonomy, has gained a seemingly ascendant position in policy circles. The decision of the Socialist Government to create a rapid intervention force (*Force d'Action Rapide*, FAR) to reinforce French units in Germany would appear to signal France's willingness to join in a forward battle for Europe against an attack from the East.

FAR has been assigned a large number of helicopters to increase France's mobile starting power, enhancing its ability to reinforce rapidly its divisions in West Germany during attack or to manifest its determination during a political crisis to fight, if necessary. Through a reorganization of its ground forces, tactical nuclear and conventional units have been more sharply differentiated in an effort to define with more clarity and articulation than in the past the escalatory rungs from conventional to tactical and strategic weapons that France appears willing and ready to mount.

These shifts in French announced and operational strategy relax somewhat, but do not resolve, the dilemmas facing France's allies and Soviet decision-makers. The conventional forces may not be sent to the front in time since their use still depends on a decision by the French President. Once French conventional forces are engaged, it is not clear when and if French tactical or strategic nuclear forces will be employed and whether France's allies will be alerted or consulted before they are used. France expects to replace its current Pluton tactical forces with the Hadès system. The Hadès has a longer range than the

Pluton which, when used from French soil, can hit targets only in West Germany. Hadès is capable of deeper strikes into Eastern Europe. The untimely use of France's tactical nuclear forces may precipitate a grave and more destructive clash than an allied-controlled response might prompt. It will almost certainly produce large-scale damage in East Germany which, Bonn insists, 'are Germans, too'.[24]

The Soviet Union will have an incentive to pre-emptively destroy these forces which are on French territory before France can use them to test Soviet determination. These tactical forces are likely to have a very limited battlefield use. The recent cancellation of the French research programme on a neutron bomb will limit the battlefield use of these forces. The destructive power of the weapons available to Hadès, ranging from 20 to 60 kilotons, will essentially confine them to testing Soviet intention and signalling French will to use its strategic nuclear forces.

The size of French or British nuclear forces, however much they will be enlarged in the 1990s, and the limited geographic territories of these two states are limits that will not be overcome in the near future. In differing measure, both countries have adopted strategies of proportional deterrence. Each seeks to deter by threatening greater damage of the homeland of the aggressor than the expected gain to be achieved by attacking their vital interests. This nuclear stance puts a premium on high-value, soft targets comprising cities and industrial centres or key civilian installations, like oil and gas fields and electrical power plants. The limited war-fighting and battlefield control strategies which are being pursued by the superpowers can be negated by initiatives of either middle-range nuclear power. Crisis and battlefield management are significantly complicated by the existence of these independent forces. The vulnerability of elements of these forces, especially French ground-based systems, makes them more a target than a deterrent. That these vulnerabilities are turned to an advantage by suggesting their utility in testing and signalling resolve appears to be a hollow rationalization of weakness rather than a positive step towards nuclear stability between rival alliances or towards internal alliance cohesion within the West. The resistance of Britain and France to entertain the notion of participating in US–Soviet arms talks adds another obstacle in the path towards developing an arms control regime in which allies and adversaries can have some degree of mutual confidence.

III.   Conditions for British–French participation in nuclear arms control talks

Four conditions have been implicitly or explicitly cited by British and French officials, with varying degrees of intensity, as prerequisites for their participation in arms control talks. First, neither will enter into talks unless the offensive arsenals of the superpowers are significantly reduced. British Prime Minister Margaret Thatcher set out this condition: 'If between the two big powers, the numbers went down massively and enormously and we moved into a totally different world . . . then there may be circumstances when ours (British nuclear forces) will have to be counted.'[25] Former French Minister of Foreign Affairs, Claude Cheysson drew a similar line in calling for 'the reduction of the superpower arsenals to levels where one might consider that the gap between capabilities had changed in nature'[26] as a pre-condition for French arms control participation.

Even if superpower arsenals were reduced, as both superpowers have proposed in Geneva,[27] there is still substantial doubt about the willingness of London or Paris to reduce their systems. Both governments currently believe that they are at the limits of minimal requirements to ensure their proportional deterrent strategies. Britain's Director of Arms Control and Disarmament within the Foreign Ministry argued that 'it is short of absurd to suggest that the British deterrent force, which is of minimal size and capacity of last resort, should be tied to an equation which links it only to one element of the threat posed by the Soviet Union to the United Kingdom. To equate the British deterrent with the SS–20 is, therefore, not only wrong by definition but unacceptable in terms of deterrence'.[28] It is difficult to discern under what conditions, if any, a French Government will be willing to lower French nuclear levels even if the superpowers choose to limit their arsenals. In a news conference on 24 September 1982, President Mitterrand asserted that France 'cannot accept that a part of our nuclear armament is negotiable'.[29] Nothing has since occurred to suggest any shift in the French position. The election of a Right-of-centre Government in 1986 solidified this non-negotiable stance.

Second, both middle-range nuclear powers oppose any incorporation of their forces into a strictly defined European zone. This reservation has several sub-conditions attached to it that should be identified to understand the British–French position.[30] Both governments consider their forces as strategic, and not as theatre elements. They reject any superpower attempt to count them as parts of a regional arms control arrangement. They prefer to be treated as coequals of the superpowers. They specifically resent having their claims to certain strategic levels depreciated by equating them with only a relatively small part of the Soviet arsenal. Similarly, they have no interest in defining theatre forces in such a way that US nuclear forces, especially cruise and Pershing–II missiles, would have to be reduced in conformity to some agreed-upon formula. The coupling and extended deterrence functions of these weapons in linking US and European security interests might be seriously compromised. Unless these sub-conditions are met, British, French and US NATO forces, as a group, would be the basis for defining and legitimating Soviet theatre capabilities. It would also imply that the Soviet Union could manipulate Western capabilities stationed in the European theatre by manipulating the composition and deployment of its theatre forces while its long-range missile force would be excluded from consideration in limiting Soviet capabilities.

Third, little progress is likely to be made in inducing French and British compromise on arms negotiations unless there are sharp cutbacks in Soviet and

Warsaw Pact conventional forces. The French are particularly adamant about this condition. Warsaw Pact forces are considered superior to those of NATO on the central front. Reductions, including US withdrawal of some of its forces, are viewed as a net loss to the West in keeping Warsaw Pact forces at bay. While US withdrawal would not only redeploy these forces thousands of miles from where they are needed, they might also signal a lowering of resolve by US officials to defend Europe.[31] The same concern applies to the possible reduction of British forces. It might also be added that the French Government is not likely to be sympathetic to conventional force reductions which might place ceilings on the German contingent to NATO at the very time that it has, at some expense and over much internal resistance from within the army, organized a rapid intervention force to bolster its treaty commitments to West Germany.

Finally, there is the threat of a breakthrough in defensive systems against nuclear offensive forces that inhibit the French and British Governments from participating actively in force-reduction talks. The two governments have responded in somewhat characteristic fashion to a commonly shared threat to their nuclear forces. The British Government has attempted to influence the US Strategic Defense Initiative (SDI) by being the first European power to sign a contract with the Pentagon for joint development of selected elements of the SDI programme.[32] But in signing defence contracts with the Pentagon, the British Minister of Defence reiterated reservations expressed earlier by Prime Minister Margaret Thatcher in her meeting with President Ronald Reagan in December 1985 and subsequently repeated by Foreign Minister Sir Geoffrey Howe in a major policy address on SDI in March 1985.[33] It is the British understanding that SDI will be consistent with four principles: (a) the promotion of parity with the Soviet Union, not superiority; (b) retention of the ABM Treaty unless otherwise jointly negotiated away by the superpowers; (c) enhancement of deterrence; and (d) retention of the aim to reduce offensive forces. If Britain can hold the SDI programme to these limiting principles, it will have played a major arms control role even without having directly participated in superpower talks. As research and development proceed on SDI, there is ample room for doubt that the British attempt to slow or constrict progress on defensive systems will actually have much effect. The likely impact of British influence is in swelling the ranks of US critics to rapid SDI development.

In contrast to the pliant response of the British Government, the French reaction was to build a backfire to SDI. Paris has succeeded in attracting European Community support for its Eureka proposal. It is defined as a strictly civilian programme aimed at improving Europe's scientific and technological capabilities and in improving its competitiveness in world markets. As the Europeans have recognized, SDI is a vehicle for developing new and promising technologies from lasers to satellites and high-speed computers. Progress in these areas is expected to have widespread civilian and military applications. Rather than lend its support to the US effort by agreeing to co-operate with US firms on SDI contracts, as Britain and West Germany have done, Paris seeks *inter alia*, to provide European firms with an alternative to US contracts without having to confront the United States directly on this issue.

IV. Relaxing the conditions for British and French participation

Finding a way to induce British and French participation in superpower arms control discussions will not be easy. The French appear particularly intractable for the reason sketched earlier. One possibly fruitful strategy might be to draw France gradually into alliance military planning. Efforts in this regard are likely to be successful only if the European component of French thinking is emphasized and if bilateral arrangements are encouraged, particularly with West Germany. Pushing France towards NATO and towards the centre of US influence in SACEUR is bound to fail. All of France's major parties are on record in opposition to France's return to NATO. There is, however, stronger sentiment for French–German defence co-operation. In weapon development, Paris–Bonn collaboration has been close and continuous for almost 30 years.[34] With Bonn as a bridge, some progress may be made on defining the conditions for French employment of their conventional and nuclear forces. Given economic and technological resource constraints, it is not likely that France will be able to build nuclear systems beyond its current plans for the 1990s. It would seem more prudent to regularize these forces within a superpower nuclear regime than to demand deep cuts in them.

The British programme appears more susceptible to influence and redefinition. The domestic consensus is deeply split over whether to have a nuclear deterrent or not. The Trident system also appears more powerful than is necessary to meet British minimum deterrent needs. The British Government may well be induced to lower its already announced limit of eight warheads on D–5 missiles. A smaller number of less powerful warheads might also be contemplated as a British gesture to facilitate a superpower accord on middle-range systems without running afoul of the conditions set down by the British about their participation in and acceptance of an arms accord. Meanwhile, British reservations about abandoning SALT I or about defence systems may prove to be a major contribution to controlling the pace and size of the arms race whether it reduces its own forces or not.

V. Conclusions

British and French nuclear modernization is an arms control issue whose time has come. Neither superpower can ignore the size and sophistication of either country's nuclear forces: the Soviet Union as a society is put at risk; and the United States will be put at risk, if British and French forces are used independently. Downgraded is Washington's ability to prevent the outbreak of a nuclear war, to limit its damage, and to bring such a calamitous event to a swift halt. One can conceive of US–Soviet ballistic missile defence systems that defy the penetration confidence and strategic relevance of other nuclear powers, by making it technologically and economically prohibitive. In lieu of this very uncertain prospect, however, the superpowers will be compelled to buy British, French (and Chinese) participation through increased recognition of these powers' quite distinct national security interests.

Notes and references

[1] The Chevaline is described in Hutchinson, R. 'Chevaline: UK's response to Soviet ABM System', *Jane's Defence Weekly*, vol. 2, no. 23, (15 Dec. 1984), pp. 1068–9.

[2] The D–5 is described in Norris, R. S., 'Counterforce at sea: the Trident II missile', *Arms Control Today*, vol. 15, no. 7 (Sep. 1985), pp. 5–10.

[3] Malone, P., *The British Nuclear Deterrent* (Croom Helm: London, 1984), p. 35.

[4] See Freedman, L., 'British nuclear targeting', *Defence Analysis*, vol. 1, no. 2 (1985), pp. 81–99.

[5] Freedman (note 4) and Hutchinson (note 1).

[6] See *The Great Soviet Encyclopedia*, 3rd edn, (Macmillan: New York, 1975), pp. 30–3.

[7] Craig, P. and Jungerman, J. A., *Nuclear Arms Race: Technology and Society* (McGraw-Hill: New York, 1986), pp. 42 and 51.

[8] Craig and Jungerman (note 7), p. 51; and Lewis, K. N., 'The prompt and delayed effects of nuclear war', *Scientific American*, vol. 261, no. 1 (July 1979), pp. 35–47. Equivalent megatonnage (EMT) is a measure of destructive capability. It does not vary at a constant rate proportional to blast or explosive power. It is measured by the formula wherein EMT varies with the cube root of the yield squared. Thus, eight nuclear weapons, each of 125-kiloton strength, is actually equal to two EMTs, not one megaton, measured by simple addition. Thus eight 125-kt nuclear devices well placed over a target will produce a greater amount of destructive power than a one-megaton bomb.

[9] Kemp, G., *Nuclear Forces for Medium Powers: Part I, Targets and Weapon Systems; Parts II and III, Strategic Requirements and Options*, Adelphi Papers Nos. 106 and 107, International Institute for Strategic Studies, London, 1974. See also Smart, I., *Future Conditions: The Prospects for Anglo–French Nuclear Cooperation*, Adelphi Paper No. 78, International Institute for Strategic Studies, London, 1971.

[10] There exists a rich literature tracing the British nuclear programme. See, e.g., Gowing, M., *Independence and Deterrence* (Macmillan: London, 1974), 2 vols. Other useful reviews are Freedman, L., *Britain and Nuclear Weapons* (Royal Institute of International Affairs: London, 1984); Simpson, J., *The Independent Nuclear State: The United States, Britain, and the Atom* (Macmillan: London, 1983); Pierre, A., *Nuclear Politics: The British Experience with an Independent Strategic Force* (London: Oxford University Press, 1972); and Malone (note 3). Also useful for early British thinking is Wheeler, N. J., 'British nuclear weapons and Anglo–American relations, 1945–54', *International Affairs*, vol. 62, no. 1 (Winter 1985/86), pp. 71–86.

[11] Arkin, W. M. and Fieldhouse, R. W., *Nuclear Battlefields* (Ballinger: Cambridge, MA, 1985), pp. 234–5.

[12] See IISS (International Institute for Strategic Studies), 'The Alastair Buchan Memorial Lecture', *Survival*, no. 20 (Jan.–Feb. 1978), pp. 2–10.

13 Malone (note 3), p. 78.
14 These conflicting imperatives of use and control of US nuclear might and policy are clearly reflected in Christoph Bertram's writings. As former director of the International Institute for Strategic Studies, Bertram's views are a useful barometer for centrist European defence thinking. See his 'Implication of theatre nuclear weapons in Europe', *Foreign Affairs*, vol. 60, no. 2, (Winter 1981–82), pp. 305–26 and 'Strategic defence and the Western Alliance', *Weapons in Space*, eds F. Long *et al.* (W. W. Norton: New York, 1986), pp. 279–96.
15 Kaufmann, W. W., *The McNamara Strategy* (Harper and Row: New York, 1964), p. 117.
16 Freedman (note 4), p. 96.
17 This trend is also traced in great detail in Freedman, L., *The Evolution of Nuclear Strategy* (St Martin's Press: New York, 1981), especially pp. 225–56. See also Kolodziej, E. A., 'Nuclear weapons in search of a role: evolution of recent American strategic nuclear and arms control policy', *Conflict and Arms Control: An Uncertain Agenda*, ed. P. Viotti (Westview: Boulder, CO, 1985), pp. 3–23.
18 Norris (note 2), p. 7.
19 For a brief summary of party positions, see Grove, E. J., *Where and When? The Integration of British and French Nuclear Forces with the Arms Control Process*, Faraday Discussion Paper No. 5, Council for Arms Control, London, 1985, pp. 13–14. Also relevant are Labour Party, *Defence and Security for Britain*, statement to Annual Conference 1984 by the Executive Committee.
20 Quoted in Laird, R. F. (France), *The Soviet Union, and the Nuclear Weapons Issue* (Westview Press: Boulder, CO, 1985), p. 48.
21 *Ministère de la Défense* (France), *La Politique de défence de la France, Dossier d'Information* No. 75 (Oct. 1984), p. 22.
22 *Ministère de la Défense* (France) (note 21).
23 See the critique of General Guy Méry, Chief of French Armed Forces, of the notion of confining French defensive preparations solely to French territory. Méry, Général G., *'Une armée pour quoi faire et comment?' Défence Nationale* (June 1976), pp. 11–34. Space limitations preclude a review and rehearsal of the complex French debate over nuclear weapons. For useful evaluations, see Laird (note 20) and especially Yost, D. S., *France's Deterrent Posture and Security in Europe; Part 1: Capabilities and Doctrine* and *Part II: Strategic and Arms Control Implications*, International Institute for Strategic Studies, London, 1985.
24 *Foreign Broadcast Information Service* (US), 19 Dec. 1981, p. K2.
25 Quoted by Dean, R., 'The British nuclear deterrent and arms control', *The World Today* (Sep. 1983), p. 321.
26 Quoted in Yost (note 23), Part II, p. 53.
27 *New York Times*, 3 July 1986, summarizes the positions of the superpowers.
28 Dean (note 24), p. 320.
29 Minister of Defence (France), *France's Defence Policy Information Bulletin* No. 69 (May 1982), p. 8.
30 See Grove (note 19), pp. 2–13 and his 'Allied nuclear forces complicate negotiations', *Bulletin of the Atomic Scientists*, vol. 42, no. 6 (June–July 1986), pp. 18–23. For background on the evolution of the British and French positions on NATO nuclear modernization, see Talbott, S., *Deadly Gambits* (Vintage: New York, 1985), especially pp. 3–206.
31 See Yost (note 23), Part II, pp. 42–50, for a discussion of conventional forces.

[32] *The Times* (London), 10 Dec. 1985.

[33] The Howe address is published in full in 'Speech of Sir Geoffrey Howe, Mar. 14, 1985' (London Press Service: Washington, DC, 1985), pp. 1–7.

[34] See Kolodziej, E. A., *Making and Marketing of Arms, The French Experience and its Implications for the International System* (Princeton University Press: Princeton, NJ, forthcoming), chapter 2.

Paper 3.2. Chinese nuclear forces: overview and ambitions

RICHARD W. FIELDHOUSE

I. Introduction

Although the People's Republic of China has possessed nuclear weapons since 1964, its impact as a nuclear weapon power is relatively unstudied and unknown. Yet, numerous developments suggest that China's nuclear forces should be carefully examined. China is the only nuclear weapon state that has engaged in armed conflict with the Soviet Union. China is the only developing country that has a full 'triad' of nuclear forces that can strike the two nuclear superpowers—the USA and the USSR—and aside from them is the only other country with ballistic missiles of intercontinental-range. China has territorial claims and border disputes with a number of countries, including the USSR; it may therefore be more likely than any other nuclear weapon country to engage in armed conflict. China and the USSR have positioned huge military forces along their common border, roughly one-half and one-quarter of their total forces, respectively. China's split from the Soviet Union (in 1960) and subsequent realignment with the USA (beginning in the early 1970s) changed the complexion of the 'East–West' competition and caused the USSR to shift much of its military might towards China. Although Sino–Soviet antagonism has abated somewhat in recent years and limited reconciliation appears likely, the USSR still deploys more than 700 'theatre' missiles and hundreds of nuclear-capable aircraft towards China. For its part, China possesses some 170–230 nuclear-armed ballistic missiles and some 120–150 bombers available for striking the USSR with nuclear weapons.

It is unclear what path China will take as a nuclear power. Some recent evidence suggests that, if China doubts the credibility of its own weapons, it may decide to pursue a broader and more flexible nuclear force posture than that of the mid-1980s. Should this happen, it could increase considerably China's nuclear prominence (in relation to the UK and France), especially as concerns the Soviet Union and in arms control matters. The prospects for arms control that includes Chinese nuclear weapons appear, for the first time, to be suitable for discussion. Since 1983, China has maintained that only after the USA and the USSR cut their arsenals by one-half would it enter into discussions with all the nuclear weapon nations to pursue disarmament—China's professed goal. Both superpowers have proposed and negotiated towards such cuts in their nuclear arsenals.

China faces an uncertain future. Although the expanded US–Chinese military relationship complicates Soviet planning and brings new technology to China, it is unclear whether China will perceive itself as more, or less, secure in the coming decade. If the USSR deploys ballistic missile defence (BMD) systems in addition to the Moscow anti-ballistic missile (ABM) system, such deployments will cast new doubt on China's relatively small nuclear arsenal. China may attempt to offset eventual superpower BMD programmes by pursuing technologies and systems such as multiple independently targetable re-entry vehicles (MIRVs) and penetration aids on its ballistic missile force, modern nuclear bombers or cruise missiles. (There is already evidence of Chinese development and testing with some of these technologies.) If, on the other hand, the USSR and the USA agree to preclude the deployment of BMD systems exceeding those permitted by the Anti-Ballistic Missile Treaty, or to reduce intermediate-range nuclear missiles (particularly Soviet SS–20 missiles in Asia), it could pave the way for China to minimize its nuclear ambitions while further reducing tensions with the USSR. Thus, the Sino–Soviet military situation could either deteriorate or improve considerably.

This paper explains the background, development and deployment of China's nuclear forces. It then examines several directions China could choose in its future nuclear weapon programmes in the light of China's nuclear ambitions and national goals. The paper concludes with a discussion of some possibilities for arms control.

Background and context

China is the most recent nuclear weapon nation and also the most obscure to outside observers. Less is known about Chinese nuclear forces than about those of the other four nuclear weapon nations: the USA, the USSR, the UK and France. This is due primarily to the extensive secrecy that surrounds all aspects of Chinese nuclear weapons; all matters concerning Chinese nuclear forces are officially considered secret in China. One must therefore rely on occasional US official statements, or the irregular and generally vague material appearing from Chinese sources. Before the USA–China rapprochement, the US Government habitually reported the developments in Chinese nuclear capabilities. More recently, the USA has remained publicly silent because of its closer ties with China.

None the less, even though China possesses a relatively small total number of warheads, they can be considered the most significant after those of the USA and the USSR. It is hard to imagine a nuclear conflict involving either Britain or France without the United States. Not so for China: it could become engaged in a war against the USSR without the involvement of any of the other nuclear weapon powers. None of these other three nuclear weapon states share a land border with the USSR, nor have they engaged in armed conflict with it. China has.

Perhaps the most significant development in the US–Soviet cold war was

China's split from the Soviet Union in 1960 and subsequent development of nuclear forces. When the vision of a monolithic Communist bloc dissolved, it changed the calculus of East–West military competition. Where once the USA feared a Chinese 'threat', it now sees China assuming the vital role of keeping a check on the Soviet military in the Far East. The USA perceives that, as long as China and the USSR remain military adversaries, the USSR cannot redeploy its forces from the Far East to Europe, even in a war. James Kelly, the principal US Department of Defense official responsible for US–Chinese military policy, told the US Congress in 1984 that the USA and China had 'a legacy of mutual suspicion from almost thirty years of considering one another enemies', but that the current US goal is 'an enduring defense relationship' with China.[1] China's role as a nuclear weapon nation is thus far more important than is apparent from a simple tally of its atomic arsenal.

Sino–Soviet relations

In 1969, a series of border disputes and armed clashes between China and the USSR led to a tense military situation that threatened war. H. R. Haldeman, then President Nixon's chief of staff, wrote that the USSR approached the USA secretly to test its reaction to the idea of a joint US–Soviet nuclear attack against China, which President Nixon declined. According to Haldeman, it appeared to the USA as though the Soviet Union intended to attack China without US help and had positioned hundreds of nuclear warheads near the Chinese border for such a strike.[2] Although no war broke out, the military buildup that followed has led, according to Kelly, to 'the largest single concentration of forces along any bi-national border', which includes Soviet deployment of 'over 750 intermediate and short-range surface-to-surface missiles ranging from the SS–20 to battlefield tactical systems'.[3]

Although Sino–Soviet relations have eased considerably since the early 1970s, China still considers the USSR its main adversary. Both nations have met sporadically since 1969, attempting to normalize relations. But official Chinese policy is that three Soviet obstacles preclude any such normalization. These three obstacles are: the Soviet invasion and occupation of Afghanistan; Soviet support for the Vietnamese invasion of Cambodia; and the large buildup of Soviet military forces along China's border. Since the early 1980s, China has also become increasingly concerned about the Soviet deployment of SS–20 missiles in Asia (over 170), which Mr Kelly reported 'has become a major issue in Sino–Soviet normalization talks'.[4] The US Defense Intelligence Agency (DIA) reported to the US Congress in 1982 that 'the SS–20s have taken over some of the missions previously allocated to those ICBMs which were targeted against China'.[5] Unless the USSR removes these obstacles, China will probably continue to view the USSR as its main adversary. However, since 1985, there have been occasional statements by Chinese and Soviet officials indicating that each side may be interested in resolving some of the obstacles, which could put their relations on a better footing.

While most observers consider China to possess nuclear weapons for purely defensive or minimal deterrent purposes, it is unclear what path China will take in the future. Since the early 1980s, Chinese officials have regularly emphasized the importance of nuclear forces. In an article in *Red Flag* in March 1983, Defence Minister Zhang Aiping called for greater Chinese concentration on nuclear weapon programmes.[6] Under China's 'four modernizations', the military has been given the lowest priority, but nuclear weapons are considered separately and have the highest priority of all military programmes.[7] China's current military reorganization plan calls for cutting regular troops by one million men, reducing overall military spending and restructuring the military districts and command system. But this massive shift in the military will not reduce China's nuclear role or capabilities; it will improve them. China will spend less money on the regular ground forces while streamlining the command and fighting structures, thus releasing proportionately more resources for nuclear forces.

II.   History

China's nuclear weapon history began with its dependence on the Soviet Union in the mid- to late-1950s for scientific and technical assistance to develop its military and, particularly, nuclear forces. China modelled its own military forces and research and development (R&D) establishment after those of the USSR. In a 1957 agreement on science and defence co-operation, the Soviet Union agreed to help China build its military forces and to share Soviet nuclear weapon designs and technology with China.[8] However, it soon became clear to China that the USSR did not intend to keep the latter part of this agreement. This was apparently the chief cause of the Sino–Soviet split in 1960.[9] China learned a lesson: never depend on another country for its own security. Thereafter, China implemented a policy of self-reliance in the military and nuclear weapon fields and set out, successfully, to produce its own nuclear forces.

Soviet assistance did result, however, in transferring many important military technologies to China, including virtually all of China'a early missile, aircraft and submarine designs. While China designed all its initial nuclear weapon delivery systems after Soviet models, it had to design its own nuclear warheads. It proceeded to design a nuclear bomb that it successfully tested on 16 October 1964. Two years later, it succeeded in testing its first missile armed with a nuclear warhead that exploded above the nuclear test site at Lop Nor. In June 1967, China tested its first hydrogen bomb, only 32 months after its first nuclear test. Chinese officials truthfully boast: 'Our development of nuclear weapons is the fastest in the world.'[10] As of October 1986, China had conducted 32 nuclear weapon tests, varying in yield from low-kiloton to about four megatons.[11] From these tests, China has produced some 300–400 nuclear weapons of at least five different yields and designs, both fission and fusion.[12] China is not a signatory to the 1963 Partial Test Ban Treaty and tested nuclear weapons in the atmosphere as late as 1980. In 1986, as part of its recognition of the United Nations Year of Peace, China announced its decision to cease atmospheric testing. This is a significant change for a nation that has always scorned the US–Soviet atmospheric test ban treaty.

III. Nuclear forces

China maintains a relatively small arsenal of nuclear forces, estimated to contain between 300 and 400 warheads, that are structured in a 'triad' of land-based missiles, bombers and submarine-launched missiles. Most of China's nuclear forces consist of ballistic missiles with ranges varying from 500 km to some 12000 km. All but a few of these ballistic missiles can only reach targets in the Asian theatre. Perhaps 10 missiles each with limited or full intercontinental range can strike targets throughout Europe or North America, respectively. All Chinese nuclear missiles currently carry only one warhead each, but China may choose to pursue MRV (multiple re-entry vehicle) or MIRV technologies in the future, especially for reasons of economy and increased targeting capability.[13] At least one missile test in 1986 appeared to be related to testing such missile advances.[14] China also maintains a bomber force of over 100 aircraft of three designs for which roughly 100 to 150 bombs are presumed to be available. The last, and most recent, leg of China's strategic triad is its force of nuclear-powered ballistic missile submarines (SSBNs) and the submarine-launched ballistic missiles (SLBMs) developed for those SSBNs. Development of this submarine force has been hampered by technical difficulties in solid-fuel production and nuclear power reactors for submarines.[15] Although China successfully test-launched an SLBM in 1982, it is not clear whether its ballistic missile submarines have begun regular operational patrols yet, or whether they are still undergoing operational testing and training.

It is possible that many of its shorter-range systems are available or intended for tactical battlefield use. Several tests of low-yield warheads and field training exercises that simulated the use of tactical nuclear weapons suggest that China has a capability to produce weapons exclusively for such purposes.[16] The US DIA has reported that atomic demolition munitions (ADMs) 'may be used' by China.[17] Each of the components of China's nuclear forces is described below.

Land-based missiles

As of 1986, China had four models of land-based ballistic missiles, known in the West by their US designations: CSS–1, CSS–2, CSS–3 and CSS–4 (CSS stands for Chinese Surface-to-Surface). It appears that China designates these missiles DF–2, DF–3, DF–4 and DF–5 respectively (DF stands for Dong Feng which may be translated as 'East Wind'). Apparently the DF–1 was an earlier model of a short-range ballistic missile (SRBM) no longer in service.[18] China's land-based missile characteristics are as follows.

CSS–1: China first began to deploy the CSS–1 medium-range ballistic missile (MRBM) in 1966. The yield of the CSS–1 warhead is thought to be about 20 kt. The CSS–1 has a range of about 1000 km.[19] According to the US Joint Chiefs of Staff (JCS), 'The CSS–1 MRBM can reach targets in the Eastern USSR, peripheral nations, and some US bases in the Far East. The deployed force has not increased significantly since 1972'.[20]

CSS–2: China's intermediate-range ballistic missile (IRBM), the CSS–2, has a range of roughly 2500 km.[21] According to the DIA, 'the system is probably intended for relatively large population targets in central and eastern Russia'.[22] It was first deployed in 1972, and the total number of operational missiles has remained roughly between 65 and 85.

China has maintained over 100 MRBM/IRBMs since the early 1980s, and they comprise all but about 20 of its land-based nuclear ballistic missiles. China has taken considerable measures to ensure that these ballistic missiles would not be vulnerable to a surprise attack. According to the JCS, 'the majority of the mobile MR/IRBM launch units will likely be dispersed to take advantage of terrain and camouflage and remain concealed during an enemy's first strike'.[23]

CSS–3: In 1976, China began flight testing the CSS–3, its first 'intercontinental' ballistic missile (ICBM).[24] The CSS–3 is unique in its 7000-km range; it falls somewhere between an IRBM and an ICBM, so it has been designated a 'limited-range ICBM' by US defence officials.[25] It is China's first multiple-stage missile, using liquid fuel and carrying a single warhead estimated to be 1–3 megatons (Mt) in yield. As early as 1976, the DIA reported to Congress that the CSS–3 could 'reach targets in European Russia' but not Moscow.[26] It was the first Chinese missile deployed in silos and, since only 5–10 missiles have been reported operationally deployed, it is widely assumed to have been a precursor to a full-range ICBM (one that could strike the Soviet capital).[27]

CSS–4: China's longest-range missile, the CSS–4, began to be developed in about 1970 and its first public appearance came with two test flights over the Pacific Ocean in May 1980.[28] The CSS–4 is estimated to have a range of over 12 000 km, which gives it the capacity to strike not only Moscow, but any target in the Soviet Union, Europe or North America.[29] It is believed to carry a multi-megaton warhead, perhaps 4–5 Mt.

Interestingly, China has reportedly deployed only 'a few' of the CSS–4 missiles, between 5 and 10, probably in hardened silos. China could have produced more of the missiles than has been the case, but has chosen to limit the programme for unstated reasons. Observers disagree in their interpretation of the very limited deployments. Some suggest that China does not want to provoke either the USA or the USSR by deploying more ICBMs, while others presume that China has simply chosen to invest its limited economic resources in more survivable nuclear forces—submarines. The DIA reported in 1984 that 'not all the decisions concerning new missiles to be developed in the next twenty years have been made'.[30]

Bombers

Bombers provided China with its first nuclear delivery capability and were used to drop at least 8, perhaps as many as 15, nuclear test 'devices'.[31] There are three types of aircraft currently available for nuclear bombing missions: the Tu–4 Bull; the Il–28 Beagle; and the Tu–16 Badger, all modelled after Soviet designs (thus the designation of Western names for Soviet models) to which China made changes. It appears that the Chinese names for these bombers are transliterated by the West as B–4, B–5 and B–6 respectively. All three models of bombers are (at best) of 1950s vintage, although China started producing them more recently. The Tu–16 Badger and the Tu–4 Bull are intermediate-range bombers, and the Il–28 Beagle is of medium range. Their characteristics are briefly described below.

• China's primary nuclear bomber is the Tu–16 Badger, which China began producing in 1968.[32] Roughly 100 Badgers are in the force, and China may still be producing a few each year as of 1986. With its combat radius of 3000 km and a bomb-carrying capacity of 4500 kg, the Badger 'can reach virtually all of the Soviet Union and US allies in Asia, but its capability to penetrate air defense systems is poor'.[33] According to the Joint Chiefs of Staff, 'about 50 Soviet urban-industrial areas east of the Urals are within its range'.[34]

• While the Il–28 Beagle is the most numerous Chinese bomber, with over 400 deployed, it is not known how many are currently configured for nuclear weapon missions, perhaps a few dozen. The Beagle is capable of carrying 3000 kg of bombs out to a combat radius of 1000 km. The Joint Chiefs of Staff have reported that 'staging from Il–28 capable airfields closest to the border areas would permit strategic operations against portions of the Soviet Union, all of South Korea, almost all of Vietnam, and parts of India. The limited range of the aircraft suggests that it also might be used in a theater support role within the PRC.'[35]

• The Tu–4 Bull is the oldest of the Chinese bombers and its obsolescence makes it 'only marginally suitable for strategic attack operations'.[36] It is thus presumed to be essentially out of the picture. It is possible that China intends to use some of its nuclear-capable aircraft, including the Tu–4, for nuclear bombing missions within Chinese territory in case of a Soviet invasion.

All told, China has some 110–150 nuclear-capable aircraft, but may be preparing to expand or modernize this force. During 1985, Chinese officials revealed that they are beginning to design a new supersonic bomber to augment or replace the existing fleet. US visitors were given tours of an aircraft design and production factory said to be responsible for the new bomber as well as the Tu–16 Badger.[37] If China does build such a bomber, it would undoubtedly be better able to penetrate air defences than the current fleet and could figure in a Chinese programme to counteract a potential Soviet strategic defence system.

Submarines

China's most difficult weapon development programme has been its SSBN force and its complementary SLBM, the CSS–N–3. The SSBN, designated the Xia Class by the West and reportedly the Daqingyu Class in China, has been under various stages of development for nearly 15 years, and the SLBM was first tested after 10 years of development.[38] In April 1981, China launched its first Xia Class submarine and the following year launched its first successful SLBM test missile from under water.[39]

China has one Golf Class ballistic-missile submarine (conventionally powered) that was assembled in 1964 from Soviet components. It has been used as a test and training vessel for ballistic missiles and submarine crews, and it was used to launch the first submerged test of the CSS–NX–3 SLBM (the 'X' is for experimental) on 12 October 1982. The Golf Class submarine may also be available as an operational submarine in a crisis, since it can launch two CSS–N–3 missiles. China's CSS–N–3 missile (the 'N' stands for naval) is a two-stage missile that carries a single warhead estimated to have a yield between 200 kt and 1 Mt. Although the missile has not been tested at full range, it is believed to have a range of 3300 km.

It is believed that China has already built two Xia Class SSBNs and is building a small fleet of them, with perhaps three more currently under construction. (Estimates vary from 6 to 12 submarines for the total programme.) The first Xia went on sea trials in 1983 and may still be serving training and testing missions, although Chinese officials reportedly have suggested that it is already 'operational'.[40] Since China has very little experience operating SSBNs, it will take some time to settle into a routine. It is quite probable that the first two submarines are armed with operational missiles and could be used if deemed necessary.

Other nuclear weapons

As mentioned above, many of China's shorter-range nuclear systems could be used for 'non-strategic' roles. There are indications that China may be considering building, or may already have built, a stockpile of distinctly 'tactical' nuclear weapons for less than all-out nuclear warfare, possibly including atomic demolition munitions.[41] These nuclear land mines could be used on Chinese territory to prevent an invading force from using the most suitable routes, by closing mountain passes, creating forest fires, and so on. In 1982, the People's Liberation Army (PLA—the general name for all of China's armed forces) conducted a large military exercise some 700 km south of the Chinese–Mongolian border, and detonated a simulated tactical nuclear airburst, complete with mushroom cloud. The local newspaper carried a photo with the caption 'An "atomic bomb" exploding deep in the ranks of the "enemy"'.[42]

It is apparent that some Chinese military officials advocate building a force of distinctly 'tactical' nuclear weapons because they fear that China's 'strategic' weapons are not sufficient to dissuade the USSR from launching a 'limited' nuclear attack and invasion of China.

IV. Future choices

In considering China's possible future choices for its nuclear forces and posture, one should keep in mind its nuclear and strategic goals, especially as they may conflict with each other. China appears to have two main nuclear goals: maintaining an assured nuclear retaliatory capability, especially against Soviet targets in Asia, and maintaining its nuclear status or prestige. China is the only Third World nuclear weapon state. It proclaimed its obligation to break the 'nuclear monopoly' of the superpowers as a justification for joining the nuclear club.

However, China clearly has a strong desire to continue its current policy priorities: economic, technological and scientific modernization. These priorities are placed ahead of military modernization for understandable reasons. China cannot afford a major military buildup and does not aspire to being a world military superpower. It has recently become clear that China is unable to afford even the cost of equipping its regular armed forces and has thus chosen to reduce its military manpower by one million. Although numerous variables comprise this decision, the conclusion is clear to the Chinese leadership: if China is to succeed in its economic, technological and scientific modernizations, it must avoid a military competition that would drain its resources. Thus China has a strong incentive to establish or maintain good relations with as many nations as possible.

Although China would rather not be forced into a military competition, it will act within its means to maintain at least a semblance of military sufficiency. In the nuclear weapons area, one can imagine that China has a mandate to be able to destroy a certain number and type of Soviet targets while assuring that some portion of its own nuclear forces would survive a surprise attack. If, in the course of superpower strategic defence developments, the USSR deploys BMD forces that would prevent China from meeting its nuclear mandate, then China could pursue several alternative military programmes: MIRVing its ballistic missile forces and developing improved penetration aids for such missiles; developing a modern nuclear bomber force to get past Soviet air defences; or developing nuclear cruise missiles for attacking relatively large, unprotected targets.

Each of these options would have different characteristics, but would likely be evaluated by the Chinese leadership using similar criteria: effectiveness; expense; technological feasibility; and so on. Some general considerations follow for each option.

- Ballistic missile modernization is probably the least expensive option since China already has the missiles and experience at hand. It would cost less to add warheads to the missile force than to the other two options. Although only ballistic missiles could have the range to strike Moscow, such missiles might not be considered effective against a major Soviet BMD system, especially one with the ability to intercept missiles in early flight. China already has considerable experience with ballistic missile technology and appears to have tested some MIRV or MRV applications.

• Building a fleet of new supersonic bombers would be quite expensive, but perhaps considered necessary in a variety of situations. Chinese officials have claimed that a new bomber is being designed to replace China's ageing fleet of obsolescent aircraft. A new bomber could, among other things, be designed to accomplish naval missions, particularly against ships. China has the personnel, air bases, infrastructure and operational experience to operate a fleet of new bombers, which may be more effective against BMD systems than ballistic missiles would be.

• Although China has relatively little experience with modern cruise missiles, it is not unreasonable to believe that it might decide to develop them as a counter to any eventual Soviet BMD system. China has deployed a coastal anti-ship cruise missile system and is reportedly testing a new sea-launched model. The technology for such missiles seems within China's grasp, especially as it imports modern electronics from the West. China would not need to duplicate the sophisticated guidance and terrain recognition technology of US cruise missiles in order to counter adversary BMD technology. Cruise missiles would be less expensive to build than bombers and would not involve the same effort or risk as with aircraft pilots. Cruise missiles designed to strike large and undefended targets might be able to reach their targets better than either ballistic missiles or manned bombers. China could probably muster the scientific and technical forces to develop a cruise missile within a decade if determined to do so.

At a minimum, China will probably keep open the option to pursue some future nuclear weapon technologies. This would result in some level of nuclear weapon R&D, but not necessarily a larger programme. It is doubtful that China could or would want to deploy more than one of these options unless political and military relations between it and the USSR worsen considerably. Current Chinese efforts with its nuclear submarine force will continue well into the 1990s. In the coming decade, China will have the time to observe the course of events between the United States and the Soviet Union, especially concerning arms control and strategic defence programmes. If arms control efforts succeed in diminishing Soviet nuclear capabilities in Asia, particularly SS–20s, it would help China to normalize relations with the USSR. If both superpowers proceed to deploy strategic defences, it will complicate the prospects for stable and peaceful relations in the region.

V.   Conclusion: arms control possibilities

It appears that China is putting its nuclear eggs in the submarine basket and not continuing to increase the numbers of deployed CSS–3 or CSS–4 missiles. If this is the case, it is concentrating on the survivability of its strategic nuclear forces, which may be both cheaper and more suitable to its retaliatory posture than trying to improve the accuracy or number of land-based missiles. If the Soviet Union pursues some widespread BMD programme, it will cause China to review its nuclear forces and consider whether fundamental changes are necessary. China has already denounced the US Strategic Defense Initiative, claiming that it will upset the 'balance' between the two nuclear superpowers and thus provoke a new and dangerous round of the arms race.[43] China is the one country that will most acutely see any such defensive system as undermining its own nuclear forces and 'credibility'.

China may soon see an advantage in pushing both superpowers on arms control, especially on measures to prevent them from proceeding with BMD systems and to reduce or eliminate intermediate-range missiles. Its first disarmament-related draft resolution to the United Nations called for peaceful space research and for the prevention of an 'arms race in outer space'.[44] Now that both the USA and the USSR are discussing such issues and have both proposed large cuts (one-half) in their own nuclear forces, China could logically become more actively involved in the arms control debate and process.

Chinese arms control policy has consistently been professed to pursue 'genuine disarmament'. China's disarmament ambassador to the UN stated in 1984:

China's position with regard to nuclear disarmament and the prevention of nuclear war is well known. We have always stood for the complete prohibition and the thorough destruction of all nuclear weapons and take this to be the fundamental way to prevent a nuclear war. We have proposed that the superpowers possessing the largest nuclear arsenals take the lead in halting the testing, refinement and production of nuclear weapons and reach an agreement on reducing by half their existing nuclear weapons and means of delivery of all types; and that thereafter a widely representative international conference be convened with the participation of all nuclear-weapon states to negotiate the general reduction of nuclear weapons by all nuclear-weapon states.[45]

If this is a sincere policy, then the time may be right for multilateral co-operation on nuclear arms reductions by all five nuclear weapon nations, the most logical approach to a regime of comprehensive arms control and disarmament. China is already involved in the US–Soviet arms control process. The USA routinely sends an envoy to Beijing to brief Chinese officials on a negotiating position or proposal before it is tabled in Geneva. Kenneth Adelman, the Director of the US Arms Control and Disarmament Agency, told reporters that 'we take Chinese views into consideration when formulating our posture with the Soviet Union . . .'.[46]

China is considered by many to have limited nuclear ambitions. However, the pattern of nuclear weapon deployments, developments and policy statements suggests that it may fall into the same pattern as the other four nuclear weapon nations: perpetually 'modernizing' their nuclear forces to overcome perceived deficiencies. If such a situation prevails, China will find it difficult to establish a final point for some putative minimum deterrent. Instead, it may feel the need to improve continually its nuclear forces and demonstrate that they are sufficient to prevent any Soviet attack, or to retaliate in the event of an attack. If the superpowers choose to develop or deploy some form of widespread strategic defence system, it would further encourage China to increase its nuclear forces in a effort to ensure continued nuclear 'sufficiency'. The result of this process would do nothing to improve arms control and war prevention efforts in the region.

Notes and references

[1] James A. Kelly, Statement before the House Foreign Affairs Subcommittee on East Asian and Pacific Affairs, 5 June 1984.

[2] See Haldeman, H. R., *The Ends of Power* (Times Books: New York, 1978), pp. 88–93. See also McNulty, A. L., 'The Sino–Soviet border problems of 1969', *Parameters, Journal of the US Army War College*, vol. 13, no. 3, pp. 59–67.

[3] Kelly (note 1).

[4] Kelly (note 1). See also 'China makes issue of Soviet missiles', *New York Times*, 7 Oct. 1983, p. 3.

[5] Statement of Wallace G. Magathan, Jr, DIA, on the 'Soviet role in Asia' before the Subcommittee on Europe and the Middle East and the Subcommittee on Asian and Pacific Affairs of the House Foreign Affairs Committee, US Congress, July 1982 (partially declassified).

[6] Reported in Weisskopf, M. 'China's defense chief calls for emphasis on nuclear weapons', *Washington Post*, 4 Mar. 1983, p. A–17; 'Going nuclear', *The Economist*, vol. 286, no. 7280 (12 Mar. 1983), pp. 46–7.

[7] The US Central Intelligence Agency has estimated that China spent 50 per cent of its military research and development funds on nuclear weapon programmes from 1965 to 1979. See Sutter, R., 'Chinese nuclear weapons and American interests', *Congressional Research Service (CRS)*, Report No. 83–187F, US Library of Congress: Washington, DC, 27 Sep. 1983, p. 12.

[8] See Mainan, K., 'Deng Jiaxian: China's father of the A-Bomb,' *Beijing Review*, vol. 29, no. 32 (11 Aug. 1986), p. 21.

[9] Nie Rongzhen, 'How China develops its nuclear weapons', (excerpts from his memoirs) *Beijing Review*, vol. 28, no. 17 (29 Apr. 1985), p. 17. Nie reported that Sino–Soviet relations were already so bad in July 1960 that he wrote a report to the Central Committee suggesting that China take a more independent and self-reliant stand. By August, all Soviet 'technical experts' had left China, thus forcing the independent Chinese research programme. Nie considered the withdrawal 'a turning point in the history of our scientific research', for which Mao Zedong commented 'Khrushchev should be awarded a one-ton medal'.

[10] Radio broadcast by Li Wen, of the Ministry of Nuclear Industry, 15 Oct. 1984, documented in Joint Publications Research Service (hereinafter referred to as JPRS)

Worldwide Report: Nuclear Development and Proliferation, JPRS–TND–84–029, US Department of Commerce, National Technical Information Service, Washington DC, 27 Nov. 1984, p. 2.

[11] See Mainan (note 8), p. 22. In 1977, the Joint Chiefs of Staff reported that China had 'recently conducted a 4-megaton test, their largest to date'. Organization of the Joint Chiefs of Staff, United States Military Posture for FY 1978 (US Government Printing Office: Washington, DC, 1977) (hereinafter referred to as JCS, FY 1978), p. 31.

[12] This fact shows that a nuclear weapon stockpile can be developed with a relatively small number of nuclear tests, contrary to many claims.

[13] Some commentators have suggested that China's successful deployment in 1982 of three separate satellites from a single booster demonstrates the ability to master MIRV technology. While the two technologies are quite similar, they require different levels of technology and testing and thus one should not infer too much from the satellite success. There is some evidence that, for the first time in 1986, China has tested MIRV technology as such on an ICBM launcher, an absolute requirement before deploying a MIRV system. For a good discussion of MIRV technology and development, See York, H., *The Origins of MIRV*, SIPRI Research Report no. 9 (SIPRI: Stockholm, Aug. 1983).

[14] See 'Chinese flight test new missile version', *Aviation Week & Space Technology*, vol. 124, no. 26 (30 June 1986), p. 16; and *China Daily*, 28 Jan. 1986 (translated article in *IDSA News Review on China, Mongolia, the Koreas*, vol. 18, no. 2, Institute for Defense and Strategic Analysis (IDSA), New Delhi, India (Feb. 1986), p. 77.

[15] US Congress, Joint Economic Committee (JEC), Hearings on the *Allocation of Resources in the Soviet Union and China* 1981, Part 7 (US Government Printing Office: Washington, DC, 1981) (hereinafter referred to as JEC, ARSUC, 1981, Part 7), p. 156.

[16] At least 7 of China's 32 nuclear tests have resulted in yields below 20 kt. See 'China shows it has tactical atomic weapon', *Washington Times*, 14 July 1982, p. 5.

[17] US Defense Intelligence Agency (DIA), *Handbook on the Chinese Armed Forces*, Report No. DDI–2682–32–76 (US Government Printing Office: Washington, DC, 1976), pp. 3–15.

[18] JEC, ARSUC, 1976, Part 2 (note 15), pp. 95–6; DIA, 'A guide to tactical nuclear weapon systems under the control of ground force commanders', Report No. DST–1040S–541–83–CHG 1, 17 Aug. 1984 (secret, partially declassified), p. 79.

[19] US Department of Defense, *Annual Report to the Congress FY 1982* (hereinafter referred to as DoD, FY 1982) (US Government Printing Office: Washington, DC, 1981), p. 48).

[20] JCS, FY 1978 (see note 11), p. 31.

[21] DoD, FY 1982 (see note 19), p. 48.

[22] DIA (note 17), p. 8–2.

[23] JCS, FY 1983 (see note 11), p. 117.

[24] JCS, FY 1978 (see note 11), p. 31.

[25] DoD, FY 1982 (see note 19), p. 48.

[26] JEC, ARSUC 1976, Part 2 (see note 15), p. 94.

[27] DIA (see note 22).

[28] Sutter (note 7), p. 19.

[29] It should be noted that while the Moscow ABM system is believed by most analysts to be capable of preventing China from successfully attacking Moscow with its current ICBMs, Chinese officials do not share this belief. For a more comprehensive

discussion of Sino-Soviet military and political relations, see Jacobsen, C. G., *Sino-Soviet Relations Since Mao* (Praeger Publishers: New York, 1981).

30 DIA, 'Chinese ballistic missile systems: trends and projections', Report No. DST–1000S–226–84 (secret, partially declassified), 17 Feb. 1984, p. 47.

31 JCS, FY 1982, p. 109 (see note 11); Gelber, H., *Nuclear Weapons and Chinese Policy*, Adelphi Paper no. 99, International Institute for Strategic Studies: London, 1973, pp. 36–7. Information is available for only the first 15 tests, so bombers could have been used for many of the following atmospheric tests.

32 JCS, FY 1978 (see note 11), p. 32.

33 JCS, FY 1980 (see note 11), p. 60; JCS, FY 1982 (see note 11), p. 109.

34 JCS, FY 1978 (see note 11), p. 86.

35 JCS, FY 1978 (see note 11), p. 32.

36 JCS, FY 1980 (see note 11), p. 60.

37 Covault, C. 'Chinese design supersonic bomber, plan joint efforts to build momentum', *Aviation Week & Space Technology*, vol. 123, no. 2 (15 July 1985); pp. 61–6.

38 JEC, ARSUC, 1982, Part 8 (see note 15), p. 111.

39 It was widely reported that China's first ocean test-launch of the CSS–NX–3 missile resulted in the destruction of the launching submarine. These reports were false and may have been politically motivated.

40 Jacobs, G. 'China's submarine force', *Jane's Defence Weekly*, vol. 3, no. 6 (9 Feb. 1985), p. 224.

41 See Wang, R. S., 'China's evolving strategic doctrine', *Asian Survey*, vol. 24, Oct. 1984, pp. 1040–55; see DIA (note 22).

42 'China shows it has tactical atomic weapon', *Washington Times*, 14 July 1982, p. 5.

43 See Zhuang Qubing, 'United States prepares for "Star Wars"', *Beijing Review*, vol. 27, no. 45 (5 Nov. 1984), also excerpted as 'Space and strategic defence: a Chinese view', in *Survival*, vol. 27, no. 1 (Jan.–Feb. 1985), pp. 35–8.

44 *China Daily*, 28 Oct. 1984, translated in *IDSA News Review on China, Mongolia, the Koreas*, vol. 16, no. 11, Institute for Defense and Strategic Analysis (IDSA), New Delhi, India (Nov. 1984), p. 315.

45 Hong Kong Standard, 11 May 1984, translated in *IDSA News Review on China, Mongolia, the Koreas*, vol. 16, no. 6, Institute for Defense and Strategic Analysis (IDSA), New Delhi, India (June 1984), p. 130.

46 United States Information Service, 'Wireless file', US Embassy, Stockholm, 8 Aug. 1986, p. 4.

Paper 3.3.   Strategy, security and advanced computing

ALLAN M. DIN

I. Introduction

The new military technology of the 1980s has catalysed the process of the restructuring of strategic thinking and of modifying the texture of international security in many ways, a trend which is likely to accelerate in the future as novel technical developments take the shape of weapon deployments. A common characteristic for most of this technology is to increase the demand for rapid and precise weapon engagement in a complex command and control environment. Precisely this feature poses fundamental problems in terms of human decision-making and intervention in present and future occurrences of international crisis and military confrontation.

The debate around the problems of the US Strategic Defense Initiative (SDI) has focused attention on a wide spectrum of weapon technologies, for example, regarding lasers, microwaves, particle beams and electromagnetic railguns, as well as on the technical challenge to the battle management structure which is supposed to make the strategic defence system work. Underlying the SDI debate is the complicated question of whether nuclear weapons can be made impotent and/or obsolete, that is, whether, besides the current nuclear deterrence doctrines, there are alternative approaches to assuring international security. The question may also be formulated differently: can strategic defence enhance security?

Some of the technologies which are being considered in the ballistic missile defence (BMD) context are already in the process of being introduced in theatre and tactical warfare arenas, in particular on the European scene; this is true both in terms of, for example, 'smart' weapons as well as of command and control stuctures. The North Atlantic Treaty Organization (NATO) doctrines like AirLand Battle and FOFA (Follow-On-Forces-Attack) rely heavily on the introduction of new technologies which are adapted to a more and more automated battlefield. As with strategic defence, a very relevant question is whether such developments really enhance the security of either of the opposing military blocs.

A common, fundamental feature in the above developments, be they on a global strategic or regional level, is the human element in the decision-making process. The weapon technologies that are now being or might be introduced in the not-too-distant future are such that little time is left for human intervention during actual weapon engagement, and this fact directly promotes the quest for automation of global and regional battlefields. As a consequence, computers must take over crucial command and control functions. Computer programming of inherently unknowable future contingencies, well in advance of any actual outbreak of hostilities, may dictate the outbreak and course of wars.

It might thus be appropriate to extend discussions of C^3 (the military jargon for command, control and communications) to C^4 when adding the computer dimension. In fact, this dimension seems to be included in somewhat different ways in Western and Eastern perspectives: in the United States, computerization in relation to data transfer and secure transmissions is considered an extension of the C for 'communications', whereas in the Soviet Union, all the Cs appear under the single heading of 'control' which, in fact, logically appears to be the real issue.

H.   The military impact of computers

The military use of computers started early in the computer age. One of the first major applications of number-crunching power was in the US development of the H-bomb design in the beginning of the 1950s; this military interest became manifest in a number of other areas and was indirectly responsible for the fast pace of the evolution of computer technology which has persisted to the present time.

The first computer generation, based on bulky vacuum tubes, developed into a second generation of more moderate physical dimension after the invention of the transistor, and then further miniaturization began with the introduction of integrated circuitry. Today, we are in the middle of the fourth computer generation characterized by much developmental work on very large-scale integration (VLSI) and very high-speed integrated circuits (VHSICs).

The consequences of these developments are already apparent on both civilian and military levels. Firstly, the miniaturization has produced a number of 'smart' weapons where microprocessors and sensors are packed into a very small volume; examples include precision-guided munitions and cruise missiles. Secondly, there is large-scale use of high-performance computers in command, control and communication posts, fixed and mobile, strategic and theatre level; and as a result, war-fighting capabilities have become vastly enhanced.

But very sophisticated technology often has a tendency to be fragile. Therefore great efforts are currently being made to improve the resistance of the computer hardware to the adverse physical effects of a hostile military environment, including, for example, the electromagnetic pulse (EMP) generated by nuclear explosions and beam weapons. Radiation hardening against such effects as EMP is now a routine element in the development of nuclear weapon systems and satellites, and various new technologies are being exploited for this purpose. Thus, for example, work is proceeding on gallium arsenide (GaAs) chips to replace the traditional silicon chips both because of

GaAs's resistance to radiation and because of its superior speed; the widespead use of optical fibres and storage media may be seen as a part of this effort.

The Soviet and US appreciations of the vulnerabilities of military systems based on advanced technology may be somewhat different, but currently they seem to be converging. On the Soviet side, the level of technological sophistication has been less manifest, which, by some observers, has been taken as a sign of a voluntary development line of robust systems; the truth is probably that sophistication is seen as a necessary development which will be implemented as soon as the technological capabilities exist, but with due regard to inherent vulnerabilities. The US approach, in particular concerning space-based systems, has been one of large-scale exploitation of the most advanced electronics but with less regard to security and robustness. However, these problems are now being addressed under the current C^3 modernization programmes.

The most important computer developments for military purposes, however, are not in the area of hardware, but software, which is the code allowing the system to perform specific tasks. Computer software is presently transforming the traditional algorithmic framework appropriate for number-crunching problems in novel directions; in fact, the military use of computers is moving towards a phase where the weapons are supposed to be not only 'smart' but also 'intelligent'. As shown by work on fifth generation computers (for example, the Japanese 'Apollo' project directed towards large-scale commercial applications), the introduction of 'intelligent' machines calls for the use of special high-level programming languages like LISP (list-processing) and PROLOG (programming in logic) as the basis for a human-like reasoning power.

The once exotic subject of artificial intelligence (AI) is thus coming back into the limelight after lying dormant for a number of years. In contrast to the high-ambition level of the 1950s and 1960s, modern AI is not attempting to develop a general theoretical framework with the abstract goal of making machines the equals of humans in terms of reasoning and intelligence. Rather, the ambition is now limited to making computers respond and act in a human-like way to complicated outside information in areas where the demands on information processing, speed and effectiveness transcend solely human capacities.

This, in particular, is the goal of expert systems which use AI techniques in combination with a rule and knowledge base relevant to the particular problem at hand. The rules and the knowledge are supposed to be extracted from human experts by so-called knowledge engineers and subsequently be translated by an inference engine into concrete answers and analysis in response to incoming data and associated queries. An expert system can thus be seen as an aid to humans in situations where decisions and actions must be executed promptly in a complicated environment which would normally require the involvement of one or several experts to make a proper assessment.

Since the military environment is mostly characterized by a certain time-urgency, expert systems would here be asked to take over a number of pressing tasks, for example assessment and action, which a single human operator cannot possibly manage in a short time. This does not necessarily imply a full automation of the battlefield because the human operator is still supposed to decide and act on some of the most essential points; but, once expert systems are implemented, there is nothing that in principle prevents 'intelligent' machines from taking over completely.

In 1983 the US Defense Advanced Research Projects Agency (DARPA) initiated a strategic computing programme which is supposed to incorporate AI techniques in a number of specific weapon systems. The programme involves developing a pilot's associate expert system which would help process large amounts of sensor data and make recommendations or decisions concerning flight and fire control. Contracts for this project have recently been awarded. They include, for example, an autonomous vehicle project supposed to be a demonstration platform for vision and image-processing technology.

More significantly, the DARPA programme is moving into the problem area of battle management. A battle management system for a naval carrier force has been on the agenda since the start of the programme; it includes, for example, the Force Requirements Expert System, and recently it was approved that a corresponding system, called FORCES/STAR should be developed for AirLand Battle management. Associated with these efforts, there is also the major work being put into battle management within the SDI programme.

In summary, military computing efforts are moving in two main directions: (a) a more traditional development line of very powerful computers, including supercomputers, for number-crunching and mass-data-handling purposes; by the very nature of such machines and their support environment, their main use is in centralized military systems; and (b) a new line of distributed, semi-autonomous computer systems that will rely heavily on the use of AI techniques. The latter line of development is considered by military planners as essential for implementing C^3 and battle management systems, in particular space-based ones, which may live up to the security demands of changes in strategy and tactics. The applications of AI techniques are admittedly still on a rather immature level, but, with the efforts currently being put in, they are bound to develop quickly in performance.

III.   Theatre and tactical warfare

The introduction of advanced computer technology in a military environment is part of a traditional modernization effort, but it may also be seen as an essential element of new strategic concepts. On the NATO side, the implementation of AirLand Battle and FOFA concepts are part of this trend. As noted above, in the Western perspective computing is most often seen in conjunction with developments in the communication aspects of C^3.

Among the relevant tactical programmes, one may mention the joint surveillance and target attack system (JSTARS) which involves an airborne radar, on board a Boeing C–18 aircraft with processing and communication equipment, looking deep into enemy territory. There is the mobile subscriber equipment (MSE) which is bringing digital technology to the battlefield in providing for secure voice, data and facsimile communications. A further programme is the joint tactical information system (JTIDS) designed to provide jam-resistant data distribution by using spread-spectrum modulation, and also the joint tactical fusion programme (JFT) which is developing a transportable, semi-automatic battlefield intelligence fusion system giving battle managers access to almost instant situation assessments on which to base decisions.

While the Western high-technology approach to C^4 problems basically emanates from underlying strategic concepts, the relationship between the two is not always very explicit. On the contrary, the Soviet approach to theatre and tactical warfare appears as a tightly knit structure which, at least theoretically, envisions the use of the most advanced technical methods even though, practically, the relevant hardware is lagging behind.

The Soviet view on C^4, as implied earlier, emphasizes 'control (*upravleniya*) which in contrast to the Western command and control terminology has an absolute and centralized connotation. Using the World War II experience, the Soviet theatre level control focuses on mission accomplishment of combined or coalitional forces and in so doing develops elaborate automatic systems for troop and weapon management using available, medium-level technology.

An interesting account on new concepts related to theatre and tactical warfare appeared in a book by General V. V. Druzinin and D. S. Kontorov.[1] The book explored the problem of bringing computer technology into the military staff process and was written for 'commanders, operators and engineers desiring to complete and deepen their knowledge in the area of means of automation for the preparation of decisions'. In a pioneering manner, the authors set out to explore the man-machine interface in order to optimize decision-making in a military environment characterized by short reaction times.

In 1976 Druzinin and Kontorov published another book which evokes the need for adapting the art of leadership to the demands of the latest developments in military science and technology.[2] Along with their first book, it may be seen as an exemplification of the Soviet cybernetics tradition, which emphasizes the inter-relationship between relevant natural and social sciences and, in so doing, it tries to present a global assessment of the problem. Their idea was, that injecting cybernetics and computing into the control process would relieve the commander of uncreative work and speed up decision-making. Even if the principles for the automated battlefield were formulated early, they have probably not been implemented in the Warsaw Pact to a very significant degree because the relevant computer hardware was lacking.

The Soviet Armed Forces are divided into five services: strategic rocket forces; ground forces; air forces; air defence forces; and navy. For operational purposes, however, these are grouped into two units: strategic nuclear forces and the forces of the theatres of strategic-military operations (the *Teatr Voennij Djejstvije* or TVD). The theoretical framework for automated control developed by various Soviet authors appears to be directed particularly towards the TVD. While the quest for automation of warfare has been expressed theoretically and practically to varying degrees in NATO and the Warsaw Pact, comparatively little effort seems to have been put into the analysis of inherent dangers and instabilities of this phenomenon.

IV.   Strategic defence

SDI was initially launched as part of President Reagan's stated goal to eliminate nuclear weapons, though early component programmes appeared instead to have the effect of further reinforcing nuclear deterrence's central dictum of Mutual Assured Destruction (MAD). Currently dominant nuclear doctrines consider it imperative to have ready a number of nuclear-strike options which must all remain intact even in the event of a hostile first-strike. At the time of the 1972 ABM Treaty, the idea of developing strategic defence to protect such options in the face of large opposing offensive nuclear forces looked futile, and unnecessary. But in the view of some analysts, the technology of the 1980s warrants a change in this conclusion.

SDI research has focused mainly on the particular weapon technologies that are supposed to constitute a future SDI defence, but lately interest has concentrated more on the problem of the so-called system architecture. This somewhat furtive term encompasses a whole range of logistic problems that must be faced and solved before the value and efficiency of any type of strategic defence system can be assessed. In military terms, one is addressing the issue by investigating the requirements for the battle management (BM) and C^3 that must be developed to make the weapon platforms of the various defence layers work together in a co-ordinated manner.

A large variety of sensors on satellites together constitute an essential element in BM/C^3; they are, for example, supposed to give warning about impending attack, to locate targets and to give damage assessment. The sensors will provide the information necessary for the action of the weapons that must perform on very short notice. The fragile sensor satellites must be considered to be prime targets in a future superpower conflict, and one therefore has to face the risk of losing essential space assets at an early stage. Without those assets, one would be left with the disturbing alternative of using the weapon platforms without full control.

The whole sequence of strategic defence operations, from the very first threat assessment to the final kill assessment, is by and large going to be under automated control. This is where the real problem of system architecture and underlying computing power enters into the considerations. No traditional algorithmic approach could possibly work in the face of so many likely and unlikely contingencies associated with nuclear war. One is therefore forced to admit the use of computer programming which makes the machines of the strategic defence system act speedily and in an 'intelligent' way at the many decision points where human intervention is unfeasible.

Thus, any strategic defence system is going to depend heavily on the use of AI techniques in general and expert systems in particular. The programming of the 'intelligent' machines that will have to be done in advance of actual deployments is bound to require a set of computer instructions running into tens of millions of lines. The requirement on the computer code of the anti-ballistic-missile (ABM) defences considered in the 1960s was probably around one million lines, but even if computer technology and techniques have developed considerably since then, it is reasonable to suppose that this requirement must be more than tenfold bigger for SDI in view of its much more comprehensive character.

Software reliability is a major problem in most areas where the computer revolution has made headway, and it is a problem which is not likely to go away easily. So-called bugs always seem to creep up when running computer programs and most often they can only be eliminated as they appear; since it is humans that are devising the computer instructions, it is improbable that a fault-free computer code applying to even a reasonably complicated problem will ever be realized. In general though, this is not of any serious consequence because there is time for a human operator to intervene and correct the problem, either stopping program execution or restarting.

However, the situation is quite different when the computer is involved in time-urgent operations which leave no possibility for human intervention. Very little is needed for things to go wrong. For example, there once was a serious malfunction in a planetary space probe because a full stop (American 'period') got mixed up with a comma in a FORTRAN program! The computer bugs expected with a strategic defence system could have very serious conse-quences indeed, and there is no obvious way to get rid of them because of the lack of possibility for testing the system under realistic circumstances.

The possible use within SDI of advanced computing in general, and AI techniques in particular, thus illustrates very well the basic problem: computers 'think' fast and are therefore in principle eminently suitable to taking over for humans in time-urgent situations; however, if the situation is so time-urgent that the humans are completely excluded from the decision-making, an uncomfortable feeling of lack of control imposes itself. The fundamental lesson to learn for military planners is to avoid the development of military systems which may lead to time-urgent situations with global ramifications!

VI. Security perspectives

The military use of more and more sophisticated technologies, in particular advanced computer techniques, is part of a general trend around the world towards nuclear and conventional force modernizations. As such, much thought is not necessarily given to the question of whether all this will actually provide the buyers of the relevant equipment with an enhanced security.

However, the vision of automatic battlefields, which may become a reality in the not-so-distant future, eventually as part of new strategic notions, ought to give rise to a number of serious concerns about its possible dangerous effects on international security in general and crisis stability in particular.

As noted in the previous sections, the danger has its origin in the reliance on technology and computer techniques which under certain circumstances may turn out to behave in unanticipated ways. The consequences of technical shortcomings may of course be of differing character, depending on the military level of conflict. On a tactical level, for example, there is the possibility that the sensors on board a plane may register a threat which is processed by the preprogrammed computer as sufficiently time-urgent to require an automatic countermeasure, thus bypassing human fire-control. If this response, following a subsequent assessment, turns out to be out of proportion to the original threat, it may already be too late to prevent a counter-countermeasure being initiated.

War-by-accident on a tactical level, or on a theatre level under a severe crisis situation, is a possibility that has to be taken seriously into account. Once hostilities have started, a further question is what kind of escalation control would be effective. On a strategic level, there are of course many safety mechanisms, but the risk of war-by-accident is already non-negligible, as indicated by the false alarms of early warning radars that have occurred.

The dangers associated with the automation and heavy use of computers inherent in strategic defence systems, as envisaged within the SDI, must be evaluated according to a somewhat different scale of judgement. Ostensibly, the intention is to reinforce the present level of security, be it in terms of enhancing nuclear deterrence or, if possible, to substitute a defence-dominated world for today's offence-dominated reality. But, one may reasonably require that it is made probable that the different security indicators, for example, arms race stability and crisis stability, should move towards confidence enhancement as a consequence of chosen system development and deployment.

If the intention of computerization and automation is to enhance nuclear deterrence, the balance sheet does not appear to favour or to foreshadow a higher degree of confidence. In fact, the new technologies may prove simply to be yet another dimension of the arms race, in which case their fragility and hair-trigger readiness can only contribute to diminishing crisis stability. The fundamental question is really whether it is possible to rely on nuclear deterrence doctrines in situations where the decision-making time for reactions to perceived threats is of the order of seconds instead of, as is presently the case, of the order of minutes.

If, however, strategic defence with its use of advanced technologies could lead to a world dominated by purely defensive technologies (if such can be conceived), then there are interesting, but also potentially dangerous, perspectives for security and stability. The issue of how nuclear deterrence could be phased out in an offence–defence transition is apt to be difficult to approach through purely quantitative security measures. Qualitatively, both the superpowers have expressed a desire for such a development, and if this desire was genuine, then it would only remain for the two parties to define the quantitative rules of the transition period. Most probably, nuclear weapons cannot be eliminated altogether; it is too easy to conceal small numbers of nuclear weapons and too easy to develop them clandestinely. Yet, the existence of this contingency is precisely one of the best arguments in favour of a defence-dominated world, consisting of specially adapted defensive buffers based on advanced technologies and combined with sophisticated technical methods for arms control and verification, where the purpose is both to satisfy genuine national security demands and to assure international security.

It must be strongly emphasized, however, that to realize a transition to a defence-dominated world would require profound changes in mind-sets and the *advance* accommodation and agreement of the superpowers concerning their mid- to long-term strategic relationship. Transition to a defence-dominated world presupposes a degree of concord that today does not exist.

Notes and references

[1] Druzhinin, General V. V. and Kontorov, D. S., *Concept, Algorithm, Decision (A Soviet View)*, original Russian edition published by the Military Publishing House of the Ministry of Defense of the USSR (*Voenizdat*: Moscow, 1972). Translated and published under the auspices of the US Air Force (US Government Printing Office: Washington, DC, 1976).
[2] Druzhinin, General V. V. and Kontorov, D. S., *Problems of Military Systems Engineering* (*Voenizdat*: Moscow, 1976).

Paper 3.4.   Emerging technology, exotic technology and arms control

PHIL WILLIAMS

I.   Introduction

The characterization of the arms race as a dinghy race in which the superpowers, especially the United States, keep moving the buoys highlights graphically, if rather crudely, the way in which technological developments impinge on the process. Although the competition between the superpowers is quantitative as well as qualitative, the dynamic of this competition has in recent years been shaped by technological innovation as well as political and strategic considerations. Furthermore, this innovation process has proved immensely difficult to manage and has made arms control a more difficult and problematic enterprise. It has been argued recently by Thomas Schelling that the failure of arms control in the 1970s was first and foremost a conceptual failure—instead of treating arms control as a means of shoring up strategic stability, the Soviet Union and the United States simply regarded it as a way of ratifying numerical parity.[1] While there is much to this thesis, it should not be exaggerated. The major problem of the 1970s, and one which, for reasons which are understandable, was not addressed early enough or explicitly enough in the Strategic Arms Limitation Talks (SALT) negotiations, was technological innovation—especially the development and deployment of multiple independently targetable reentry vehicles (MIRVs). Indeed, MIRV proved a short-lived advantage for the United States but contributed to the long-term problem of land-based missile vulnerability. In many ways the history of MIRVs provides what may well be a taste of things to come, as unrestrained technological developments make deterrence less stable. The paradox is that such developments underline the importance of arms control while simultaneously making arms control much more difficult to achieve.

This is not to imply that technology is invariably malevolent or destabilizing in its impact. The technologies which made possible 'national means of verification', for example, were crucial to the SALT process. Even more important, the technologies which resulted in the ability to disperse strategic forces in submarines and to provide a degree of protection in hardened silos did more than any arms control agreement to produce a high degree of strategic stability in the 1960s and early 1970s. Furthermore, the trend towards mobile intercontinental ballistic missiles (ICBMs), which is becoming evident in both the United States and the Soviet Union, may help to lessen—even though it is unlikely to eliminate—the concerns over the vulnerability of the land-based component of strategic forces. Although such examples are familiar, they nevertheless make clear that technology can be stabilizing as well as destabilizing, and that technological advancement can ease as well as exacerbate the superpower relationship. They also caution against a 'strategic Ludditism' which sees technology as an unmitigated evil.

If some of the trends which are currently discernible promise to improve strategic stability, however, other developments may work in the opposite direction. Indeed, the whole strategic environment of the late 1990s and the early part of the twenty-first century could be much more volatile and dangerous than it is at present. There are several elements in what might prove to be a long-term deterioration in the strategic environment. These include nuclear proliferation, the spread of more sophisticated conventional weapons to Third World states, and the increasing prevalence of regional conflicts and instabilities. At the superpower level, the development and deployment of both emerging and exotic technologies could pose a new, unprecedented and intractable set of problems.

Although emerging and exotic technologies are very different—with the former usually referring to smart conventional systems, often associated with the concept of deep attack in the context of a North Atlantic Treaty Organization (NATO)–Warsaw Pact conflict in Europe, and the latter used to cover systems that are related primarily to defence against ballistic missiles—it is contended here that in some respects at least they pose similar problems for arms control and conflict management. Furthermore, it is necessary to set them within the broad context of technological change and development. With this in mind this paper is divided into several parts. Section II identifies what appear to be some of the main trends in military technology—at least as they appear to the non-technical observer. Section III, while acknowledging the difficulties inherent in assessing the implications of new technology, examines the implications of these developments for the strategic environment of the 1990s and beyond. Section IV considers those factors which drive the qualitative arms race—as an understanding of the sources of technological momentum is crucial to any attempt to manage the innovation process. Section V considers ways in which technology might be constrained or channelled by arms control and attempts to assess the feasibility of an arms control regime in the 1990s and beyond which would deal effectively with both emerging and exotic technologies.

II.   Major trends in technological development

One of the problems with any discussion of technology concerns the number of definitions that are available. For present purposes, however, technology is perhaps best understood as the final product of scientific and engineering research and development.[2] Seen in this way it clearly encompasses not simply weapons but also the capabilities for command, control and communication, which have a crucial role in battle management whether it be at the level of conventional, nuclear or space warfare. Within this broad concept of technology, it is possible to discern several distinct trends, which seem likely to have a profound, if incalculable, impact upon both the battlefields of the future and the deterrent postures of the superpowers. The problem, of course, is that different developments work in different, and in some instances potentially contradictory, ways. Nevertheless, any attempt to assess the strategic environment of the 1990s must take account of the following trends in technology:

1. *Increasing miniaturization.* Weapons are becoming smaller and more mobile. At the strategic level this may offer a reprieve to land-based strategic retaliatory forces, although because of the problems posed for verification by increasing reliance on mobile ICBMs, it may hinder the cause of negotiated arms control. Furthermore, even in terms of deterrence, greater mobility does not seem likely to provide a complete answer to the vulnerability problem. This is partly because even mobile missiles might be vulnerable to certain kinds of barrage attack. It also reflects the continued improvements in accuracy, which mean that the gap between target acquisition and target destruction is getting smaller.

2. *Improved accuracy.* Advances in the techniques of target acquisition, precision guidance and discrimination have increased the potential lethality of weapons at much greater distances than in the past. This, in turn, offers opportunities to reduce yield and thereby minimize collateral damage. It also seems likely to provide some opportunities to substitute conventional for nuclear systems. This is particularly important for the Western Alliance and has led to a belief that emerging non-nuclear systems provide relatively safe options which could be integrated into the NATO force posture in ways which reduce dependence on nuclear weapons and provide greater opportunities for escalation control. In addition, there is growing interest in the development of non-nuclear strategic weapons, capable of travelling intercontinental distances and striking targets with what a recent RAND Corporation analysis described as 'surgical precision'.[3] Such a development would make it possible to implement roles and missions, which have hitherto required nuclear weapons, with advanced conventional systems. This leads on to another trend which seems likely to be increasingly evident during the 1990s.

3. *A move towards greater fungibility.* One important development that has been discussed most explicitly in relation to cruise missiles is the ability of particular weapon systems to fulfil several different roles and missions. Cruise missiles can be used on a variety of launchers and for purposes which may be tactical or strategic, and which may require conventional or nuclear warheads. This increased versatility is a considerable asset in military planning, although it poses immense problems of discrimination and makes efforts at regulation immeasurably more difficult. It seems likely that as accuracies improve and conventional munitions become more sophisticated, the same kinds of development will occur with ballistic missiles. There could well be an increasing reliance on systems which are not only dual-capable but dual-purpose. In

other words, conventionally armed ballistic missiles, with an extremely low or even zero circular error of probability, could acquire an increasing number of missions at both the tactical and strategic levels. Indeed, the aforementioned RAND study has suggested that over the next 15 years non-nuclear strategic weapons will become readily available, and possibly widely deployed by one or both superpowers.[4]

4.   *Improvements in surveillance techniques, data processing, and information and communications technologies.* These seem likely to be reflected in augmented capabilities for command and control, and indeed for battle management. Fifth generation computers combined with increasingly sophisticated satellites may provide an unprecedented ability to monitor—although not necessarily to control—hostilities whether they occur at the conventional or the nuclear level. At the same time, it has to be acknowledged that improvements in anti-surveillance technologies and tactics designed to confound the adversary's imaging and detection techniques are also quite considerable. Indeed, it seems that the convergence between surveillance capabilities and readily detectable weapon systems, such as heavy bombers and fixed ICBMs, which has existed since the early 1960s, may be disappearing, making it more difficult to verify a peacetime arms control regime.

5.   *The development of exotic technologies.* Exotic technology may be defined as 'the employment of unconventional principles and approaches in the solution of military problems'. This unconventional application of principles may relate either to the novel use of existing knowledge to solve military problems or to the exploration, development and application of new principles to overcome those problems.[5] It is even possible that unconventional solutions to military problems will be found without high technology. The difficulty with current discussion of exotic technology, however, is that the term is used mainly in relation to research and development activities that are part of the Strategic Defense Initiative (SDI). This is understandable. Such technologies as plasma weapons, X-ray-generated lasers and railguns—all of which involve the extremely rapid transfer of considerable amounts of destructive, if precisely focused, energy—have been brought under the SDI umbrella. Yet research into all these systems pre-dated 1983. Indeed, conceptually it is possible to distinguish exotic technology as something which is not only separate from the specifics of the SDI programme but which, potentially at least, has relevance far beyond the mission of ballistic missile defence. Exotic technology involves a range of approaches to weapon design that at present is being applied largely to defence against ICBMs but may eventually be utilized for a much broader range of strategic purposes.

This summary of major trends in technology is both partial and simplistic, adopting as it does a macro rather than a micro approach to technological change. It also focuses on the near term (i.e. the next 15 to 20 years). Longer-term developments in mathematics, physics and computing will almost certainly have a profound and incalculable impact not only on narrow questions on military strategy but on the broader issues of national and international security. Any attempt to assess the effects of these longer-term changes, however, would make an already difficult undertaking impossible. Similarly the paper omits developments in chemical and biological warfare. This is an area in which new technologies could well be available as the United States and the Soviet Union make substantial advances in genetic engineering. Although this might become an increasingly important area of superpower competition, its analysis requires highly specialized knowledge and expertise. Consequently, this chapter does not attempt to offer a comprehensive discussion. It simply provides a starting point from which to consider what the strategic environment might be like in the late 1990s and the early years of the next century.

III. The strategic environment

The full implications of these technological trends are not easily discernible or readily predictable. This should not be surprising. Even a brief survey of the history of strategic doctrine reveals how often the dissonance between expectations and the reality of technological change has resulted in disaster and defeat. Innovation may have all sorts of unforeseen as well as unintended consequences. Furthermore, there is a constant dialectic in most of the areas identified. Improvements in command, control, communications and intelligence (C^3I), for example, could be nullified by advances in technologies designed to create an electromagnetic pulse without the use of nuclear weapons, and thereby black out communications while avoiding heavy collateral damage. At the very least, however, the trends identified above seem to portend a strategic environment which is highly complex, in which the movement towards war-fighting strategies and weapons have gone much further, and in which both superpowers deploy a mix of offensive and defensive systems. It is arguable that in such an environment the problems of crisis management and escalation control will be even more formidable than they are at present, while arms control will be even more marginal than it has been in the 1980s. The real danger, though, is that the improvement in command, control and communications as well as the development and deployment of more discriminate and less-destructive weapons seems likely to foster an illusion of controllability when, in fact, control is likely to become increasingly tenuous. Indeed, one of the paradoxes of the 1990s and beyond is that as weapon systems become more discriminate, conflict may become less manageable.

The illusion of controllability is likely to be encouraged by enhanced capabilities for monitoring developments during hostilities. This enhancement is a result of both improving technology and the increasing resources devoted to command, control and communication in response to concern over the potential vulnerability of national command authorities to decapitation strikes. The belief that even hostilities between the superpowers could be controlled may well be strengthened by the introduction of more discriminate weapon systems which appear to provide a variety of discrete options. Indeed, this is part of the rationale for the introduction of conventional strategic missile forces. According to the RAND study on non-nuclear strategic weapons, such systems 'offer the prospect of a slower pace of warfare. By adding a rung to the escalation ladder, they could provide a "nuclear firebreak" at the strategic level of conflict. This means increased opportunities for bargaining and crisis resolution in the early stages of war'.[6] By offering more usable options, it is argued, these weapons would also restore or enhance the credibility of extended deterrence in Europe.

The drawback, however, is that of the introduction of such systems into the force postures of the two superpowers can hardly fail to result in a blurring of thresholds and an erosion of firebreaks—developments which will make hostilities much more difficult to manage and control. The nuclear age so far has been dominated by simple concepts, clear-cut distinctions and ready categorizations. Much strategic analysis, for example, is based on the idea of distinct levels of hostilities or categories of warfare and weapons. The nuclear threshold in particular has been seen as something which would provide a highly salient limitation in any conflict between the superpowers. Crossing this threshold would require careful consideration and deliberate choice. Similarly, going from the tactical or theatre level of warfare to the strategic is something which has traditionally been seen as a very major step. Yet the increasing reliance on weapons which are dual-purpose and dual-capable could result in steps being taken without full awareness of how they might appear to the adversary. The use of weapons such as conventionally armed cruise missiles during intense conventional hostilities in Europe would create unprecedented and urgent problems of discrimination and attack assessment for the Soviet Union—which defines as strategic any weapon which lands on its territory regardless of the source or location of its launch. The greater the distance beyond the forward edge of the battle area NATO would attack with these systems, therefore, the greater the problem. In the confusion of hostilities, when both sides are concerned about threats to command centres and the danger of strategic capabilities being degraded, such an attack might be difficult to distinguish from nuclear pre-emption. At the very least, it would confront the Soviet Union with 'use them or lose them' dilemmas and might thereby precipitate a major Soviet escalation. This possibility is even greater in relation to strategic conventional forces. Any idea that these could be used with relative impunity against the Soviet homeland displays not only a remarkable ethnocentrism and a total disregard for Soviet history, but also a series of outrageously optimistic assessments about Soviet willingness to see its strategic assets degraded while leaving those of its major adversary intact. This is not to suggest that the problems are caused only by the United States. The same kinds of dilemma not only confront NATO already but seem likely to intensify rather than abate. There is much concern in the West about the possibility of conventionally armed Soviet missiles being used against NATO's short-range and long-range theatre nuclear forces.

The point about such actions, whether initiated by NATO or the Warsaw

Pact, is that even though they would not directly involve the use of nuclear weapons they would effectively and critically erode the nuclear threshold. Crossing this threshold has traditionally implied the direct use of nuclear weapons. It seems probable, however, that, during rapidly moving hostilities, attacks on nuclear weapons (or even nuclear power plants) by whatever means would be seen as a major escalatory move and generate a nuclear response. This problem exists at sea as well as on land. The strategy for the US Navy enunciated by Admiral Watkins makes explicit that Soviet ballistic missile-equipped, nuclear-powered submarines (SSBNs) would be a legitimate target during conventional hostilities between NATO and the Warsaw Pact. The problem with this, however, is that it is effectively a counterforce strike, and one which would seriously increase the risk of escalation.

To some extent, of course, these developments are as much a matter of strategy and tactics as they are of technology. Nevertheless, technology seems likely to encourage what might be termed a compression effect, whereby the various stages of warfare become much more closely linked, and movement towards full-scale nuclear war takes place because of a series of incremental decisions. The problem with multiple options is that by appearing to provide relatively safe alternatives they make choices less awesome, and thereby contribute to an escalatory slide. If thresholds are blurred or eroded, they are more likely to be crossed than when they stand out in bold relief and when the consequences of one's actions are clear and dramatic. What is perhaps most interesting about such a development is that if it occurs, it will not be because of revolutionary advances in technology but because of a 'trickle down' effect as technologies of precision guidance and so on, which were developed initially for strategic nuclear forces, are integrated into other systems and into operational strategies and force postures without full assessment of the possible consequences. Although these developments seem likely to strengthen deterrence, the advantages might be outweighed by the reduced capacity for crisis management and escalation control they seem likely to engender.

In addition to force postures which provide a seamless web of options, it is conceivable that by the end of the century both superpowers will have deployed or be in the process of deploying defences against strategic missiles. Whether such defences will be based on existing as opposed to exotic technologies—or most likely of all some combination of both—is not certain. It does seem likely that if exotic technologies prove promising, there will be attempts to move very quickly from the research and development stage to an initial operating capability. Furthermore, in so far as defences incorporate exotic technology and are space-based as opposed to ground-based, then it is unlikely that they will be restricted to terminal defence of silos. Point defence has limited rationale, and either on its own or in combination with the move towards mobile systems discussed above, seems more likely to add to rather than detract from strategic stability. Exotic technologies, though, tend to be discussed far more in relation to boost phase, post-boost phase, and mid-course phase interception than in relation to terminal phase. By its very nature, a multi-layered space-based defence system goes well beyond the requirements for silo protection and, as a result, could have serious repercussions on strategic stability. An extensive system coupled with offensive forces with a substantial capability for hard-target kill is a recipe for strategic instability. Should this be coupled with the compression effect identified above, then the possibilities for managing superpower confrontations would be seriously reduced. During even a relatively minor superpower confrontation, the pre-emptive pressures might prove overwhelming and escalation control would be difficult if not impossible.

Another possibility with weapon systems that incorporate exotic technologies is that they might be used for offensive as well as defensive purposes. The most obvious aspect of this, of course, is the use of SDI technologies for anti-satellite weapons. Not only is there considerable overlap between SDI and anti-satellite (ASAT) technologies, but the relative softness and vulnerability of satellites makes them much more vulnerable targets than ICBMs. Even if the superpowers did not deploy extensive ballistic missile defences, therefore, their current efforts could give them a capability for destroying each other's satellites—another development which would have adverse implications for stability.[7]

Although the ASAT spin-off is perhaps the most immediate and urgent issue associated with multi-purpose weaponry, there is a more pervasive concern that space-based lasers and other systems capable of destroying ICBMs in the boost phase would also be capable of destroying targets on the ground. Indeed, as William Kincade has argued: 'Any device that can accurately and reliably transfer significant amounts of destructive energy over long distances by beam or projectile will have clear offensive implications.'[8] Once this is acknowledged, a whole host of contingencies opens up. The possibility that systems based on exotic technologies might contribute directly to the potential, or the perceived potential, for first strike could certainly not be excluded. In other words, exotic technologies could add a further layer of unpredictability and instability to what, in any event, will be a highly volatile environment. Unless it is somehow checked or reversed, the trend certainly seems to be towards what is sometimes termed strategic deterioration. This is made all the more likely by the difficulties the trends seem likely to create for arms control, at least as it has traditionally been conceived.

Arms control concepts have been predicated upon the assumption that there are clear categories of weapons which provide obvious foci for negotiations and which facilitate agreement on mutually acceptable limitations. The experience of the 1970s however, suggests that, if not patently false, this assumption was at the very least wildly optimistic. In fact, many of the problems in the Soviet–US negotiations in both the 1970s and the 1980s stemmed from differences in each side's understanding over what was or was not a strategic system. Such differences were—and are—compounded by geographical asymmetries between the superpowers. US forward-based systems in Europe, for example, proved a major obstacle to a comprehensive and permanent agreement on offensive forces in SALT I. Far from disappearing, such difficulties seem likely to intensify as new kinds of weapon are developed and deployed which do not fit easily or neatly into traditional categories and defy agreement between the superpowers.

The implication of all this is that current trends in technology, if left unchecked, will not only create formidable difficulties for strategy but will render arms control irrelevant to the major issues of national and international security. What though are the prospects for halting or reversing the trend before this point is reached?

IV.   Technological momentum and arms control

In assessing the future prospects for arms control, it is necessary to consider whether new weapon systems result from technological pull or political push. If the question is straightforward, however, the answer is more complex. Much appears to depend on circumstances. Where technological advancement obviously and explicitly involves revolutionary changes in military capabilities, the political factor may be dominant. This was certainly the case with the development of the hydrogen bomb and the change of emphasis, if not yet of direction, in US strategy which resulted from President Reagan's Strategic Defence Initiative.[9] Other cases, however, suggest that technological momentum, generated by a competitive and highly dynamic research and development process, and by a persistent tendency to think in terms of matching future and potential—rather than present and actual—threats, is what primarily drives the procurement of new weapon systems—as was the case with MIRVs. Furthermore, a series of incremental improvements in several distinct areas of technology may be combined in novel ways to produce new capabilities even though there is no strategic requirement for such systems. The strategic rationale may be developed after the weapon itself. The strategic cruise missile, for example, became a major element in the US strategic posture as a result of 'uncoordinated, integrative and synthetic technological innovation, rather than a deliberate effort at an epochal breakthrough'.[10] There is yet another category of research and development, which may occur incrementally and with little attention paid to it apart from the specialists involved, which for one reason or another is given a major boost as a result of political decision. In other words, the relationship between the research and development process on the one side and the formal decision-making process on the other can vary considerably. In some cases it will be very close; in others extremely tenuous. Some weapons result from technological push, other from political pull, and yet others from a mixture of both.

What cannot be denied though is the importance of the prevailing attitudes. It is possible to identify two broad mind-sets in regard to military technology. The first emphasizes the idea of strategic stability and the dangers of unbridled technological enthusiasm. It treats much of the new technology as a threat to stability and, therefore, a potential source of strategic deterioration. In this view, which evokes considerable sympathy in Western Europe, technology can have effects which are both unexpected and undesirable. Diametrically opposed is an approach which treats technology as something to be managed and manipulated for unilateral strategic advantage. This second approach has considerable support—and is probably the dominant strand—in the Reagan Administration. Indeed, many members of the administration contend that a focus on the systemic aspects of security is misguided and that the real concern must be national security: measures which will augment US power or provide security through strength should not be surrendered simply because they jeopardize a concept of stability which is not shared by the Soviet Union. In addition to this unqualified unilateralist approach to security there is also a more moderate, if more muted position, in the Reagan Administration which suggests that unilateral measures are important in developing bargaining power—and that SDI has already been of considerable value in getting the Soviet Union back to the bargaining table and in eliciting possible concessions from Moscow on offensive force reductions. Indeed, much of the debate within the US Government can be understood in terms of differences between these two groups—the unqualified technological enthusiasts who want to use US programmes to maximize the USA's competitive advantage and to 'squeeze' the Soviet Union into retreat, exhaustion and possible internal crisis; and those who acknowledge the importance of US technological advantage but prefer to use this as bargaining currency in their efforts to reach a 'deal' with the Soviet Union on arms control.[11] One of the problems facing the dealers is the fact that systems which begin as 'bargaining chips' may be deemed vital to national security. The result is an unwillingness or inability to bargain them away—an outcome which is all the more likely if the 'squeezers' remain the dominant faction within the administration.

The difficulties of establishing a consensus in favour of a deal with the Soviet Union highlights one of the most important problems which confront any scheme for qualitative arms control—the belief by many groups and individuals in the national security community in the United States that technology is the USA's salvation in the continued strategic and political competition with Moscow. To regard new technologies, whether conventional or exotic, as a threat is to engage in self-denying ordinance that is not only unnecessary but inimical to the long-term national security of the United States. The tendency to see technology as a solution rather than a major part of the problem clearly underlies much of the enthusiasm for SDI in the United States. Indeed, this fundamental attitude as much as the dynamics of the research and development process itself, or the vested interests of the weapon designers and producers, drives the qualitative arms race. Furthermore, unless there is, somehow, a shift in attitude, away from what might be termed an entrepreneurial approach to technological advancement, or a shift in the political balance between 'dealers' and 'squeezers', the prospects for inhibiting the development and deployment of systems based on emerging and exotic technologies must be negligible. Technological enthusiasm is not conducive to the restraints and constraints embodied in either existing or future arms control agreements.

The difficulty is that even if successor administrations adopt a different approach, the SDI and the effort it has galvanized may have created such momentum that it will be difficult to halt or reverse the trend. Interest in the exotic technologies now encompassed in the SDI programme existed prior to March 1983. Nevertheless, the technological push was modest. President Reagan's initiative offered an unprecedented degree of political pull. It is possible, however, that this will create such technological momentum that future administrations which have a different approach to technology and to arms control may find it extremely difficult to prevent a move from research and development to production and deployment. In other words, technological push will once again come to the fore, and the prospects for arms control will recede further. The desire of the scientific and technological community to rise to the challenge—and the infusion of large funds associated with the SDI programme—has already led to the identification of technologies which, in the view of their proponents, promise to make a substantial contribution to strategic defence.

The other consequence of SDI is that it will inevitably create vested interests within the defence industry in favour of at least some deployments. Getting from the testing stage to deployment will not be easy for many of the systems currently being discussed. If these systems show promise, however, the pressures for their exploitation could prove virtually irresistible. These pressures will be strengthened further by the belief that the technologies involved in SDI will provide a boost to the US economy and help restore US technological supremacy over its economic competitors in Western Europe and Japan.

There are some countervailing pressures, however. Concerns over the budget deficit mean that the US defence budget will grow far less in the next 5 to 10 years than it has in the past 10 years and in real terms may well decline. Consequently, the battle for funds within defence will be intense. In these circumstances, SDI will have to face tough competition from organizations concerned with maintaining existing roles and missions. Furthermore, it is far from certain that future presidents will have the same degree of commitment as Ronald Reagan has to SDI. There has been much criticism that SDI, at least in the President's conception of 'astrodome defence', is based on 'the fallacy of the last move'—rather than giving the United States permanent advantage, it will simply elicit Soviet countermeasures. If future administrations accept this judgement, the programme may not go beyond research to the extent that its proponents desire or its critics fear. Even technological push can be held in check by political decision.

Such caveats notwithstanding, the current dominance of a mind-set that sees security as something to be achieved exclusively through unilateral effort; regards technology as something to be exploited for unilateral advantage; and views arms control agreements (actual or potential) as a hindrance could result in a strategic environment which is far more intractable and dangerous than that of the 1980s. It is essential, therefore, to consider ways in which exotic technologies in particular might be regulated or constrained as part of an arms control regime.

V.   The arms control dimension

Even if there is an attempt in the 1990s to restore arms control to a central place in US security policy and in the superpower relationship, the task will not be an easy one. At the most fundamental level, the problem is one of establishing rules for dealing with technological change, while the particular technologies involved will severely complicate efforts to devise a new arms control regime.

A major problem is that emerging and exotic technologies will further blur and confuse the traditional boundaries of arms control. Brand new categories will have to be devised if arms control is to progress along traditional functional lines in which certain kinds of weapon system are neatly categorized as strategic or theatre and delimited accordingly. Yet this may prove impossible. In a complex strategic environment characterized by multi-purpose weapon systems, the tasks involved in categorization may prove insurmountable. Distinguishing between conventional and nuclear systems will be much more problematic than it has been in the past. The difficulties of categorizing weapons, which could be used over a range of distances and against targets ranging from tanks to ICBMs, are immense. Such weapons as the laser, the particle beam and the railgun have far wider potential application than ballistic missile defence, and the inherent potential of these new forms of weaponry could make arms control as traditionally conceived and compartmentalized a thing of the past. It also seems likely that the increased complexity of arms control negotiations in an environment containing advanced systems based on emerging or exotic technology would accentuate the adversarial nature of arms control negotiations, make asymmetries harder to trade off, and render the verification problems virtually insuperable. In short, exotic and emerging technologies seem likely to undermine the arms control process further by exacerbating the problems created by technical advance in the 1970s.

A further difficulty concerns the kinds of limitation that might be imposed. Assuming that there is agreement on the inadequacies of a *laissez-faire* approach to emerging and exotic technologies, questions arise about whether to opt for discriminating control or a more comprehensive prohibition. The discriminating approach would attempt to identify those technologies and weapon systems that would enhance strategic stability and to facilitate their deployment while somehow inhibiting those which are deemed to be destabilizing in their impact. The advantage of this is that it might have political appeal to those who believe that US security lies in technology and who would therefore resist a more comprehensive prohibition. It might also obtain the approval of those who were anxious that the other side would cheat on an agreement: the development and deployment of some systems incorporating exotic technologies would provide a basis from which to respond to any 'breakout' by the adversary. Yet another argument in its favour is that of realism. It may be impossible to stop the march of weapon technology. If so, the only feasible approach is to attempt to channel technological progress in directions that are stabilizing. But there are difficulties with what might be termed the 'colander' approach to arms control. Distinguishing 'benign' from 'malevolent' technologies would be a formidable task, especially given the multiple uses of the systems involved. In view of this, a prohibition approach might appear attractive.

One problem here, however, would be what kinds of activity to prohibit and how to verify that the prohibitions are being observed: at what stage in the process of research, development, testing, production and deployment should the restrictions impinge? Three stages of intervention seem plausible: at the research or embryonic stage; at the development and testing stage; and at the deployment or evolving stage.[12] The implication of much of the previous discussion is that the earlier the better. Once they are a feature of the strategic environment, weapon systems based on new technologies would be enormously difficult to regulate. In other words, emerging and exotic technologies are best dealt with well before the deployment stage is reached. Because of the different time frames involved, the advanced state of development of emerging technologies, the need for replacements for existing weapons and the preoccupation with nuclear arms control, however, it may be that emerging technologies are already beyond the stage at which significant limitations can be imposed.

What though of exotic technologies? The difficulty with trying to control these at the embryonic stage is that a prohibition would be difficult or impossible to verify. Furthermore, given the continued adherence to worst-case analysis, both sides will want to continue research for fear of a breakthrough by the adversary. The implication is that prohibition has to occur after the research phase, that is, before actual testing is undertaken. The clear model or this approach is the ABM (Anti-Ballistic Missile) Treaty of 1972. The crucial elements of the Treaty in relation to exotic technologies are article 5 and Agreed Statement D. Article 5 prohibits the development, testing and deployment of sea-based, air-based, space-based, or mobile ground-based ABM systems or components, while Agreed Statement D makes clear that ABM systems 'based on other physical principles and including components capable of substituting for ABM interceptor missiles, ABM launchers, or ABM radars' could not be deployed without discussion in the Standing Consultative Commission and amendment of the ABM Treaty itself.

Both these elements have become controversial. Much discussion has revolved around the definition of 'development'. In fact, Gerard Smith's testimony before the US Senate Armed Services Committee in July 1972 offered a clear statement of the position: 'The prohibitions on development contained in the ABM Treaty would start at that part of the development process where field testing is initiated on either a prototype or breadboard model . . . the prohibition . . . applies to activities involved after a component moves from the laboratory development and testing stage to the field testing stage wherever performed. The fact that early stages of the development process, such as laboratory testing, would pose problems for verification by national technical means is an important consideration in reaching this definition'.[13] In spite of this, members of the Reagan Administration have contended that the ABM Treaty is in many respects very permissive. In a sense, however, this brings the argument full circle. There is already a basis in the ABM Treaty for preventing development (at least beyond a certain stage) and deployment of exotic technologies. Yet, there are many in the administration who appear to believe that the Treaty is an impediment to the full expression of US technological prowess. A crucial problem, therefore, is not how to devise restrictions but how to change the dominant attitudes.

Assuming that there is no success in this in the immediate or short term, then the problem will be one of devising means of dealing with exotic technologies once full-scale testing has been initiated or even after development has started. The problem here will be similar to that which occurred with MIRVs. If one side has an advantage—even if it recognizes that it will be only temporary—it will be reluctant to give it up for the sake of agreement, while the adversary will be equally reluctant to enter into any accord which freezes its inferiority. The prospects, therefore, seem very dim. The question of exotics has a degree of urgency about it which is to some extent obscured by the futuristic nature of some of the technologies.

IV.   Conclusions

There is a considerable temptation to follow a gloomy analysis of this kind with positive recommendations and a degree of optimism that if these prescriptions are followed the dangers will be avoided. The problem, however, is that the impulses which have been identified do not readily admit easy solutions. It is possible to offer platitudes and pieties about the desirability of inculcating an arms control philosophy into the weapon acquisition process, or about the need for a more managerial and intrusive form of arms control which attempts not simply to ratify the main elements of the strategic environment but to shape that environment. The problem is that where minimum forms of effective regulation have proved elusive, the feasibility of maximalist versions of arms restraint must be in even greater doubt. Without depreciating the difficulties inherent in the details of arms control negotiations, however, the major problem seems to be one of attitude. Unrestrained technological enthusiasm can only result in a long-term and fundamental deterioration of the strategic environment. The reassertion of a more apprehensive approach to technology is essential if this eventuality is to be avoided. A change in attitude would facilitate a reaffirmation and strengthening of the ABM Treaty. It might also make it possible to contemplate the creation of a forum in which the superpowers engage in joint surveillance and assessment of new technologies. If technological development cannot be halted, then at least an attempt could be made to introduce it in ways which are not excessively destabilizing. There are few signs, however, of the requisite shift in attitude. Technological enthusiasm may be a luxury which can no longer be afforded, but is nevertheless likely to prove enduring. The implications for strategic stability and international security are likely to be as profound as they are disquieting.

Notes and references

1 See Schelling, T. C., 'Arms control: what went wrong?', *Studies of War and Peace*, ed. O. Osterud (Nobel Insitute: Oslo, forthcoming).
2 For a fuller analysis of the various meanings of technology, see Kincade, W. H., 'The future of Star Wars and arms control', paper prepared for the Conference on Strategic Defence and Soviet–American Relations, the Woodrow Wilson Centre, Washington, DC, 10–11 Mar. 1986. See also paper 2.1 (pages 69–77).
3 'The challenge of non-nuclear strategic weapons', *RAND Research Review*, vol. 9, no. 3 (Fall 1985), p. 1.
4 Rand (note 3).
5 The definition and analysis here relies heavily on Kincade (note 2).
6 Rand (see note 3).
7 See Jasani, B., 'Outer space being turned into a battlefield', *Bulletin of Peace Proposals*, vol. 17, no. 1 (1986), pp. 29–39.
8 Kincade (note 2).
9 See Stein, J. B., *From H Bomb To Star Wars* (D. C. Heath: (Lexington, MA, 1984).
10 Betts, R., quoted in Thee, M., *Military Technology, Military Strategy and the Arms Race* (Croom Helm: London, 1986), p. 35.
11 Horelick, A. L. and Warner III, E. L., 'US–Soviet nuclear arms control: the next phase', *US–Soviet Relations: The Next Phase*, ed. A. L. Horelick (Cornell University Press: Ithaca, NY, 1986), especially pp. 250–1.
12 These distinctions are adapted from Kincade (note 2).
13 Quoted in Longstreth, T. K., Pike, J. E. and Rhinelander, J. B., *The Impact of US and Soviet Ballistic Missile Defence Programs on the ABM Treaty*, A Report for the National Campaign to Save the ABM Treaty, Mar. 1985, p. 26.

Part 4. Beyond the security dilemma

Paper 4.1.   Battle management: the control of war, crisis and armed peace

WILLIAM H. KINCADE

I.   Introduction

Three continuing trends have, over the past four decades, presented civil and military authorities with serious new challenges that further stress their always uneasy relationship in the direction of armed forces. These related developments are: the advent of nuclear and thermonuclear weapons; the increased tempo, scope and potential destructiveness of modern warfare; and the resulting changes in the nature of combat and the use of force. As technical innovation continues to improve the capability for waging war, the challenge to political and military command and control of the use of force will only intensify in the future.

Indeed, one of the most significant consequences of secular technical change in the post-war period is the increasing tension between the improved capability and controllability of weapons, on the one hand, and, on the other, the growing difficulty of controlling conflict itself as a means to achieve political ends. The time which physical limits on military capability formerly provided for political adaptation and thoughtful decision-making has been drastically foreshortened. According to one US official:

Decisions will be made by computers that have been taught, i.e., programmed, all that humans know about war as they hypothesize it will be fought with modern weapons. The computer will perhaps have expanded upon that knowledge. Humans will oversee and override rather than execute. War will not only be 'come as you are', but will also be preprogrammed.[1]

While perhaps excessively sanguine about the use of computers or, more specifically, artificial intelligence, in the larger direction and management of combat, this view is essentially correct in pointing at the fact that the speed, range and lethality of modern weaponry require reaction times that can only be achieved by automatic means. Already, the strategic nuclear and the conventional battlefields are at the point where the response to most detected threats could be automated, subject to human override.

As a result, to simplify, the political task of conflict management has become even more tightly related to the military function of battle management, with significant implications for both. And the intimacy of this relationship will continue to grow. Yet, for reasons that are well known, military objectives, strategy, and practices often diverge from or conflict with political purposes and needs. Military objectives, operational repertoires, and doctrines are oriented to winning engagements and wars. In the nuclear age, political objectives and practices are increasingly directed to the attainment of policy ends without actually resorting to war, but only the threat of it. The difficulty, of course, lies in using, for more subtle purposes, a command system geared to war and operated largely by the military.

Thus, while the systems developed for the control and management of armed forces present many faces for scrutiny, the primary test of effectiveness must finally be their adequacy in ensuring the primacy of political purposes and objectives.[2] Hence the question for officials and independent analysts is whether current or foreseeable systems (human, institutional and technological) for the management of war, crises and armed peace will be equal to the growing challenges they face in these areas.

II.   The brains of the system

Command and control systems are often likened to the human brain and the central nervous system, which provide the direction for most human activity. The analogy is apt in other ways. Command and control systems are similar to the brain and the central nervous system not only in that they direct rational, purposive activity, but also because they are highly complex, not fully comprehensible and often reflexive, owing to routines that have been programmed into them for a variety of purposes but which are no longer appropriate or inappropriate to certain purposes.

What makes command and control systems of supreme importance in modern conflict is primarily the fact that the effectiveness of weapons and fighting forces generally is now determined more by information limitations than by energy limitations. The underlying trend that has caused the great increase in the speed, range and lethality of weapons and the parallel increase in the ability to transport fighting forces is the reduction of the barriers of space, time and physical obstacles through the more and more efficient use of energy.

As fighting forces and their weapons have become more and more energy-efficient, emphasis has shifted to their information effectiveness. This principle applies whether the problem is improving the target location, discrimination and acquisition capability of a missile or artillery shell; improving the capacity of a company commander or destroyer combat information centre to fulfil their functions; or improving the ability of political and military leaders to guide selective nuclear strikes, conduct operations in space, management crises or direct conventional campaigns.

Great strides have been made, of course, in these and other areas of command and control. More and more complex information systems and programmes have been developed to direct projectiles and operations. In short, warfare, and operations short of war, have become information-intensive as well as energy-intensive. And, battle management or command

and control systems are, in effect, information systems on a very large scale.

Wars, campaigns and battles have often been won or lost on the basis of the adequacy of a commander's information and hence his information system. What has changed is that the stakes in many conflicts are now much higher. Also, the scope and tempo of conflict may be such that neither the commander nor the political leader will have an opportunity to remedy errors they make out of poor judgement or poor information: the first mistake may be the only one. The adequacy of command and control from the level of the battlefield to the capital may mean, not just the difference between success and failure in war or crisis, but the difference between survival and catastrophe.

The information revolution in both civil and military spheres leaves the erroneous impression, though, that information technology has solved the age-old problems of fog of war or battle, which arise when tactical or strategic information is disregarded, incomplete, unconfirmed, deceptive, untimely, unavailable, contradictory or misinterpreted. To the contrary, however, in the potentially information-soaked environment of the modern battlefield, fog of war may prove to be an even greater problem but for different reasons.

All of the old information problems that create fog of war or battle will still be possible. But to them will be added the problems of information overload and of making sound judgements amid too much information, rather than, as was usually the case in the past, too little. Furthermore, the very technology that has created the information revolution is also effective for disinformation, that is, for disrupting or deceiving the information systems on which weapons, forces and leaders are so dependent.

A distinguishing characteristic of information systems is, in fact, their vulnerability compared to other types of equipment employed in battle. The technology for gathering, analysing, displaying and communicating information that lies at the heart of command systems is intrinsically susceptible to disruption by attack, deception or various internal failure modes (design defect, operator error, equipment malfunction or all three). This inherent vulnerability is the basis of the scenario for a 'decapitation attack', where the first and perhaps the only blow in a nuclear conflict would be against command and control centres, intelligence, collectors, communication links, and so on.[3]

Hardening of such technology against blast or radiation effects is difficult. This leaves redundancy, camouflage and dispersal as the primary means of protecting the hardware. Yet the size, complexity and requirement for energy radiation of the systems limit even these expedients. Protection against deception is also problematic in a time of constant innovation. A further vulnerability arises from the fact that this type of equipment requires operation and maintenance by well-trained and highly skilled personnel, whose constant availability in adequate numbers may not be assured in combat conditions.

Thus, on top of the problems of adaptability and misuse or miscalculation by decision-makers, there is the possibility that this most crucial weapon of all— the central nervous system for prosecuting wars and crises—will function at only a fraction of its peacetime or design capability. Given the vulnerability of highly complex, interactive, elecronics-based systems, it is perhaps not going too far to assert the principle that, under conditions of intense conflict, their effectiveness will decline more rapidly than that of the forces, weapons or other equipment they are supposed to control.

Because of this vulnerability, attention has increasingly focused on both the protection of information systems at the tactical and strategic levels and on ways of countering such protection. This will likely continue to be a 'growth area' in military-technological innovation, so much so that the terminology now in use (electronic warfare, electronic countermeasures, electronic counter-countermeasures, and so on) could be replaced with a single term, 'information warfare'.

What is important about information warfare is that it will be difficult to integrate into methods for calculating military balances and for simulating combat. Far from being clear-cut 'force multipliers', a quality that is claimed for command systems, they could be force dividers. Since the quality of information systems and the impact of information warfare are intrinsically difficult to quantify, calculate and integrate with other variables in battle analysis or war games, it is likely that information warfare will be a great unknown that looms over conflict and makes estimates of weapon capabilities, force balances, and so on, of even less relevance to the prediction of outcomes.

The challenges to equipment designers and operators, to troops and commanders, to services and other defence institutions, and, above all, to political and military leaders posed by the information revolution and the advent of information warfare are vexing indeed. The challenges are compounded by the assumption that the information revolution in military affairs is positive, on balance, since it solves so many military problems, and also by the lack of recognition of the seriousness of the difficulties it creates. Also challenging are the problems which these developments create for independent specialists in military studies.

III.   Conflicts and requirements of command

Despite the fact that military command and control systems can be differentiated in many ways, they tend to be unified in that they are designed to cope with a variety of military contingencies that cannot be precisely known in advance. While the system can be divided into functional or other components, its components are required, in theory at least, to serve the overall objective of carrying out national policy, particularly its military dimension. Hence a superpower like the United States establishes a Defence Communications Agency and creates a World-Wide Military Command and Control System, although the principle of the unity of command reflected in these designations may be honoured more often in the breach than in the observance.

When we consider the command and control of armed forces in the present or the future, therefore, we must look, not only at how contemporary or anticipatory systems will function under conditions of conventional or nuclear war or conflict in space, if that possibility becomes a reality. Equally important is the question of how command and control systems operate in the context of the ongoing superpower competition for influence in the world and especially in the context of the crises that punctuate the larger contest.

Also to be considered is the use of command and control systems in special operations, such as the Israeli actions at Entebbe, against the Osirak reactor, or in the Six-Day War and the US actions against Libya in the Gulf of Sidra or its invasion of Grenada. Thus, these systems must be examined in terms of their capacity to manage the use of military forces across the spectrum of battles, campaigns, wars, crises and the continuing strategic competition, including the superpower involvement in many of the so-called low-intensity conflicts that smoulder or flame around the globe.

Of particular importance, if still little recognized, is the role that battle or conflict management systems have acquired in terms of escalation control. That is, the increasing use of force or the threat of force for political purposes, as distinct from launching or repelling an attack, has made the political direction of military operations more immediate and significant. Escalation potential has raised the importance of political control of low-echelon operations; information technology has made it possible. Leaders may be immediately privy to events, as Presidents Ford and Carter were in the Mayaguez incident and the Iranian raid, or even 'call the shots', as Lyndon Johnson did in bombing Southeast Asia. Thus, a major function of overlapping systems for conflict and battle management has become the direction of military means for political ends, usually in a way that restrains the inherent escalatory propensities of combat operations.

It is in this area that military routines are likely to conflict most directly with political objectives. Increasing the level of violence is the normal way to attain a stubborn military objective. And the *threat* to increase the level of violence has always been an axiom of the political use of military force and is now the foundation of deterrence dogma. Yet the larger political purpose continues to be to attain policy objectives while avoiding or minimizing conflict, not stimulating it. In this situation lies the essential dilemma of command and control in the nuclear age: can a system used for both implementing violence and communicating threats be effective in restraining conflict and controlling escalation? It is this dilemma that justifies assessment of command and control effectiveness at the lower levels of conflict, including crises. Among these less intense conflicts may lie the fuse of nuclear war.

IV. Analysis of command systems

To date, however, most of the open research in this area has focused on the management of nuclear war and, in particular, on the US command and control system (usually called command, control, communications and intelligence, or C^3I), for which the most information is available.[4] This emphasis results, in particular, from concern about whether command and control for nuclear war has kept up with the capabilities of the weapons themselves and, indeed, whether the command systems themselves might contribute to inadvertent nuclear war.[5]

Doubts about the adequacy of contemporary command and control are made more acute at the official level because of the technical possibility of protracted nuclear conflict and because of the symbolic aspects of command systems in a strategy of nuclear deterrence, as it has come to be conceived. If a nation's command and control arrangements for nuclear war are clearly inadequate to the exigencies of common scenarios, then, according to deterrence dogma, there will be reason to doubt the national resolve; that country's deterrent or coercive power may thus seem diminished.

Regarding the other concern—unintended nuclear conflict—it is interesting to note that this has virtually replaced concern for a premeditated nuclear war. The Reagan Administration, not otherwise successful in negotiating with the Soviet Union, has completed an ageement to upgrade the Washington–Moscow Hot Line and undertaken quiet talks on risk-reduction centres, both of which reflect the perceived need to provide counterpoises against a rapid and unintended escalation to or beyond the nuclear level.

Since the US command and control system for nuclear war is largely undifferentiated (that is, only a few elements are dedicated solely to the nuclear contingency), however, its adequacy has been in part judged on how well it fared in non-nuclear operations or episodes. Indeed, as Desmond Ball points out, command and control failures surrounding the Israeli attack on a US signals intelligence ship, the USS *Liberty*, during the Six-Day War and the subsequent crisis provoked by the North Korean seizure of a smaller such ship, the USS *Pueblo*, prompted greater attention to the command and control problem.[6] Thus, other levels of conflict have been addressed in the growing but still scant literature on the subject; yet the treatment has been *ad hoc* rather than systematic.

The subject did not gain widespread public, or even high-level, attention until a series of widely reported false nuclear alerts in the late 1970s and early 1980s, although it had begun to be an issue among specialists after the 1974 announcement by the then Secretary of Defense Schlesinger of the New Strategic Doctrine of Limited Nuclear Options. Since President Reagan accorded priority to command and control requirements in his October 1981 press conference on nuclear forces, the issue has been a prominent one, occasioning considerable commentary in the military press and at meetings of specialists, as well as in often sensational treatments in the popular media. It remains unclear, though, how much has been accomplished by such attention.[7]

In addition, much of the research on command and control dwells heavily on the technical dimensions of the problem and their adequacy. Less attention has been paid to the questions of human and institutional performance for the understandable reason that these dimensions, however critical, are inherently difficult to analyse due to a paucity of information and appropriate analytical techniques or agreed criteria. Nevertheless, most analysts of US command and control arrangements question the stress on the 'machine' in the system, to the neglect of the 'man' or the institution and the complex features of the man–machine interface.

In terms of an agenda for research and analysis, therefore, specialists in security studies are faced with multiple problems. There is a need to move beyond the technology to look at human and institutional questions. There is likewise a need to expand research to include the North Atlantic Treaty Organization (NATO) and Warsaw Pact command and control arrangements, those of the other nuclear weapon states, primarily the USSR, and those of key actors in regional hot spots.

Yet each of these tasks involves formidable obstacles. Nor, as suggested, do we have at present the analytic techniques and common criteria to judge the adequacy or performance of complex systems which have not been truly tested under all the conditions they potentially face. For now and the foreseeable future, very few persons other than officials, consultants and analysts at contract research firms hired by governments to design or review their command and control systems will have the information and techniques needed to study these arrangements.

Even if information on the major aspects of command and control arrangements could be obtained and appropriate tests applied, there remains the possibility that, in an emergency, the formal system would not be used as planned; instead an *ad hoc* arrangement might be adopted to fit the particular circumstances, using some of the institutions and technology available in an expedient rather than programmed or 'text book' way. Precedents are legion.

V.   An approach to command systems

If there are thus drastic lmits to what can be done in terms of independent research and analysis, the need to take this vital area of politico-military activity into account is no less great. Future calculations of military balances, of the relative efficacy of weapon systems or of military preparedness in general that do not attempt to address systems for command and control will yield an incomplete, and possibly an irrelevant, image of reality.

The first step towards developing a foundation for such analysis is to adopt an approach that is sytematic, multivariate and conceptual, that is, one which will permit examination of a given command system across the range of elements it includes and the functions it performs, as well as allow comparison across different options or existing systems. Table 4.1.I. reflects an attempt to formulate such an analytic framework.

This framework suggests that command system analysis pays attention to at least 10 aspects of the management of military forces and operations. This does not mean that each of these aspects is of equal importance in evaluating the overall system but that each merits attention.

Although there is clearly room for refinement, most of the basic aspects of command systems shown in table 4.1.I. are sufficiently commonplace or self-

Table 4.1.I.   Elements of command system evaluation

1. Interactions	Politico-military interactions; functional interactions; service interactions; alliance interactions; interactions with foe
2. Functional elements	Surveillance and intelligence collection; early warning; attack and damage assessment; communications and data transmission; analysis and display; command, control and co-ordination
3. Components	Institutional; human; technical; procedural
4. Dimensions	Land; sea; air; sub-surface; global; space
5. Scenarios and contingencies	*Nuclear*: tactical, theatre, strategic; first or second strike; limited or unlimited. *Conventional*: major and short; limited and long; special operations. *Crisis*: prolonged; episodic
6. Phases	*Nuclear*: pre-attack, trans-attack, post-attack. *Conventional*: pre-war, wartime, war termination. *Crisis*: pre-crisis, onset, peak and resolution of crisis
7. Substantive	Decision-making; decision-execution
8. System qualities	Adaptability; reliability; responsiveness; resistance; survivability; durability; reconstitutability; inter-operability; capacity and comprehensiveness
9. Areas of concern	Generally same as or closely related to System Qualities but dependent on scenario and contingencies within scenario, as well as vulnerabilities to external disruption or internal failure modes
10. Idiosyncratic factors	Impact of individual, institutional or national culture, tradition, experience and technological or strategic styles on the design and operation of command systems

explanatory as to need little justification. The particular role each plays in command and control is perhaps less obvious. The human element in data display, for instance, could be more important than might be imagined. As one officer has commented: 'I just hope that some operator doesn't think an empty cell in the matrix on his screen necessarily means there is no activity going on in that area.' Rather than take up each item in detail, however, focus will be on selected aspects.

Interactions

The interactive relationship between political and military authorities has already been addressed as a critical variable in command and control. Equally clear, under conditions involving more than one service or country, are the interactions among services or alliance partners. The weaknesses of US command and control systems in the former area are notorious; some have questioned whether the US Armed Forces are capable of carrying out effective joint operations at any level—and, despite its success, the invasion of Grenada did not allay these doubts. The prognosis for NATO command and control is nearly as poor, both in terms of technical and institutional or procedural capability.

The importance of the interaction of the functional elements of command systems should be obvious as well. History is replete with cases, for example, where intelligence that was available was not disseminated to the people who needed it in a timely way and with adequate emphasis, or its import was not understood. US unpreparedness at Pearl Harbor was partly a product of holding intelligence too closely in Washington. The National Security Agency claimed, after the *Pueblo* incident, that it had warned the Pacific Command of the possibility of North Korean action against this vessel. The Israeli command system seems to have worked well during the October War of 1973 but failed an initial test in not providing tactical or strategic warning of the Egyptian attack.

Less obvious, and far less controllable yet vitally important, are the interactions between adversary command systems, especially in crises. Authorities on one side may make a special disposition of forces or take similar action with the intent of sending a particular message to the other, perhaps an implied threat to escalate or an implied offer to parlay. Yet the opposing command system may not register this information correctly or at all; it may fail to send it up the line to the decision-making level; or it may interpret it in a way other than intended.

In combat, while opposition command system elements may make tempting, even imperative, targets, their disruption or destruction could well induce escalation, as the more damaged side seeks to retrieve its military position and resort to a level where control can be re-established. Though it is not possible to evaluate these aspects of command system interaction fully in advance, neither can they be left out of account as variables in sensitivity analysis or after-action review of performance.

Scenarios and contingencies

Perhaps the most important variable in assessing command and control, however, is the particular circumstance under which the system is to perform. A command system that is deemed inadequate for the prosecution of a nuclear war may be fully effective for other purposes, such as a limited conventional conflict or a crisis. Or vice versa.

Without making any judgements about the effectiveness of Soviet command and control under greater stress, it seems to have failed to operate effectively in peacetime conditions in the case of the Korean jetliner shot down after wandering into Soviet airspace. The possibility that the local commander thought Korean Airlines flight 007 was a US military intelligence aircraft does not mitigate the judgement that an enormous miscalculation occurred. This incident and the subsequent shooting of Major Arthur Nicholson in East Germany suggest a command system that is overprepared for a very frigid cold war and incapable of dealing with what were, at worst, minor provocations. Part of the problem appears to be a rigidity in military routines that excludes larger political considerations from overriding well-drilled procedures.

System qualities

Discussion of scenarios and contingencies immediately raises the question of desired system features or qualities. Among the major qualities a command system should have are the following:

1.   Adaptability—can it be converted readily from a peacetime footing to meet the specific requirements of a variety of contingencies short of but including war?

2.   Reliability—is it as free as possible from internal defects and failure modes, including design defects, invitations to operator error and equipment malfunctions?

3.   Responsiveness—is it sensitive to the direction of decision-makers, that is, can it provide information and react to commands different from standard or pre-programmed routines?

4.   Interoperability—does the system permit effective exchange with other military services, including those of friends or allies?

5.   Resistance—is the system secure against external jamming, spoofing, electronic warfare, sabotage, or other intrusion and interference?

6.   Survivability—is there a high probability that the crucial elements of the system will remain effective through very severe conflict conditions?

7.   Durability—can it function effectively under the continued stress of intense conflict?

8.   Reconstitutability—is there sufficient redundancy or other inherent features to allow the system to be readily reconstituted if it suffers direct damage?

9.   Capacity and comprehensiveness—can the system manage the volume of directives and data associated with a particular scenario and does it extend to the areas where it may be called upon to operate?

Some of the desirable qualities mentioned in this short list, such as reliability, resistance and adaptability, will be important under all circumstances. The value of others will vary with different scenarios. Survivability, durability and reconstitutability matter little during crises or special operations, but a great deal in nuclear or space conflict scenarios. The contingencies that may arise in the context of general scenarios also influence requirements of the command system. Responsiveness and durability will be crucial in launching a limited first strike, whereas the survivability of the system is the first consideration when the task is nuclear retaliation.

Areas of concern

Likewise, as suggested in table 4.1.I., particular concerns vary with scenarios and contingencies, as well as with the particular vulnerabilities command systems exhibit under different scenarios. And since different scenarios or contingencies tend to be associated with specific services, there is institutional variance, which adds to the complexity of developing a cohesive command system. The concern of the US Army is with maintaining tactical command and control in what is euphemistically called a 'nuclear-stressed environment', which poses different kinds of durability and resistance problems from those faced by US Air Force elements charged with the command and control of strategic nuclear forces.

Not surprisingly, there is relatively little concern for how command systems function in situations short of actual conflict, although it is out of such situations that conflict is likely to grow, especially if there are major unseen deficiencies in the system itself.[8] Neither those who believe that the command system is inadequate to the heroic demands of fighting a limited but protracted nuclear conflict or a short and unlimited nuclear war, nor those who fear the command system itself may contribute to an inadvertent nuclear war have closely examined its performance in other contingencies, such as crises.

On the official level, there seems to be an assumption that a system optimized to fight a nuclear or space war, a conflict at sea or a major conventional land campaign could easily manage a crisis. Yet this is far from the case. Indeed, as command systems are driven more and more in the direction of the automatic or semi-automatic decision-making and decision-execution that may be required on the battlefield of the future, their ability to deal effectively with less apocalyptic but more common events (terrorist incidents, guerilla warfare or aggravated crises) may suffer.

Even a brief discussion of the elements of command systems would not be complete without reference to the phases of scenarios, the major substantive dimensions of command, or the idiosyncratic factors that bear on the design and performance of command systems. In the US case, just as the reference to the National Command Authorities in military directives supports the illusion that all questions of succession and the delegation of political and military power have been resolved in advance (though they have not), the establishment of alert levels, or 'defence conditions', leaves the impression that moving from one level or type of preparedness to another is a simple feat when it is not.

Instead, the conversion of very large, complex and widespread institutions from one footing to another is always problematic. What Clausewitz called 'friction' and what the Anglo-Saxons dubbed Murphy's Law (if anything can go wrong, it will) are potentially as operative in increasing preparedness as in combat itself. The problem is inherent. During the prelude to war or the peak of a crisis, military forces are usually being heavily used for political purposes—demonstrating resolve, indicating thresholds, staking positions, and so on—which entail especial adroitness in the command system. At the same time, they are also trying to achieve a state of readiness for combat operations that may follow, which means rehearsing routines or taking other actions that may be in conflict with the political aim of showing or using armed forces so as to avoid combat.

A pertinent example occurred during the Cuban Missile Crisis, when the Chief of Naval Operations took exception to the 'political' interference of the Secretary of Defense in connection with the way the Navy was operating its blockade of the waters around Cuba. The aim of the naval chief was to conduct an effective blockade in line with standard procedures; the aim of the secretary was to give the Soviet leadership enough 'wiggle room' to slip off the hook on which it had impaled itself.

This case also reflects the gulf that can exist between decision-making and decision-execution. Had not the Secretary visited the war room from which the blockade was being monitored, the decision to pursue this seemingly more moderate option might have been implemented in a way entirely contrary to the intent of the senior officials of government. In this instance, the command lines were foreshortened and a misstep was avoided. But in other crises, the on-scene commander may have a very different interpretation of the orders he receives without the opportunity of checking or being checked as to its congruence with political intentions.

Regarding idiosyncratic factors affecting the performance of command and control systems, we are once again in a realm where only retrospective analysis is possible. Yet a review of past cases from the standpoint of the possible influence of distinctive individual, institutional or national traits should provide a sense of how important these might be. Language, after all, is the medium of command and control. While military practice tends towards developing a synthetic language that is as free as possible from idiosyncratic elements, and hence opportunities for misinterpretation, it cannot wholly eliminate the variance, especially where operations involve the forces of different nations. Moreover, what standardized military language gains in freedom from ambiguity, it loses in terms of the nuance and subtlety of political discourse.

Future demands

In response to the technical conditions sketched at the beginning of this chapter, organized violence and the use of force have acquired a somewhat different character in the nuclear age. As between the major powers, resort to the *threat* of the use of force has predominated over its actual employment. Meanwhile, the rest of the world has been deeply scarred by limited wars, proxy wars, terrorism, guerilla warfare, wars of national liberation, military raids and other forms of what is now called low-intensity conflict, though that term hardly does justice to the suffering and destruction experienced, individually or cumulatively, in these conflicts.

So long as these conditions obtain without sparking a general conflagration, the more dire predictions about the shortcomings of command systems may never be realized. What is troubling about the current prominence of command and control issues is that priority is accorded to preparing for the more extreme scenarios (space warfare, limited or unlimited nuclear war, and alliance conflict in Europe under AirLand Battle scenarios) rather than to assuring that command systems are well suited to keeping armed violence at its current if regrettable level.

The problems of algorithms for improbable systems to intercept intercontinental ballistic missiles (ICBMs) or of connectivity among system components in a protracted nuclear war—either of which may prove insoluble—reduce attention to the questions of clarity and responsiveness in command systems during crises or when operations are underway in or near trouble spots. Yet the record of command system performance in crisis and low-intensity conflict is not such as to breed confidence in its operation at this level of violence, much less under conditions as extreme as those of major conventional war or nuclear exchanges.

This unbalanced approach suggests that, in the United States at least, command systems are now unequal to either set of tasks. The hardening and redeploying of airborne civil and military command posts, development of hardened mobile communication centres for strategic conflict, and improvement and exercising of civil–military facilities for post-attack contingencies will likely prove futile against a determined attacker. Meanwhile, the *ad hoc* conglomeration of service or special-purpose command systems that is rationalized as a global command system often lacks the capability to respond quickly and effectively to political direction, even in instances where laborious advance preparations are made.

The introduction of more and more high performance information technology in the command equation, moreover, has a differential impact across various conflict and crisis scenarios. At the present stage of information system development, high-performance equipment is most beneficial in maintaining peacetime readiness, prosecuting special operations or conducting limited wars. In terms of nuclear conflict, major conventional warfare, crisis control or space operations, high technology has a double-edged impact owing to the relative utility or desirability of high-speed and high-volume information systems for decision-making, implementation and escalation control. In these cases, high-performance technology may aid in decision-execution, but prove counterproductive as regards making sensible decisions or retarding escalation.

In short, high-performance information systems can be very effective in limited or isolated actions and against a weaker party. But 'set-piece' operations are a relatively poor reflection of how the larger battle management system will function when all components are under stress simultaneously. Hence, they remain a large unknown in terms of the circumstances where their performance will be most critical.

'In warfare', Lord Mountbatten noted, 'the unexpected is the rule and no one can anticipate what an opponent's reaction will be to the unexpected.' What automatic decision-making and decision-execution neglect are the awful uncertainties attendant on crises and combat. It is not so much a case of whether decision-makers will be able to override automatic command systems (although that could prove far more difficult than enthusiasts will admit), but whether they will know when to override and when not.

In addressing future demands on command and control, what seems to be needed is, first, a better way of thinking about the subject, one that is more comprehensive and more sensitive to non-technical problems. Second, more attention to the political dimensions of command and control is required; it is clear that political leaders will have to continue to rely on military command systems to carry out their decisions. Yet civil authorities must assure that these systems—hierarchically organized, drilled in standard operating procedures, and oriented to the prevailing doctrines of separate services—will be responsive to political direction. This involves the recognition that command systems will most often be used in an expedient and selective way, putting a premium on adaptability, and that intermediary or on-scene commanders are presently schooled in military tactics, not political ones.[9]

Third, the application of new and emerging technology to the problems of command and control should be pursued judiciously, less in terms of what the technology can do and more in the context of the multiple and often subtle demands of command and control. In short, the future effectiveness of systems for managing war, crisis and armed peace depends more on perspective than on hardware.

Notes and references

[1] Colvard, J. E., Deputy Chief, Naval *Matériel* Command, 'Technological transformation of defense', *Bureaucrat: Journal for Public Managers*, vol. 14 (Sep. 1985).

[2] This formulation of the problem, of course, appears to ignore the reality that it is sometimes military authorities who have to remind political leaders of the risks and ramifications, both political and military, of the use of force or the threat of its use, for it is often politicians who are most anxious to use the military resources available to them. Still, this would seem to be a special case of assuring the paramountcy of the political purposes in the use of armed forces.

[3] Steinbruner, J. D., 'Nuclear decapitation', *Foreign Policy*, no. 45, Winter 1981–1982.

[4] The relevant major studies are: Ball, D., *Can Nuclear War Be Controlled?* Adelphi Paper No. 169 (International Institute for Strategic Studies: London, 1981); Blair, B. G., *Strategic Command and Control: Redefining the Nuclear Threat* (The Brookings Institution: Washington, DC, 1985); Bracken, P. J., *The Command and Control of Nuclear Forces* (Yale University Press: New Haven, CT, 1983); and Ford, D., *The Button: The Pentagon's Strategic Command and Control System* (Simon and Schuster: New York, 1985).

[5] Studies which touch on this possibility include: Frei, D., *Risks of Unintentional Nuclear War* (UNIDIR: Geneva, 1982); George, A. L., Bernstein, D. M., Parnell, G. S. and Rogers, J. P., *Inadvertent War in Europe: Crisis Simulation*, Special Report of the Center for International Security and Arms Control, Stanford University (Stanford University: Stanford, CA, 1985); and Roderick, H., (ed.), *Avoiding Inadvertent War: Crisis Management* (University of Texas: Austin, TX, 1983).

[6] Ball (note 4), p. 5.

[7] See the critique of Blair, B., 'Solving the command and control problem' *Arms Control Today*, vol. 15, no. 1 (Jan. 1985).

[8] An exception is the very fine paper by Bouchard, US Navy Lt Commander J. F., 'Crisis management and the control of military operations' (unpublished paper, Apr.

1985), to which I am heavily indebted in terms of my thinking about the range of demands made on command systems.

[9] The paper by Lt Commander Bouchard (note 8) contains cogent suggestions for improving crisis response capability, including development of service doctrines for this purpose.

Paper 4.2. Beyond the security dilemma: technology, strategy and international security

NICHOLAS J. WHEELER AND KEN BOOTH

I. Introduction

We are inundated by technological changes. In the defence field the headlines are dominated by the Star Wars debate and the increasing sophistication of conventional weaponry, while the penetration by new gadgetry of all corners of civilian life is an everyday occurrence. Our sheer amazement at the speed and output of contemporary technological innovation frequently deflects attention from first-order questions, even in the defence field. Confronted by a new weapon, we are too busy asking 'What can we do with it?' to ponder the most fundamental strategic-philosophical question of all: 'What is it all about?'[1] There is therefore a need for us to step back from too close an involvement in current debates about particular items of new technology, and attempt to understand more generally the various interrelationships between technological change, strategy and international security. Some historical perspective will help.

II. Engineers and unilateralists

Two apparently simple themes will run through our discussion. First, it will be argued that future international security will depend upon reciprocity between states: it will not emerge as it sometimes did in the past, from the unilateral pursuit of national security. And second, it will be stressed that international security is at root a political and not a technological problem. These themes might seem trite at first sight. Many, if not most, practitioners and commentators would find themselves able to accept them. However, a sizeable proportion of that group, while nodding approval at the idea that international security is a reciprocal and political phenomenon, continue to act and write as if it is not. Among the latter have been the policy-makers of the superpowers. The simple themes of this paper have been antithetical to the 'engineering approach' to foreign policy of the United States and the traditionalist 'strategic culture' of the Soviet Union.

Because the pace of military technological change has greatly accelerated since the middle of the last century, strategists have been increasingly burdened by the pressures of innovation. Indeed, strategic life has become one technological problem after another. As a result, there has been a tendency to exaggerate the significance of technological considerations. Since we have grown up in a world in which technology shapes so much of what we do, as individuals and groups, we almost intuitively come to invest it with a significance in international security that is not justified by the historical record. US strategists in particular have been prone to this. They have tended to believe that since technological change throws up the problems, it can also provide the solutions. Out of the fact of technological innovation has been born a faith in the technological fix.

The characteristically American faith in the technological fix is an element of that 'can do' attitude which runs so strongly through US life, and indeed much of the success of the United States. Foreign policy has not been immune from its effects, and over 30 years ago Stanley Hoffmann dubbed it the 'engineering approach' to international politics. It was an approach, he said, which was not steeped in history or psychology, 'which are sciences (or arts) of the complex and uncertain'. Indeed, this approach involved a quest for 'mathematical formulas that tend to give a reassuring sense of certainty even when they measure the immeasurable'. According to Hoffmann, the engineering approach contains several drawbacks that 'operate as blinders' on US policy-making. In particular, the quest for certainty leads to an 'over-simplification and overrating of purely technical but calculable elements over intangible ones'. Such faith in 'human engineering', he argued, was both misplaced and liable to disappointment. Hoffmann's words were written over 20 years before President Reagan's Star Wars speech, but they could have been written the day after.[2]

Running in parallel with this engineering approach to foreign policy problems has been the theme of US 'unilateralism'. This describes the nationalistic desire to act autonomously on the world stage to secure the values and interests of the US political community. Such unilateralism has been even more a feature of Soviet international behaviour. Indeed, unilateralism in its approach to foreign and defence policy has been a basic element in the Soviet 'strategic culture'. The main features of the latter have included a deep suspicion of outsiders, and therefore a belief that the nation has to rely on its own strength for security, and an understanding of the dangers of being weak, and hence a belief that safety is best secured by preponderance rather than parity with an adversary. Alongside these characteristics has been a habit of seeing the struggle in international politics in crude power terms, as is illustrated by Stalin's famous or infamous question: 'How many divisions has the Pope?' Not surprisingly, therefore, such an outlook has nurtured a tradition of military overinsurance. All those attitudes have been perpetuated by what is probably the most security-conscious leadership in the world and one which is overwhelmingly reliant on the advice of a conservative military establishment. The United States is confronted by a superpower which also interprets security in unilateral rather than reciprocal terms.

The already formidable problem of international security in the last part of the twentieth century is therefore compounded by the mind-sets which have dominated the two superpowers. The basic issue we continue to face is whether the interplay of the new technological challenges and the old ways of thinking will preclude the possibility of a stable international order.

III.   Revolutionary powers versus international security

International security can be defined as an arrangement whereby the evolution of the international system is managed through the common consent of the players as to the essential 'rules of the game'. This consent can be tacit or explicit, and when it occurs the states in the system can have a justifiably high expectation that there will not be a major war, and that their core values will not be under threat.

In the past the greatest challenges to international security have come from the rise of those revolutionary powers which have been determined to destroy the existing order, and so deny to other states either the right to exist or the right to exist in their preferred ways. Such revolutionary powers as those represented by Charles V, Louis XIV, Napoleon and Hitler challenged the established rules of the states system in their bids for absolute power.[3] The major breakdowns in international security have therefore grown out of political ambition rather than technological innovation. Nor were the ambitions of these revolutionary powers created by new technological possibilities; in each case the technology of the day was employed, more or less well, in their attempt to destroy the existing order.

Henry Kissinger has argued that lasting international security depends upon the creation of a 'legitimate' international order. This condition requires that all the major powers agree on the 'permissible aims and methods of foreign policy . . . at least to the extent that no state is so dissatisfied that, like Germany after the Treaty of Versailles, it expresses its dissatisfaction in a revolutionary foreign policy'.[4] A revolutionary power is one which believes that it can be secure only if others are insecure, or for practical purposes do not exist as international actors.

One state's search for absolute security implies the absolute insecurity of all other states. And every search for a new order on this basis has proved to be self-defeating. Since all states seek to maximize their security, the net effect of any drive for absolute security is to provoke countervailing efforts and thus a competition for security which brings about additional insecurity for all. Such a prospect confirms the Realist characterization of international politics as a Hobbesian world in which law and morality can have little place, where crises and wars are ever-present possibilities and where the narrow pursuit of self-interest is king. Robert Jervis in a major contribution to our thinking about these matters has described the gist of the problem as the 'security dilemma'.[5]

IV.   Security dilemmas, insecurity traps and security communities

The security dilemma, according to Jervis, describes those situations in which one state's increase in security brings about a decrease in the security of others. This formulation undoubtedly provides a useful contribution to our understanding of the reason that co-operation has proved to be so difficult in the international system. However, it must be questioned whether it fully captures the reality of global politics and whether it is helpful in thinking about how to minimize the dangers inherent in the system. We will argue that characterizing our problem as a security dilemma is, in analytical terms, either tautologous or mistaken, while as a guide to action it is regressive.

The essence of the security dilemma argument is that policies designed to increase one state's security inadvertently decrease the security of others. A particular state may not have aggressive designs on others, but the interplay of military behaviour and mutual mistrust tends to produce a reciprocal fear, competition and insecurity. The 'prisoner's dilemma' is a useful analogy; as in the security dilemma the pursuit of individual self-interest by the players leads to a sub-optimal outcome. It is the primacy of security, the perceived costs of not playing the self-help game and the chronic uncertainty which attends inter-state interaction which combine to make the promise of co-operation so difficult for the actors involved. The dynamics of power competition produce the security dilemma which Realists believe to be the inevitable by-product of living in a self-help system.

But the Realist conception is too crude. Clearly, the notion of the security dilemma—an increase in one state's security decreases the security of others—is mistaken in relationships where there is a stable expectation of peace between particular states. Such relationships have been categorized by Karl Deutsch and others as 'security communities'.[6] Thus, when US security increases, Canada does not feel threatened. Similarly, when Norway feels more secure, Denmark does not shiver. In relationships where there is no expectation of peaceful intercourse, on the other hand, the label security dilemma is merely tautologous, that is, in a logical sense it is a proposition which is always true. An 'enemy' is a state which manifests hostility to another by actively trying to thwart its purposes and damage its interests. It naturally follows from this that if one state in a hostile relationship becomes more secure, then it must be at its enemy's cost. If security involves not feeling that one's core values are threatened, then it is obvious that any rise in Syrian power and self-confidence, for example, will be seen as a direct threat by Israel and so will increase the latter's sense of insecurity. The same is true in reverse. Such outcomes are always to be expected between sworn enemies in a 'state of war'.

Between friendly states, therefore, the notion of the security dilemma is mistaken, while between enemy states it is tautologous. But even in the latter case too much significance should not be read into the same label 'enemy', for when this label is attached to some state or other at least as many questions are raised as are settled. Unfortunately, in the always complex world of international relations, labels sometimes suffice for analysis.

In international politics, as in consumer affairs these days, we must be more careful with our labelling. This means, in connection with our present discussion, that we must be careful before accepting the label 'enemy', for once we do, we have gone a long way to conceding the validity of the pure security dilemma syllogism. This is not to say that the syllogism is always invalid: indeed it is sometimes entirely appropriate, for pure enemy relationships obviously do exist. Even so, for the most part the real world is greyer, and its processes more complex than the action–reactions suggested by the pure security dilemma formulation. It is not enough merely to describe a particular state as an enemy. Numerous considerations must qualify the meaning of this term. There are questions relating to the extent of the antagonism: is it limited or total? There are issues of intentions and capabilities. And geographical matters pertaining to distance and accessibility need to be raised. All these considerations interact in different ways to give different meanings to the label 'enemy'. As a result, even between 'enemies' the pure security dilemma does not always operate. The United States never shivered at increments in Albanian security.

Few states exist in 'security communities', where they do not have each other targeted and where there is a stable expectation of peace. And few are in the pure security dilemma relationship where there is a real incompatibility and where all the characteristics of a zero-sum game are exhibited. Most relationships in international politics fall somewhere between; many states are unable to be 'friends' with others because of real or imagined incompatibilities, but they are unwilling to fight because of the limited benefits and excessive costs of such an outcome. This situation, in which most states find themselves, might be called the 'insecurity trap'. States cannot live in positive peace with others, but they do not see any profit in war. Insecurity is normal, but there are grounds for coexistence. When states believe that their security depends upon others being insecure, there is little prospect of escape from an enemy relationship: however, if states can accept that others might be willing to coexist in a legitimate order, and that part of the mistrust and antagonism which states show towards each other is in part a direct consequence of living in a self-help system rather than being the result of aggressive intent, then there exists the possibility that states can manage insecurity within an anarchic system.

V.   Security and anarchy

It was argued earlier that fundamental challenges to international security have come from those actors determined to overthrow the existing rules and restraints. But international history also offers more hopeful experiences. There have been times, for example, when international order has been robust and when states have placed a common value on security. This occurred in a particularly notable fashion in the period known as the Concert of Europe. The explanations for this development are varied, but of major importance was the fact that the states involved had just fought a most destructive war and that all the participants were determined to prevent any recurrence. The governments concerned therefore placed a common value on moderation and restraint in inter-state politics.

The Concert system institutionalized reciprocity between states. Governments took a long-term view of their predicament. They believed that short-run sacrifices would yield long-term gains and that others would not exploit their restraint for immediate ends. They realized that all were sharing equally in the costs and benefits of restraint. Self-interest still motivated states, of course, but they believed that their national interests would be best served by co-operative behaviour. The Concert was a form of enlightened self-interest, and Robert Jervis has characterized it as a 'security regime'. He defines the latter in terms of those principles, norms and rules which permit actors to be restrained in the belief that others might reciprocate.[7] By posting the need for security regimes there is the implicit assumption that international security will not automatically flourish in a self-regulating anarchic system. In fact the Concert developed from the realization that the self-regulating order of eighteenth century Europe had made possible the destructive experience of the Napoleonic wars.

The international order of 1815–23 had to accommodate different political ideologies. Then, as now, the restraint that is required for a security regime— or something approaching it—is not one based on the countries concerned sharing a political ideology: instead, restraint is rooted in shared ideas about external conduct. Hoffmann has wisely argued that the key to a legitimate international order is not whether one achieves one's preferences regarding domestic orders, but whether 'one behaves moderately on the world stage'.[8] Thus, coexistence is necessary of different ideologies in the same legitimate structure. Whether such restraint and accommodation will be possible in the future, as it was during the Concert, remains to be seen. In this process, balances of relative military capability are obviously important, but stability ultimately rests on self-limitation and reciprocal restraint—a mixture of unilateral and multilateral actions.

A major obstacle in building legitimate orders arises from the fact that nations evaluate situations in terms of their own domestic culture and traditions. But as Henry Kissinger argued, in the conclusion of *A World Restored*, any effort to identify international order with a particularist concept of justice is likely to lead to international insecurity.[9] This is a verdict which goes to the very heart of our contemporary predicament: are the superpowers incapable of creating a legitimate order because of their particular political and strategic cultures? The Concert system was able to last (for a time) because the statesmen who came to share in the drama of working out co-operative solutions to complex problems were conscious that those things which united them were much greater than those issues which separated them. So far, the leaders of the United States and the Soviet Union have not developed a similar consciousness.

The record to date—more than 40 years after the ending of the common struggle against Hitler—does not give us great confidence for the future. But neither must it lead us to bleak despair. As we have seen, co-operation is possible, even in an anarchic setting; but it must also be accepted that international co-operation has always proved to be a fragile blossom. Every period of co-operation has proved transitory and every period of order and equilibrium has, eventually, broken down into war. This verdict for obvious reasons casts a depressing shadow over life in the nuclear age, but it should be a sharp spur to our efforts to attempt to understand the conditions and dynamics of international co-operation. In this regard it must be pointed out that one of the oddest aspects of proponents of the Realist ideology in international politics is that although they constantly rub our noses in the gloomy history of human behaviour, they above all others today seem to believe that more of the same, this time, will 'work'.

VI.   Travelling hopefully

The most important single bilateral relationship of our time is obviously that between the Soviet Union and the United States. It has accurately been described by Marshall Shulman as a 'limited adversary' relationship,[10] to indicate their competitiveness in many fields, but also the fact that their competition has been limited by a mutual recognition of the irrationality of war. Part of the adversarial character of their relationship has been structurally determined: history provides several examples of bi-polar confrontations between the most powerful states in the system. But some part of the adversarial character of their relationship has been the result of misperceptions. Today what we have is not an eschatological conflict between absolute enemies. We have competitive coexistence infused with excessive mistrust on the part of some powerful bodies of opinion in both states. Objectively speaking, the relationship does not necessarily fall into the pure security dilemma formulation—'an increase in one state's security decreases the security of others'—because the superpowers are limited rather than total adversaries.

Empirical support for the preceding argument is suggested by the fact that when Soviet security increased through the 1960s, after the alarms of the Cuban missile crisis, it was not accompanied by a proportionate increase in feelings of insecurity in the United States. Indeed, this rise in Soviet security helped to establish the conditions in which both states thought it profitable to explore the relatively co-operative relationship implied by their search for détente at the end of the 1960s. In addition, at least some US observers of Soviet affairs recognize—what has always been clearer to Western Europeans—namely that when the Soviet sense of insecurity sharply increases, the outcome may well be a rise in militant and unco-operative behaviour. This was obviously the case in the 1958–62 period.[11] This recognition of the threat to the West represented by Soviet insecurity is well illustrated by the old adage that there is nothing so dangerous as a Russian on the defensive.

In addition to its analytical weakness, therefore, the security dilemma concept can be regressive as a guide to policy, that is, backward-looking and fatalistic. It plays into the hands of the Realists by offering a static view of the world. It suggests that any effort to increase international security is destined to be counter-productive, and that life in international politics is bound to be 'nasty, brutish and short'. Thus, this is seen as the best of all possible worlds because it is the only possible world. By characterizing our predicament as basically an 'insecurity trap', we hope to emphasize the variety of paradigm conditions in what Bull dubbed the 'anarchical society'. Few states have the luxury of living in a 'security community', and few face the clear-cut impera-tives of the pure adversarial security dilemma. For most, the condition is that of the 'insecurity trap', where states have to manage insecurity, to a greater or lesser degree. The use of war as an instrument of policy is a possibility, but a distant one.

Realism in international politics is regressive: it is ideology masquerading (having captured a persuasive title) as truth. At the same time, dwelling on distant utopias is a distraction from the actual problems we face. In such circumstances our efforts should concentrate on what Joseph Nye, Jr, has called 'process utopias'.[12] He defines these as 'hypothesized benign or pacific trend(s) though the end point of the trend is uncertain'. If one were certain that a process was consistently reducing the risk of war, then one would be more optimistic than if one concentrated on some infeasible 'end point' utopia. When thinking about the problem of security, it is therefore advisable to adopt the minimalist perspective of the utopian process; this should give some grounds for modest optimism and some encouragement for action. Changing the game is not presently an option. Travelling hopefully is as near as one can presently hope to get to utopia in international politics.

The certainties sought by some groups in the superpowers—the new right in the United States and the old left in the Soviet Union—are bound to end in disappointment and frustration. At the same time, the unilateralism of their operational strategies will do nothing to loosen the ties of the insecurity trap. Consequently, if the present international system is to be saved from that cataclysmic breakdown which has characterized all those in the past, a major shift of opinion is required. Influential opinion-formers and policy-makers in these two countries must accept that although some degree of insecurity will remain the norm in their relationship, it need not be an impediment to limited co-operation, particularly on the matter of war avoidance. The fact is that the superpowers have no alternative but to remain dependent on each other for what relative security they enjoy. Recognition of such strategic inter-dependence is alien to the Realist ideology. But not all Realists are immune from either change or longer-term perspectives. It is not sufficiently well known, for example, that the founders of Realism in the study of international politics, Hans J. Morgenthau and Edward H. Carr, both recognized its limitations. Towards the end of his life Morgenthau warned of the great dangers of realism, while Carr stressed the need for diplomacy to be based on 'elements of both utopia and reality'.[13]

Despite the prevalence of the ideas fostered by the disciples of the Realist ideology, it should be apparent from empirical investigation that the condition of global anarchy (the absence of a legal superior) does not automatically mean that inter-state relations are characterized by chaos and violence. The existence of co-operative elements in international politics is generally over-looked by those who look at the world almost exclusively through strategic spectacles. The prevalence of these Hobbesian thinkers have skewed our understanding of the game of nations towards the law-of-the-jungle end of the spectrum and in so doing have created expectations which have a self-fulfilling aspect to them. If policy-makers believe that the world is nasty, brutish and short, and act accordingly, their behaviour will almost certainly ensure, by an action–reaction process, that their images become translated into reality. Such 'doctrinal realists', in William T. R. Fox's phrase, do not see the need to examine how nation states behave because they have already posited how they must behave by virtue of their 'nation-stateness in a multi-state world system'. Fox contrasts this approach with that of the 'empirical realist' who 'by contrast looks to see how they actually behave' and, perhaps beyond, examines the possibilities 'for tolerable coexistence'.[14] Doctrinal realists, according to Fox, act on the assumption that security depends upon strength and preponderance and, as a result, 'a gigantic and unending negative-sum game' follows. This mind-set has the potential to turn uncomfortable and difficult 'insecurity traps' into pure security dilemmas in which states become locked into self-defeating and potentially self-destructive strategies of confrontation. The objective conditions of the international system naturally promote power and force to the top of the agenda, but the obsessive primacy which they are accorded by doctrinal realists is often (though not always) the result of the malignant effect of mutually reinforcing myths and illusions about the game of nations.

VII.   Escalators and dampeners

Although it was suggested that it has been the movement of political factors rather than the innovation of technology which have proved most disturbing to international security, this problem cannot be ignored, and a revealing ex-ample of the possible interrelationship between technological change and international security can be seen in the collapse of international security in 1914.

Consider the interplay of technology and perception in terms of 'escalators' and 'dampeners'. Escalators are those pressures which encourage crises between states to take on a greater momentum. They might include domestic insecurity, élite intransigence, faith in one's first-strike weapons or confidence in one's ability to prevail at the higher levels of confrontation. Such conditions are likely to turn tests of resolve into major crises and so increase the risks of war. Dampeners, on the other hand, are those brakes and constraints which reduce the escalatory potential of crises and encourage co-operation between adversaries in the task of disaster avoidance.

Although meaning slightly different things to the main actors, a 'Cult of the Offensive' gripped military minds in the decade before 1914. The offence was believed to be dominant, victory was perceived to be dependent upon pre-emption, and there was a belief that to strike second was to be lost. These are classic escalators, and as Schelling has put it, 'military planning which encourages haste encourages war'.[15] In such an environment, with measures for defence indistinguishable from those for offence, there was considerable suspicion in the capitals of Europe. Someone was likely to crack, and it was the particular psychological realities of the German leadership which started the deadly ball of competitive mobilizations rolling. Even so, it was not at root the mobilization plans with their dependence on railway timetables which pushed Europe over the abyss into war: rather, it was the underlying political struggle between Germany and Britain for dominance of the international system, or, more accurately, the reciprocal perception in Berlin and London that the other wanted preponderance and hegemony.

In evaluating the costs of going to war in 1914, the decision-makers had also to consider the costs of not acting, and for Germany's leaders it was the latter which loomed large. They believed that a quick and decisive blow was possible and that war could be won. They also believed that there was a finite time limit within which to act because a Russian rearmament programme was beginning, and if Germany was to escape encirclement, it was thought necessary to act before the situation became worse. Thus, a deadly combination of ambition, pressure to act and faith in success through offensive strength led German leaders to risk all in a desperate bid to resolve their problems and advance their power by means of brute military force.

The insecurity which motivated the German inner circle was well illustrated by a note from the Kaiser which read: 'The net has been suddenly thrown over our head, and England sneeringly reaps the most brilliant successes of her persistently prosecuted, purely anti-German world policy, against which we have proved ourselves helpless.'[16] Here is chronic paranoia, fear and desperation. It was this collective mind-set which led the Germans into believing that there was a military escape from what they saw as a tightening noose. Had they learnt what now seems to have been the 'lessons' of the US Civil War, instead of being preoccupied by the Prussian successes of 1866 and 1870, they might have appreciated the growing advantages which were accruing to the defence. With this understanding, they would have known there was little chance of winning a war but also that there was less urgency in risking trying to break out and fight one. The encircling noose which they feared was primarily in their heads rather than in the diplomacy of the day. But it was no less 'real' for that.

Against the background of the political struggle between Germany and Britain, and in the midst of an intense crisis, Germany's leaders were faced by the choice of dampening the situation, or escalating it. By believing that their opponents were intent on destroying Germany, they engaged in worst-case thinking about their political situation while, at the time, they were tempted into engaging in best-case thinking about their prospects of military victory.

The 1914 experience illustrates that the fundamental problem lies not in some autonomous process of technological change as such, but in the hopes and fears, the perceptions and misperceptions, and the values and biases which infuse national policy-makers.

VIII.   Technological change and strategic prognosis

Our argument is not that technological change is irrelevant to questions of international security, only that it rarely deserves the centrality which it is usually accorded. The latter has been encouraged by the pre-eminence of strategists in the contemporary debate about East–West affairs, and by the way they have made 'strategy' and 'security' almost synonymous. In the post-war period, security has too often been interpreted in an almost exclusively military fashion. When this occurs, 'security' and 'strategy' can be antithetical. When strategy is seen as it frequently is by Realists, simply as the pursuit of national military strength, then the outcome in terms of security might well be the opposite of that intended. On several occasions in the post-war period, one or other superpower has attempted to push for preponderance in some area or other of the strategic confrontation. Arms races ensued. There was more cost, more tension and more overkill. But there was no more security at the end of it.

The major feature of the relationship between technology and strategy in the past 150 years has been change itself. The Concert of Europe just preceded the era when the industrial revolution spawned the processes of military innovation which every few years since then have changed the sights and sounds of the battlefield or war at sea. It appears self-evident that a legitimate international order is more likely to grow on a technological plateau than on slopes where all the major actors are scrambling to acquire the best of newly discovered weapons and trying to guess their implications. Unfortunately, the advantages of such a technological plateau are not those that we have enjoyed in the last generation, nor are we likely to see any in the years ahead if the trends outlined in this book continue. Nevertheless, there can be no doubt that mutual national restraint in weapon innovation can make a positive contribution to political restraint.

Estimating in peacetime the implications of technological change has been one of the most consistently difficult tasks for strategists. It has been suggested by writers such as Herman Kahn that in the past technological changes largely occurred within wars rather than between them. Technologically speaking, the next war usually began where the last left off. It is different today. Weapon innovation is now a constant peacetime condition. Furthermore, the speed of modern wars, in most circumstances, has led to the 'go as you are' phenomenon. What you fight with is what you have on mobilization day. Industrialized states, engaged in war, can no longer expect Britain's traditional luxury of the 'long haul'. The latter gave the British the opportunity to mobilize relatively slowly, and subsequently experiment and develop the weaponry, tactics and strategies as appropriate. Technological change has not only made strategy an increasingly peacetime preoccupation, it has also made it more bureaucratic. This has found its ultimate expression in the huge and permanent staffs of the North Atlantic Treaty Organization (NATO) and the Warsaw Pact, two organizations which help underpin a military confrontation but also help freeze those political factors which constitute the problems of European security.

Echoing our theme that the major breakdowns of the states system have not been determined by changes in technology is the fact that some of the most significant developments in the evolution of strategy, according to writers like Bernard Brodie, have been the result not of the arrival of new weaponry as such, but rather as a result of political and social changes.[17] The institution of limited wars, which characterized the century preceding the Napoleonic era, were overthrown not by revolutionary weaponry, but by the spread of revolutionary ideas, including that of nationalism. None the less, it is undeniable that particular innovations in military technology have occasionally had a decisive effect on events, as with the use of shells by the Russians against the wooden ships of the Turks at Sinope in 1853. But such breakthroughs are rare and have not been the cause of the major breakdowns of the system. Today, the strands which bind together the system of states into a society, however anarchical, are more likely to be unravelled by the spread of Islamic fundamentalism, and the challenge it represents to Western norms, than the development of any particular piece of technology, even an excellent ballistic missile defence system.

When experts in defence policy confidently discuss the implications of new technology, our historical memories should encourage us to be sceptical. The war cemeteries of the world are memorials, among other things, to the errors of our strategic forefathers. Establishment strategists in the past were often slow to adjust to the implications of new weapons, and this record is such that we should not automatically invest great confidence in the assessments of their counterparts today. New weapons have sometimes been developed with great expectations in relation to some immediate national problem, but with little or no thought to their long-term implications for international security. In recent years the US promotion of multiple independently targetable re-entry vehicles (MIRVs) is the best example of how a technological quick-fix can turn out to be counter-productive.

Historically, military establishments have frequently adjusted tomorrow's weapons into yesterday's doctrine. Those Harold Lasswell called 'the specialists in violence'[18] have tended to perpetuate a conservative, conflict-oriented and ethnocentric view of the world. It is unlikely to help the cause of international security if policy-making is unduly under the influence of strategists in general and those with a technological rather than political outlook in particular. Unfortunately, the arrival of nuclear weapons tended to encourage this trend. In the superpower relationship, as a result, the role of politics and diplomacy has diminished.

Since the middle of the nineteenth century, military planners have swung from a general scepticism about the impact of technological change (as witnessed by the survival of the cavalry) to the very opposite extreme. Strategists have frequently exaggerated the political significance of new technology. This was evident in the inflated expectations of the early airpower theorists, through those who believed that nuclear weapons would change everything down to those today who invest the technology of Star Wars with a potential which is not remotely manifest in metal and mirrors. The former predisposition towards technological scepticism has given way to the contemporary predisposition to excessive technological faith. The latter detracts attention both from thinking about the past and what can be learned from it, and overestimates the possibility of finding technological escapes from fundamentally political predicaments.

Without doubt, the pace and character of technological change has been remarkable over the past 160 years, and especially during the past 50 years. Most obviously, this change has increased the potential destructiveness of wars. The industrial revolution allowed wars to grow in terms of the manpower which could be mobilized and kept fighting. Bigger wars occurred, which proved to be more difficult to control politically, and were therefore less useful as instruments of policy. War at the highest levels of violence became decreasingly useful as instruments of policy. The Western allies had justifiable cause for engaging in the two world wars, but in neither case did their overwhelming military victories produce a harmonious peace.

The two world wars of this century have led some to argue that war—certainly total war—does not pay. Germany's victims, or potential victims of those wars, knew that this view was premature. But there is no doubt that the advent of a world of nuclear plenty has changed this. Total war between the major powers, which was already threatened with becoming an obsolete instrument of policy, has finally come to be seen as such, save for the false beliefs of some 'strategic fundamentalists' in the camps of both superpowers.[19] These fundamentalists apparently believe that even nuclear wars can be fought and in some sense 'won'. To them the Clausewitzian paradigm is still seen to be relevant, even when contemplating nuclear war.

The arms spiral of the past 150 years which has increased the potential destructiveness of war has had the effect of elevating deterrence to a new doctrinal prominence in both the theory and practice of strategy. Between the major powers there is peace in the negative sense, meaning the absence of war, but there is no positive or 'stable peace'. Kenneth Boulding described peace as stable if it is based not on deterrence but on a political relationship in which there is no expectation of war.[20] Such peace is impossible when the adversaries give such prominence to the nuclear dimension of their relationship, when they have each other constantly targeted and when the characteristic feature of their relationship over a period of 40 years has not been the search for the foundation of a legitimate order, but rather confrontation, suspicion and vigorous arms-racing.

The arms race phenomenon and its relationship with international security is a complex one. Arms races are always costly and mostly generate tension, but they do not inevitably lead to war. Nor are their products necessarily destabilizing; sometimes weapons are produced which help the participants move from relative instability to relative stability. The development of Polaris, which enabled the United States to move on from the vulnerability of the 'delicate balance of terror' is a prime example of this. But it sometimes works the other way, and most wars are preceded by arms races.[21] Even so, this proves little, for an arms race is an obvious symptom of a growing conflict of interests between states; it would be difficult to prove that arms races were fundamental causes rather than symptoms of conflict. Between powers or groups of powers of roughly equal potential, arms races tend towards equilibrium. Nevertheless, the balances of military power which can develop as a result of a mutual arms buildup do not automatically produce a stable equilibrium. The year 1914 taught that to the world. And in the aftermath of the breakdown of that competitively armed peace, an extravagantly destructive war occurred.

Armaments competition is inherent in mistrustful relationships between nations. In such circumstances it has been thought essential for military planners to be conservative in their assessments: this has resulted in the process of worst-case forecasting, that is, making pessimistic assumptions about the other side's intentions and capabilities. When both sides practice this, the outcome is what Robert McNamara called the 'action–reaction phenomenon'; from this comes arms-racing, the continuous modernization of weaponry, and also a pendulum-swing in the characteristic of that weaponry. The latter results in first the offence having the advantage, then the defence and so on, as counters and counters to counters are found.

The idea that the 'offence' or 'defence' have 'superiority' or 'dominance' at some period or another is a common idea, but its theoretical validity and historical accuracy is easily exaggerated. It wrongly implies a technological determinism to the history of war, it neglects circumstantial factors, and it ignores the human dimension in clashes of violence. Let us consider the paradigm case of World War I. In what sense, for example, was the 'defence' superior in that war, when a great victory was eventually achieved as a result of offensive power? And what if the Schlieffen plan had succeeded at the outset— and who is foolhardy enough to say that the plan was bound to fail? Furthermore, we must not forget the Eastern Front, where the density of manpower to front was much less. Technological change does give relative advantage—other things being equal—to the offence and defence in turn, but one cannot say much more than that. The outcome invariably rests on a combination of such factors as the skill of the operators, the strategic doctrine around which their weapons are organized, the geographical environment in which the battle(s) take place, morale and leadership, relative willingness to suffer casualties and, last but not least, the comparative size of the forces employed.

The exception to the preceding argument is the nuclear-tipped ballistic missile. This does appear to have given an inherent superiority to the strategic 'offence'. But even this apparent exception is not relevant, since intercontinental ballistic missiles (ICBMs) and submarine-launched ballistic missiles (SLBMs) cannot be regarded as traditional 'weapons' of war. Their indiscriminate destructiveness when used in any war between the superpowers would negate the Clausewitzian connotation of the word weapon. ICBMs are instruments of deterrence, not weapons of war.

The problem of distinguishing between inherently 'offensive' and inherently 'defensive' weapons is well known. It has plagued disarmament efforts. If one adds to this problem the criticism of the idea that offence or defence can achieve 'superiority', the weakness of those who would assert technological fixes to long-term political problems is further exposed. It follows that the so-called Strategic Defense Initiative (SDI) is neither inherently defensive nor can it guarantee absolute security to its possesser. Shields can be used in attack as well as defence, and no defensive system can give the guarantee of being leak-proof.

While weapon innovation has shown a pendulum effect, the secular trend has been towards increasing the destructiveness of war, and hence hastening its obsolescence at the higher levels of violence. Although the destructiveness of nuclear stockpiles has been reduced in recent years by the introduction of lower-yield nuclear weapons, both sides nevertheless retain massive stocks of nuclear overkill. Some would argue that there must be a move towards a 'defence dominant' world, as a result of new space-based 'defensive' systems. Nevertheless, the reality is that we will live for the foreseeable future in a world in which the cost-exchange ratio will favour nuclear-armed ballistic missiles. There is no escape from a situation in which nuclear war between the superpowers would lead to mutual assured destruction (MAD). Whatever the doctrinal labels, MAD will remain a fact of strategic life.

IX.   Deterrence and reassurance

It is notoriously difficult to learn 'lessons' from the past, but what the preceding discussion brings out is the critical importance in strategic life of evaluating perceptions, which in turn involves the ever-difficult task of trying to see into men's minds. This has been evident in the way conventional strategic studies have approached the problem of deterrence, for example. Endless time has been invested in trying to work out the requirements for the effective deterrence of rational opponents, but there has been a neglect of those factors which might motivate a state to gamble all on one desperate throw. We have refined deterrence into a sophisticated tool, but we have paid insufficient attention to avoiding those situations where desperate gambles are conceivable. It was desperation and ambition which resulted in the willingness of Germany to take high risks in 1914. And if Germany was beyond reassurance in 1914, was it not also beyond deterrence?

After 1918, as ever, military planners in different countries learned different lessons from the changes which had taken place in the methods of war. By the

1930s, the reaction to the Western front had produced Maginot-mindedness on the part of the French, while Germany had moved towards the blitzkreig strategy. Neither offence nor defence were 'inherently' dominant in 1939. What mattered was where and how well the technology was used, and this depended as much as anything on why. On this occasion the German propensity to engage in high risk-taking was more the result of naked ambition rather than desperation, but the Hitlerite challenge also grew out of the oppressive nature of the Versailles settlement, which seemed to rest on the premise that European but especially French security depended on German weakness and insecurity. In such circumstances the policy of keeping Germany weak fanned the flames of the nation's pride and ambition. By the time the policy of appeasement was tried, Hitler was already in the driving-seat and beyond conversion to moderation. Chamberlain mistakenly tried to appease the unappeasable.

Thus, as in 1914, Germany in 1939 was beyond both reassurance and deterrence. Such historical events are of considerable significance for deterrence theory. History shows that in the midst of an intense crisis, when a particular state most needs its military power to provide an effective deterrent, this self-same 'deterrent' can provoke desperation on the part of the adversary. When a particular 'deterrent' is sufficiently intimidating to excite intense fear, but not powerful enough to curb ambition, the result will be war. If the leaders of the challenging state believe that the costs of inaction will be punitively high, they may at the same time convince themselves either that the adversary will back down in face of higher levels of threat, or can be defeated by aggressive action. Thus, deterrence may well be irrelevant in stopping an aggressor which at that point, because of desperation and ambition, has convinced itself that the status quo is unacceptable and that 'victory is possible'. Thus, deterrents might not only fail to deter, but they might also actually elicit those very responses they were designed to prevent.

Deterrents, historically, have regularly failed to deter, but in the nuclear age the MAD condition has induced a novel caution on decision-makers. Nevertheless, not everyone believes that this rules out war. Some US strategists have, for example, argued that the Soviet Union does not accept MAD, and that it believes that it can fight and win a nuclear war.[22] Paul Nitze is one of those who have argued that the Soviet leaders are the real 'Clausewitzians' and that they have carried the classical principles of war into the nuclear age. He has commented:

It is a copy book principle in strategy that, in actual war, advantage tends to go to the side in a better position to raise the stakes by expanding the scope, duration or destructive intensity of the conflict . . . The other side is the one under greater pressure to scramble for a peaceful way out. To have the advantage at the utmost level of violence helps at every lesser level.[23]

If both sides believe that their security depends upon escalation dominance at all levels, then there is no escaping a pure security dilemma. The problem is illustrated by the case of mobile Soviet ICBMs. In a MAD world, mobile Soviet missiles could be interpreted as making both sides more secure. However, while US policy is dominated by strategic fundamentalists and counterforce targeters, the prevailing belief is that US security will decrease if it cannot hold Soviet 'hard target' capabilities hostage. Thus, depending on the mind-sets concerned, mobile Soviet ICBMs can be seen as either stabilizing or destabiliz-ing. Moreover, if the United States is determined to hold Soviet ICBMs hostage, then any US targeting policy designed to deny military opportunities to the Soviet Union could in fact increase Soviet insecurity. Of course, this one possibility does not mean Soviet leaders will suddenly stake all on a single nuclear gamble. Nuclear weapons generally impose prudence and restraint. But does the experience of 1914, or of the record of Soviet behaviour between 1946–50 and 1957–62, suggest that the best route to Western security lies in Soviet insecurity?

X. 'Desperado geopolitics'[24]

The belief that US security is assured by Soviet insecurity was held by the members of the Committee on the Present Danger, which so dominated the defence debate in the United States in the late 1970s. Subsequently, many members of the committee went on to hold key posts in the Reagan Administration. In the second half of the 1970s, the Committee was preoccu-pied with the Soviet missile threat to the US land-based ICBM force. They postulated a Soviet attack scenario which they argued created various political dangers for the United States as a result of the 'window of vulnerability' which was supposed to exist. Despite the serious weaknesses of this idea, it neverthe-less attracted widespread support. It necessitated a view of the Soviet Union which was reductionist and mechanistic and which made Soviet propensities for risk-taking almost entirely dependent on the details of the strategic 'balance'. As one analyst observed:

The period of peril theory is a self-contained system of thought. If its basic assumption of technological determinism and its projections of Soviet capabilities are accepted there is almost no way in which it can be invalidated. The argument therefore has a powerful persuasive appeal. Its ramifications can be derived in a seemingly logical way. No knowledge of Soviet history or the complex structure of Soviet goals and motivations is required.[25]

The reason for the prominence of such views in US defence circles in the late 1970s was a mixture of the resurfacing of rightist elements in US ideology and disappointment with the result of superpower détente.

Stanley Hoffmann has accurately criticized the flaws of the Nixon–Kissinger strategy of détente. In its design, the United States never intended to recognize the Soviet Union as a political as well as military equal.[26] Soviet leaders understood this. As a result they came to believe that they were largely bearing the costs of détente: restraint seemed to be a one-way street in which the

United States promised much but delivered little. From the Soviet viewpoint, détente was undermined by US arms-racing, its lack of seriousness about arms control, its failure to follow through on the spirit of détente (as revealed by its attitude to human rights and trade agreements), and by its pursuit of unilateral advantage in the Third World.[27] These, of course, are the very complaints which the United States has levelled against the Soviet Union. From Washington's perspective, the 1970s were characterized by Soviet assertiveness and US restraint.

In addition to having a diametrically opposed interpretation of events, important opinion-formers in the United States believed that nuclear parity with the Soviet Union was the cause of what they perceived as their relative geopolitical failure. In the 1970s the United States experienced vulnerability and did not like it: Viet Nam, the Organization of Petroleum Producing Countries (OPEC) and the Iranian fiasco contributed to a feeling of impotence which was deeply unsettling to the American psyche. Americans wanted a definition of the 'problem' to which they could give a successful solution. It was therefore hardly surprising that they were seduced by the ideas of those technical strategists who popularized the notion that US impotence and Soviet momentum were a consequence of growing Soviet strategic power. It was a short step from this to the assertion that US reverses were a function of US nuclear self-denial, the so-called decade of neglect.[28] If the problem was caused by growing Soviet military power, the solution was obviously for the United States to build more and better; in short, the United States must be restored to what it saw its rightful place as 'Number One' in international affairs. The experiment with restraint and reciprocity, represented by détente, proved short-lived and was discarded.

Richard Falk has made a powerful indictment of this 'technological determinism' in US attitudes to foreign affairs. He has argued that the 'supposed "linkage" between strategic levels and assertiveness in foreign policy is impossible to validate or invalidate . . . if strategic strength (or weakness) correlates with "resolve" toward Third World threats or crisis confrontations then assertiveness may indeed follow from a perception of strategic build up'.[29] If one or both superpowers believe that strategic superiority is the key to national security, then the 'adversary partnership' will tend towards a 'state of war'. But we have argued that the pure security dilemma is not inevitable in all relationships in international politics. The Soviet–US competition is rooted in the dynamics of an anarchic system, but it belongs to our category of insecurity traps rather than pure security dilemmas. The former, as we argued, can be managed. Securing recognition of the need for reciprocity and restraint in the superpower relationship is the challenge of our time.

XI. Conclusion

'Reciprocal security' implies that security should be a value which is consciously exchanged or shared. The basis for it exists since in the nuclear age there is an unavoidable strategic interdependence between the superpowers. Whether they like it or not—and many groups within each country do not—the ultimate security of each of them rests upon the restraint of the other. As David Holloway has put it: 'In the end, the prevention of nuclear war and the survival of the human race cannot be secured without the cooperation of the Soviet Union'.[30] Such a conclusion is anathema to the strategic fundamentalists who comprised the Committee on the Present Danger, and who happen to have been the forefront of support for Star Wars/SDI. Some of the more visionary fundamentalists—notably the President himself—look forward to a situation in which US security is not based upon a mutual hostage relationship. The move towards strategic defence is in line with an increased US emphasis on damage limitation, both to enhance deterrent threats, and also to prepare for the possible breakdown of deterrence. There is a depressing strategic fatalism in the attitudes of the strategic fundamentalists. They assume a simple and continuous Hobbesian world and their actions are calculated to create a self-fulfilling prophesy. The early cold war vision of the US National Security Council directive 68 has been reincarnated, which projects the idea that the Soviet Union is a revolutionary power and that improvement in the character of East–West relations can only take place if there are fundamental changes in the Soviet state. As long as views such as this dominate US policy-making, a long-term détente relationship with the USSR is impossible.

The Soviet Union has its own strategic fundamentalists whose importance, as in the United States, varies over time. Like their US counterparts, they resent the fact that their security rests on a tacit or explicit relationship with the imperialist West. Once again, it is not technological change which is at the heart of the international security problem: that is but the symptom. The trouble for the strategic fundamentalists in both superpowers is their unease in finding themselves dependent on their adversary for their continued existence; such a state of affairs is the antithesis of all Realist and unilateralist preferences. As long as the leaderships of both sides believe that the landscape of East–West relations is shaped by the devil character of their adversary, the prospects for a legitimate order based on shared ideas about external conduct will be remote.

History leads us to expect a cataclysmic breakdown of the system. It has always been so, and to believe that the future will prove any different is to hold an optimism unjustified by any historical perspective. The problem is compounded by the prevalence in superpower thinking of such old and unhelpful attitudes as the 'engineering approach', dogged unilateralism, a belief in safety through strength, and a propensity to seek security through technological fixes. Against these pessimistic points, the threat of a nuclear catastrophe has so far proved to be uniquely restraining on superpower behaviour. However, prudent behaviour has not always been forthcoming, as the outbreak of the Cuban missile crisis shows.

That some combination of muddle and management saw us through the Cuban missile crisis and the other alarms of the post-war period is some comfort. But would such a dangerous crisis have arisen had deterrence been as robust as some of its supporters would have us believe? Moreover, those who would maintain that the nuclear age has witnessed the subordination of military/technological necessities to political control have to explain why, during the crisis, the United States Navy interpreted Presidential Directives in such a coercive fashion against Soviet submarines.[31] The continuing problem of competing political and military logic can also be seen in what many regard as the Achilles' heel of modern strategic forces, namely their command and control systems. If the superpowers ever find themselves again embroiled in an intense crisis, a critical determinant of peace or war will be the extent to which either of them believes that war is inevitable. In such circumstances, the pressure to launch a 'decapitation' strike against the opponent's command and control system could prove irresistible.[32]

If planners on one or both sides come to believe that a decisive advantage can be gained by an aggressive damage-limiting blow, then there may be a pressure to act which could once again provide the trigger which could unleash a cataclysmic conflict—this time on a scale never before seen. But the pressure to act will be all the greater if those same planners believe that the subsequent conflict can be fought in a controlled manner. We cannot completely escape the command and control Achilles' heel; the dilemmas entailed remain integral to modern strategic forces. Consequently we must recognize the critical import-ance of reshaping the superpower relationship in such a way that the chances of an intense crisis progressively diminish.

When contemplating crisis prevention, it is important to remember that the Soviet Union challenged the United States in 1962 because it feared that the US Administration was determined to exploit its nuclear superiority. The Kremlin was worried by the Kennedy Administration's early emphasis on superiority, and appears to have taken seriously the President's refusal to rule out a first strike and US Air Force statements about 'prevailing' in a nuclear war.[33]

In the aftermath of the Cuban missile crisis, the superpowers moved towards détente. As with previous crises and wars, this one shifted inter-state relations from overt conflict to tentative co-operation. But, in turn, the superpower détente of the late 1960s and 1970s, like others in the past, proved to be transitory. The failure of this détente had various immediate causes, but there is a more basic question: does co-operation under anarchy contain the seeds of its own destruction? The past shows that fear and insecurity can produce international co-operation, which for a time makes international politics seem safer. However, this expectation of safety leads states in the course of time to believe that the structure is so stable that co-operation need not be such a transcendent value. The belief grows that national interests can more effectively be pursued by unilateralist means. The powers test the limits of safety, and the result is a collapse of whatever edifice of co-operation has been built.[34]

The past suggests that the superpower relationship will continue to be characterized by cycles of competition and co-operation. But how many crises can the world face before Murphy's law finally operates? The idea of 'cumulative risks' is relevant here: that is, the more crises we face, the greater the cumulative risk is that one will end in disaster.[35] Furthermore, the larger the number of crises we successfully 'manage', the more the temptation will be to minimize the risks inherent in them. We will become confident that nuclear weapons are gadgets which any rational strategic man can manipulate and control. In the future it may well be that he who lives by faith in crisis management may well die by faith in crisis management.

Nobody or policy can guarantee a successful escape from our predicament. Nevertheless, it would be fatalistic simply to assume from past failures that we are doomed to apocalyptic collapse. And while there is no magic formula, there is a choice: between the self-defeating strategies of the past and what the strategic fundamentalists would call the 'pieties' and 'platitudes' which this paper has emphasized, notably the belief that international security demands restraint and reciprocity rather than the narrow pursuit of national strength and self-interest. It is one thing to state these evident 'lessons' of history but another entirely to turn them into actual operational policies. The caution of policy-makers and the grip of enemy stereotypes conspire to prevent even a modest reform in old attitudes. From the Western viewpoint, change must begin by adopting a more realistic attitude towards the Soviet Union, one based on empirical realism and empathy rather than on doctrinal realism and outdated Sovietology.

Unless there is reciprocal annihilation, the United States and the Soviet Union will be 'adversary partners' for the foreseeable future. But greater co-operation and more security is by no means unthinkable. In speculating about the conditions for reciprocal security the West must accept that co-operation is not a favour we do the Russians. It is a basic necessity of international security. Furthermore, we have to take some risks, and we do not have the time to wait for internal changes in the Soviet Union. Henry Kissinger made mistakes, but he was shrewd enough not to insist that changes in internal Soviet politics be a condition for the superpower détente of the early 1970s; this was a lesson which was lost on his successors. In addition—and here Kissinger was less sensitive— the Soviet Union must be treated as a legitimate superpower with global interests and responsibilities. This will involve, for example, the extension of more understanding towards natural Soviet ambitions and interests in the Third World, and particularly in the unstable borderlands to their immediate south.[36] It is not sufficiently realized that the Middle East is to the Soviet Union the geopolitical equivalent of Central America to the United States.

The road to reciprocal security will be bumpy, for it involves changing men's minds, and it is always easier to dump rusty technology than to transform obsolete ways of thinking. In both superpowers there are groups who will always be opposed to accommodation. However, there are also more open-minded and rationally responsive elements in both countries and their allies who recognize the need for fundamental changes in the relationship.[37] Since the grip of conservatism is powerful, it is all the more important that no opportunity is lost to encourage whatever hesitant steps towards co-operation are made.

Among the changes in attitude necessary to encourage reciprocal security, the following are the most important:

1.   If both sides could accept that an important element of their hostility stems from the fact that each can do the other the most harm in the international system, there would be a chance to reduce the moralizing and self-righteousness that now characterize both sets of attitudes.[38]

2.   If both sides could control their mutual proclivity to portray the antagonist in demonic terms, they might better appreciate the extent to which they share a number of common interests (such as nuclear non-proliferation); these could provide the political cement of a legitimate superpower order.

3.   There is a need for military advisers and others to eschew their fixation with 'balances' and symmetry in the strategic relationship. While the balance is less robust than in the 1970s, it is sufficiently stable that neither need worry at present about 'windows of opportunity'. What they must worry about is the interplay between present technological trends and possible shifts in political factors. Fear and insecurity combined with destabilizing technologies could be the ingredients of a nuclear age Sarajevo.

4.   The superpowers must learn to emphasize reassurance rather than intimidation in strategic doctrine. In this regard there are a variety of measures presently on the agenda that could begin to initiate an action-reaction process in tension reduction.[39] Of these, a Comprehensive Test Ban Treaty, the strengthening of the Non-Proliferation Treaty, and a superpower freeze have been on the agenda for some years. Even more pressing is the problem of the international politics of space.

The current US Administration is unwilling to deal seriously with the Soviet Union on arms control. They assert that the Soviets cannot be trusted. On the other side, some within the Soviet leaderhip fear the United States and believe with some justification that the Reagan Administration is not interested in technological restraint, only in bankrupting and undermining a Soviet state already unable to compete on equal terms with a resurgent United States. In such circumstances is there any basis for hoping for reciprocity and reassurance? Perhaps there is not much. But might the United States be willing to show technological restraint, even though it goes against the national grain, in return for the Soviet Union showing more openness concerning arms control verification? Such a deal would be what reassurance and reciprocation are all about: each shares in the costs and benefits of the relationship.

If reassurance is the key to the next stage of superpower relations—if they are to improve rather than deteriorate even further—then space is the key arena. As long as present policies continue, space will become weaponized, but there will be no increment in security on earth. Indeed, the opposite will be the case. There will be no perfect ballistic missile defence system in the years ahead, but we will see new first-strike threats. Star Wars systems, together with viable anti-satellite weapons, will strengthen the damage limitation potential of the technologically superior, and together these capabilities will make strategic doctrines more pre-emptive and therefore more dangerous. If, by tacit or formal agreement, such an outcome could be avoided, we would not have guaranteed international security: but if we continue to pursue the present path in space—unilateralism, technical fixes, the bargaining-chip mentality and the search for peace through strength—we can be confident in arguing that we will seriously erode the prospects for lasting order. The weaponization of space is an urgent issue, and successful reassurance there would be highly symbolic. But if we are to succeed in this task, the policy-makers of both sides must realize that the real challenge of the 'high frontier', like that on earth, is not technological. It is intellectual, diplomatic and spiritual.

Notes and references

1 See Brodie, B., *War and Politics* (Cassell: London, 1973), p. 1.
2 Hoffmann, S., *The State of War* (Pall Mall Press: London, 1965), p. 178.
3 Holsti, K. J., 'The necrologists of international relations', *Canadian Journal of Political Science*, vol. 18, no. 4 (Dec. 1985), p. 684.
4 Kissinger, H., *A World Restored—Metternich, Castlereagh and the Problems of Peace 1812–22* (Houghton Mifflin: Boston, MA, 1957), pp. 1–2.
5 Jervis, R., *Perception and Misperception in International Politics* (Princeton University Press: Princeton, NJ, 1976). Also see Jervis, R., 'Cooperation under the security dilemma', *World Politics*, vol. 30, no. 2 (Jan. 1978), pp. 167–214. The classic encapsulation of the security dilemma in the literature of international relations theory was in Butterfield, H., *History and Human Relations* (Macmillan: New York, 1952), pp. 19–20.
6 The concept was first defined by Deutsch, K. W., Burrell, S. A., Kann, R. A., Lee, M., Lichterman, M., Lindgren, R. E., Loewenheim, F. L. and Van Wagenen, R. W., *Political Community and the North Atlantic Area* (Princeton University Press: Princeton, NJ, 1957), p. 5.
7 Jervis, R., 'Security regimes', *International Organisation*, vol. 36, no. 2 (Spring 1982), pp. 357–78.
8 Hoffmann, S., *Primacy or World Order?* (McGraw Hill: New York, 1978), p. 39.
9 Kissinger (note 4), conclusion.
10 This is the theme of M. Shulman, *Beyond the Cold War* (Yale University Press: New Haven, CT, 1966).
11 Lebow, R. M., 'Clear and future danger: managing relations with the Soviet Union in the 1980s', *New Directions in Strategic Thinking*, eds R. O'Neill and D. M. Horner (George Allen and Unwin: London, 1981), pp. 221–45.
12 Nye, Jr, J. S., 'The long term future of deterrence', *Journal of Strategic Studies* (special issue in honour of Bernard Brodie), forthcoming.
13 On Morgenthau's volte-face see Boyle, F. A., *World Politics and International Law* (Duke University Press: Durham, NC, 1985), pp. 70–4; Carr's own words are in Carr, E. H., *The Twenty Years' Crisis, 1919–1939: An Introduction to the Study of International Relations* (Macmillan: London, 1940), pp. 89 and 94.

[14] Fox, W. T. R., 'E. H. Carr and political realism: vision and revision', *Review of International Studies*, vol. 11, no. 1 (Jan. 1985), p. 13.

[15] Schelling, T., *Arms and Influence* (Yale University Press: New Haven, CT, 1966), pp. 227–32.

[16] Quoted by White, R., *Fearful Warriors* (Free Press: New York, 1984), p. 203.

[17] Brodie, B. and Brodie, F. M., *From Crossbow to H-Bomb* (Indiana University Press: Bloomington, IN, 1973).

[18] See Lasswell, H., 'The garrison state and the specialists on violence', *American Journal of Sociology*, vol. 47 (1941), pp. 455–68.

[19] The phrase was coined by Booth, K., 'Nuclear deterrence and World War III. How will history judge?', *Journal of Strategic Studies* (special issue in honour of Bernard Brodie), forthcoming.

[20] Boulding, K., *Stable Peace* (University of Texas Press: Austin, TX, 1979).

[21] Naroll, T., *Military Deterrence in History* (State University of New York Press: Albany, NY, 1974); Wallace, M., 'Arms races and escalation: some new evidence', *Journal of Conflict Resolution*, vol. 23, no. 1 (Mar. 1979), pp. 3–16.

[22] The standard reference is Pipes, R., 'Why the Soviet Union thinks it could fight and win a nuclear war', *Commentary*, vol. 62 (July 1977).

[23] Nitze, P., 'Is SALT II a fair deal for the United States?' (Committee on the Present Danger: Washington, DC, 1979), p. 6.

[24] Falk, R., 'Introduction' in Aldridge, R. C., *First Strike! The Pentagon's Strategy For Nuclear War* (Pluto Press: London, 1983), p. 8.

[25] Johnson, R. H., 'Periods of peril: the window of vulnerability and other myths', *Foreign Affairs*, vol. 61, no. 4 (Spring 1983), p. 951.

[26] Hoffmann (note 6), chapter 2.

[27] Shulman, M. D., 'US–Soviet relations and the control of nuclear weapons', *Rethinking the U.S. Strategic Posture*, ed. B. M. Blechman (Ballinger Publishing Co.: Cambridge, MA, 1982), pp. 77–100.

[28] This and other false ideas about the 1970s are discussed in Booth, K., and Williams, P., 'Fact and fiction in U.S. foreign policy: Reagan's myths about détente', *World Policy Journal*, vol. 2, no. 3 (Summer 1985), pp. 501–32.

[29] Lifton, R. J., and Falk, R., *Indefensible Weapons: The Political and Psychological Case against Nuclearism* (Basic Books: New York, 1982), p. 206.

[30] Holloway, D., 'Soviet policy and the arms race', *The Choice: Nuclear Weapons Versus Security*, ed. G. Prins (Chatto and Windus: London, 1984), p. 127.

[31] See Sagan, S., 'Nuclear alerts and crisis management' *International Security*, vol. 9, no. 2 (Spring 1985), pp. 99–139.

[32] See Steinbruner, J., 'Nuclear decapitation', *Foreign Policy*, no. 45 (Winter 1981–2), pp. 16–28.

[33] Scheer, R., *With Enough Shovels: Reagan, Bush and Nuclear War* (Secker and Warburg: London, 1982), p. 216.

[34] Robert Jervis has pointed out the difficulties of sustaining co-operation under anarchy (see note 7), p. 184.

[35] Deutsch, K. W., *The Analysis of International Relations* (Prentice-Hall: Englewood Cliffs, NJ, 1968), p. 128.

[36] In any case, the West has much less to fear from Soviet policy in the Third World than the present US Administration claims. The Soviets did not make great gains with their so-called adventurous behaviour in the Third World in the 1970s. See Booth and Williams (note 28), p. 516.

[37] See, e.g., the multinational input into *Common Security: A Programme for Disarmament*. The Report of the Independent Commission on Disarmament and Security Issues under the Chairmanship of Olof Palme (Pan Books Ltd: London, 1982).

[38] Note Bowker, M. and Williams, P., *Misperception in Soviet–American Relations*, Faraday Discussion Paper No. 6, The Council For Arms Control, London, 1986.

[39] White (note 16), pp. 295–319.

Index

DATE DUE
